The Social Psychology of Ethnic Identity

European Monographs in Social Psychology
Sponsored by the European Association of Experimental Psychology

Series Editor:
Professor Rupert Brown, Department of Psychology, University of Kent, Canterbury, Kent CT2 7NP

The aim of this series is to publish and promote the highest quality of writing in European social psychology. The editor and the editorial board encourage publications which approach social psychology from a wide range of theoretical perspectives and whose content may be applied, theoretical or empirical. The authors of books in this series should be affiliated to institutions that are located in countries which would qualify for membership of the Association. All books will be published in English, and translations from other European languages are welcomed. Please submit ideas and proposals for books in the series to Rupert Brown at the above address.

Published

The Quantitative Analysis of Social Representations
Willem Doise, Alain Clemence, and Fabio Lorenzi-Cioldi

A Radical Dissonance Theory
Jean-Léon Beauvois and Robert-Vincent Joule

The Social Psychology of Collective Action
Caroline Kelly and Sara Breinlinger

Social Context and Cognitive Performance
Jean-Marc Monteil and Pascal Huguet

Conflict and Decision-Making in Close Relationships
Erich Kirchler, Christa Rodler, Erik Hölzl, and Katja Meier

Stereotyping as Inductive Hypothesis Testing
Klaus Fiedler and Eva Walther

Intergroup Relations in States of the Former Soviet Union
Louk Hagendoorn, Hub Linssen, and Sergei Tumanov

The Social Psychology of Ethnic Identity
Maykel Verkuyten

Forthcoming Title

The Passionate Intersection of Desire and Knowledge
Gregory Maio

The Social Psychology of Ethnic Identity

Maykel Verkuyten

Psychology Press
Taylor & Francis Group

HOVE AND NEW YORK

First published 2005 by Psychology Press,
27 Church Road, Hove, East Sussex BN3 2FA

Simultaneously published in the USA and Canada
by Routledge
270 Madison Avenue, New York, NY 10016

Reprinted 2006

Psychology Press is an imprint of the Taylor & Francis Group, an informa business

Typeset in Times by Keystroke, Jacaranda Lodge, Wolverhampton
Printed and bound in Great Britain by MPG Books Ltd, Bodmin
Cover design by Amanda Barragry

British Library Cataloguing in Publication Data
A catalogue record for this book is available from the British Library

Library of Congress Cataloging-in-Publication Data
Verkuyten, M.
 The social psychology of ethnic identity / Maykel Verkuyten.
  p. cm. – (European monographs in social psychology)
 Includes bibliographical references and index.
 ISBN 1-84169-532-7
 1. Ethnicity. 2. Ethnopsychology. 3. Social psychology. I. Title. II. Series.

 GN495.6.V48 2004
 305.8–dc22

                                                      2004011672

ISBN 10: 1-84169-532-7
ISBN 13: 978-1-84169-532-7

To Wietse and Ella

Contents

About the author

Maykel Verkuyten is an associate professor of social science at Utrecht University, the Netherlands. He also is a senior researcher at the European Research Centre on Migration and Ethnic Relations (ERCOMER) at Utrecht University. By training, he is a social psychologist (graduated from the Catholic University Leuven, Belgium) and an anthropologist (graduated from the Catholic University Nijmegen, the Netherlands). He did his PhD at Erasmus University in Rotterdam, the Netherlands, and worked as an academic at that university for 10 years. For the past 12 years he has been working at Utrecht University. He has published extensively in the fields of ethnic identity and interethnic relations.

Acknowledgements

Many people have directly or indirectly influenced my interest in and thinking about ethnic identity. I am grateful for their support, suggestions, and stimulating comments. Several of my colleagues have been involved in particular studies that in one way or another addressed issues related to ethnic identity. In this regard, I am indebted to Peary Brug, Kadir Canatan, Louk Hagendoorn, Wiebe de Jong, Kees Masson, and Katarina Pouliasi.

I also have had the pleasure of working with a number of undergraduate and graduate students who chose to work with me on ethnic identity for their master's theses or dissertations, or for extracurricular research. Thank you, Esther Aelbers, Sophie van de Calseijde, Anna Cieslik, Barbara Kinket, Fatuma Köker, Ineke Kwa, Wieger de Leur, Shervin Nekuee, Jochem Thijs, Angela de Wolf, and Aslan Yildiz.

One person in particular has been responsible for much of the theoretical development of my thinking through many stimulating discussions and comments, so I would like to specially thank Rob Wentholt for his constant support and constructive criticism, not only in relation to this book but during my whole academic career.

I am also indebted to Rupert Brown, the editor of the European Monographs in Social Psychology Series, for his detailed and insightful review of the manuscript.

A word of thanks goes to Marijke Schoenmakers, who was involved in the first stages of preparing the manuscript, and to Rachel Kress, who edited the text for language and suggested many improvements.

Finally, I would like to thank Christel for her continuous intellectual, emotional, and practical support. Her interest and belief in me is an irreplaceable source of energy.

Zeist, March 2004

Introduction

Ethnicity has become a major feature of social structure, everyday interactions, self-understanding, transnational networks, and political debates and conflicts around the world. Processes of globalization are drawing people from different places and with different backgrounds into close relationships. The continuing and increasing flow of migration, the growth of diasporas, and the emergence of Internet communities have raised all kinds of new and pressing questions. Most societies around the world are, or are rapidly becoming, ethnically and culturally plural. Ethnic diversity challenges the existing social hierarchies and exclusionary conceptions of citizenship, but also leads to a new tribalism that threatens democracy and social cohesion. Hence, questions of ethnicity, migration, identity, and multiculturalism are hotly debated in many countries. These concepts are frequently employed in and by the media. Given the increased importance of ethnicity and migration in contemporary public and political debates, it is not surprising that these have become major topics in academic debates in a number of different disciplines, including philosophy, political science, sociology, and anthropology. For example, in the past decade, political scientists, (moral) philosophers, and sociologists have paid increasing attention to the questions and dilemmas surrounding migration, citizenship, and multiculturalism (e.g. Barry, 2001; Favell, 1998; Goldberg, 1994; Kymlicka, 1995; Parekh, 2000; Taylor, 1992). Philosophical, ideological, and pragmatic arguments are being put forward in order to defend or challenge notions of the 'politics of identity' or 'modes of belonging'. In comparison to all this work in different disciplines, social psychologists, particularly in Europe, have to a large degree ignored ethnicity.

Ethnicity can be studied from various perspectives and in different ways. The emphasis can be on economic restructuring and ethnic entrepreneurship, on demographic changes in response to migration, on political factors such as minority policies and identity politics, and on ethnic self-organizations. This book focuses on ethnic identity. The emphasis is on some of the complexities of real-world ethnic phenomena and particularly on the ordinary understanding and behaviour of people in their everyday social settings. To do so, I use a social psychological perspective. The central aim of the book is to show that while, on the one hand, social psychology can be used to develop an understanding of ethnicity, on the other hand, an increased attention to ethnicity has benefits for social psychology.

In contrast to other disciplines, social psychology has been slow in making a contribution to questions of ethnicity. This is somewhat surprising given its focus on issues of social identity and intergroup relations. Social psychology has produced many concepts, theories, and empirical findings concerning these issues that are central to debates on ethnic minority identity and the management of cultural diversity. For example, part of the rationale behind social identity theory (Tajfel & Turner, 1986) was to analyse large-scale groups or 'imagined communities' (Anderson, 1983) in which members are geographically dispersed.

The study of ethnic identity offers the possibility of asking new social psychological questions, considering neglected issues, and filling theoretical and empirical gaps. For example, studying ethnicity inevitably raises questions about the role of history, culture, ideology, and power as well as issues of multiple identities and hybridity. These questions and issues are relatively neglected in social psychology. However, their importance has been pointed out by earlier social psychologists, and there are increasing signs of a renewed interest (e.g. Chryssochoou, 2003; Deaux & Philogene, 2001; Flick, 1998; Huddy, 2001; Jost & Major, 2001; Wolsko et al., 2000).

There is another reason behind the writing of this book, and that is that the study of ethnic identity offers an interesting opportunity to combine or reconcile the more mainstream or perceptual with the more critical or discursive social psychologies. In general, the former are more interested in mental processes or what happens 'inside' individuals, whereas the latter are more concerned with what happens in interactions and societies. I will argue that these approaches predominantly focus on different questions and different levels of analysis that cannot be reduced to one another. Each approach has its pros and cons, its limiting and insightful viewpoints. The one, for example, focuses on the psychological or behavioural consequences of existing ethnic categorizations, whereas the other examines the actual construction and use of these categorizations themselves. Some researchers examine the stable and continuous aspects of ethnic identity, whereas others focus on its variable and situational character.

There certainly are important epistemological differences between perceptual and discourse-oriented social psychologies, and I will discuss these in the next chapter. However, an emphasis on differences ignores the possibility of engagement and reconciliation. Bringing different approaches together helps to identify and articulate their distinct differences but also their possible commonalities. There is little to be gained by arguing about which approach to social psychology is the better one. I want to show that the questions asked differ and that much of the debate between these psychologies can be reformulated in an 'and-and' rather than an 'either-or' way. Furthermore, I think that such an engagement and reconciliation are necessary to develop an adequate understanding of ethnic identity. For example, discursive and rhetorical approaches have convincingly argued that social identities should not be taken for granted (see Antaki & Widdicombe, 1998). They have shown how identities are defined and used in interactions, and what the discursive consequences of different definitions are.

However, it is also relevant and important to know what it actually feels like to occupy a stigmatized, ethnic minority position or to be defined as an asylum seeker yet not receive refugee status. These identities have all kinds of consequences, including important emotional ones (e.g. Sinnerbrink et al., 1997; Verkuyten & Nekuee, 1999b). Asylum seekers, for example, often suffer from high levels of uncertainty and fear about their legal status and the possibility of being repatriated. These feelings and experiences should not be ignored and examined only as discursive practices. Doing so would bring us close to the dehumanizing methods used in the more positivist approaches criticized by discourse analysts. It is possible to examine how ethnic identities are socially established and negotiated, but also to ask what belonging to an ethnic group 'feels like' or means to a person. Ethnic identity is socially defined and constructed, but it also provides a foundation for self-understanding and a source of positive or negative self-feelings.

This book has one additional objective and that is to make use of the broader perspective that cultural and social anthropology can provide. In anthropology, ethnicity has been a key concept since the late 1960s (see Banks, 1996; Cornell & Hartmann, 1998; Eriksen, 1993; Fenton, 2003, for reviews). Anthropologists have provided many detailed descriptions of the way that ethnicity is created and re-created at the level of everyday interaction and in relation to broader social and cultural circumstances and developments. In addition, more general theoretical and conceptual positions for the study of ethnic identity have been developed. Anthropologists have traditionally also been interested in psychology. For example, there have been attempts to give a more social psychological account of ethnicity and to theorize the self (e.g. Cohen, 1994; De Vos, 1995; Jenkins, 1996). However, this interest is not reciprocated by most social psychologists. Some reject anthropological work because of what is regarded as methodological inadequacies, and others are indifferent to or ill-informed about it.

In studying real-world ethnic phenomena, it is important not to ignore anthropological contributions. Liebkind (1992) has argued that a crossing of disciplinary boundaries is necessary in order to achieve an adequate understanding of ethnic identity processes. Further, Jahoda (1982) has shown that psychologists can benefit from considering anthropology. Similar arguments have been made by Moscovici and Tajfel among others. As someone who has formal training in both social psychology and anthropology, I wholeheartedly agree. Hence, although the emphasis is on social psychology, I make references to anthropological perspectives and research. This is particularly the case in Chapter 3, where I focus on the concept of 'ethnicity'. In this chapter, I discuss anthropological ideas and debates in order to have a better understanding about what ethnicity means and how it can be examined. Doing so implies that I consider the relationship between ethnicity and culture, and discuss transactional, circumstantial, and primordial approaches.

However, I think it useful to focus on the different social psychological approaches first. In Chapter 1, I discuss the way social psychology typically tends to investigate ethnic identity, and I present a model with three levels of analysis.

Using this model, I identify and discuss various social psychologies and examine the possibilities for engagement and combination. These possibilities raise epistemological questions, which I discuss, while also addressing questions of research methods and reflexivity. I end the chapter by arguing for the importance of defining the key concepts 'identity' and 'ethnicity'.

Chapter 2 is on social identity. In this book and following most scholars, ethnic identity is conceptualized as a particular social identity. This raises questions about how social identity can be understood and what the implications are of such a conceptualization. Three related components of social identity are discussed, and it is argued that the distinction between these three components allows us to examine ethnic identity issues more adequately. In addition, the distinction relates to differences in emphasis and interest in social psychological work. Other questions considered in this chapter are those of the context dependency of social identities and identity formation. Furthermore, it will be argued that it is important to make a clear and concise distinction between social identity and sense of identity and between social identity and social identification. These distinctions are important, but unfortunately they are all too often ignored in social psychology.

After I consider the notion of 'ethnicity' in Chapter 3, in Chapters 4 to 7 the focus is on particular questions and issues. I make use of the empirical findings of research that we have conducted over the last 15 years among ethnic minority and majority groups in the Netherlands. It is not my intention to give a description of the variety of identity phenomena among these ethnic groups. In view of the great number of groups and the huge diversity within them, this would be an almost impossible task. Rather the intention is to discuss different social psychological ideas and approaches in relation to various examples from our research. In this way, both the limits of the discipline and the contributions that social psychology can make to an understanding of ethnic identity become clear. The use of empirical examples allows us to identify the distinctive differences and commonalities of social psychological approaches in a concrete rather than only a theoretical and more abstract sense.

In Chapter 4, the focus shifts to ethnic categorization in relation to place, space, and time. Place is the concrete site of everyday interaction in which identities are flexibly managed and negotiated in relation to different persons and groups. Hence, ethnic identity can be studied in relation to local circumstances and conditions. However, because of technological developments in transportation and communication, it is also possible to define and sustain identities through space, leading to transnational communities and diasporas. Furthermore, there is an important time dimension to ethnicity. Ethnicity locates people in history and often involves comparisons in time and 'intergenerational' obligations. The discussion of place, space, and time widens the social psychological perspective from its typical focus on the 'here and now' by adding the 'there and then'.

Chapter 5 examines the nature of ethnic identity in terms of essentialism and inherentism. Interest in essentialist thinking has been growing in social psychology. Essentialist ideas about social groups can be examined as cognitive processes but also as social practices performed in discourse. In many of these studies, a critique of essentialist positions in relation to ethnicity and race is developed. This chapter examines essentialism in relation to multiculturalism and group status positions. Here, my main argument is that essentialism is not by definition oppressive and that de-essentialism is not by definition progressive.

In general, social psychologists are not very interested in the messier categories of human affairs. In Chapter 6, I focus on questions related to hyphenated identities and hybridity. Social identities are predominantly studied as 'pure' categories, for which there are clear-cut boundaries and a simple, mutually exclusive structure, such as black/white, and majority/minority. However, in social reality, the number of identity options proliferates, and these options are combined and mixed in various ways, leading to more 'problematic' categories. Theories of hybridity reject the notion of homogeneous, uniformly defined identities and subscribe instead to notions of heterogeneity and multiple identities. However, in the social sciences, the theoretical studies on hybridity greatly outnumber the empirical work. Hence, it is unclear whether these new identities are really as multiple and fragmented as they are posited to be. It is also unclear how people actually manage their belonging to different social groups. These questions will be discussed in relation to our empirical work in the Netherlands and on the Polish Tatars.

In our research, we have often found that the same person defines himself or herself in one context as, for example, Turkish and in another as Dutch. That is to say, in one context, individuals may stress their Turkish background and culture, while in another they may downplay its importance in favour of their 'Dutchness'. Chapter 7 discusses different interpretations of this apparent inconsistency by focusing on self-definitions and the ethnic self. The emphasis is on the various ways in which ethnic self-definitions can be examined and understood. In doing so, the strengths and weaknesses of different social psychologies are laid bare.

Chapter 7 also examines ethnic identity formation from a psychological perspective. Here, the emphasis is on the individual meanings of ethnic identity and the ways in which a sense of ethnic identity develops and structures mental life. Different theories have tried to describe and explain the psychological correlates and consequences of belonging to an ethnic group. These theories focus on how discrimination, stigmatization, and cultural differences affect the development of a positive and secure minority group identity. This line of work is important for understanding the psychological predicaments of a minority position. However, it is also limited because it does not have much to say about the ways that ethnic identities are communicated and used in interactions.

Finally, in the last chapter of the book, I try to bring the main points and arguments together. I discuss how social psychology can improve our understanding of ethnic identity and ethnicity, and show how increased attention to ethnicity has benefits for social psychology. I also put forward the possibilities for combining or reconciling different social psychologies. These social psychologies often try to establish a distinctive position within the field of 'social psychology' by refuting or criticizing other approaches. The result is a kind of either/or thinking that does not really help to push the field and our understanding of ethnic identity forward.

The Dutch context and terminology

Most of the research that I will discuss has been conducted in the Netherlands. This does not mean, however, that this book has no implications outside this country. It is certainly the case that the particular national context has an influence on the ethnic groups considered, the ideas and questions asked, and the research conducted. This is true for any national context including, for example, the USA, where most social psychological findings are produced. Hence, it is important to say something about the Dutch situation and I will return to this shortly. However, I have written with a wider audience and applicability in mind. This is evidenced and, I hope, achieved by the theoretical emphasis taken and by the use of examples from other countries. Firstly, those aspects of the claims made that have a certain generality to them are more theoretical than empirical. Existing notions and theories are used as starting points from which to examine ethnic identity, and, in the process of doing so, to scrutinize and evaluate the notions and theories themselves.

Secondly, examples from different countries are used as evidence and to illustrate the claims that are made. There are many similarities between the situation in the Netherlands and other European countries, such as Belgium, Germany, and the UK. Furthermore, despite the important differences, there are also similarities with the USA. For example, prejudice and discrimination against ethnic minorities are well documented in many countries around the world, and similar processes of exclusion seem to be operative among different minority groups in trying to deal with these negative circumstances.

However, I do want to focus on examples of our research in the Netherlands. The main reason is that the studies have been conducted within the framework of the ideas and perspective that is presented in this book. In terms of methods, this implies that in the research various techniques have been used, including experiments, surveys, interviews, focus group discussions, and ethnographic work. However, I will not discuss all the technical details of the different studies. These can be found in various journal articles that are indicated in the text. Here, I am concerned with the examples and the evidence that these studies provide in relation to the central concern of this book.

As already mentioned, it is worth saying something about the Dutch situation. Chinese and Italian migrants came to the Netherlands before the Second World War, and in the 1950s and 1960s a few thousand workers came from Spain, Portugal, and Greece. In addition, in 1951, around 12,500 South Moluccans arrived in the Netherlands, on the basis of their status as former military personnel of the Royal Netherlands Indies Army. It was not until the late 1960s, however, that Dutch industry started recruiting migrant labour on a large scale. Most of these migrant workers were Turkish and Moroccan men who were either single or had left their families behind in their home country. At first, all parties concerned imagined that these migrants would remain in the Netherlands for only a limited period of time. Events proved otherwise, however, and in the mid-1970s, a process of family reunification began, as first the Turks and later the Moroccans were joined by their wives and children. At the same time, large numbers of Dutch nationals from Suriname (both Hindustani and Creoles) settled in the Netherlands. In the 1990s, many refugees and asylum seekers who had fled countries such as Iraq, Iran, Sudan, Ghana, Somalia, and Ethiopia sought refuge in the Netherlands. For example, in 2000, around 130,000 people came with the intention of settling in the Netherlands.

In 2002, there were approximately one and a half million immigrants resident in the Netherlands (10% of total population), of which the Turks formed the largest single group (320,000), followed by the Surinamese (309,000), the Moroccans (273,000), and the Antilleans (117,000). More than half of these ethnic minorities live in the four largest cities, and in many neighbourhoods in these cities the majority of the population are members of ethnic minorities. Where there are relatively large concentrations of immigrants, the immigrant population itself is ethnically heterogeneous. The different groups live together with Dutch people in the same areas. There are, however, areas with a large concentration of (particular) ethnic minority groups, and there are, for example, many Islamic primary schools attended only by Muslims.

In terms of housing, schooling, and the labour market, the position of most ethnic minority groups is worse than that of the ethnic Dutch. For example, studies indicate that ethnic-minority-group students consistently perform less well in school. The Moroccans and Turks have the poorest academic results, irrespective of how academic performance is defined (e.g. Martens & Verweij, 1997; Tesser et al., 1996). The Turks and Moroccans have the highest unemployment rates and are around twice as likely to be unemployed as the Dutch. Furthermore, these groups are at the bottom of the ethnic hierarchy, or, put differently, they are the least accepted by the Dutch (Hagendoorn, 1995). In the Netherlands, there is a notable pattern of relatively low levels of blatant prejudice and high levels of subtle prejudice towards ethnic minorities (Jackson et al., 1998; Pettigrew & Meertens, 1995). This pattern changed with the general election of May 2002 and the rise of right-wing parties and politicians, in particular the populist Pim Fortuyn, who was murdered a few days before the election. Prejudice became more blatant and involved stigmatization as well as more open hostility towards ethnic minorities in general and Islamic groups in particular. In only two years' time, the political and social 'climate' has changed dramatically from a tolerant and more multicultural perspective to one that emphasizes Dutch national identity and the need for assimilation of minority groups. This change is most evident among political parties on the right of the political spectrum, but it also involves left-wing parties such as the Social Democrats.

To conclude this introduction, a few terminological remarks are in order. After all, an ethnically heterogeneous society is particularly sensitive to the way language is used. Each label has its own connotations and implicitly reflects a certain position. Social psychological research has shown that the evaluation of an object depends on the way in which it is named (e.g. Eiser, 1990). Labels are important and can be subject to strong disagreements. We will see examples of this in later chapters. Words such as migrant, guest worker, and foreigner point to different characteristics and also reflect a standpoint about the relationship between the groups. Thirty years ago, 'guest worker' was a common term in the Netherlands, whereas today it is unacceptable.

Using the concepts of ethnicity and ethnic minorities seems self-evident in a book on ethnic identity. I will discuss the ethnic aspect of this in Chapter 3. The minority aspect can refer to the numerical size, but is usually used to indicate a disadvantageous social position. The term 'minority' is adequate to describe the situation at the societal level where ethnic groups form a minority in a social and political sense. However, at a local level, in old urban quarters and multiethnic schools, the situation can be quite different. Here, immigrant groups often do not form a minority in the numerical sense of the word, and also not in the sense of having less influence and power. I will come back to this in Chapter 4.

Finally, this book will discuss specific ethnic groups living in the Netherlands such as Turks, Moroccans, Chinese, South Moluccans, and Dutch. The use of the term 'Dutch' should be understood in an ethnic, and not a legal, sense. Many people from ethnic minority groups are Dutch nationals. Hence, the term 'Dutch' refers to the Dutch as an ethnic group, in relation to other ethnic groups. In the Netherlands, the terms 'race', 'racial group', and 'whites and blacks' are not often used. The distinction between ethnically Dutch and non-Dutch is made most often by the terms 'autochthonous' and 'allochthonous'. These terms are also common in, for example, Belgium and Germany, but are unusual in English-speaking countries.

1 Social psychologies

At a neighbourhood centre somewhere in an old part of a city, six locals are having a friendly chat about their neighbourhood. They are discussing the primary schools located in the area. Gradually their discussion moves to family affairs and how difficult it is to raise children in the present society. At some point in the discussion, one of the neighbours says that 'among us' women are in charge of the house. 'Among us' points to the Hindu background of these neighbours. The pleasant, relaxed atmosphere of the conversation changes into a fierce discussion about what is typically Hindu and what is not. Numerous characterizations enter the stage, but are also challenged again by the others. All neighbours agree that their Hindu background is very important, but they do not agree on what this background actually means.

A municipal anti-discrimination centre has organized a festive get-together with various activities such as people talking about each other's experiences. Guests from various backgrounds are present. One of them is a young Turkish woman wearing a headscarf. She explains that people often look at her in a special way. Because she is wearing a headscarf, people categorize her and expect certain things of her. She feels that she constantly has to justify herself, which results in her paying less attention to the things that she herself thinks are important. Sometimes she likes getting the opportunity to explain her headscarf, but the fact remains that there *is* something to explain. For many people, a headscarf is not so self-evident.

In a team meeting at a multiethnic secondary school, teachers are discussing the relationships between students. One of them states that in the higher classes students form groups along ethnic lines. He talks about segregation within the school and feels something needs to be done about this, both within the school and also with respect to the development of a ethnic diverse society. A discussion arises about the feasibility and desirability of taking action and how they should go about it. Some teachers point out that interaction with others from the same ethnic background is also important for students, in that it provides support, trust, and recognition. Others propose that ethnic group formation leads to conflicts between groups. The teachers decide they need first to think carefully about whether something should and can be done about this situation before returning to it at a later date.

Farouk is a 39-year-old Iranian refugee who has been living in the Netherlands for more than 15 years. He has great difficulty in living the life that he wants, involving family, work, and leisure. He has many social and practical problems, and he does not feel at home in the Netherlands. He explains that he is insecure and confused about what his Iranian background means to him. He thinks a lot about his former life in Iran, and he struggles to find an acceptable and fulfilling idea about himself. He also feels not really accepted by the Dutch and has the impression that it is always he that has to adapt and that he can never be himself. He lacks confidence, often feels depressed, and finds it very difficult to commit himself to anything.

The National Institute for Multicultural Development (FORUM) asks researchers to investigate ethnic identity among young South Moluccans in the Netherlands. The published final report is presented at a conference. In light of the results of the project, FORUM decides to organize some discussion evenings with South Moluccan young people. Both authors of the report are present to explain the results. Soon, however, a problem arises. Both authors are ethnically Dutch persons and are consequently subjected to much criticism. How could they know what preoccupies the South Moluccans, what do they know about the problems of the young people, and why did South Moluccans not carry out the project themselves? The ethnic background of the researchers appears to be sufficient reason for dismissing the report.

In all of these examples, taken from our own research in the Netherlands, ethnicity plays a role. Who and what people are is established and discussed, is interpreted and justified, is explained and serves as an explanation, structures situations and relationships, and affects well-being and mental health. In short, it has meaning and consequences in many different ways. Although these examples can be painful for those involved, they relate to relatively innocent events. Nevertheless and depending on circumstances, belonging to one ethnic group or another can also have far-reaching consequences. It could mean having the right to social security provisions and to get a residence permit, but it could also make the difference between life and death, as in the case of ethnic cleansings or suicides committed by desperate asylum seekers. Increasingly, ethnic distinctions play a role in every-day life in all sorts of ways. They are accompanied by and determine rights, duties, chances, expectations, forms of exclusion and conflict, and feelings of insecurity, uncertainty, and fear about, for example, stigmatization and discrimination.

Although today many discussions involve the topic of ethnic identity, its popularity is relatively recent. Gleason (1983) has shown that the concept of identity has a short history when it comes to ethnic and migration issues. The concept became popular in the 1950s. Until that time, questions around immigration were treated and studied in terms of alienation, loneliness, and uprooting. Concepts such as identity crisis and identity conflict were introduced only later.

In the past decade, the number of writings and studies on (ethnic) identity has increased enormously. Several reasons can be given for this. Identity is the key word for conceptualizing the relationship between the individual and society.

Identity is 'the best device I know for bringing together "public issues" and "private troubles"' (Jenkins, 1996, p. 3). The concept tells us something about how people place themselves and others in their social environment, and how such positions get personal meaning and value. This makes it understandable that in a period of important societal changes, issues of identity are in the spotlight and that concepts such as identity crisis and the search for one's own identity are frequently brought up. Political, economic, cultural, and demographic transformations go together with changes in the relationship between the individual and society, placing issues of identity at the forefront.

Hence, many authors have argued that questions of identity have become more urgent and profound in our late modern and global era. Economic and cultural changes, the disappearance of dominant ideologies and of traditional symbols, the extremely rapid exchange of information, the large mobility of goods, services, and people, and the increasing number of national and international conflicts are all seen as responsible for the growing importance of identity issues. Globalization processes mark the way in which people see and place themselves and others. Events happening on the other side of the world can influence local definitions and self-understandings. Transnational developments on the one hand and regionalization and localization on the other hand, it is argued, reduce the importance of national borders. In many cases, globalization goes together with an increasing emphasis on localities and a reference to descent and origin. Cultural heterogeneity and mixture often have their counterpart in strivings for homogeneity and purity.

Ethnic, religious, and cultural diversity has become a reality in many countries around the world. This diversity forces both citizens and authorities to deal with the thorny question of identity. Many debates address multiculturalism, pluralism, and enhanced diversity, and these developments pose numerous new questions for the authorities. Ordinary citizens also struggle with differences and similarities. People from ethnic minorities, for example, are confronted with the question of just what their ethnic background entails and how they should act towards members of not only their own group but also the majority and other minorities. The consequences of that diversity and the choices made by ethnic minorities constitute a rich source for reflection and discussion. Especially young people from ethnic minority groups try to give their own meaning to their ethnic background. The world of their parents often does not correspond to their position and future in the country in which they live. Furthermore, a situation of feeling unaccepted or only partially accepted by (persons from) the majority group hampers an orientation towards that group.

The ethnic identity of members from the majority group is typically more self-evident, since it is linked to their dominant social position. Members of this group often do not have to think about their ethnicity and what it consists of. They constitute the implicit norm against which others are measured. Hence, not so long ago, Dutch identity was less explicit but at the same time it constituted an indispensable source of value. However, 'whiteness' and the sense of belonging to an ethnic majority group has become increasingly less of a given and more and more a question, not only for people in multiethnic schools and neighbourhoods but for the populace in general. The arrival of new groups has changed the situation in such a way that one's own ethnic or national background is no longer invisible or taken for granted. More and more, what it means to be 'just Dutch' is something that is and feels challenged and problematic. In some situations, being Dutch has been gradually reduced to one ethnic group among other ethnic groups, with the consequence that people are confronted with the question of how exactly do the Dutch differ from other ethnic groups attending the same school, living in the same neighbourhood, or coming to the Netherlands. In that sense, majority group identity has become vulnerable and problematic. The multiethnic situation confronts people directly with the question of boundary construction and with the value and meaning of what is considered typical of one's own group.

Not only are questions of identity heavily discussed, but also the terminology with which these discussions take place has changed dramatically (Grossberg, 1996; Hall, 1996), as has the way in which identity is viewed. Not so long ago, the term 'identity' was used to refer to something private and clearly defined, whereas nowadays it is considered to indicate something public and variable. In the past, words such as 'stability', 'unity', 'certainty', and 'essence' were said to describe identity phenomena accurately, but now, 'variability', 'multiple', 'fragmentation', 'uncertainty' and 'ambivalence' are considered to be much more appropriate terms with which to describe the way identity functions. Increasingly, questions of identity are viewed as the result of a continuing process of construction, choice, and negotiation. In this process, cultural meanings are used situationally to define differences and similarities. The focus is on the flexible and ambivalent ways in which people define themselves in relation to others. Since this is happening in a constantly changing global, national, and local context, identity is an always unfinished project and temporary state. In this line of argument, questions that focus on more enduring and stable aspects of identity are ignored or disqualified by branding them as examples of essentialism and primordialism.

One main objection to this typification of the present-day situation is its general and abstract character (e.g. Mac an Ghaill, 1999). The abstract descriptions contain assumptions on how identities have changed and are shaped, but have led to relatively little research about the everyday life of ordinary people. Very little research has been done on how people give meaning to their life in actual situations. According to critics, the late- or postmodern condition refers mainly to a small elite of cosmopolitans or to styles among certain groups of young people (Friedman, 1997; Smith, 1994). These descriptions are said to fit mainly Western individualistic cultures in which personal choice and self-responsibility are emphasized. People living in cultures with a more group-oriented collective character in which obligation and duty are the basis for self-definition, would, it is argued, have more stable and clear identities.

Social psychology and ethnic identity

In the USA, increased interest in ethnicity and related issues is evident in psychology (see Phinney, 1996; Sue, 1999; Sue et al., 1999). For instance, the field of 'ethnic psychology' has developed from the principle that culturally appropriate methods should be employed to describe and explain the experience of ethnic minority groups. Furthermore, in 2003, the American Psychological Association published its 'Guidelines on Multicultural Education, Training, Research, Practice, and Organizational Change for Psychologists'. And the interest of the American Psychological Association's division, Society for the Psychological Study of Ethnic Minority Issues, is mainly focused on questions of mental health and personality development. These are the main topics of their journal *Cultural Diversity and Ethnic Minority Psychology*.

In the USA, there is also a well-established research tradition in issues of racial identity and racism. For example, the early research by E. L. Horowitz (1939), Clark and Clark (1947), and Goodman (1952) inspired many studies on racial identity, and much work has been done on racism (Duckitt, 1992). In addition, although there are some older studies (e.g. Giles et al., 1976), American social psychologists have shown an increased interest in questions of ethnic identity (e.g. Gaines et al., 1997; Gurin et al., 1994; Judd et al., 1995; Lorenzo-Hernández & Ouellette, 1998; Prentice & Miller, 1999; Wolsko et al., 2000). In Canada, interest in these questions started in the 1970s with the country's adopting multiculturalism as an official ideology, and several studies have been conducted since (e.g. Berry, 1984; Berry & Kalin, 1995; Moghaddam & Taylor, 1987; Montreuil & Bourhis, 2001).

In contrast, European social psychologists have devoted relatively little attention to ethnic issues (but see, for example, Christian et al., 1976; Hutnik, 1991; Kitwood, 1983; Liebkind, 1992; Tajfel, 1978; Ullah, 1987). However, there are clear signs of an increased interest in ethnicity, such as special journal issues (e.g. Chryssochoou, 2000), books (e.g. Chryssochoou, 2003; Reicher & Hopkins, 2001), and an increasing number of articles by European scholars in major social psychological journals, such as the *European Journal of Social Psychology*, *Personality and Social Psychology Bulletin*, and *Journal of Personality and Social Psychology*.

Social psychology can offer a valuable and important contribution to the understanding of the complexities of ethnicity. For example, in social psychology, there is a long tradition of studying categorization and social identity processes and stereotypes, prejudice, and racism. Numerous studies have been conducted on these issues, and relevant cognitive and emotional underpinnings have been identified. Important theories have been developed, and solutions for group conflicts have been proposed. However, there are at least two related restrictions when studying ethnic identity from this perspective. These restrictions have to do with social psychologists' preoccupation with mental processes and the failure to theorize ethnicity as such. In general, the emphasis is on intrapersonal procedures, and ethnicity is examined as just another social category that mainly results from information processing. Social psychologists have typically theorized processes and operations that act on categories such as ethnicity. As Sherif and Sherif (1969, p. 223) argue, 'if there is a *social psychology* of intergroup relations, it should not be altogether different when we consider small groups, ethnic groups, labor or management groups, or nationalities. What may be different, of course, are the sets of factors to be included in our analysis. In the rivalry between two churches, economic considerations may be very slight, whereas they may dominate labor–management negotiations.'

Many social psychologists examine the cognitive tendency to form and evaluate categories. In doing so, political, cultural, and other social factors are considered in so far as they determine which events and features are worth processing. The focus is, for example, on the general tendency to favour members of one's own group or the exaggerated perceived similarities and differences within and between social categories. This emphasis on cognitive analyses in the intergroup literature fails to address the fact that intergroup relations and behaviour are fundamentally interactive phenomena (Shelton, 2000). It is in the day-to-day contacts between people in concrete and localized circumstances that group distinctions are produced and used to make sense of lives and to accomplish certain goals.

The focus on general processes has for a long time led to a relative neglect of content and context. However, within the field, it is increasingly acknowledged that more attention should be paid to social context and content (e.g. Ellemers et al., 1999; Jost & Major, 2001). For example, from their research among African-American and white students, Judd et al. (1995, p. 479) concluded that 'group perceptions are guided not only by the fundamental cognitive processes that we have come to understand reasonably well in our laboratories but are also guided by ideological beliefs that our society has taught us all about the role of ethnicity and the extent to which ethnic differences are to be valued or denied.'

Groups and group membership derive their specific identity from a particular context, and approaches such as self-categorization theory (Turner et al., 1987) try to give a systematic account of the role of context. However, ethnicity cannot be examined only as a consequence of the way information is contextually processed. Ethnic identity can also be seen as a socially produced, contingent category. The focus can be on the legal, political, and societal definitions, practices, and conditions, and on the way ethnicity is used and lived by people in the context of everyday interactions. Specific forms of ethnic (self-)definitions can be explained not only by psychological tendencies and dispositions but also by political and cultural discourses and local discursive practices. Taking the content of social categories seriously implies that the nature and meaning of ethnicity should be considered. Otherwise, ethnicity becomes similar to national, gender, religious, class, or whatever (artificial) social identity. To be sure, ethnic identity has many things in common with other social identities, but at the same time there is the question as to what is special about *ethnic* identity?

What is predominantly offered in social psychology are theories of social categorization and intergroup relations, but ethnicity as such is not theorized. The question of what distinguishes ethnic identity from other social identities is, typically, not asked (Brown, 2000). People, however, have been found to make distinctions between different types of groups that affect normative expectations about in-group relations (Hong et al., 2003; Lickel et al., 2001). Furthermore, there can be differences between social categories in terms of psychological investments and social and institutional 'grounding'. In addition, an emphasis on processes has led to a focus on the more stable and clear categories that are often implicitly taken for granted (Reicher, 2001). Social psychologists as a whole are not much interested in the messier categories of human life and the ways in which these are socially defined and negotiated. The neat distinction between in- and out-group predominates, whereas, for example, in reality the number of hyphenated, or 'in-between', identities increases. Mexican-Americans, Chinese-Canadians, Turkish-Germans, Moroccan-Dutch, and Polish-Tatars are examples of groups reconstituting and negotiating their identities. These identity definitions take place in the context of histories, cultural differences, transnational migration, and (inter)national political debates and developments. These identities bring into sharp relief the sense of constantly managing and negotiating between tradition and modernity, past and present, local place and global space, and self and other.

Social psychologies

I have been writing about social psychology as if it were a unitary discipline. This reflects the dominance of the individualistic and mentalistic perspective. However, it is of course more appropriate to speak about social psychologies. Already in the 1970s, there was criticism and talk about the crisis in social psychology (e.g. Armistead, 1974). Many of the critics felt that the discipline was not getting anywhere in understanding social phenomena. It was argued that the individualism and experimentalism of the dominant form of social psychology ignored the social embeddedness of the person and the complexities of human life.

In the late 1980s and 1990s, social psychology saw the emergence of theoretical and empirical approaches that have formulated a more or less radical alternative to the dominant cognitive approach. Scholars such as Tajfel and Moscovici emphasized the social nature of the individual but were also interested in cognitive and motivational processes. In contrast, those writing from within critical social psychology (e.g. Ibanez & Iniguez, 1997) and discursive psychology (e.g. Edwards & Potter, 1992) have taken a more anticognitivist stance, focusing on collective constructions and social interactions.

There is much boundary drawing and little dialogue between these different social psychologies, particularly between the more cognitive and interactive approaches. According to Burr (2002, p. 21) this is 'the most recent incarnation of the long-standing division between psychological and sociological forms of the discipline'.

Historically, two kinds of social psychology have developed: psychological social psychology and sociological social psychology. According to Stryker (1987), the difference is mainly metatheoretical. The former approaches social psychology from the standpoint of the individual and examines basic tendencies and cognitive processes that underlie perceptions, evaluations, and behaviour. The focus is on explaining what individuals do and why they do it. In contrast, the latter emphasizes social relationships and interactions and examines meaningful actions in their social and historical context. Here the focus is on the social world itself and in trying to understand how social life is possible and changes over time. The former is more bottom-up and explains social reality by starting with the individual and moving outwards, whereas the latter is more top-down and starts with society and how it affects the lives of individuals.

Many of the differences between these two kinds of social psychology are to be found in the current debate within European social psychology between more mainstream and more discursive social psychological approaches (e.g. Stainton Rogers, 2003). This debate tends to lead to independent frameworks that either ignore each other or defend their opposing positions by contrasting the own favoured approach with that of the other. It is usually argued that there are fundamental epistemological differences between these frameworks and the emphasis is on that which the other fails to address. For example, mainstream social psychologists emphasize that discursive psychologists ignore important cognitive and affective processes, whereas discursive psychologists argue that mainstream approaches fail to address the practical activities entered into by people in interactions.

Rather than joining this either/or discussion, I would like to argue that, despite the epistemological, theoretical, and empirical differences, it is possible and necessary to engage with these approaches, particularly for developing a multi-dimensional understanding of ethnic identity. These approaches can be combined because they tend to have different emphases, are concerned with different questions, and focus on different levels of analysis. These levels are not simply right or wrong but more or less useful and appropriate depending on what is being analysed. Before elaborating on the levels of analysis, I will first consider the 'structure versus agency debate'.

Structure and agency

The notion of identity forms a link between the individual and society. This easily evokes a choice for the one or the other: that society determines the individual or that the individual constitutes society via its own meaningful actions. In the first case, the starting point is a rather deterministic image of humans, in which the moulding of people is emphasized. In the second, the starting point is a voluntary-like image of humans, in which the autonomy of people is stressed. The choice of the starting point has important consequences for research on ethnic identity.

In approaches that take society as their starting point, sociocultural circumstances and structures are central. People's characteristics are considered the result of the situations and positions in which they find themselves. The social environment determines or at least structures what people do, feel, and think. Ethnic identity is then studied at the societal and social level, in terms of economic, political, cultural, and ideological factors. For example, people are viewed as bearers of their culture, so that those who belong to one culture differ from those who are part of another. The result is a society with different cultural groups that determine what people are and how they act. Or people are seen as the passive recipients of imposed or assigned identities whereby the sense of ethnic identity is structured by the dominant discourses, meanings, and images that are attributed to the wider society.

In approaches that start with the individual, the emphasis is on one's own meanings and autonomous actions. Changes in society do not happen on their own, but are the outcomes of concrete actions and interactions. Ethnic identity is, then, considered to be the result of individual choices, personal meanings, and assertions. For example, Hollinger (1995) argues that people's affiliations with an ethnic or racial group should be wholly voluntary. The individual is seen as the fundamental unit of social life, and in research the thoughts, feelings, and actions of individuals are the starting point.

While both approaches are valuable, each has its limitations. The society approach rightly points to the fact that people are influenced by their circumstances. However, at the same time, people are not only reflections or 'photocopies' of the culture in which they have been raised or of the social positions assigned to them. Humans and their identities are not simply an effect of social structures or discourses. The danger of an 'oversocialized concept of men' is great (Wrong, 1961).

The individual approach implies the opposite: people are not passive victims of circumstance. They are able to think about their situation, do something about it, reflect, assert, react, and create. However, here we face the danger of an 'under-socialized concept of men'. The issue of belonging to a particular ethnic group is not determined by an individual's desires or choices alone. Circumstances are important since they provide possibilities and create limitations. The space for personal meaning and action is limited and prestructured. A quotation from Morris (1997, p. 328) summarizes this well: 'The emphasis on social structure indicates the way in which cultural schemas (language) and social institutions come, through social praxis, to shape and modify human consciousness and behaviour. The emphasis on human agency highlights the degree to which humans change social structures and cultural frameworks.'

People make their own lives, negotiate meanings, and change prevailing views and ideas to their own insights and desires. People do not simply reproduce the circumstances they are in, but appropriate them. At the same time, people are capable of doing this only because of the particular circumstances in which they are in and by which they have been shaped. The one cannot go without the other: Each presupposes the other. The emphasis on structure indicates the way in which discourses and institutions come to shape and modify human consciousness and behaviour, and the emphasis on human agency highlights the degree to which humans change cultural frameworks and social structures. Neither aspect can be reduced to the other. The fact that social changes are the result of people's concrete actions does not imply, for instance, that these changes are in line with the intentions behind those actions. Social changes may have little to do with what people intend to do or aim to achieve. And the fact that, for example, politicians or (local) policies try to influence people's thinking and behaviour does not mean that they succeed. In discussing ethnic identity, Nagel (1994, p. 154) argues that ethnicity is 'The result of a dialectical process involving internal and external opinions and processes, as well as the individual's self-identification and outsiders' ethnic designations—i.e. what *you* think your ethnicity is, versus what *they* think your ethnicity is.'

Ethnic identities are not simply the products of ethnic assignments imposed by others or assertions made by people themselves, but the result of the interaction between the two.

Hacking (1999) makes a distinction between natural and human (or interactive) kinds. The latter are categories by which people are classified. These categories have a profound impact on people's lives. Being categorized in a particular way implies being treated or institutionalized in that way. However, people are most often aware of this and can act in response to how they are being classified. In contrast to natural kinds, human kinds may exhibit a feedback cycle or what Hacking calls a 'looping effect'. The categorization affects those categorized, and their response brings about a change in the meanings and functions of the categorizations. Categorizations and beliefs about ethnic minorities as kinds of persons become known to the people classified, and this changes the way individuals present themselves and behave. This then loops back to force changes in the categorizations and beliefs about them. Because of the looping effect of human kinds, the targets of the social sciences are always on the move. This does not mean, however, that categorizations cannot appear or be treated as natural kinds or that changes in categories occur easily. In principle, there is an ongoing process, but distinctions and meanings can become more stable and institution- alized. They can become self-evident and taken-for-granted ways of understanding the world and oneself.

Three levels of analysis

The usefulness of a distinction between levels of analysis has been suggested by several social psychologists (e.g. Doise, 1986; Duckitt, 1992). Here I want to focus on the personality and social structure model as proposed by House (1977, 1981). This is a comprehensive and heuristically useful model for explaining and situating different approaches to social identity. It has been used recently by Coté and Levine (2002) in their attempt to give a synthetic view of identity formation. For my examination of ethnic identity, I will present an adapted version of this model.

House distinguishes between three levels of analysis: personality, interaction, and social structure. For my purposes, I will refer to these levels as individual, interactive, and societal. The first level involves intraindividual processes and personal characteristics which are studied in terms of the self, sense of identity, cognitive structures, and so on. In studying ethnic identity, the focus is, for example, on identity status, self-schemas, self-esteem, and identification. Developmental and most social psychologists are typically interested in this level of analysis.

The level of interaction refers to the dynamics of both concrete and everyday contacts in many different situations. The emphasis is on the emergence and maintenance of identity in situated interactions. Ethnic identity, for example, can be examined in terms of an ongoing process of social definitions and negotiations. These dynamics of interaction are studied by symbolic interactionist and discursive psychologists, and are also the main topic of interest of anthropologists.

Political, ideological, cultural, and economic features make up the societal level of analysis. This is the level of the broad or macrosocial and historical developments that are examined, for example, in terms of (post)modernism, globalization, and dominant discourses. Here, ethnic identity is investigated in relation to state regulations, transnationalism, economic changes, and ideologies. Sociologists and scholars in cultural studies have done much work on this level just as have social psychologists that build on the work of Foucault and Althusser.

Figure 1.1 is an adapted version of figures presented by Coté and Levine (2002) and is closely related to Berger and Luckmann's (1966) discussion of the social construction of reality. It illustrates the three levels of analysis along with their interrelationships, and it can be used to explain the different social psychological approaches to social identity and ethnic identity in particular.

There are a number of assumptions underlying this model. The first one is that the level of interaction mediates between the other two. Society and the individual are taken to influence each other indirectly. There is no society without actions of individuals and there is no individuality outside society. It is in interactions that societal relations, beliefs, norms, and values are reproduced and changed, actualized, or challenged. And it is in interactions that a sense of self and identity

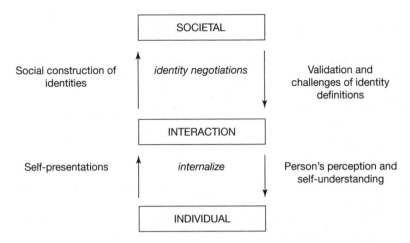

Figure 1.1 Social identity formation and maintenance processes.

is formed. Many social psychologists share a strong interest in actions and interactions, but not to the same extent. Condor (1996, p. 292), for example, argues, 'In general, social identity theory posits a direct line of communication between the individual and the macrosocial by effectively cutting out the microsocial middle-man.'

The second idea behind the model is that the different levels cannot be reduced to each other. The three levels are, of course, interdependent, but each level is analytically different from the other two. It is only by making this analytic distinction that the particularities of each as well as the relationships between the three can be examined. For example, issues of ethnic identity management and negotiation in interactions are related to institutional and psychological processes, but they cannot be reduced to either one. And psychological aspects of ethnic identity are, of course, strongly related to and influenced by societal and local circumstances, but also have their own processes and characteristics. In the next chapter, I will argue that it is important to make an analytic distinction between social identity as a social construction and sense of identity as an intrapsychic phenomenon. Doing so allows us, for example, to examine identity conflicts in terms of the potential misalignment between a person's self-definition and others' definition(s) of who one is considered to be. These kinds of identity problems can easily occur among ethnic minority group members. For example, the way a Turkish girl living in the Netherlands understands her Turkishness can differ from the way the Turkish community defines this, which can also differ from the way the Dutch majority sees her. The result can be that her sense of ethnic identity is disrupted, making her confused and insecure. Psychologically, her ethnic identity can become a dominating and distracting issue, and, socially, she has to struggle to establish and affirm an acceptable ethnic identity. Hence, social processes of identity maintenance and negotiation should not be confused with psychological processes of identity development and formation. Both are important to examine in their own right and in relation to each other.

The third aspect of the model is that it allows for a systematic conceptualization and investigation of the interrelationships and influences among the three levels. The beginning point for describing these influences is arbitrary. In Figure 1.1, the right-hand top arrow indicates how cultural definitions and structural positions in a society provide the limits and possibility for processes of identity maintenance and negotiation in interactions. Laws, socially shared values, discourses, images, and conventions, as well as status and power differences, influence everyday behaviour. For example, institutionalized practices, stereotypes, and labels used for ethnic groups on the level of society will affect how people define and position themselves in interactions. Ethnic options are constituted by the nature and range of socially available positions that can be taken up in interactions. These options construct particular versions of migrants and ethnic minorities as real. For example, the discourse about asylum seekers and refugees as being 'fortune seekers' produces a particular reality about immigrants which has consequences for how they can speak and behave, as well as the rights they are entitled to (Verkuyten, 2005).

The lower arrow on the right-hand side in Figure 1.1 represents the person's perception and self-understanding that results from everyday interactions with others. Social identities are managed and negotiated in interactions, and the outcomes of this are internalized. That is to say, people develop an individual understanding of social reality. The social definitions of what it means to be a member of an ethnic minority group are apprehended and developed into an individual understanding. For example, children learn that they are considered members of a particular ethnic group. The social location or ethnic place in the world assigned to children by parents, peers, and others is subjectively appro-priated. It becomes part of their self-understanding and affects the way they perceive and approach the world. The content of internalizations comes from the concrete contacts with others within a particular context. However, internalization is not determination, just as enculturalation is not cultural 'cloning'. Children from the same ethnic group living in the same family can give different personal meanings to their ethnic identity. Children are active participants in learning to understand their social world and themselves.

The lower left-hand arrow in Figure 1.1 indicates that an individual's behaviour is in part a product of the internalized abilities to produce self-presentations and to act appropriately in a given situation. People can present themselves in a certain way and learn how to respond to social expectations that may differ situationally. Individuals struggle to establish and affirm their sense of identity in interactions. The idea of who one is or wants to become requires behavioural and emotional confirmation by others. To possess ethnic options implies that one is able to claim some desired images and understandings that are recognized and validated in social interactions. The way people present themselves in interactions can be accepted by others and correspond to what is expected by others. However, it is also possible to question and resist these expectations. One's sense of identity can differ from the general conception of the group. Identity management and negotiation require an internalized understanding of the relevant social meanings and the ability to produce the expected or personally valued and desired behaviour. An ethnic minority group member with a secure and strong sense of what her ethnic background means to her will fulfil the task of self-presentation and identity management differently from someone with an insecure and negative ethnic self-understanding.

In Figure 1.1, the upper arrow on the left-hand side represents the social construction of reality. Social reality is the product of human interactions, and social identities are socially produced and defined. Distinctions that people make and things that people do in everyday life can evolve into socially assigned identities. As people repeatedly engage in particular activities, they become typified as the sorts of persons that do those sorts of things or that simply are that way. Social distinctions and practices become objectified and institutionalized. Socially shared ideas and beliefs are created by people in interaction, but, once created, they have a seemingly autonomous life. They become the self-evident and taken-for-granted assumptions about the nature of human beings and the social world. In addition, social construction processes culminate in the creation of institutions, conventions, and (in)formal norms that are enforced through social control. The socially constructed reality becomes objective or factual. People of a certain ethnic group just are the way they are; they reflect 'what everybody knows about them'. The stereotypes and beliefs are socially shared, and there is the tendency to see them as accurate reflections of the nature of ethnic groups.

Social psychological approaches: Perception and discourse

The model described emphasizes the dialectical nature of the relationship between individual and society. Both are not pre-existing entities but are inevitably and intimately connected; the one constitutes the other. In the words of Berger and Luckmann (1966, p. 79; their italics), '*Society is a human product. Society is an objective reality. Man is a social product.*' The model can be used to situate different social psychological approaches to identity and to show that these approaches are concerned with different questions and levels of analysis. Examples of these approaches will be discussed more fully in later chapters where empirical studies on ethnic identity are presented.

Some social psychologists are particularly concerned with discourses as producing and maintaining people within particular positions and relationships (e.g. Burman & Parker, 1993; Parker, 1992). Influenced by the work of social theorists such as Foucault and Althusser, the focus is mainly on the societal level of analysis (see Willig, 2001). Foucault analysed how people are created by the discursive formations and regimes of truth within which they live. Discourses are seen as systems of representation that construct subject positions and constitute social interactions. All discourses affect the field of possible actions by enabling and constraining what can be done and said, and what cannot. Hence, the analytic interest here is in the ways that historical and cultural resources that are grounded in dominant institutions construct people's lives.

These representations are predominantly examined by deconstructing or taking apart the language in which definitions and representations appear. The consequences of discourses are examined by analysing textual constructions in terms of the diversity of social positions and relationships that are being defined and provided or denied and ignored. For example, one can examine how discourses are used to reify, legitimate, and dissimulate patterns of social power and ethnic dominance. However, in making textual deconstructions, the extent to which devices and interpretations actually affect people's actions and self-understandings in everyday interactions is often left unexamined. The focus is on 'unmasking' the nature and origin of the discourses and discursive regimes that constitute 'the subject'. The subject is seen as produced within discourse and as a bearer of a discursive system that creates him or her. This focus can result in an unnecessarily deterministic stance, in which people have hardly any room for manoeuvre. There is the real danger that one could lose sight of the possibility for reflexivity and resistance.

Discursive psychologists tend to focus more on the level of social inter-actions. For example, in their analyses, some discursive psychologists use an ethnomethodological and conversation-analytic perspective on social action (Antaki & Widdicombe, 1998; Edwards, 1997; Potter, 1996). In these studies, the focus is on the everyday practice of language use in which actions are conceptualized in terms of the range of practical and interpersonal tasks that people perform. Construction is examined through talk and texts in which specific versions of the world are developed or challenged. Identity is seen as something that is actively accomplished within a particular context.

Discursive psychologists acknowledge that there are basic mental capacities necessary for discourse work to occur, but they have a particular understanding of these inner, or psychological, processes (e.g. Edwards & Potter, 1992; Harré & Gillett, 1994). Psychological processes are seen as constituted through discursive social activity, and substantive cognitive claims are rejected on epistemological grounds. The analytic focus is on the sequential organization of interactions and on what is made relevant by the participants themselves (Schegloff, 1997). Discursive consequences are examined in terms of the visible consequentiality in social interactions. To examine the functions of an interpretation or account, discursive psychologists focus on the observable responses of the other participants in a conversation. Assumptions about underlying psychological processes or mental states are rejected in favour of an analysis of the interaction itself.

However, discursive studies do not demonstrate that differences in psychological tendencies and feelings do not exist or are of secondary importance. The focus on everyday interactions is crucially important but draws attention away from the question of the relationship between the social and the psychological. Discursive psychologists largely ignore this question but implicitly tend to characterize the person as self-interested and motivated in order to build an acceptable account (Hammersley, 2003). The result is a kind of interactionist—if not behaviourist —reduction.

Developmental (social) psychologists are concerned with questions of identity formation. The focus is on the way that individuals achieve a sense of identity and form a particular self-understanding. Identity formation is not seen as a cognitive and emotionally isolated process but as depending on the interplay between a developing individual and his or her social context. However, the emphasis is typically on how a person assimilates social influences and the intrapsychic outcomes of this interplay. The dominant concern focuses on, for example, self-organization and self-feelings. Researchers talk about psychologically strong or weak, secure or insecure, elaborate or simple, and positive or negative self-concepts. These terms are also used to think about ethnic identity and to provide an understanding about how negative social circumstances have an adverse effect on people's self-understanding. Furthermore, the identity status paradigm developed by Marcia (1966) has been used to examine the development of ethnic identity in terms of identity diffusion, identity foreclosure, identity moratorium, and identity achievement (e.g. Phinney, 1989).

This line of research can provide valuable insights, for example, into how belonging to a stigmatized ethnic minority group affects people psychologically.

Questions of psychological well-being, the development of self-feelings, and the way people try to form a secure sense of identity are important issues to consider. Although these issues are inevitably and closely related to social circumstances, they cannot be reduced to these. The fact that the person is embedded within society does not mean that there is no inner world or that the psychological is not relevant. However, the danger of a focus on the psychological is that the dynamic and complex ways in which people present themselves across different situations is neglected. A psychological perspective tends to frame the causes of action in terms of inner structures, motivations, and cognitive processes. These are assumed to act as the real, underlying, causal hand behind behaviour. Ethnic identity then becomes understood in terms of mental issues, and the way people account for their ethnic identity as an ongoing, negotiable process within particular social contexts is ignored.

As is common in the social sciences, the approaches on these three levels often situate themselves in opposition to one another, leading to a kind of either/or thinking. Ethnic identity becomes, for example, an issue either of cognition or construction, of stability or variability, of continuity or change, of unity or fragmentation, of voluntarism or determinism, of the individual or of society.

Each of these positions is not so much wrong as it is limited. In an either/or approach, an opposite is created in which the other kind of analysis is dismissed as inadequate. Discursive psychologists tend to take a strong anticognitive stance, and cognitive psychologists ignore or reject the turmoil of everyday life. Either the one *or* the other has to be right, and with that the possibility that both are useful disappears. There is often a clear tendency to treat one's own kind of analysis and explanation as *the* appropriate one. Time and energy are spent in asserting the value and priority of one's own approach, and criticizing the value of others and defining these as peripheral. There is a danger that social psychologists, preoccupied with pursuing and protecting their own particular approaches, theories, and methods, will neglect to understand real-life social phenomena and problems, such as those related to ethnicity and race.

For example, social psychologists studying interactions focus on the emergent and changing qualities of identity definitions. The emphasis is on flexibility and variability in the use of language to produce a given account in particular conversations. This means, for example, that the interest is on the actual accomplishment and manifestation of ethnic self-definitions in talk.

Similarly, in the postmodern literature (e.g. Gergen, 1991; Michael, 1996), the emphasis is on the self as decentred, relational, contingent, and lacking any core or essence. It is argued that the declining modernist institutions, based on logic, reason, and reality, have been replaced by more relativistic, subjective, and nonrational social forms. As a result, identity has become a question of temporary choice and the strategic consumption of images, fashion, and illusions. Because of the multiplicity of incoherent and disconnected relationships and 'voices', the self has become fragmented, 'dialogical', and without substance. However, not all identities should be considered as equivalent. As Billig (1995, p. 139; his italics) writes, 'One can eat Chinese tomorrow and Turkish the day after: one can even dress in Chinese or Turkish styles. But *being* Chinese or Turkish are not commercially available options.'

At the institutional or societal level, statuses and positions are often more enduring and stable. There are clear structural and cultural constraints on individual activity which can be investigated. Power and status relations, as well as predominant discourses in society, do not change very easily, and they affect the way that individuals can position themselves and others. The continuous negotiation on the level of everyday interactions does not imply a similar level of flexibility and variability on the level of society. Institutional and cultural features associated with ethnicity and race persist and do not change very easily. The importance of distinctions between ethnic and racial groups has not disappeared, and the political dimension of 'identity politics' requires more stable and identifiable ethnicities. In addition, the postmodern perspective is rather individualistic and voluntaristic. The emphasis is on choice, rather than on duty and obligation, as the basis of self-definition. However, the latter can be important among ethnic minority groups with a more collectivist cultural background.

Moreover, the emphasis on flexibility and variability does not imply that psychological or inner resources are no longer relevant. According to Gergen (1991, p. 150), 'The pastiche personality is a social chameleon, constantly borrowing bits and pieces of identity from whatever sources are available and constructing them as useful or desirable in a given situation.' However, this does not have to imply that people do not develop a particular, structured sense of who they are. Variation in self-description and self-presentation does not necessarily imply an equally flexible self-concept. One can have a relatively stable sense of oneself and still describe oneself in flexible and context-sensitive ways. Self-understandings are invested with cognitive and emotional meanings, in which particularly the latter can be important. In postmodern accounts, situated-cognition and changing self-definitions predominate, and affect and sentiments tend to have disappeared. However, emotional investments, feelings of loyalty, and self-feelings are, in general, much more persistent than cognitive understandings. Furthermore, the psychological problems related to a lack of inner structure should be neither ignored nor celebrated, just as a subjective sense of identity confusion and low self-regard among ethnic minority group members should be taken seriously.

The distinction between levels of analysis is useful for examining the nature of the processes at these different levels and the interrelations between them. It is also useful for situating and characterizing the main focus of different approaches. As indicated, of course, this does not mean that these approaches are inadequate or wrong in placing a relative importance on one or another level. They simply focus on different levels of analysis that are related in certain ways but are not reducible to one another. The questions asked differ, as do the concepts, theories, and methods employed. There are also social psychological approaches that try to take different levels into account. This is the case not only in sociological social psychology as developed in the USA, but also in European approaches.

For example, some social psychologists try to combine the societal and interaction level of analysis. Thus, Deaux and Martin (2003) specify the levels of social representation and interpersonal networks that act as independent settings of identity work. Further, critical social psychologists (e.g. Billig, 1995; Edley, 2001b; Wetherell, 1998) examine how shared cultural understandings structure the everyday life of people. The interest is not so much in the sequencing of activities in talk among discursive social psychologists that adopt a conversation analytical perspective on social action. The issues highlighted by speakers in the sequential organization of their talk often do not help us to understand why a particular argument works as an adequate justification. Speaker orientations move beyond the previous turns in a conversation by drawing on 'argumentative threads', or socially available patterns of meaning in organizing accounts and formulating accusations and justifications (Wetherell, 1998). These patterns can be regarded as shared, pre-existing discourses, interpretative resources, or cultural narratives with which accounts are constructed in order to achieve particular ends. For example, social psychologists using this approach will examine how discursive devices and specific constructions are used to reify, legitimate, and dissimulate patterns of social power and ethnic dominance.

Gramsci (1973) argues that elements of common sense have their own history, so that common sense is situated within a wider context than that in which the actual talk is situated. Interactions, for example, are resourced by elements of (moral) philosophy which have passed into common sense and are taken as natural and self-evident. A detailed analysis of situated talk does not tell us much about the nature and history of the resources from which people construct versions of themselves and others. Talk of the present is linked to discussions of the past, making it possible for ideological notions to function as an argument. Hence, what is required in examining, for example, racialized talk or ethnic self-definitions is to 'be prepared to look at the microprocesses of present interaction in terms of the long reach of history' (Billig & Sabucedo, 1994, p. 141).

This does not mean that these resources have fixed meanings. For example, Wetherell and Potter (1992) have shown how arguments couched in terms of individual rights and equality can function as starting points not only for antiracist talk but also for racist discourse (Verkuyten, 1997a). However, certain interpretations are more likely to be accepted than others, and certain constructions (e.g. racism and equality) need much more discursive work than others. Notions may have social default values which imply that more work has to be done to use them in another way. The fact that they can be used in different ways and in various contexts indicates, however, that these resources do not determine people's talk and understanding. Attention can be given to what people are doing when they use particular resources for producing an account. These doings can be examined in terms of fulfilling interactional functions, such as blaming, excusing, and defining subject positions. For example, claiming personal agency and responsibility is more difficult in a discourse about essential ethnic differences and cultural moulding than in a discourse that emphasizes change, hybridity, and self-determination.

Another example of a combination of levels of analysis is Moscovici's (1984) theory of social representations. This theory tries to link cultural discourses with individual cognition, affect, and understanding. Social representations are seen to exist at the social as well as the individual level. They are part of social reality but also of a person's psychology. It is the shared ideas and assumptions about the world that enable people to make sense of experiences, to formalize their activities and to communicate effectively. Hence, the theory has a clear cognitive component and examines the psychological processes involved in the (re-) production of socially shared ideas and images. However, Moscovici stresses that social representations are not just ideas inside people's heads, because they influence the actual, situated interactions and are objectified at the level of society.

Philogene (1994) has used this theory to examine 'African-American' as a new social representation. The change from 'blacks' to 'African-Americans' marks the elaboration of a new social reality. Rather than race, it is ethnicity and cultural distinctiveness that is emphasized. A transformation of a social representation requires that the object can be seen from a new perspective. This became possible with the predominance of discourses in the USA about ethnic and cultural diversity. The ethnic revival in the 1970s and 1980s made the possession of an ethnic identity an acceptable and normal part of society. Ethnic groups started to demand increased visibility and recognition. This created the possibility for some black Americans to redefine and reconceptualize themselves. Philogene (1994, p. 94) quotes Jesse Jackson as saying, 'Just as we were called "colored", but we were not that, and then "Negro", but we were not that, to be called "black" is just as baseless. Just as you have Chinese-Americans who have a sense of roots in China . . . or Europeans, as it were, every ethnic group in this country has a reference to some historical cultural base.' The term 'African-American' was used by a socioeconomic subgroup that elaborated its distinction to other blacks. However, it became familiar and common and started to influence (self-)perceptions and interpretations. Furthermore, the term started to appear in interactions and became part of ordinary language. The use of the term in conversations validated the ideas associated with it. Gradually, the term 'African-American' became part of a shared, taken-for-granted reality in which its nonexistence became more and more inconceivable.

Epistemological issues

When social psychologists focus their attention on trying to understand the actual complexities of real-world ethnic phenomena, they will probably tend to become more eclectic in their orientation. In general, an understanding of specific social phenomena or problems requires a broad and multidimensional perspective. Any concept, theory, or method that improves our understanding is worth learning about and using. Hence, in later chapters, I will discuss various theories and methods that we have used in our research. However, this raises questions of epistemological consistency and reflexivity. These questions are also raised by efforts to try to engage and reconcile different approaches that have different epistemological positions and by the simultaneous use of various research methods for examining questions of ethnic identity. Hence, a short discussion on epistemology, methods, and the role of the researcher is essential to this book.

It has become common to argue that the pursuit of knowledge is not value free and that there is no unmediated relationship between the world and consciousness. The issues involved in the debate about the underlying philosophical assumptions of knowledge are diverse and extensive. In general, however, this debate is presented in terms of contrasting positions or world-views that are captured in the prototypical statements, 'reality constructs the person' or 'the person constructs reality'. The former is akin to an epistemology based upon logical positivism that argues that reality has its own properties and is objectively accessible. The latter is closely related to a constructionist orientation in which any attempt to describe the nature of the world is seen as depending on the discourses we use. Buss (1975, 1978) has argued that psychology, as a discipline, has shifted back and forth between these two world-views. Furthermore, this difference in epistemological framework has been found in investigations among members of the American Psychological Association (Coan, 1979), social scientists, and college students (e.g. Unger et al., 1986). In addition, this difference appears to be related to personal experiences, political views, and social identities. For example, members of marginalized and minority groups are more likely to hold a constructionist point of view in which empiricist claims are criticized and multiple interpretations of reality are considered valid.

These different epistemological frameworks also underlie the debate between the more mainstream and the more discourse-oriented social psychologies. For example, many discursive psychologists have developed a relativistic approach to knowledge. They focus on what counts as knowledge in different social and cultural settings. The emphasis is on identifying the functions of knowledge claims rather than on refuting these claims. In contrast, by examining general processes and causal relationships, mainstream social psychologists tend to have a more positivistic orientation. Their emphasis is on trying to test ideas and claims rather than showing the functions and interests they serve. These positions are often seen as polar opposites, but there is also a long philosophical tradition of defining a defensible middle-ground position between them (see Fay, 1996; Morris, 1997). This position is consistent with both the idea that reality constructs the person and that the person constructs reality.

The starting point for this position is that knowledge is always a *relationship* between description and the world. It is a relationship between person and reality in which both are crucial. This means, on the one hand, that we should not prioritize 'reality' and assume that it is possible to have unmediated access to how the world really is or that knowledge is a mirror or reflection of it. However, on the other hand, it does not mean that we should assume that there is no connection between description and the world. Nor should we prioritize the 'person' and assume that no correspondence with reality is possible. A rejection of the idea that language mirrors or reflects things in the world does not entail a complete rejection of representation or truth as correspondence. Just because the world as we know it is a construct of our language does not mean that it is an arbitrary construct. Both a crude realism (or positivism) and a pure (linguistic) idealism (or relativism) should be rejected in favour of a dialectical approach to knowledge.

Acknowledging that science is a human social practice does not deny the validity of empirical claims or the possibility that one kind of claim can be more accurate or more in touch with reality than another.

Fay (1996) makes the analogy between science and cartography. In cartography, map-makers attempt to delineate certain aspects of a terrain. This is typically a physical terrain, but can also be a historical or social one, such as that of Wetherell and Potter (1992), who have been 'mapping the language of racism'. The aspects of the terrain that are mapped are not simply given but depend on the interests, questions, and intentions of the map-makers. The same terrain can yield road maps, vegetation maps, and maps showing the distribution of ethnic groups, racist incidents, and so on. Furthermore, the mode of representation employed depends on conventions, concepts, and the perspective taken. There is no 'one true or best map' of a particular terrain, and map-making is not discovering a pre-existing map. However, it does not follow from this that a distinction between more accurate and inaccurate maps cannot be made or that any map is as good as any other. 'Mapmaking is not a wholly imaginative activity; it is constrained by facts as they can be best ascertained, and by the demands of the practice of mapmaking in both the construction and use of maps' (Fay, 1996, p. 211). Maps can be evaluated in terms of being better or worse, more or less accurate, without needing the 'one true map' as a standard.

The fact that all thinking occurs within a conceptual framework, and thus that unmediated access to the world is not possible, does not mean that all truth claims are entirely relative or subjective. And the fact that descriptions and explanations are given from a certain perspective or standpoint does not mean that social reality does not matter. If that were to be the case, there would be no difference between fact and fiction, myth and history, or judgement and prejudice. The notion of wrong implies the notion of right. A group of people can be defined as vermin, as the Nazis did the Jews, and this definition is constitutive for how these people are understood and treated. But the fact that it becomes a social reality with profound consequences does not imply that it is true.

Doing research from a certain perspective is not the same as being subjective. In the former case, reality does matter and the research tells us something about those under study. In the latter case, it is only the researcher that matters—his or her standpoints and preoccupations—and the research predominantly reveals something about the researcher.

Discursive psychologists emphasize that there is no way of apprehending the world outside language. We cannot step outside our language system and see reality as it is. However, as Edley (2001a) points out, discursive psychologists do not deny the existence of an extradiscursive reality, and he gives the following quotations from Potter and Edwards (with his italics):

Descriptions are not *just* about something but they are *also* doing something: that is, they are not *merely* representing some facet of the world, they are *also* involved in that world in some practical way. (Potter, 1996, p. 47)

> Emotion categories are not graspable *merely* as individual feelings or expressions. . . . They are discursive phenomena and need to be studied as such, as part of how talk performs social actions. (Edwards, 1997, p. 187)

These quotations stress that when people talk about their (outer or inner) world they are doing a lot more than only describing how it is, or expressing how they feel inside. In discourse studies, the analytic interest is in this 'doing a lot more'. Priority is given to the pragmatic aspect of language. For example, identity is studied in terms of stories and linguistic forms that define people's positions and responsibilities. A description of an event or feeling is taken as a construction of that event or feeling rather than as an unobtrusive neutral reflection of mental processes and states. There is always more than one description possible, and the one or the other description has particular consequences; for example, one's own privileged position is justified or rendered self-evident, and the position of the other is rendered unacceptable or reprehensible. Hence, interviews and conversations can be analysed in terms of actions. The language itself is then the subject of analysis instead of an instrument that provides access to what people really think and feel, as is done in survey and experimental research. The utterance 'I feel Moroccan', for example, is seen not as indicative of an underlying attitude, but as a position in a debate on Moroccans living in the Netherlands. The utterance is taken to reflect a position against, for example, those who criticize Moroccans. Hence, it has a social and not merely a psychological meaning.

An emphasis on the performative aspects of language and language use is important and central to understanding people's lives. However, it does not mean that each reference to, for instance, cognitive processes, motives, and attitudes can be put aside. The fact that language is performative does not imply that it is not also expressive and descriptive. Only paying attention to the effects of language use is as limited as only looking at what is expressed or described. The psychological can be thoroughly discursive and social, but that does not mean that it can be reduced to that. Even though cognition and emotion are socially shaped, shared, and used in crucial ways, they are also psychological realities that can conflict with social demands and expectations. Furthermore, the organization of the social world affects the categories people use, as for example, by shaping and limiting the ways in which we can address ethnic phenomena. The three levels of society, interaction, and psychology are highly interdependent but also distinct, each having emergent properties that are irreducible to one another. It makes perfect sense to concentrate on one level of analysis, but it becomes a problem if it is used to replace analyses on the other levels. There is also nothing wrong in focusing on how broad social and cultural contexts affect human actions and understanding as long as doing so is not used to replace an analysis of the path from human understanding to the social construction of reality.

Research methods

Questions of ethnic identity are examined in many disciplines, from different perspectives and by using various research methods. Surveys, interviews, group discussions, participant observation, and experiments are used for gathering data. For example, and as mentioned earlier, in this book, I will discuss our own research in which we have used these different methods. This diversity of methods can be seen as necessary for an adequate understanding of the different issues and levels involved in questions of ethnic identity. However, the use of diverse methods raises important issues. The debate over the relative virtues of more quantitative and qualitative types of research also affects ethnic studies. The distinction between these two research types is not always clear because there is often quite some overlap between the two as well as much diversity within them. However, the terms are common, and I will use them here to outline the different positions that are taken in this debate and to explain the differences between social psychological approaches. In doing so, it is helpful to make a distinction between philosophical and technical issues related to the quantitative/qualitative distinction (Bryman, 1992). This allows us to identify four different positions in the debate.

One position is the argument that a particular epistemology implies a particular methodology. Quantitative methods would follow from a preoccupation with more positivist features such as operational definitions, objectivity, and causality. Surveys and experiments would be adapted to these concerns and would therefore be the preferred instruments. In contrast, the commitment to trying to see the social world from the point of view of the actor and to address the complexities and reflexive nature of interpretative processes leads to the use of, for example, unstructured interviews and participant observation. This link between episte-mology and method has the advantage of presenting a consistent framework for doing research. However, one problem is that in the practice of research this link is one of convention, and not necessity (see Bryman, 1992). Survey research can be used in different ways and for different purposes, and participant observation has also been located in the same epistemological space as the survey.

A second position is to see qualitative studies as having a more secondary role in the overall research process. These studies can be taken as preparatory in providing ideas, leads, and hypotheses that are subsequently tested using more rigorous quantitative frameworks. For example, a pilot study on ethnic identity involving unstructured interviews can result in particular predictions that are confirmed or rejected by an experimental design. It has also been argued—although to a much lesser extent—that quantitative techniques are preparatory in mapping the general terrain or context, which is then studied in more depth and from the inside (Schuyt, 1986). The idea that one is preparatory to the other places both within the same epistemological framework and is attractive to those engaged in the 'real' work. However, qualitative researchers, especially, have presented their work as epistemologically distinct and as an alternative to positivist frameworks. They stress the significance of their research per se by emphasizing the need for contextual understanding from the perspective of the people themselves.

A third possibility is to argue that the proper method of research is dictated by the problem under investigation. The use of methods becomes more a question of appropriate techniques: a technical matter in the sense that the researchers seek to identify those issues and domains in which particular research methods are either adequate or not. This position suggests that a particular technique will be more useful in some contexts than in others, and for some research questions than for others. For example, it is difficult to see how a survey can be used in a situation of fierce ethnic conflict or how interview data can be used to establish the causal relationship between ethnic discrimination and ethnic identification. The implication of this position is that no one technique is inherently superior. Different techniques just have different things to offer.

A fourth position is to shift the debate even further from an epistemological focus to matters more technical. This is the position where an argument is made for the combination or mixing of methods as a form of triangulation. The idea is that such a combination can in principle provide a more elaborate, reliable, and valid view and understanding of, for example, ethnic identity and interethnic relations. The virtue of a combinatory strategy would be that the strengths of different techniques are used and that the familiar methodological parochialism is avoided. The difficulty, however, is that the argument for combination and mixing is essentially a technical one: combination would lead to a superior piece of research. The suggestion seems to be that techniques are epistemologically neutral and therefore commensurable. The results derived from, for example, survey data are cross-checked against observations in order to present a single, comprehensive, and reliable picture of social reality.

The debate about quantitative and qualitative research involves philosophical and technical issues that are sometimes mixed up. The preference for a particular method is closely connected to questions of epistemology. However, the everyday practice of research is not only about philosophical assumptions. There are also habits, training, practical (financial) possibilities, and professional identities that are (implicitly) defined in terms of methods. For example, anthropologists often present participant observation as the hallmark of their trade whereas psychologists emphasize the need to (be able to) do experiments.

The distinction between epistemological and technical issues is also useful for explaining the difference between the more mainstream and the more discursive psychologies. The latter focus on action and interaction or the range of practical tasks that people perform with specific descriptions and definitions. Their criticism of research methods focuses on the interpretation of the data rather than the particular technique of data gathering. They treat data as forms of social action rather than as reflecting inner or outer realities. For example, an interview is seen as a conversation in which both the interviewer and interviewee are responsible for any interaction, although from a different position. Hence, interviews are analysed as interactions rather than as elicitations.

This approach is valuable and useful for examining questions of ethnic identity, particularly at the level of social interaction. It is important to address the range of discourses related to ethnic and cultural diversity and then to examine how they are used to manage one's social world. In doing so, one should try to stay as close as possible to the actual lives people lead, with their complex and messy interpretations. That is why discursive psychologists favour the collection and analysis of natural talk.

However, this does not imply that other kinds of data or analyses are not useful. For one thing, social life is not only about conversational complexities. People often have to avow personal opinions and are asked to personally support or reject a particular proposal or decision. There are many moments in people's lives where a relatively simple response is required to a particular construction of a complex reality, such as for elections, referenda, policy decisions, and practical recommendations. Particular discourses or constructions may engage psychological mechanisms that have consequences other than discursive ones (Hopkins et al., 1997). In these situations, supporting one or another construction of reality has important social and political implications. Using different ideological notions to frame a particular issue may lead to different evaluative reactions and actions, and these can be examined experimentally (e.g. Augoustinos & Quinn, 2003; Katz & Hass, 1988; Verkuyten, 2005).

Furthermore, questions of ethnic identity should not be limited to issues of identity management and negotiation. It is also important to examine and understand the experiences and feelings related to ethnicity as well as to describe the discourses predominant in society. This can be done by using different techniques depending on the research questions and practical considerations. For example, societal discourses on migration, ethnicity, and multiculturalism can be examined by analysing public debates, newspapers, and other media, but also by using questionnaires and interviews. And ethnic self-feelings can be examined by using in-depth interviews, structured questions, and unobtrusive measures.

A multilevel study of ethnic identity requires a range of methods. Discursive analyses are most appropriate at the level of interaction, where everyday encounters have emergent qualities and people are in the process of managing their social world. These analyses are less appropriate, however, at the societal level, where positions and ideologies are relatively more fixed and stable, or at the psychological level, where a sense of identity develops with its concomitant self-feelings, and feelings of belonging and commitment.

Reflexivity

Studying ethnic groups and ethnic relations inevitably raises questions about one's own categories and claims in relation to those of the people that are being studied. There is always a variety of analysts' categories available to interpret the data. As an analyst, one employs analytic categories and decides about focus and presentation of the research material. This can differ from what the people themselves consider relevant and important.

One of the examples from the beginning of this chapter concerned the reactions of the South Moluccans to the presentation of our research. The reproaches from the South Moluccan young people had to do with our being ethnically Dutch. How could we know what it is like to belong to another ethnic group, and, moreover, to a minority group? How could we ever know what it is like to be discriminated against, to live between two cultures, or to feel displaced in a foreign country? In short, the reproach in the example was, 'You have to be one to know one'. This is a familiar argument that is, for example, also printed on T-shirts with 'It's a black thing, you wouldn't understand' or 'You're white, you wouldn't know'. In philosophy, this thesis is known as 'insider epistemology': To know other insiders, one has to be an insider oneself.

The implication of this thesis is that traditional anthropological research, in which the researcher studies an unfamiliar group, is almost impossible. Another implication is that an ethnic group can be studied only by a researcher with the same ethnic background. Turks should be studied by Turks, South Moluccans by South Moluccans, and the Dutch by the Dutch. But what does having the same ethnic background mean? Is being of a similar ethnicity and having a similar group history enough, or should one also be of the same generation, gender, location, and social class? Is the ethnic background so uniformly determining that having that in common is sufficient?

Pointing out the implications of a thesis or argument, however, is not a refutation. Fay (1996) addresses the tenability of the thesis extensively. He points out that the core of the problem lies in the question of what is understood by 'knowing'. The South Moluccan young people seem to understand it as having the same experiences. However, such an interpretation is problematic for two reasons. Firstly, what is a 'same experience'? Experiences are determined by so many factors, such as ethnic background, age, concrete circumstances, and the unique individual life history. Experiences differ from person to person, from situation to situation, and from day to day. In that sense, each experience is different, although similarities do occur.

Secondly, 'having' an experience is not the same as 'knowing' that experience. People have many experiences that they are unable to articulate. And people do all sorts of things, although they often do not know how and why they are doing them. Knowing can be understood as describing and explaining the meaning of experiences and events. In that case, it is not about the experience or the event itself, but about understanding and interpretation; in other words, about gaining knowledge. Knowing in this sense requires a certain distance, reflection, and systematization. In order to understand experiences, there must be distance, more distance than those who have the experiences typically have. Fay (1996, p. 25) puts it as follows, 'The interpretation of meaning is rather like the process of trying to decipher a difficult poem rather than trying to achieve some sort of mental union with its author.' However, the comments made by the South Moluccan young people can also be taken less literally. If they refer to the necessity of an open-minded, interested, and responsive attitude, they are certainly right. To gain insight into ethnic identity phenomena, it is necessary to be involved with and to be sensitive to the lives of those that are studied. In order to find out what concerns and preoccupies people, what their life looks like, and how they see themselves and others, it is important to gain in-depth knowledge of their world.

In anthropology, the necessity of both involvement and distance is a central issue. Involvement and openness are necessary to learn about other people's lives, just as keeping enough distance is necessary for the production of knowledge. What 'enough' means in this respect is not fixed, but depends upon, for example, the aim and questions of the research. What is also not predetermined is that only one research method can be used to achieve this, such as participant observation.

There is a third way in which the comments of the South Moluccan young people can be understood. As discussed, knowledge is always related to a conceptual framework or meaning system with which social reality is described and explained. The researcher's perspective might differ from that of the participants, as for example, when the latter do not recognize themselves in the description and analysis presented. This could mean that the perspective of the participants is distorted or ignored. The emphasis on one's own perspective often has a political meaning. The political aspect finds expression in what is called *identity politics* or the politicization of identity. Here minority groups demand that their own voice or perspective is acknowledged and taken seriously. The socially common terms and concepts would not reflect their world. If you are listened to only when you speak in the words of the dominant group, then your own perspective would get lost or distorted (Sampson, 1993). From an epistemological point of view, a form of relativism seems to underlie the politicization of identity. I will come to this debate in Chapter 2.

However, it is clear that the role of the researcher is important. There are at least two possibilities here. The emphasis can be placed on identity as an analytic concept of the researcher, or identity can be studied in terms of those being investigated. Most social psychological, and also sociological, approaches tend to use the first method. The concept of identity is used to divide people into ethnic groups and to study the social and psychological consequences of belonging to a particular group. The key questions are which ethnic group a person belongs to, how that person feels about that, and what the possible consequences (e.g. intergroup relations, participation in the educational system, and psychosocial problems) might be. In research, this usually comes down to starting from existing ethnic categories and offering prestructured ethnic labels to people. People are given clear categories from which they have to choose and to indicate how strongly they identify with their group. Subsequently, the individual answers are used to compute more general, statistically significant patterns. In discursive approaches and anthropology, the emphasis is on what people themselves say and do. Here ethnic identity is a topic that those involved in an interaction define, can bring up, or orient to. The participant, not the researcher, is the one determining whether identity issues are at stake. The definitions and reactions of the people themselves are used as the main source from which to derive meaning. The focus is, for example, on the way the speakers define themselves and construct definitions of others. The discourses are analysed in terms of the varying ways in which ethnic identities are presented and argued over. Here the central questions are whether, when, and how people define, use, and orient to ethnic definitions. Both approaches have their pros and cons. A danger of the first approach is that in imposing ethnic categorizations the range of possibilities is restricted and the category of 'ethnicity' is taken for granted. Thus, a socially constructed feature of the world can be reproduced and transformed into an obvious fact. In the second approach, the possibility exists that ethnicity as an important structuring principle can escape the researcher's attention. Ethnic categories can be so self-evident to the people involved that they do not talk about them explicitly.

However, these two ways of approaching things are less contradictory than they seem and can complement each other. It can be argued that we live in a world where ethnic categories are often deeply embedded in different spheres of life, and that we should examine the many consequences of these categories. But, at the same time, we should not take ethnic categories for granted. Rather, we should try to problematize the very category of 'ethnicity' and examine how and why ethnic distinctions are defined and used (Reicher, 2001). Ethnic identity can be examined in terms of how category definitions are arrived at as well as in terms of the consequences of forms of ethnic organization that have developed into more stable and institutionalized distinctions.

The importance of definitions

In the literature, terms such as 'identity', 'self', and 'ethnicity' are used extensively, in a wide range of situations and in many different ways. As a result, there is a tendency for these terms to lose all significant and coherent meaning. Considering the conceptual inflation and vagueness, one could expect that authors would try to give clear and precise definitions. Unfortunately, this is often not the case. Most authors use these concepts without pointing out what they mean by them. Implicitly, they seem to assume that the concepts speak for themselves or are plainly understood. Sometimes the vagueness of the concepts is discerned, but this does not seem to be a sufficient reason for clarification. The following statement by Moscovici and Paicheler (1978, p. 256) seems to be illustrative of many scholars' attitude. 'The concept of identity is as indispensable as it is unclear. This is why no attempt will be made to define it and we shall keep it in the zone of shaded obscurity.' And in a book about European identity, MacDonald states that a definition of identity '(would be) contrary to the guiding spirit of this book, which is to explore the ways in which identities are defined and experienced by various people themselves' (quoted in Vermeulen & Govers, 1997, p. 24).

The same can be said about the concept of ethnicity and related terms. Cohen (1978), for instance, notices that only a few authors explain what they mean by ethnicity. In an essay titled 'Terminological Chaos', Connor (1994, p. 91) shows that the concepts are 'shrouded in ambiguity due to their imprecise, inconsistent and often totally erroneous usage'. Despite conceptual ambiguity, all authors seem to agree that ethnicity has something to do with group distinctions and group relations. As argued earlier, for many social psychologists but also for some anthropologists (e.g. Chapman, 1993; McDonald, 1989), this is a sufficient reason for studying ethnicity as another example of social categories and categorization processes. In this way, ethnicity becomes similar to national, gender, religious, class, or whatever (artificial) social identity. The emphasis is on general processes that would work similarly for each category so that the content of each category can be ignored. To be sure, ethnic identity has many things in common with other social identities. At the same time, however, the question arises as to what it is that makes a category 'ethnic', or what is special about *ethnic* identity?

Some authors explicitly object to definitions and clear descriptions, especially those working within the postmodern and critical perspective, who consider definitions to be unimportant, limiting, and even obscuring. Identities, for them, are characterized by contradiction, ambivalence, and fragmentation. Hence, fixing meanings by means of definitions is to be avoided. Rather, definitions of identity and ethnicity should be criticized by exposing or unmasking their underlying assumptions and ideological consequences. Two related objections to definitions are being made here. The first is the assumption that a definition entails a claim to be the only right one and thereby provides an essentialist understanding. A definition is taken to indicate what something really is, and with that the core or essence of it is fixed. This is a misunderstanding, however. Definitions do not refer to essences but are used to make distinctions. This enables us to distinguish between phenomena and to describe and explain them. Definitions are some of the most powerful methodological tools for mapping reality. The use of unclear definitions leads to ambiguous descriptions and in turn to inadequate explanations. The question is not whether one definition is right and the other is not because one grasps the essence of a phenomenon. Rather, the question is to make distinctions in an unambiguous and consistent way and to use them to improve our understanding. Social analysis requires relatively unambiguous analytic concepts. The usefulness of definitions depends on whether they help to provide a more accurate description and explanation of social reality.

Second, definitions are rejected because they are supposed to have a homogenizing effect. Identities would be characterized by diversity, contradiction, and change. Depending on the groups, circumstances, and local situations, identity or ethnicity would take on many different forms. To define identity or ethnicity would stress commonalities and deny diversity. Hence, definitions would be incompatible with observed variability. However, such an observation is difficult to make without at least some idea about what identity or ethnicity means. After all, what justifies the idea that 'identity' or 'ethnicity' is at stake here? These claims presuppose a certain view of what identity and ethnicity entail, and this is what the question of definition is about. Contradictions and changes can be understood only once it is clear exactly what it is that is considered to be contradictory and changing. Definitions are rejected, yet at the same time there is an inevitability to revert to an implicit idea about the phenomenon, which is, however, simply ignored or forgotten.

I think it is useful and important to try to explain how particular concepts are used. This makes it clear what the argument is about and gives the reader the opportunity to disagree and voice criticism. Hence, the next two chapters will discuss ethnic identity by elaborating first the 'identity' and second the 'ethnic' aspect. This discussion will provide the conceptual framework for the ensuing chapters in which empirical examples from our research will be presented.

2 Social identity

This chapter is concerned with the 'identity' aspect of ethnic identity. Chapter 3 will focus on 'ethnicity'. The following, still relevant quotation from Gleason (1983, p. 910) expresses the reasons for this chapter very well:

> Today we could hardly do without the word *identity* in talking about immigration and ethnicity. Those who write on these matters use it casually; they assume the reader will know what they mean. And readers seem to feel that they do—at least there has been no clamor for clarification of the term. But if pinned down, most of us would find it difficult to explain just what we do mean by identity. Its very obviousness seems to defy elucidation: identity is what a thing is! How is one supposed to go beyond that in explaining it? But adding a modifier complicates matters, for how are we to understand identity in such expressions as 'ethnic identity', 'Jewish identity' or 'American identity'? This is a question to which the existing writings on ethnicity do not provide a satisfactory answer. (original italics)

In this chapter, I will discuss the concept of social identity and present my approach, which is based on the work of Wentholt (1991).[1] I will do so by, first, discussing the conceptual confusion and the necessity to clarify the concept. Then I will present three components of 'social identity' that can be used to situate different lines of social psychological research. Subsequently, I will discuss the importance of context, social processes of identity formation, the difference between social identity and sense of identity, and the distinction between identity and identification.

The identity concept

Identity has become one of the main concepts in social science thinking. The term is used frequently, in different circumstances and for different reasons. Although the concept has a history in the social sciences (see Weigert et al., 1986), its current popularity is unique. Indeed in our globalizing and late-modern days, questions of identity have become both more salient and more urgent than ever before, and 'identity' provides a prime explanatory principle (e.g. Gergen, 1991;

Michael, 1996). Identity processes also seem to have replaced economic self-interest as prime movers of human history in political and sociological theories (e.g. Huntington, 1993). The formation and maintenance of identity has become both vital and problematic.

While the term 'identity' has acquired great suggestive power, it must still be asked whether the use of the concept is helpful in understanding social reality. Weigert et al. (1986, p. 29) note that identity has become an indispensable analytic term but also a cultural buzzword. They conclude, 'The widespread acceptance of the concept of identity does not imply agreement on or even a clear understanding of its various meanings.' Brubaker and Cooper (2000, p. 1) argue that identity 'tends to mean too much (when understood in a strong sense), too little (when understood in a weak sense), or nothing at all (because of its sheer ambiguity)'. And Bendle (2002, p. 1) concludes that 'accounts of identity are inconsistent, under-theorized and incapable of bearing the analytical load required'. Furthermore, while in social psychology a large mass of empirical work has been devoted to its causes and consequences, the concept of social identity per se has traditionally received relatively little attention.

The reputation of 'identity' as a cultural buzzword is not surprising. As Gleason's statement indicates, popularly the meaning of the word seems self-evident, but it becomes quite elusive as soon as one starts to think about it. At first, the meaning of the term seems simply to refer to who you are. But what is meant by that pinpointing essence, 'who you are'? As Gleason argues, very quickly all certainty evaporates, and the disagreements about what the defining characteristics may or may not be proliferate.

As soon as the popularity of a term increases, conceptual inflation seems inevitable. This is also the case for 'identity'. Nowadays, identity seems to be everywhere; as a consequence, it is nowhere. Its overuse leads to confusion, misunderstanding, and conceptual vagueness which makes the term lose its analytic purchase. The result is an undifferentiated vocabulary that is used in many different ways. For example, the identity concept is used in a descriptive, an explanatory, and a normative sense.

Descriptively, an incredibly varied and dissimilar range of phenomena is widely held to be a matter of identity: nationality, gender, individual character, personality, psychological needs, social memberships, personal preferences, likes and dislikes, prejudices, projections and identifications, group characteristics, intergroup conflicts, and personal uniqueness. All these and more are relevant to 'who you are' and therefore are defined as identity issues. In using the same term, there is a tendency to assume that all these things are somehow of the same kind. However, although each of these descriptions of 'identity' may tell us something, they do not tell us the same thing.

Used in an explanatory way, the concept is often granted an omni-explanatory status; whenever no clear explanation is available or the impression exists that it has got something to do with self-understanding or psychological well-being, or with societal changes and circumstances, the identity concept appears. For example, identity problems are held responsible for diverse forms of deviant behaviour and for various educational difficulties among young people from ethnic minority groups. A lack of identity is also held responsible for the malfunctioning of organizations and the falling apart of communities. An organization or community without a clear identity is considered weak, without direction, and confused, comparable to persons facing identity problems.

Identity is also used in a normative sense. 'Having an identity' is considered good and desirable, whereas the situation of 'no identity' is evaluated negatively. Everyone has the right to his or her own identity, whatever this means. Especially the discussion on the politics of identity gives the concept a normative and moral value. In this discussion, identities are seen as historical and political constructions in which power differences play a decisive role. Ethnic minority groups claim the right to be different and to define who and what they are, or want to be themselves. Identity has become a legitimate topic in human rights and democracy discourses. This politicizing of identity emphasizes the unstable, contingent, and dominating aspects of identity. Identities are seen as subject to struggles and changing power relations, interests, and positions. Ethnic and cultural identities should be recognized and respected, particularly when they are denied or repressed by others.

The fact that the term 'identity' is used in different ways is not, however, only because of its being a modern cultural buzzword. Erik H. Erikson is largely responsible for the increased scientific and general popularity of the identity concept in the latter half of the twentieth century.[2] He was one of the first to investigate the incisive significance of identity processes in social reality. However, the way he uses the identity concept is not always very clear and sometimes invites misunderstanding (e.g. Bosma & Graafsma, 1982). An example is an article in which Erikson (1966) examined the identity concept in race relations. In the article, in the same passage, identity, taken by Erikson to mean specifically the very essence of a person, is applied both to Freud's Jewishness and to the heightened consciousness of himself as a unique person that William James once had in a rare moment of ecstatic, oceanic experience. Erikson (1966, pp. 147–148; his italics) tells us how James had written to his wife about this experience, 'at such moments [of feeling most deeply and intensively active and alive] there is a voice inside which speaks and says: "*This* is the real me!"'. He also tells us how Freud had said, in an address to a Zionist society in Vienna in 1926, 'What bound me to Jewry was (I am ashamed to admit) neither faith nor national pride . . . [but] . . . many obscure emotional forces, which were the more powerful the less they could be expressed in words, as well as a clear consciousness of inner identity, the safe privacy of a common mental construction.'

Erikson concluded that this was, 'a statement of that unity of *personal and cultural* identity which is rooted in an ancient people's fate'. Hence, in the one case, the essence of personal self is held to be one's membership of a social category or ethnic/religious group; that is, being like a number of other people. In the other case, it is the most individual sensation of a person's unique sense of self; that is, being utterly unlike anyone or anything else. Using the concept in these two different ways is not very helpful and invites misunderstanding.

Of course, Erikson did not think that Freud was, as an individual, exhaustively characterized in 'who he really was' by only this one particular collective membership. Emotionally significant though it undoubtedly was, it was but one of a number of others that were also important for him. And of course Erikson was well aware that William James possessed a number of social memberships essential to who he was. Yet that particular collective membership of Freud's, permanently significant though hardly encompassing him, and that one fleeting moment, the opposite of permanent, of a uniquely individual sense of self experienced by James, seemed to Erikson a question of identity. In his own words (1966, p. 14; his italics), 'for here we deal with something which can be experienced as "identical" *in the core of the individual* and yet also identical *in the core of a communal culture*, and which is, in fact, the identity of those two identities'.[3]

The Erikson example reminds us of the fact that there are many conceptual problems in thinking about questions of ethnic identity. This has led some scholars to argue that the concept ought perhaps to be removed from the scientific vocabulary (e.g. Brubaker & Cooper, 2000). However, this does not seem very helpful. The term does refer to real phenomena which need to be investigated somehow. If we fail to do so, a particular range of both societal and psychological processes just cannot be grasped. The Erikson example also serves as a reminder that the identity concept is not about individuals as such, nor about society as such, but the relation of the two. It is about the intricacies, paradoxes, dilemmas, contradictions, imperatives, superficialities, and profundities of the way individuals relate to and are related to the world in which they live. This is what, perhaps more than anyone at the time, Erikson was sensitive to and what the concept of identity was meant to illuminate. Hence, the term 'identity' refers to important realities. Although identity is now a problematic and vague term, it is the one we have at our disposal. What we can do is to try and handle it in an analytically useful way.

In the following sections, an attempt at conceptual clarification is made. In doing so, I will not present an overview of existing ideas and approaches about identity.[4] An entire book could be written about this, and it would lead us too far away from questions of ethnic identity. Most scholars agree that ethnic identity is a kind of social or collective identity, and ethnicity is typically analysed in these terms. Hence, my focus will be on ideas that have been developed on social identity, and, particularly, on the approach taken by Wentholt (1991). In my view, he has presented a clear, coherent, and useful framework for examining social identity.

Social identity

Social identity is about the relationship between the individual and the environment. Social identity refers to the question of what someone is taken to be socially (Stone, 1962). Hence, what is at stake is not that which distinguishes a person as an individual from other individuals, but that which is shared with others. The emphasis is not on what makes a person unique, but on similarities to some and differences from others.

The social identity concept indicates what a person is, how she or he is socially defined. It is about categorical characteristics—such as gender, age, and ethnic background—that position or locate people in social space. These characteristics distinguish a person from people that do not have that characteristic and puts him or her together with those that do. Your identity as a member of an ethnic group, a particular culture, or one or the other sex is a designation placing you by what you, in a particular respect, simply are taken to be.

Social identities involve social categories and designate the person's position(s) in a social structure or social space that is larger and longer-lasting than any particular situation. Social identity 'locates a person in social space by virtue of the relationships and memberships that it implies' (Gecas & Burke, 1995, p. 42). This localization has led some scholars to reinterpret the traditional identity question, 'Who or what am I?', into the question, 'Where am I?' (e.g. Hall, 1996). To know the particular identity of a person means to know in which social category he or she fits. The membership of this category *is* the particular social identity. It indicates what a person is from a social perspective; one's location or place in society (Simon, 1997). This is all there is to it, and, apparently, all there is in this respect to know. This does not say anything, however, about, for example, the cultural meanings of the categories and who is involved in defining the social categories, about the day-to-day negotiations and management of social identities, or about how one personally feels about a particular social identity.

But the implications are many. For one thing, the information provided by the identity leaves one, in general, in no doubt about both what an individual in some respect is and all the things he or she is not. A girl is not a boy, a Turk is not a Moroccan, an Irishman is not a Scot, and a Dutchman is not a German. In this way, a person is joined as it were to the people she or he belongs with or is considered to be like. These are the people who share the same particular identity. And the person is separated from all the ones he or she does not belong with in this respect, who have different identities. Hence, these identities are by definition divisive although not necessarily oppositional or antagonistic.

At the same time, the information provided by social identities is limited. It tells us nothing about the individual so designated, apart from the characteristics going with or supposed to go with the membership of the particular category. In talking about social identity, attention shifts away from personal identity. We are not interested primarily in how a particular individual is to be known, but in what there is to be known about social categories. Social psychology has clearly shown that these are different things. An individual fits into many different categories, some of which are shared with some people, some with others, never all of them with anyone else. A social category lumps together people who may be very different in all other respects. But what they share in characteristics through membership of the category, at least for the moment and for the purpose or circumstances of the designation, is supposed to outweigh all those differences.

Three components

Social identity is about socially defined and recognized distinctions and designations. However, not all classifications into which a person fits and not all of his or her memberships become established and socially recognized identities. We make lots of temporary and generalizing distinctions about ourselves and others all the time, such as in terms of mood, taste, and preference. Social identities related to ethnicity, nationality, race, and religion involve more enduring collective definitions and understandings. According to Wentholt, for the membership of a collectivity of some sort to form a social identity, a combination of three related components is needed: 1) *social classification,* or the sociostructural component; 2) specific *behavioural and normative consequences and expectations* bounded to the category, or the cultural component; and 3) *judgements of an ontological nature,* or the ontological component. Together, these three are the necessary components of social identities. Obviously, the three are closely linked. It is the combination of the three that gives a social label the required 'identity depth'. Hence, the distinction is an analytic one that allows us to ask specific questions and examine interrelations.

Gender identity is a ready example. There are no cultures in the world which do not make a clear distinction between men and women in their classification of things, in the way the two sexes are allowed to behave, and in what they are supposed to be like as human beings. The identity potential of the gender difference is enormous. This does not mean that the characteristics imposed or expected to exist are in any way natural or inevitable. Even here, though the role differentiation is to a certain extent biologically given, there are extreme differences between cultures in prescribed behaviour for the sexes and in gender-related development. I will elaborate on these three components in the next sections.

The sociostructural component

First of all, there is the social classification of people into categories or groups. All social psychological theories recognize social categorization as a basic cognitive or discursive process in identity and intergroup relations. The social world is divided in many different ways, and those divisions are used to say something about individuals. Socially defined categories are used for labelling and pigeonholing. People are classified in terms of sex, age, ethnicity, race, culture, nationality, religion, legal status, and so on. It is these categories to which one is socially recognized as belonging and which are used for self-definition. Social identity is a public reality, an assignment that divides people on the basis of all kinds of criteria that can be used in different combinations. Hence, people can be included or excluded on many different grounds.

It is a characteristic of the human mind to classify and use categories, but this says little about what kind of distinctions are being made and what kind of features are being used to do so. Categorization always implies selection, because only certain characteristics are made meaningful. The arbitrary character of social categories does not imply, however, that the characteristics used are unimportant. For example, the term 'visible minorities' is used to indicate that the extent of visibility is important. Groups that look different from the majority group may face difficulty in being accepted and may constantly be approached or judged in terms of their ethnic background. Once visible characteristics form the basis for social classification it is, in general, quite easy to determine to which category someone belongs. Features such as skin colour or striking clothing are immediately visible. One glance is enough to categorize people. Other characteristics—such as language, accent, and behaviour—are somewhat more difficult and often require more careful watching and listening.

Differentiating between and hence categorizing people happens everywhere in society and for a variety of reasons. It not only occurs in everyday life, but is also a prerequisite for the functioning of society. For example, from a legal point of view, people are constantly treated differently on the basis of their positions, life circumstances and situational needs and/or desires. The entire social security system consists of classifications based on distinctions made between a large number of categories of people, who are then treated differently on the basis of these categories. Such distinctions are justified by the doctrine of reasonable classification. The criteria on the basis of which the distinctions are made have to be adequate with respect to the purposes they serve. Persons and circumstances that are in fact different should not be treated as if they were equal, whereas similar cases should be treated in a similar way.

Making distinctions is not a problem, but it can become one if it occurs without adequate basis. Differential treatment is quite different from discrimination. In the latter case, a distinction is made on the basis of a characteristic—gender, age, or ethnicity—that is considered irrelevant to the situation. What is considered socially (ir)relevant is of course subject to change and depends on historical and cultural circumstances. Not so long ago, refusing a job to a black person or a woman (or both) was far less controversial than it is today.

People can object to the fact that category distinctions are made because they consider these inadequate and irrelevant, but they can also criticize the fact that no distinctions are made between groups. In studies in ethnicity, the former situation represents an emphasis on similarity and a plea for a general perspective that can involve assimilation or colour blindness. Here, it is argued that ethnic categories should not be utilized in, for example, the formulating of policies because it is considered simply wrong or inadequate to make ethnic distinctions and to take account of ethnic categories. This argument can be put forward by majority group members who on the basis of liberal principles or racist tendencies reject the idea of special measures for ethnic minorities, but also, for a variety of reasons, by minority group members themselves.

The second situation tends to translate itself into ethnic pluralist and multicultural thinking, in which it is argued that existing differences should not be denied or ignored but rather acknowledged and respected. It is argued that the idea of similarity and commonality is an ideological device to mould groups in the direction of the majority. However, being treated in a similar way does not have to mean equality. Equality should involve the full recognition of relevant ethnic differences, and not only the rejection of irrelevant ones.

The cultural component

Not all possible classifications constitute social identities, such as categorizations based on the colour of the eyes or on the preference for a certain holiday destination. Under certain circumstances, such divisions can grow into real identities (see below), but usually they are superficial, quite meaningless, and temporary. As long as these are not socially recognized bases of classification, they do not constitute social identities. A label—or what Jenkins (1996) refers to as the nominal—does not suffice for a social identity. A label alone does not constitute a social identity, and the meaning of ethnicity cannot be reduced to a mere ethnic classification. A second component is necessary: accompanying manifestations of behaviour, behavioural consequences, and normative expectations. Certain activities are connected with particular categories, and this boundedness provides a shared or common-sense understanding of the social world. This cultural component of identity—which Jenkins refers to as the virtual—is sometimes institutionalized in roles, and it gives a certain categorization its social meaning or relevance. Categorizations have to have content or substance, if they are to be more than just a label. The cultural component is what the category means, in practice and over time. The position assigned to a person—for example, Turk, asylum seeker, or elderly person—implies behavioural expectations and opportunities. This can vary from the legal exclusion of certain categories of people to approaching others in a patronizing way. As soon as someone is put into such a category, there are stereotypical expectations about how that person will and should behave. These are the expectations not only of outsiders, but also (similar or different) of people belonging to the same category. For example, members of one's own ethnic group, or co-ethnics, expect a degree of conformity and similarity in normative values and behaviours. Ethnic identities are associated with particular (implicit and explicit) 'scripts', or recognized norms of behaviour, which stipulate forms of behaviour and adherence to values.

The emphasis in objecting to and criticizing social distinctions can relate more to this second component; that is, to the consequences and expectations rather than to the distinctions or categorization as such. People can agree with the fact that ethnic or other distinctions are made and used, but the cultural meanings and consequences of the categories can be challenged, disputed, or rejected. For instance, the gay movement does not challenge the distinction between homosexuals and heterosexuals, but rather the stigmatization and unequal treatment that results from it. Another example is the 'black is beautiful' movement of the 1960s, which did not fight against the distinction between blacks and whites, but rather against the cultural meanings and consequences that were connected with this. In the words of James Brown, the movement meant, 'Say it loud, I'm black and I'm proud.' A further example is ethnic groups that claim public affirmation of the value of their distinctive culture by stressing the need for multiculturalism.

All these groups rebelled against the consequences and expectations of the categorizations. They have succeeded for the most part in taking control of the content of the category, at least for themselves. Instead of being homosexuals, they are now gay or lesbian; instead of being blacks, they are now African-Americans.

Ontological definition

Labels for social categories are powerful not only because of the related behavioural expectations and consequences, but also because of the way that members of these categories are seen. The third component is the accompanying judgement of the nature of the people that are categorized. This concerns the ontological definition that is prominent in the sense of 'this is what you are—you cannot deny that this identity tells something about yourself, about the kind of person you are'. Knowing to which category someone belongs leads to an ontological judgement about that person. It tells something about what that person is. Among other things, the ontological definition implies that not all social classifications have to be social identities. For instance, all legal classifications involve social distinctions with behavioural consequences, but they often lack the third component. An example is the Dutch tax system in which tariff groups 1, 2, and 3 are used. These categorizations do have clear consequences, but they do not constitute any social identities. After all, in everyday social life, they do not function for defining or indicating what a person is. People do not greet each other with 'hi, second-tariff-group person'.

This third component of social identity also implies that a distinction between, for example, 'looking' and 'being' can be made. Someone who looks Dutch would be considered Dutch if ethnicity was nothing more than visual features. But the practices of ethnic classification do make this distinction. Although a person can appear to be Dutch, he or she will be regarded as a Turk if both parents are Turkish. The way one looks can differ from what one is. Another example is Jews who tried to pass as non-Jews in the Second World War. Success in passing hinged on their 'Aryan' looks and familiarity with non-Jewish culture, but was never certain. One could always be detected and arrested for being a Jew.

An ontological definition is not about a gradual difference in terms of more or less of something, but about an absolute difference in the sense of being or not being. Social identities are expressed in the language of nouns (Rosenberg, 1979). Social categories are 'nouns that cut slices' through our environment (Allport, 1954, p. 174). Someone is a Turk, a Moroccan, or a Chinese. In using such words, no quantifiable qualities are defined, as there would be with adjectives. Nouns reflect separate social types, with characteristics and boundaries that suggest a more than superficial difference. Men differ from women and Turks differ from Surinamese in many ways.

People that belong to the same group are supposed to share invisible characteristics and to differ from others in a more than superficial way. If we define someone as belonging to another ethnic group, we expect that person to be different from us on many important points. Social psychological research has shown that people tend to infuse an essence—biological, cultural, or religious—into social groups in order to explain their differences (e.g. Haslam, Rothschild & Ernst, 2000; Hirschfeld, 1996; Rothbart & Taylor, 1992). Psychological essentialism argues that 'People act as if things (e.g. objects) have essence or an underlying nature that make them the thing they are' (Medin, 1989, p. 1476). By attribution of an essence to a group, the very nature of the group is defined. Members of such a group would display deep similarities and differ thoroughly from others: they really *are* or are presumed to *be* different.

People can object to social distinctions for what they presumably tell us about the kind of people concerned. In these cases, it is not so much the social categorization or the related behavioural consequences that are at stake, but rather the assumed underlying ontological characteristics. To a greater or lesser extent, ethnic groups can be thought of as possessing inherent characteristics. For example, in a classically racist way, these groups can be seen in biological terms in which the way people are is inescapably part of their 'nature'. Nowadays, what is more common is a form of 'cultural or new racism' (e.g. Barker, 1981) or what anthropologists call 'culturalism' (Vermeulen, 2001). This is the argument for a cultural essentialism in which people who belong to a particular ethnic group are just the way they are because of their culture. In both cases, ethnic differences are seen as relatively fixed and final. Ethnic categories are taken to represent human types, specifying that an individual is fundamentally a certain sort of person.

It is also possible to attribute inherent characteristics to the spirit of a people or nation. This idea was central among prominent nineteenth-century philosophers such as Herder and Hegel. Blum (2002) calls this 'metaphysical inherentism', and in a later chapter we will see that this line of thinking also can exist among ethnic groups.

Essentialistic or inherent notions of ethnic groups can be challenged and rejected. For example, ethnic group differences can be understood not in inherent cultural terms but in terms of social and structural conditions that produce culture. And generalized or stereotypical views of groups do not have to imply the idea of a necessary or natural link between categories and characteristics. Turkish people living in the Netherlands can be seen as traditional, conservative, and community oriented, but this can be understood in terms of their current position and situation in society, rather than in terms of 'their culture'. Hence, there can be disagreement not so much about the ethnic distinctions themselves (first component) or about the particular meanings and consequences (second component), but rather about the nature or internal characteristics of the people concerned.

An example: Blue and brown eyes

In reality, the three components are interrelated and intermingled, and the importance of making an analytic distinction between the three is not always easy to see. The connotations, meanings, and histories of existing social identities are complex and elaborate. An example of the formation of a new social identity is helpful here.

In 1968, Jane Elliot, a primary schoolteacher in Iowa, carried out a famous classroom intervention, which was recorded in a documentary film, *The Eye of the Storm* (1970). All of her students were white, and to teach them something about race and racism, Elliot divided the class into two groups, brown-eyed and blue-eyed. Hence, she used a particular characteristic for making a distinction, and she could of course have used others. In order to make the distinction clearly visible she had the two groups wear collars of a different colour. This process of classification changed the situation from one in which there are individual pupils, to a situation of two 'racial' groups. Hence, two discrete subsets were created, and this was accompanied by accentuation of perceived intracategory similarities and intercategory differences.

Because eye colour does not ordinarily have any significance, this distinction can be used to make it meaningful in all kinds of ways. Elliot proceeded to treat the one group as if they were inferior, and the next day she subjected the other group to the same treatment. She did this by defining clear behavioural consequences and expectations. For example, the 'inferior' group had to sit at the worst places in the back of the class, had to go last in line, were not allowed to use paper cups to drink from the water fountain, got no extra minutes at recess, and were not allowed to go for seconds in the cafeteria. The categorization was made normative, and having blue or brown eyes was no longer an insignificant feature but became consequential and meaningful.

Teachers often make functional distinctions between groups of pupils, but these do not have to develop into social identities. Elliot turned the distinction into real social identities by starting to use the terms 'blue-eyed' and 'brown-eyed' people and by defining the two groups as deserving their inferior or superior treatment. She made the distinction factual by giving concrete examples that would prove that 'blue-eyed' (or 'brown-eyed') people are smarter, nicer, or simply better people.

Interestingly, in class and in the playground, the children started to use the labels themselves for self-definition and for describing and treating others. The labels became inductively potential or informative about the nature of the two groups of children. For example, when the class went to lunch, a blue-eyed child suggested to Elliot that she alert the servers in the cafeteria because brown-eyed children might go for seconds. Another example comes from when Elliot tried to explain something in front of the class and one child was not ready:

Ms Elliot: Page 127, ready? Everybody ready? Everybody ready but Laury. Ready, Laury?
Pupil: She's a brown-eye.
Ms Elliot: She's a brown-eye. You may have begun to notice today that we spend a great deal of time waiting for brown-eyed people.

The pupil's remark shows that the category has become meaningful. It says something about the supposed nature of the people concerned and therefore can be used to interpret their behaviour.

Another example occurred after recess when one child was withdrawn and agitated because he had gotten into a fight. Elliot asked what had happened.

Ms Elliot:	What happened, John?
John:	He called me names.
Ms Elliot:	What did he call you?
John:	Brown-eye.
Pupils:	They always call us that. 'Hey brown-eye, come here, brown-eye.'
Ms Elliot:	What's wrong with being called a brown-eye?
John:	It means we're stupid and all that.

The categories had become real social identities that pupils used to define and place themselves and others. They became part of the way the children started to live their lives. The one group started to feel superior and the other group inferior, and the children started to act in terms of the way the categories were understood.

Questions of categorization, cultural norms, and essentialist thinking are, of course, closely related, and many researchers inevitably address all three. Furthermore, a similar topic, such as stereotypes and stereotyping, can be examined in terms of cognitive devices that simplify reality, but also as social normative expectations and beliefs, and, in addition, as linking specific attributes to the essence of what people are assumed to be. However, despite the relationships and commonalities, there are differences in emphasis and questions asked. Studies on categorization processes do not inevitably involve questions of essentialism, and an investigation of essentialist thinking can start from and compare particular social categories. Similarly, in examining ethnic identity or social identity in general, it is possible to emphasize one or the other component.

Partial identities

Every individual simultaneously belongs to a great number of social categories and can thus be flexibly categorized in a multitude of ways. That is, people have multiple identities they or others can focus on. Social identities are always 'among other' identities. Besides being a Turk, a person may be, for example, also a male, a Muslim, a father, and a 'Rotterdammer' (someone from Rotterdam). Seeing each specific social identity as a partial identity prevents all the things that people are, all the categories that they belong to, from being reduced to but one single identity that is considered pre-eminent. There is often a tendency to think that one knows quite a lot about a person on the basis of one particular social identity. For example, in studies on ethnic minorities, it is not uncommon to assume that ethnic identity is central or decisive for what people consider themselves or others to be. However, there are always more social identities that, depending on the circumstances, are psychologically salient and sociologically prominent. These identities can to a greater or lesser degree correspond to each other or, on the contrary, present contrasting ideas and pose conflicting demands.

The number of social identities with which people are placed in their social world depends on many factors, such as the stage of life and one's social network. The number also varies between societies and cultures. The identity options that are socially available and common are in some societies and cultures more limited than in others. A socially complex society has great diversity in positions, tasks, and roles, and people frequently change these. In more traditional societies, the positions and roles are usually more limited. For instance, for many women in Islamic cultures, being a mother is the identity that predominates. Their position and tasks are relatively clearly defined, and in public life there are few other options available to them.

Among other things, this means that there are few opportunities for what could be called 'identity-compensation', if necessary. Linville's (1985, 1987) work on self-complexity has shown that people who have a large number of social identities can deal with difficult and stressful situations more easily. They are less dependent on one particular social identity and are able to find compensation in other social identities when one identity is adversely affected. Shifting identities may also be an effective strategy for deflecting threatening social comparisons (Mussweiler et al., 2000). And Roccas (2003) shows that identification with an in-group is stronger when there is simultaneous membership of a low-status group.

However, multiple social identities can raise questions of how to accommodate or reconcile different social identities. It is not always simple to be a good mother, devoted wife, and successful career woman all at once. And it is not always easy to be a Moroccan, a Dutch citizen, and a Jew at the same time. These identities can be more or less contradictory, depending on the circumstances and the way they are defined and articulated.

Having multiple social identities brings with it the possibility of combinations. Social identities are usually not independent of each other, but are closely connected or articulated in relation to each other. Such an articulation has, for instance, been described in racism, which very often gets intertwined with nationalism and sexism (Miles, 1989); divisions on the basis of 'race' are linked to distinctions based on nationality and gender. Social distinctions can influence and interfere with each other. Ethnicity can become 'gendered'. That is, ethnic differences can be understood in terms of the positions and responsibilities of men and women, as happens often with Turks and Moroccans in the Netherlands. In this case, what it means to be Moroccan or Turkish is closely linked to ideas and notions about the nature and role of men and women. Women can be defined as the symbolic bearers of the continuity and integrity of the ethnic group, making them subject to scrutiny concerning friendships and relationships and their behaviour more generally. Another example is that a strong emphasis on masculinity and macho behaviour is self-defining for some ethnic subgroups (Sansone, 1992).

However, it is also possible that both identities have their own meaning. For example, one of the distinctions can dominate, while the other is used to subcategorize or refine the former. Someone is then a Turk in the first place and a woman in the second, or the other way round. In social psychology, work on crossed-categorization examines the effects of crossing one dimension of categorization (e.g. Dutch–Turkish) with a second (e.g. male–female). Different correlated or orthogonal dimensions can be used to make distinctions and, depending on the positions on these dimensions, stronger or weaker group distinctions can be made. Many models of cross-categorization patterns have been delineated and examined (e.g. Brewer et al., 1987; Hewstone et al., 1993; Urban & Miller, 1998). And recent work focuses not only on patterns of responses predicted by these models, but also on factors that moderate crossed-categorization effects (see Crisp & Hewstone, 2000).

Although there are always multiple social identities, in specific circumstances, one of them may become central and highly absorbing to the individual. I am not referring here to the cognitive process of situational and momentary identity salience central to self-categorization theory (Turner et al., 1987), but rather, to circumstances in which a particular identity dominates thoughts and actions and starts to play a role in almost every situation—not only as a guiding line in the interpretation and judgement of other people's behaviour ('you only say and do those things because I'm black'), but also in the experience of all other aspects of what someone is. The identity at issue constantly plays a role, eclipses other identities, and is announced or communicated in all kinds of situations.

A specific social identity can become chronically accessible because of the motivations, desires, and experiences of the person; that is, compulsively from within. This is the case with the typical macho, who exaggerates the importance of his masculinity in relation to other social identities and always tends to think in male/female terms. Or with the notorious racist, for whom a difference in skin colour or ethnic background determines his or her judgement of others and self-presentation. Following Goffman (1959), anthropologists also talk about group memberships being *overcommunication*. This means that the ethnic or racial identity is 'shown off' and indicated or claimed in almost all situations. A more positive example is the African-American concept of 'race man' or 'race woman', which expresses that one's racial identity is the centrepiece of one's self-understanding and that one is devoted to the advancement of black people.

Specific social identities can also become overwhelming or unidimensional when the society obliges people to place a particular identity in the forefront of their minds and central in their behaviour. A simple example is a nation at war when national identity forcibly takes precedence to almost all other ones. Another example is a society in which race or ethnicity is used as the principal criteria for social distinctions, as in apartheid South Africa. In that case, skin colour or ethnic background is the first and predominant characteristic in determining (un)equal possibilities and opportunities. Ethnicity and race can develop into stigma identities, which provide a chronically salient distinction or a master status that cannot be ignored and serves to define the essential character of those who are classified. An example of this is the identity 'Gypsy' in many east European countries. A person can be a doctor, an engineer, or a teacher, but as soon as she or he is known to be a Gypsy, this identity tends to become the definitive one.

Importance of the context

Specific social identities can predominate to such an extent that they are relevant in almost all situations. In general, however, processes of social identity are highly context-dependent. For example, in most cases, ethnic identity is not continuously and overwhelmingly present. To what extent and how a particular identity is considered relevant and important is not fixed. According to Wentholt (1991), this depends, firstly, upon the circumstances or *situations* under which the distinctions are made, and, secondly, upon the *relations* between and within the groups that are socially categorized under those circumstances. As Phinney (1990, p. 510) concludes in her review of theory and research on ethnic identity, 'Adolescents report that their feelings of being ethnic vary according to the situation they are in and the people they are with.' In line with this, Rosenthal and Hrynevich (1985), for example, have observed that adolescents of Greek or Italian origin in Australia feel strongly Greek or Italian in some situations (as at home or with family), whereas they see themselves as Australian in other contexts (as at school). Another example is ethnographic studies in urban settings that show that ethnic and racial distinctions are either emphasized or ignored depending on circumstances and relationships (e.g. Baumann, 1996; Conquergood, 1994). For example, studying youth in two London areas, Back (1996) shows that ethnic identity is actively denied in favour of local and subcultural identities, but at the same time there also exist divisive and exclusive notions of ethnicity.

Hence, the social context, in terms of concrete situations and relations, is of great importance for the question of whether and how particular social identities become meaningful. Depending on the context, a specific social identity becomes relevant and others recede into the background. However, this is not an automatic process in which people are completely determined by the existing social influences. Situations and relations are not self-evident, but become meaningful through individual and collective *interpretations*.

Context not only refers to the immediate, local environment but can also be taken to refer to broader historical, economic, and political circumstances (Ashmore et al., 2004). The way in which ethnic identities are defined in local places occurs in relation to past events and the broader social space. The importance of this for understanding ethnic identity will be discussed in later chapters in terms of history, diaspora, and transnationalism.

An example that can be given here is that there is an obvious link between the former colonial subjection of groups and present negative stereotypes. Minorities from former colonies are typified in very similar ways in different Western countries, such as being lazy, criminal, stupid, and unreliable (e.g. Grasmuck & Grosfoguel, 1998). In the USA, there are many negative stereotypes about African-Americans and Puerto Ricans, but this is much less the case in countries like the Netherlands and France. In these countries, African-Americans and Puerto Ricans may be approached negatively and discriminated against because of the colour of their skin or their appearance, but not so much because of their ethnic background. In the Netherlands and France, on the other hand, there are negative stereotypes about Surinamese and Algerians, whereas these groups are much more accepted in the USA.

The relevance of history not only indicates that local circumstances are important. It indicates also that there is often stability and continuity. Identities are not only context-specific positions and meanings that change situationally. The flexible processes of categorization and boundary drawing for defining an identity are not more important than the contents of that identity. Social identities should not be treated as phenomena without a history and without defining characteristics. The crucial emphasis on situation and change should not lead to ignoring continuity and stability. As Jenkins (1996, p. 62) writes, 'social identities are neither remorselessly permanent nor frivolously malleable'.

The importance of the latter is not the same for every social identity. For national, ethnic, and religious identities, a focus on continuity and stability is, for instance, more important than for voluntary memberships in sports clubs and social movements. Some identities are more interwoven in the structure and culture of a society (e.g. gender), offer an encompassing view of the world (e.g. religion), or have a long history (e.g. ethnicity). These 'primary' identities (Jenkins, 1996) are socially and culturally more robust than other identities and are also learned at an early age. At a young age, people learn specific categorizations that provide a first and basic understanding of the social world. These categories are not only used to distinguish between others but also develop into particular self-understandings. As a participant in one of our studies said, 'We can leave Morocco but Morocco does not leave us.' The social identity becomes a self-evident and basic framework for thinking, feeling, and doing. Of course, this does not imply that the social psychological meanings of these identities are fixed once and for all. On the contrary, people are actively involved in defining and dealing with these identities, and they interact and negotiate with each other to come to new understandings. In that sense, identities are never finished but are rather like unresolved issues in an ongoing debate.

Gender identity is again an appropriate example. Gender has a physical component, has consequences for almost every facet of life, and is taught at a very young age. Hence, it is no surprise that being a man or a woman is for most people a central aspect of who and what they are. In many cases, this identity is self-evident and is accompanied by habitual response patterns. And as soon as this identity is threatened, emotional responses are evoked. What it means to be a man or a woman is, however, dependent upon social and local circumstances that are shaped and defined by people themselves. The fact that certain social identities are of primary importance from a psychological point of view does not mean that they are fixed and unchangeable from a social point of view. However, there can be many restrictions and limitations on change, such as ideological representations, existing discursive regimes, institutional arrangements, and power relations.

Identity formation

The previous discussion of social identity may give the impression that people are subject to the social circumstances they find themselves in. After all, in the approach presented, the emphasis is on the social environment in which identities are being defined, institutionalized, and assigned to people in all kinds of ways. Social identities are public realities; they are the result of social processes of group definitions and assignments. This emphasis carries with it the danger of a socially deterministic account in which the way individuals actively and in interaction with each other assert, (re-)define, and negotiate identities is ignored.

However, the emphasis on social circumstances does not imply determination. These circumstances are always the outcome of human actions and therefore changeable. Common meanings and requirements are appropriated and adjusted to concrete situations, existing understandings are rejected and resisted, and initiatives for change are always there. Individuals are not simple bearers or victims of social positions, discourses, or situations, although the room for change and manoeuvre is predefined and limited. Social categories can be questioned, behavioural expectations can be challenged, and existential definitions can be rejected. People are able to say 'no' to counter meanings and images and to take up a critical stance. Although some individuals and groups have a wider range of choices than others, there are always ethnic options available (Song, 2003).

Social identities are socially constructed and therefore neither inevitable nor fixed. Although they often appear and feel solid and overwhelming, they are the contingent outcomes of social processes. Change and renewal are inherent to social life. Categorizations that appear to be self-evident and natural can become the subject of discord and lead to new or adjusted distinctions. Social identities are continuously under negotiation. These negotiations can involve the question of whether a certain distinction should or should not be created and emphasized. They can also concern the cultural meanings and expectations that are linked to the existing divisions and situations, or to the ontological definitions that follow from these. In identity formation, the emphasis can be on one of the three distinguishable components of identity.

Political classifications, for example, can lose their predominant legal status and start to function as categorizations in everyday social life. An example is the term *Hispanic* in the USA. Originally used for statistical and political reasons, it gradually evolved into a social identity for some of those categorized by it. Eriksen (1993) refers to the usage of the term *West Indians* in Great Britain, which initially functioned only as an ascribed label for people coming from Caribbean islands such as Trinidad, Jamaica, and Barbados. These people regarded themselves as members of different groups. Gradually, however, they started to regard themselves as West Indians. At first, this occurred mainly in contacts with the majority group, but very soon it also started to play a role in contacts between and within the groups involved. The same goes for *Asians* in the USA and Britain. A further example is the anthropological term 'allochthonous' that predominates in the Netherlands. This term was introduced in 1989 by the Scientific Council for Government Policy as an alternative to terms such as 'guest workers' and 'foreigners'. Nowadays, the term is commonly used by the Dutch as well as by different ethnic minority groups for classifying themselves.

Clearly distinguishable behaviours can also be the starting point for identity formation. People can do particular things together and have reciprocal expectations. Recognizable shared activities are conducive to the development of a social identity. An obvious and important example is the language spoken. The observation that a number of people do the same thing in the same way, or speak the same language, easily leads to the conclusion that it is a distinguishable group of which the members differ in a certain way from other groups. But this observation is by no means self-evident. It is not enough to assert or claim an identity. The fact of doing things differently or of speaking a particular language has to be recognized and validated by the wider society; it has to be turned into a social identity.

The starting point for identity formation can also originate from the idea or feeling that one is basically a different kind of person. For example, on the basis of shared interests or preferences, one can try to establish common activities with like-minded others and use symbols to differentiate and distance oneself from others. In that case, the commonality is socially stated, 'proved', and a social categorization and ontological judgement can follow. For instance, the identification with certain musicians and music (such as rock and rap) is typically accompanied by a characteristic behaviour and appearance. This can lead to a social categorization with the related identity definitions (rockers or rappers). The Rastafarian movement with its typical hairdo, reggae music, and use of green and yellow colours is an example of identity formation within certain categories of young people.

Among other things, identity formation has to do with the question of who is able to construct socially relevant categorizations. A familiar distinction that is often used in this respect is between ascription and self-ascription. This distinction is sometimes used to distinguish an ethnic category from an ethnic group. In the former case, people are put together by others on the basis of assumed common characteristics, as in political and legal classifications. In the latter case, people see and define themselves in ethnic terms and their own norms, rules, and goals are involved. Ascription and self-ascription, or assignment and assertion, are of course strongly related to each other. Ethnic minorities are not simply the passive recipients of imposed identities but rather actively respond to unwanted and negative images. Individuals and groups act in response to how they are being classified, and this in turn leads to reactions by the original classifiers. There are many looping effects here (Hacking, 1999).

For example, in the Netherlands, the abusive term 'cunt-Moroccans' (in Dutch, 'kut-Marokkanen') was used by an alderman of Amsterdam in an informal talk with the mayor to describe some groups of Moroccan youths. By accident, the talk was recorded by the media and became public. The alderman apologized publicly but emphasized that Moroccan youths cause many social problems, particularly related to criminality. People of the Moroccan community were obviously offended and hurt. However, when the song 'kut-Marokkanen' by the rap artist Raymzter reached the top of the charts, the term started to be used by some Moroccan youths in a proud and defiant way.

Another example is the process of ethnic self-description among Louisiana Cajuns. Henry and Bankston (2001) analyse how contemporary Cajuns' self-image is rooted in stereotyped descriptions given by outsiders. Those who consider themselves Cajuns have taken up, reworked, and revalued the negative and stereo-typical portrayals developed by outsiders. Hence, the Cajuns have actively responded to the negative representations and images which are attributed to them by the wider society.

These examples also show that despite the many looping effects, differences in emphasis on ascription (assignment) or self-ascription (assertion) can exist. To illustrate this, the distinction between ethnicity and 'race' is useful. These two concepts are heavily debated, especially in the British and North American literature (see Banks, 1996; Cornell & Hartmann, 1998). Here, I am not concerned with this discussion, but rather with the example. Banton (1988) argues that ethnic identity is the result of self-definition. Ethnicity would involve a 'voluntary' identity that is typically not developed in response to oppression but taken up and defined by the group itself (ethnicization).

In contrast, 'race' would be a categorical distinction based on phenotyp-ical characteristics that, from a historical point of view, has been imposed by outsiders (racialization). Race categorization is a division that white people used to distinguish all nonwhites from themselves; race is a basis for a shared fate. To Banton, this renders race an external construction, an ascription in which only black people would have a racial identity and white people would not.[5] In that sense, 'black' is a derived category that has no real meaning in itself but indicates 'nonwhite', including all the negative connotations and stereotypes. However, in the 1960s, those classified in this way brought about a change in this identity. For the black consciousness movement, the term *black* became the expression of unity of black Americans in their battle against racism, and it was considered a positive counterpart to *white*. This led, for example, to black leaders arguing strongly that pride in being a person of colour should lead people of mixed parentage to regard themselves as black. Any other identity was seen as a rejection of one's black ancestry and a betrayal of the black community and cause.

According to Banton, the difference between race and ethnicity has mainly to do with the question of who categorizes and defines. Hence, it is understandable that the terms used to label groups are often quite sensitive and that the use of a particular term is not neutral. The labels express and symbolize how outsiders see a group or how a group understands itself and wants to be seen by others. The choice of one or another label reflects in many cases a social or political position. The term 'ethnic minorities' has different connotations and implications from terms such as 'immigrants', 'guest workers', or 'foreigners'. Waters (1990), for example, tries to show how in the USA whites' privileging of ethnic over racial identity, with regard to both themselves and others, can lead to ignoring or rejecting racial inequalities.

Strong debates can arise about the used and to-be-used terminology. For example, in the USA, there is a 'battle of the name' over how Spanish-Americans should be referred to. There is some disagreement on *Hispanic*, a term that according to some people should be replaced by *Latino* or by referring to the country of origin, as in 'Mexican-American'. In addition, groups with a clearly political agenda tend to favour the term 'Chicano'. Furthermore, the USA has witnessed a transition in the use of the term used to refer to 'black' Americans, from *coloured* to *Negro*, to *blacks*, and currently to *African-Americans*.

The introduction or change of a term is of course not enough to accomplish an actual change in the thoughts and behaviour of people. In 1988, at a conference of black leaders in Chicago, the president of the National Urban Coalition proposed the term 'African-Americans' to refer to black Americans. Hence, an ethnic term was proposed to replace a racial one. Most leaders accepted the proposition, and the new name spread quickly. Nevertheless, identity formation needs the label to become the prevailing and functional term in everyday social life. It has to grow from idea, notion, and expectation into a social reality. That is, it has to become a term with which people define themselves and each other, use to interpret behaviour, and is part of the social beliefs and practices of a collectivity. As Philogene (1994) shows, the change has to be accepted and become self-evident, so that a certain uniformity and formalization in meanings and interpretations exist.

This is not self-evident. For example, in academic circles in the 1970s, the term *Afro-Americans* was used, but this term did not become the prevailing one among the population and was associated with a particular hairdo and racial differences. Another example, is the Dutch term 'medelanders' ('fellow country-men') that was proposed as an alternative to 'allochthonous'. The term is a nice variation on the Dutch word for Dutchman ('Nederlander'), but it has not been socially adopted.

The question of ascription and self-ascription is central in 'identity politics' or the 'politics of difference' (e.g. Parekh, 2000; Sampson, 1993; Taylor, 1992). People derive meaning; purpose; feelings of belonging; and status, prestige, and esteem from their social identities. Hence, it is not strange that different groups, such as ethnic minorities, homosexuals, and women, have been raising their voices and claiming a space in which to define their own identity. In identity politics, not only equal treatment and rights are at stake, but also the social recognition and public affirmation of the value of a particular, history, culture, or lifestyle. The emphasis is on group identities and the necessity for societal change. In the name of one's history and 'own culture', claims are made and justified. It is argued that one's particular perspective should be recognized and respected, because, 'If, in order to be heard, I must speak in ways that you have proposed, then I can only be heard if I speak like you, not like me' (Sampson, 1993, p. 1220).[6]

The politicizing of identity shows that social identity phenomena are closely related to power. This is certainly the case for ethnic identities, which typically express power constellations. Several authors have pointed out that people who are part of the dominant 'white' group often do not consider themselves members of an ethnic group (e.g. Bonnett, 1993; Frankenberg, 1993; Mills, 1997). This is also the case in the Netherlands, where the term 'ethnicity' is typically used to refer to minority groups. The majority group members are the ones who can more easily deny the psychological importance of ethnicity. They view themselves as the rule rather than as the exception, as invisible and normal rather than visible and out of the ordinary, as the ground against which the figures of other ethnic groups appear. The majority group identity has a strong normalizing effect. Their ideas, beliefs, and attributes are the self-evident and undiscussed criteria against which the behaviour of minority groups is measured (Mummendey & Wenzel, 1999). This normalizing effect makes problems caused by minorities of central concern, whereas the implicit and dominant understandings of group identities are not considered (Verkuyten, 2001a).

Understanding ethnic identity requires an analysis of power relations. Chances, opportunities, and interests depend not only on social positions and decisions of particular individuals, but, typically, also on the fact that social mechanisms, principles, and opinions are represented as logical and inevitable. Power hides mainly in the everyday, self-evident understandings of how things are and should be. The consequence is that inequalities become invisible or are considered normal and just.

Ideological notions are important here, and we will discuss some of these in later chapters. In addition, as system justification theory argues (Jost & Banaji, 1994), cultural stereotypes can play an important role in the normalization and legitimization of relations and behaviour. An example is the idea that in Turkish and Moroccan families the relationship between parent and child is characterized by the authoritarian and command-like behaviour of the father. Teachers can use this idea to justify their own authoritarian actions toward Turkish and Moroccan students. As a Dutch teacher remarked in one of our studies, 'You shouldn't negotiate with Turkish and Moroccan students because they always have a story. I just follow the situation at home, what they're used to. So in other words: "Shut up and work!"'

Power can be reflected in language, and language can constitute and perpetuate power. The placing of people occurs within a discourse, vocabulary, or story in which social positions are defined and rendered (un)acceptable. In these discourses or 'texts of identity' (Shotter & Gergen, 1989), positions are presented in such a way that they imply and perpetuate power differences. A particular discourse implicitly attributes, for instance, control and competence to some group of people, and not to others (Laclau & Mouffe, 1985). In addition, depending on the discourse, different rights and obligations can be attributed to the same group of people. For example, one can talk about illegals (Dutch: 'illegalen') in the language of the constitutional state. Illegal individuals are then represented as lawless persons that are not allowed to stay in the country, because they have, for instance, performed illegal labour. However, one can also speak of illegal persons in economic terms, in which they are defined as employees and workers. In that case, the labour performed offers the opportunity to stay in the country, for example, as what are referred to as 'white illegals'.

Social identities are not given or fixed. Old identities lose their social meaning and new ones arise. The processes of identity formation are complex and involve many different actors and factors, such as the limitations and possibilities constituted by ideological frameworks, institutions, and authorities; economic circumstances; relations between groups; characteristics within groups; and the effort and creativity of elites and other individuals (Cornell & Hartmann, 1998). Historical circumstances are also of huge importance. Historians and many anthropologists study ethnic identity formation from a historical perspective. Their focus is on the changes and developments that explain why and how ethnic groups have originated. These processes of ethnogenesis have been described for many groups. For example, van de Vyver (1998) gives a historical analysis of the tense relationship between Romanians and Hungarians in Transylvania, western Romania. He goes back to the ninth-century social-political circumstances in the region and shows how the Romanians and Hungarians have constructed and presented their own histories in opposition to each other. Another example is offered by Kappus (1997), who examines the transformations of social identities in Trieste, Italy. She argues that it was the nineteenth-century principle of nationalism that created the modern ethnic and oppositional identities of Slovenes and Italians. Another example comes from Stallaert (1998), who examines the genesis of the Spanish as an ethnic group. She starts with the Moorish period and shows how the imagery of Christians versus Moors is still part of Spanish identity today.

In later chapters, I have more to say about the role and importance of history. From a social psychological perspective, it is particularly interesting to examine how ideas about the past are shaped by the present and influence present perceptions and arguments. One reason why history affects ethnic identities and the perceived nature and legitimacy of ethnic relations is that history is never finished but is constantly reinterpreted in terms of present situations.

Social identity and sense of identity

Social identities are formed and defined in the social world, independently of the particular individual that is located by them. He or she has hardly anything to say about this, and there is nothing individually subjective about establishing a social identity. In an interview, the sociologist Norbert Elias gave the following answer to the question of whether he still felt Jewish, 'Yes, I am a Jew and even— like I have said before a German Jew, that's how I look, that's who I am. If you ask me whether I still consider myself Jewish, it seems as if that is a choice. But to that I can only answer: I have no choice, I am a Jew—whatever I do or say.'[7] Another example comes from the novelist and legal scholar Steven Carter, who states, while writing about his own experiences, 'To be black and intellectual in America is to live in a box. So I live in a box, not of my own making, and on the box is a label, not of my own choosing' (quoted in Deaux, 1996, p. 789).

Identity as a social fact is not the same thing as how people experience themselves. For example, a Chinese girl in one of our studies, asked to describe herself, stated, 'From the outside I am Chinese but from the inside I am Dutch.' Another Chinese girl said, 'I am not Dutch from the outside and not Chinese from the inside.'[8] Social identity as a basic social phenomenon and public thing is decided for the individual externally, by his or her environment. Since this externally established identity comes about regardless of the wishes, preferences, and needs of the person in question, the internal appreciation of it, that is the way the person *thinks and feels* about a particular social identity, is obviously something else. The subjective experiencing (who you think and feel you are) may or may not tally with the 'objective' designation (of what you are taken to be). And it is the conceptualization of a subjective, interiorized sense of identity that suggests some scope for agency and control. Hence, an analytic distinction is needed between the subjective experience or sense of identity and the social identity itself.

Identity as a social fact—who and what somebody is socially—should not be confused with the sense of identity or the way that identity is psychologically meaningful. The latter is basically a subjective phenomenon, although this does not mean, of course, that the psychological meaning is formed independently of the social world. On the contrary, identity as a social fact concerns the social constructions or the way in which categorical distinctions are made meaningful, collectively and in interaction. Individual interpretation is central to which personal features, such as wishes, desires, needs, and experiences, are important. The fact that these personal features have been socially formed and attained and that they are socially shared and used does not alter that. The distinction between social reality and subjective experience is a difficult but analytically necessary one. This allows us to examine the discrepancies between subjective interpretation and the 'cultural designs into which they are woven' (Keesing, 1982, p. 31). Berger and Luckmann (1966) argue that there can be a 'slack' between an individual's understanding of the group of which she is a member, and the general conception of that group or the 'identity-type'. They use the distinction between sense of identity and identity type to examine the dialectic between subjective understanding and social reality, the latter being beyond the person's direct control. This interplay allows for changes in the individual as well as in the group and the society in which the person is situated.

Identity issues concern both personal interpretations and sociocultural constructions, and these issues cannot be reduced to one another. This dual aspect is quite often neglected, not only in approaches that emphasize subjective interpretations and individual choice, but also in approaches that stress the role of, for example, social representations, public images, and cultural models that define and impose particular identity types.[9]

Concerning the former, people can, of course, try to distance themselves from particular identities, and not pay any attention to them. Neglecting these identities, however, is often quite difficult, as social reality almost rubs their faces in it. From a psychological point of view, one can take many directions, but, sociologically, one's freedom is limited. Although a Turk may not consider his ethnic background an overriding feature, the moment he is turned down for a job because of his ethnic background, his Turkish identity becomes very present, as much for himself as for others. The political refugee offers another example of this, she may feel herself to be just that, but it is not easy to get that self-understanding accepted as a social identity in the country to which she has fled.

The second type of approach often assumes that there is a simple correspondence or little or no distance between social representations, public images, or cultural models of identity and subjective experience. Hollan (1992) argues that this assumption poses at least three problems. First of all, cultural models give a simplified and idealized image of identities in which much of the dilemmas, contradictions, and buzzing complexity of daily life is suppressed or ignored. Secondly, cultural models are more like socially shared examples, premises, and propositions than fixed and coercing frameworks for how individuals (should) view themselves. The extent to which people's inner life is influenced by them is an empirical question. There is always the possibility that the model (or parts of it) is not integrated in everyday experience. Thirdly, there are personal desires, preferences, experiences, and social interactions which may actually run counter to, or even contradict, the social representations or cultural models.

Identity and sense of identity are closely connected and often coincide with each other. However, these are different phenomena, and discrepancies and tensions can occur. The subjective experience of a social identity cannot simply be derived from the establishment of a categorical membership. The personal interpretation can differ from that which is defined socially. Others in the social environment can agree that a person belongs to a certain group, but the person himself might think quite differently about this. An example of this is the homosexual who struggles with his coming out or the transsexual who socially is a man but feels that he is a woman and takes measures to acquire the desired social identity surgically. Furthermore, there can be considerable individual differences in the way a particular social identity is experienced.

Most social psychologists are mainly interested in subjective experiences and much less in identity as a social construction. The emphasis is on the psychological meaning of group membership and the process of identification. This can be illustrated by Tajfel's (1981, p. 63) well-known and often-cited definition of social identity, 'that *part* of an individual's self-concept which derives from his knowledge of his membership of a social group (or groups) together with the value and emotional significance attached to that membership' (original italics). In this definition, social identity (in singular) is taken to be a psychological phenomenon. It is part of the self-concept, namely that part that relates to group membership(s). People know that they are members of a group, and it is this 'knowing', in combination with evaluative and affective aspects, that forms the social identity.

Like most social psychologists, Tajfel focuses on the sense of identity as part of the self-concept. Hence, social identity is not considered to be the same as the self-concept or the self.[10] The term 'self-concept' is typically used to refer to the sum of the thoughts and feelings that a person has about him- or herself (Rosenberg, 1979). The content of the self-concept can relate to many different things, such as unique preferences, desires, attitudes, skills, and also group memberships.

In the literature, the terms 'self' and 'identity' are used extensively and often as alternatives. Many authors do not make a distinction and use both notions interchangeably. The choice of 'self' or 'identity' becomes coincidental, because they seem to mean the same. This is not a very helpful situation (see Coté & Levine, 2002). It is interesting to note that this interchangeable use does not lead to the conclusion that identity (or 'self') has no separate meaning and that we might as well do without it. There remains some sense that these notions, although closely connected in one way or another, point to different things. This becomes especially apparent in those cases in which identity is used to indicate that self-understandings also imply social roles, category memberships, discrimination, social adjustments, status, or whatever else that is described as 'societal'. The notions 'self' or self-concept are considered not very appropriate to indicate this. In other instances, however, both notions are used interchangeably again.

Using the term 'social identity' in the sense of self-understanding, self-feeling, or 'self' is often misleading. If social identity coincided with self-understanding, this would imply that an identity can change only when one's self-understanding changes for one reason or another. But of course it is not that simple. People can start to understand themselves differently, while from a social point of view they are still categorized and treated as if no change has occurred. Furthermore, losing or acquiring another social identity does not have to mean that one's self-understanding changes equally. One can lose or receive a certain social identity, know and accept this, but need time to incorporate it in the way one understands and feels about oneself. For example, immigration involves leaving a situation in which one's sense of identity has been enacted and supported to enter a situation in which it must be redefined and 'remoored' (Ethier & Deaux, 1994). This is also clearly illustrated in changes that result in becoming an 'ex' or 'former' of some kind, such as an ex-worker in the case of retirement, or an ex-foreigner in the case of naturalization, or a former bachelor in the case of a wedding (Ebaugh, 1998). A relatively sudden change in social position is often accompanied by a gradual change in self-understanding. It takes time to get used to one's new social location and to forget the internalized meanings related to the previous one.

Thinking about the sense of identity raises questions about identity development. How do people come to a more or less structured and consistent self-understanding? The idea that one of the central developmental tasks is to achieve a coherent and healthy sense of identity has been widely accepted. Erikson's work has contributed most to this acceptance, and his theory has been elaborated by others, particularly Marcia (1966). This line of thinking has also been applied to the psychological development of ethnic and racial identity. Examples are offered by Cross (1991), Helms (1990), Phinney (1989), and Weinreich (1986). I will discuss some of this work in Chapter 7.

Identity and identification

Being seen and approached by others as a member of an ethnic group has its consequences. There are expectations, interpretations, and the possibility of discrimination and exclusion. In these cases, whether people identify with their ethnic group does not matter very much. The person is looked upon, addressed, and treated as a member of that group, both by in-group members or co-ethnics and by outsiders. However, it is obvious that identification does matter in many cases. After all, identification establishes the link between the individual and the group. As soon as people identify with their group, that group becomes the basis for thinking, feeling and acting.

'Identity' and 'identification' are terms typically mentioned in the same breath. A conceptual distinction is often not made. For example, for social psychologists working within the tradition of social identity theory, the essential questions are, '*how* do people identify with a group, and precisely what are the consequences of such identification?' (Hogg & Abrams, 1988, p. 2; their italics). Turner (1982, p. 18; his italics), similarly, states, 'The sum total of the social identifications used by a person to define him- or herself will be described as his or her *social identity.*'

However, since people have only a limited say in their social identities but can still choose what or whom they identify with, we should be careful not to treat the two notions as following inevitably from each other. Identification entails a psychological—intentional or unintentional—process, no matter how socially influenced and shaped this process is. Individuals identify with a group, and the process of identification depends on personal characteristics, preferences, needs, experiences, and circumstances.

According to Wentholt (1991), the relationship between identity and identification can take at least four forms. Identification can correspond to an existing social distinction. This is, for instance, the case when, in Belgium, a Flemish person identifies with the Flemish cause and everything that is Flemish. Or when a Chinese person in the Netherlands, who is very aware of his or her Chinese background, starts to identify strongly with Chinese culture. In both examples, there is identification with a group to which one is taken to belong. Identification can correspond with social identity.

Identification with the group to which one belongs can also be resisted or denied. In that case, someone does not want to belong to that group but rather wants to opt out or keep a distance, somewhat or entirely. De- or dis-identification rather than identification is the issue here; a distance is kept from the ethnic in-group and the expectations and demands that follow from the group membership. This often results in criticism from the co-ethnics, as is indicated by terms such as *bounty bar, coconut* or *oreo* (black on the outside, white on the inside), and *banana* (yellow on the outside and white on the inside) and by the reproach of *acting white, selling out, mental corruption,* and *treason.*

It is also possible to identify with an ethnic group that one does not belong to. A white person can identify with blacks. However, this does not change the identity that someone simply has. As much as I can identify with Surinamese or with Chinese people living in the Netherlands and as much as I can try to be one of them in what I do and how I think, others will not see and recognize me as such. I will remain an outsider who 'acts as if' and whose acceptance is provisional. It is not enough to claim an ethnic identity. One must be able to enact or perform it satisfactorily. The possibilities of this are of course not the same for each social identity. In the examples of cross-racial identification, a clearly visible feature (skin colour) plays an important role. However, there are also identities that are much easier to change, such as an identity related to membership of a sports club, and sometimes there is the ability to 'pass' and neither take up nor accept an identity.

Lastly, identification can be independent from existing social divisions. People can identify with a certain cause or person, such as a pop star or a top athlete. In that case, identity is not the issue but rather identification based on admiration and involvement. Identification cannot directly 'cause' a social identity. Identity has to 'work', meaning that significant others have to recognize and validate the identity claim. Based on identification, one can of course develop shared activities, use symbols to distinguish oneself from others, and try to get one's self-understanding accepted and recognized by others. In that case, identification is made explicit and objective, and a social division and ontological definition can follow.

Identification as and identification with

Identification does not have to correspond with social identity. These are often closely connected but distinguishable phenomena. Identification is a psychological process whereas social identities involve processes of social construction. This distinction raises the question of how the concept of identification can be understood. 'Identification turns out to be one of the least well-understood concepts —almost as tricky as, though preferable to, "identity" itself; and certainly no guarantee against the conceptual difficulties which have beset the latter' (Hall, 1996, p. 2).

As Hall states, identification is almost as complicated a concept as identity and has been taken to mean many things. For example, it is sometimes understood as liking someone (Barker, 1989; Graham, 1972).[11] As a term 'identification' is complex and ambiguous and requires clarification. Yet, most scholars use the term as if it were self-evident, and its use by different authors does not imply a common understanding.

It was Freud (1955) who introduced the term 'identification' to the social sciences. He mainly focused on the role of identification in the development of children. He saw identification as something that occurs between a child and a parent and that has long-lasting, virtually permanent consequences. However, the process of identification is not restricted to a particular other but gradually expands to include a wide range of persons and groups. For example, most people identify with an ethnic or national group, from which they derive a sense of involvement, concern, and pride as a result.

According to Freud, identification is more than imitation, because the former makes someone think, feel, and act as though another person's characteristics belong to him or her. Identification is a process whereby others' beliefs, values, and standards are adopted as one's own. For Freud, although identification may be a pre-eminently emotional process, it is based on observed similarities. Identification 'arises with any new perception of a common quality shared with some other person' (Freud, quoted in Deaux, 1996, p. 778). That is, it is observed similarities that are the starting points for identification, just as observed differences can lead to distancing. A definition or sense of similarity is accompanied by a tendency to become emotionally involved with those with whom one is identifying, whereas difference would lead to de-identification.

Freud argues that identification has both a cognitive and an affective aspect. This dual aspect of identification is also emphasized in the social psychological literature on the topic, and the increasing empirical evidence for this distinction (e.g. Ellemers et al., 1999; Jackson, 2002; Jackson & Smith, 1999; Smith et al., 1999) applies to minority groups as well (e.g. Phinney, 1990; Verkuyten & Nekuee, 1999a). In discussing ethnic identity, Lange (1989) uses Stone's distinction (1962) between identification *as* and identification *with*. The former involves the cognitive act of categorizing and defining oneself as a member of an ethnic group. One recognizes one's membership of an ethnic group and uses an accurate label to define the group and oneself.[12]

Identity theory (McCall & Simmons, 1978; Stryker, 1980) may be regarded as addressing this aspect of identification insofar as role identities are considered self-referent cognitions or self-definitions, and insofar as the focus is on the process of labelling or naming oneself as a member of a social category.[13]

Social identification as conceptualized in self-categorization theory (Turner et al., 1987) also refers mainly to identification of oneself as a member of a social category. According to this theory, social categories influence behaviour when individuals define themselves in terms of those categories, because self-definition in collective terms typically involves self-stereotyping of how one's category is defined in relation to other categories. When, in a particular situation, people see themselves as members of a group, they will act *as* members of that group. That is, the norms and beliefs characterizing the group provide the famework within which people act. Hence, the cognitive aspects of identification include the process of self-categorization ('I am a member of a particular ethnic group') and depersonalization ('I think about myself in terms of ethnic group attributes').

Self-categorization starts with giving oneself a name or a label; I am a Moroccan, a police officer, a father, a 'Rotterdammer'. Each label carries different meanings, and changing labels means taking on a different set of expectations. Or, as Foote (1951, p. 17) states, 'a person by another name will act according to that other name'. Buriel (1987) argues that Americans of Mexican origin that define themselves as *Chicano* tend to act, think, and feel differently from those that describe themselves as *Hispanic*. *Chicano* has a clearly political connotation that points to exclusion and discrimination, whereas *Hispanic* is originally a policy term (see also Banton, 1998; Isaacs, 1975).

Defining oneself as a member of an ethnic group, however, does not necessarily imply that one identifies *with* that group. A person may recognize and accept an ethnic group as self-defining, but he or she does not have to consider this definition personally important or be emotionally involved. Self-categorization can exist without feelings of belonging or the group membership having emotional significance. Identification *with* refers to what Rosenberg (1979, p. 179) calls 'introjection'. This is 'the degree to which the group is experienced as an integral and inseparable part of the self. Introjection . . . refers to the adoption of externals (persons or objects) into the self, so as to have a sense of oneness with them and to feel personally affected by what happens to them. For the group identifier, the distinction between me and my group is unclear; the fate of the group is experienced as the fate of the self.'

Freud emphasizes the emotional aspect of identification. For him, it is about 'the earliest expression of an emotional tie with another person' (Freud 1955, p. 134). Identification is more than placing oneself in the same category as others with whom one is identifying. It is about wanting to be and feel at one with an other; it is a kind of emotional fusion or mergence in which the self and this other are experienced as inextricably intertwined. The success of the other person or the group becomes one's own success and increases positive self-feelings, whereas failures become one's own failures that diminish positive self-feelings. Identification implies a—temporary or more permanent—reorganization of one's emotional life. Various emotions can be involved here, such as solidarity and loyalty, but also compassion and anger. However, the presence of the emotions pride and shame are typical of identification, as these emotional reactions only reference the self (Rosenberg, 1979). I can admire or despise a particular person or group, but that does not mean that I take pride in that person or group, or feel ashamed by them. However, when I identify with that person or group, they are capable of arousing feelings of pride and shame in me.

Esteem and belonging

For many social psychologists, the emotional meaning of identification lies primarily in the resulting self-esteem. People prefer identifications that bring positive social identities, and thereby positive collective self-esteem (Luhtanen & Crocker, 1992). Intergroup differentiation is one strategy for achieving positive social identity, but there are others, such as meeting in-group expectations. Negative self-esteem as a result of group membership is thought to lead to a tendency to dis-identification with the group or to seek more favourable intergroup comparisons. Identification and self-esteem are assumed to be closely related, and often they are not distinguished but taken as indicators for each another.

Group identification, however, does not have to imply positive self-esteem but can involve vicarious shame. People can feel (emotionally) closely connected to their ethnic in-group, while that group membership brings them social contempt and discrimination or induces feelings of collective guilt (e.g. Doosje et al., 1998; Iyer et al., 2003). This shows that a distinction is required (e.g. Rubin & Hewstone, 1998). Identification with a group can serve other functions than positive self-esteem. Particularly for ethnic and racial minority groups, identification can provide, for example, a buffer against the effects of stigma (e.g. Branscombe et al., 1999), a source of bonding and belonging with other minority members and their experiences (e.g. Cross & Strauss, 1998), and a condition for effective political action (Reicher & Hopkins, 2001).

The need for self-esteem plays a central role in human affairs. A sense of identity implies an awareness not only of who and what one is, but also of the value, recognition, and respect that particular identities bring. Self-esteem develops in interaction with others and is strongly dependent on the esteem granted socially. Negative judgements about who and what one is are painful, whereas positive evaluations affirm that one is a person of worth, a person that counts. Positive self-esteem does not have to involve the feeling of being better than others. This feeling, however, is never far away, particularly not in group relations (Brewer, 2001). The idea that as a group 'we are good' because, for example, we live up to our cultural standards or historical obligations can easily develop into the idea of 'we are better'. Social categories typically differ in status, prestige, and worth so that the mere category membership implies a certain amount of social esteem. Standards of evaluation depend on social comparisons that may result in social competition for positive identity.

The social psychological focus on self-esteem is important but also limited because the role of feelings of belonging and attachment tends to be ignored. People do not only want to distinguish themselves positively from others. There is also the striving for affective relationships with the social environment. Identification and a sense of identity also encompass feelings of belongingness and an aware-ness of togetherness and unity: 'We belong together', 'I am part of this', I am one of them'. In their review, Baumeister and Leary (1995, p. 497) conclude, 'Existing evidence supports the hypothesis that the need to belong is a powerful, fundamental and extremely pervasive motivation.' This need to belong means an outer-directedness, an affective involvement in other people and things. Humans want to attach themselves to someone or something, want to belong and feel at home in their world. Feelings of belongingness, connectedness, security, solidarity, and loyalty can be the result, but a sense of being lonely, isolated, separate, and a stranger or outsider without ties and a home can also develop. Without a web of attachments, life becomes empty and shallow.

Belonging is outer-directed, but not in a disembodied way. It is something concrete that evokes the awareness of connectedness and the associated feelings—the sight of the national flag, rituals, ethnic symbols, particular persons, landscapes, sensory experiences, pictures, and so on. These are the materials or anchoring points of belonging that can result in unreflected and direct feelings of affection for those who are like oneself, members of the same social group. However, questions of belonging, like esteem, can also become more conscious and politicized.

The politics of identity and modes of belonging are prominent themes in contemporary academic debates. The latter has been used extensively in racist discourses and tends to produce arguments and definitions about who belongs and who does not ('They don't belong here, but we do. So they have to go'). This happens at the level of the nation state and institutions but also at local levels where people argue about who authentically belongs to a particular neighbourhood or place and who does not. However, increasingly, the notion of belonging is being put forward as a useful political category by all kinds of minority groups (e.g. Bromley, 2000; Christiansen & Hedetoft, 2004). The notion stresses that participation in society is not necessarily founded on a particular ethnic membership, and it brings sentimental and symbolic dimensions in the discussion. Furthermore, the term can be used in plural, suggesting that one can have several coexisting attachments. The variety of attachments constitute different modes of belonging, such as civic, civil, local, national, and global.

Identity politics is about the recognition of one's status as rightfully belonging and the public manifestation of modes of belonging. In addition, identity politics is about recognition by others of who and what one is (e.g. Taylor, 1992). It is concerned with the emancipation from repressive, ignored, or denied social identities, and with the equal value of groups and the equal respect to which they are entitled. For many, this does not simply imply equal treatment but rather that specific experiences, histories, cultures, and contributions of groups are publicly affirmed and recognized.

The foregoing discussion of group esteem and belonging is a good example of the necessity to distinguish between the three levels of analysis that were indicated in Chapter 1. Questions of belonging and the recognition of social identities can be examined at the societal level where immigration and integration policies are formulated and implemented, organizations and institutions function, cultural discourses and historical memories exist, and public debates take place. At this level, there are highly important decisions about and implications of belonging and recognition. These questions can also be examined in everyday interactions where people negotiate about belongings and the meanings of social identities (Bell, 1999). It is in interactions that identity claims are made and modes of belonging are announced and performed, and these can correspond to or contradict the placements and interpretations that others make. Analyses of these social processes are of course centrally important, but there is also the psychological dimension.

Feelings of belonging and a positive identity are psychologically important. It is possible, for example, to examine how ethnic minorities cope with stigmatization and discrimination (see Major et al., 2002; Schmitt & Branscombe, 2002). And many immigrants and asylum seekers are troubled not only by (perceived) lack of recognition and respect but also by feelings of uprooting and loss. It can also be examined when and how one's own ethnic group offers a sense of belonging with the related feelings of commitment, involvement, solidarity, and loyalty. A sense of belonging can (partly) compensate for negative stereotypes and discrimination, but can also lead to inner conflicts. The attempt to achieve an esteemed position and higher status in society can imply a far-reaching adjustment that can result in isolation and alienation from one's own ethnic group.

Stability and variability

In the literature, identification is seen as a rather stable individual difference characteristic, but also as a highly contingent process that varies in time and across context. Both approaches make sense phenomenologically. Most people will be familiar with situations in which their ethnic group membership is temporarily at the forefront of their thoughts, making them feel ashamed or proud. At the same time, most people are aware that there is something permanent and enduring about their group identity which has developed in a process of socialization. Although a sense of ethnic identity is more salient and important in some situations than in others, there also seem to be more stable understandings and affective meanings.

Hence, it is not surprising that some approaches focus more on the situational nature of a sense of identity, while others examine the psychologically more stable features. For example, anthropologists and sociologists use the concept of situated identity to indicate that identity is primarily a matter of establishing and maintaining social location in interaction (e.g. Hewitt, 2003; Okamura, 1981). Discursive social psychologists have a similar focus on situational interactions and they emphasize the practical consequences of variable identity definitions (e.g. Antaki & Widdicombe, 1998).

Another example of this is self-categorization theory (SCT), which emphasizes the situational and cognitive aspects of self-definition. This theory is more concerned with the contextually sensitive ways in which self-categorizations become salient and less with group identification or the degree to which group membership is psychologically central and valued. Hence, the concept of ethnic self-categorization emphasizes the significance and consequences of a person's ethnicity within a particular context, whereas the concept of ethnic identification emphasizes individual differences in the degree to which ethnicity develops in a psychologically central and valued group membership.

SCT does not deny the existence of more stable individual differences in the tendency to define oneself by in-group terms (Turner, 1999). Some people are more inclined than others to see themselves as a group member, and some to value their group membership more than others. From a self-categorization perspective, measures of identification or sense of identity are useful for assessing the centrality and emotional value attached to a group membership. Group identification is an important factor affecting a person's readiness to use a social category for self-description. Identification reflects one of the psychological resources—together with individual motives, needs, and goals—that are used to make sense of oneself and others in a particular context. For example, in our research among Iranian refugees living in the Netherlands we examined which factors determine whether they categorize themselves as (typical) Iranians (Verkuyten & Nekuee, 1999a). It was found that both perceived negative circumstances (discrimination) and ethnic identification were independent positive predictors.

An emphasis on context and variation is crucially important. The understanding of who and what someone is depends on those who are present and on the way in which the context is interpreted. However, this does not mean that questions of individual differences in group identification or the affective commitments to, for example, the ethnic group can be neglected. Tajfel (1981) stresses that social identity is connected to and derives from the membership of emotionally significant social categories or groups. Social meanings and messages are internalized, and most people develop a more or less elaborate and coherent sense of ethnic identity. This does not mean that this identity constantly frames the behaviour or that one thinks and feels the same about this identity in every situation and in any period of life. It is very possible that people are proud of their ethnic identity in one situation, while they are ashamed of it in another (Brown, 1998). However, this does not imply that, in general, some people will not feel emotionally more attached to their ethnic identity than others.

The debate about stability and variability in social identity is often conducted in an either/or fashion in which both 'sides' are talking only partially about the same issues and questions. For example, where one side will stress the flexible and continuously changing self-definitions, the other will accentuate the emotional investments and loyalties that make identity changes difficult. For one, cognition and detachment are the rule and emotional involvement and intensity the exception; for the other, things are simply the other way round. While one stresses short-term or temporary changes, the other has a more long-term perspective. Furthermore, one is claimed to reflect our late-modern or postmodern world whereas the other would characterize the (pre)modern situation.

Kunneman (1996) makes a metaphorical distinction between the postmodern 'walkman-ego' and the traditional 'tea-cosy-culture'. In the latter, people's identities are rooted locally in kinship and community networks and linked to a tradition with a clear moral order. Such a situation provides stability, predictability, and emotional solidarity, but is also limiting and oppressive. Obligation and duty are the basis for self-definition. In people's thoughts and actions, one social identity is central, that of the local community to which they belong.

In contrast, the postmodern Walkman ego is characterized by ambiguity, plasticity, and personal choice. Identities are linked to the globalizing mass culture, where images dominate and in which 'you are what you consume today'. Identities, so the argument goes, change with each new tape played on one's Walkman. Individual choice and the rapid proliferation of trends and styles are central. There are no investments in affective relationships. Rather, the investment is in ever-changing, multiple, and new self-images (Michael, 1996).

This emphasis on multiplicity, fragmentation, and personal choice is important because it relates to the many changes in our globalizing world. Nowadays, a great diversity in meanings, messages, and images is available, and this is used to manage and negotiate identities. Furthermore, with this emphasis, attention is given to agency or to the individual as a reflexive and critical agent engaged in defining his or her own social location.

However, not every social identity is the same. Ethnic, national, and racial identities provide for many people vital horizons of meaning rather than being just superficial and temporary images. These identities are substantial sources of self-understanding and meaningfulness in life, which find expression in the dynamics and essentialist claims of contemporary identity politics, modes of belonging, and conflicts. They are typically more than a style or trend to be adopted or discarded according to how one momentarily feels. In thinking and imagining, much is possible, and the options one can take are many and interchangeable, but emotions and loyalties are much less easy to change and combine (Ahmad, 1995). Furthermore, these identities are often embedded in supportive and oppressive social relationships. Changing relationships is not easy, because they need to be developed and maintained or challenged and replaced. This requires investment in time and means and brings with it expectations, obligations, and reciprocity.

In postmodern thought, identity tends to be reduced to personal taste and choice or constantly changing identifications and cultural orientations. It is more about what people choose and want themselves than about what they are taken to be socially. But possession of a social identity comes at least in part from being placed socially by others and having one's identity claim recognized and validated by others. Self-identification can differ from the categorization of oneself by others. Furthermore, there can be a difference between identification and sociocultural orientation.

An orientation toward particular styles and trends does not have to imply identification. For example, young people from minority groups can strongly identify with their own ethnic group and at the same time orient themselves toward (parts of) Dutch society and culture. Taking over and appropriating styles, images, and ideas does not need to involve a feeling of oneness or a kind of emotional mergence. With identification, however, the characteristics and concerns of others become personal issues. Group threat becomes a personal threat, and group success becomes one's own success. The identification itself is important and does not have to serve something else.

A sociocultural orientation implies that ideas, trends, and styles are examples for one's own behaviour. But this does not have to evoke the same emotional involvement as with identification. The orientation can be rather superficial and serve only one's own ends. The cultural meanings that are spread throughout the world by the mass media are used in specific local circumstances and adjusted to existing interpretations. Hannerz (1992) talks about a 'creolisation of cultural styles', and others use terms such as 'syncretism' and 'hybridization'. For example, cultural expressions of black culture in the USA are used and adapted by many different young people in the West. And parts of American mass culture are appropriated by youth in Islamic countries, although there is no identification with America or Americans.

A final word

This chapter has addressed various issues and questions, many of which will be developed in later chapters. I have tried to argue that the relation of what is social and what is psychological in social identity is inherently intricate. Social identities are social in origin, are socially defined and communicated, and serve social functions. And although their psychological impact on the people carrying them varies, may be complicated, and is always complex, in one way or another the psychological relevance of these identities is often overwhelming.

This is so for the simple reason that even when people are not moulded (which they usually are) by the patterns of behaviour a social identity imposes on them, their freedom is restricted and their actions are influenced by the expectations prevalent in their social world. And even where people do not judge (as they usually do) their personal worth at least partly on the basis of the prestige or other values generally accorded the social identities they possess, many others will pass such judgements about them whether they like it or not.

But all this may vary with circumstances, as may the demands social identities make on a person's time, energy, and thoughts. Ethnic identities may be more a matter of self-ascription or ascription by others, of assertion or assignment; they may be positively or negatively valued—though by different categories of people differently and for different reasons. There is a great deal that varies a great deal, but there are always also inertia and continuity. Questions of variability and stability depend on many different factors and conditions, including the particular social identity, such as ethnicity.

3   Ethnicity

In anthropology, ethnicity has been a major research focus since the 1960s and has remained so to the present day. A wide variety of cases, groups, and circumstances have come under examination, such as ethnic conflicts, nonviolent ethnic movements, multiethnic neighbourhoods and schools, and indigenous populations, as well as immigrants and refugees to Europe and North America. Despite the obvious and important differences between these situations, an ethnic framework is considered a useful instrument for understanding (parts of) what is going on. This raises the question of the conceptualization of ethnicity. Although less has been written about ethnicity than about identity, clarification is necessary.

'The whole conception of ethnic groups is so complex and so vague that it might be good to abandon it altogether.' This statement by Max Weber (1968, p. 385) illustrates the elusive quality of ethnicity. Although Weber was not enthusiastic about the concept, he actually did not abandon it but tried to give a precise definition that, subsequently, has been adopted by many scholars. How can ethnicity be conceptualized, what is the relationship with culture, how do ethnic distinctions function, and why is ethnicity so important in many instances? All these questions are, among others, central in the anthropological literature. However, I will not give an overview of this literature, as this would lead away from the intention of this book.[1] My main concern is to discuss some of the anthropological debates and to show that these have similarities with social psychological ones, but also to raise some interesting issues that are considered only marginally in social psychology.

Defining ethnicity

It is common nowadays, following Anderson (1983), to argue that national, ethnic, and other large-scale groups are imagined communities.[2] According to Anderson, these communities can be distinguished by the way or style in which they are imagined.

Many authors argue that it is the reference to descent and common origin that makes a group an ethnic one;[3] that it is the idea and belief in a common origin, descent, and history that distinguishes ethnic identity from other social identities. This emphasis on descent and origin can already be found in Weber (1968, p. 389). He defined ethnic groups as human groups (other than kinship groups) which cherish a belief in their common origins of such a kind that it provides a basis for the creation of a community. . . . We shall call 'ethnic groups' those human groups that entertain a subjective belief in their common descent because of similarities of physical type or of custom or both, or because of memories of colonization and migration; this belief must be important for the propagation of group formation; conversely it does not matter whether or not an objective blood relationship exists . . . ethnic membership does not constitute a group; it only facilitates group formation of any kind, particularly in the political sphere. On the other hand it is primarily the political community, no matter how artificially organized, that inspires the belief in common ethnicity.

A number of things are interesting in this description.[4] One is that the *belief* in common descent and shared origin is central. Weber stresses that ethnic membership is a presumed identity or a claim based on putative shared descent. Whether or not the common descent and history have been (partly) made up is of less importance than whether people regard it as plausible and experience it as real. Hence, ethnicity has to do with a subjective belief in common origin, descent, and history. This belief is of course never finished but always subject to reinterpretations and adjustments, depending on the present circumstances. In that sense, ethnicity is dynamic, changeable, and socially constructed. However, the idea itself of common descent and continuity with the past is central. In defining where one has come from, ethnicity provides a particular historical and social location within the complex world.

Furthermore, Weber indicates that the idea of descent and history can be made *plausible and acceptable in different ways.* Criteria for ethnic identity vary, and this has important consequences. Physical similarities, cultural characteristics, language, religion, and historical events and myths can all play a role in the definition and justification of a common origin. Justification, however, is necessary, both for in-group members and for outsiders. Ethnic claims have to be 'proven' if they are to become meaningful identities. Many things are possible here, but not every possibility is intellectually plausible and morally acceptable. Although ethnic identities are malleable, they are not complete fabrications. In order to create an ethnic identity, it is not enough to invent traditions (Peel, 1989). An imagined community is not an imaginary one.[5] History is continuously reinterpreted in light of current circumstances and interests; the present shapes the past. Nevertheless, it is not enough to invent traditions independently of historical facts; the past also shapes the present.[6] The story of one's own ethnic identity has to convince and satisfy emotionally. It should resonate with everyday experiences in order to give people an understanding of the present situation and future events (Eriksen, 2001). Redefinitions of the situation are always possible and happen regularly, but these should not contradict people's everyday experiences too obviously. An interesting case in point is Duijzing's (1997) analysis of a specific group of Gypsies who, in the 1990s in Kosovo and Macedonia—for mainly political reasons—started to define themselves as 'Egyptians'. At first, this seemed a case of pure invention and fantasy. However, Duijzing shows that the choice of the Egyptian identity was not wholly accidental but was related to at least some historical facts and some oral traditions of this group.

Finally, Weber emphasizes that ethnicity *does not imply ethnic group formation*. Rather, the belief in common ancestry is likely to be a consequence of collective political action. Furthermore, ethnicity is a (powerful) basis for group formation, which can occur depending on the circumstances. Group formation in terms of ethnicity is not limited to minority groups but also occurs among majority groups, such as the Dutch. That is, majority groups can also define themselves in terms of a belief in common descent and shared origin. Hence, the term 'ethnicity' also applies to the identity of the majority. In most research on ethnicity, the emphasis is mainly on processes of group formation. Anthropological studies focus particularly on interactions, ideologies, and the social (re)production of group boundaries. One of the reasons for this is the paradigmatic influence that the Norwegian anthropologist Barth (1969) has had.

Ethnic boundaries

The book *Ethnic Groups and Boundaries*, edited by Barth in 1969, was an important break with the then prevailing ideas of cultural groups. Up to that point, the notion of culture had been treated relatively statically, and ethnicity ('tribalism') and culture were considered to be more or less the same thing. Ethnic groups were typified on the basis of lists of common cultural characteristics. However, Barth and many others made it clear that such lists are never finite and that there is no one-to-one relationship between ethnic differences and cultural ones.

Culture is not a very useful basis for the definition of ethnicity. An important reason is that such a definition leads to a static and reified notion of culture. For example, the notion of 'multicultural society' quickly leads to the idea that cultures are bounded entities, clear-cut wholes, clearly distinguishable from other entities that are linked to other groups. As social psychologists would predict, the consequence of this is that the differences and contrasts *between* groups are emphasized and that similarities and commonalities are neglected. Moreover, the similarities *within* groups are easily exaggerated, and differences are forgotten. If people belong to the same group and each group has its own culture, then there is usually not much attention to in-group differences and to cultural change, mixture, and renewal. However, a great number of researchers have shown that there are considerable cultural differences within ethnic groups, but also similarities between groups.

Furthermore, a cultural definition of ethnicity would imply that each group that distinguishes itself culturally should be considered an ethnic group. An example of this is provided by Cohen (1974), who regards the stockbrokers who work in the City of London as an ethnic group. The result of this is that the specific character of ethnicity disappears and ethnicity is treated as any other group that shares some patterns of normative behaviour.

In addition, a sense of ethnic identity can remain strong, although from a cultural point of view numerous changes take place. Acculturation as the process of becoming more similar culturally does not have to imply a change of group membership and self-definition (Liebkind, 2001). People often hold on to their ethnic group identity, to what they feel is a continuity with the past, although their culture becomes intermingled with that of others. Contact between ethnic groups almost always leads to an exchange of cultural characteristics and mutual adjustments, but at the same time it often results in enhanced ethnic consciousness and stronger group differentiation. Ethnic groups remain more or less 'equal' to themselves, despite the fact that their culture is constantly changing. Cultural content and ethnic identity are, to an important degree, functionally independent. For example, in Trinidad, the distinction between African and Indian is regarded as a critical one, despite the fact that few if any cultural differences remain (Miller, 1994). Furthermore, we have found in many studies that young people 'Dutchify' in a cultural sense, but not at all in an ethnic sense. They are and remain proud of their ethnic background and strongly define themselves as, for example, Moluccan, Turk, or Antillean (Verkuyten, 1999).

Barth did acknowledge the importance of the belief in descent and origin, but treated ethnic groups as social groups that are the result of self-definition and definition by others.[7] For him, ethnicity is a principle of social organization and ethnic identity an issue of the way that ethnic boundaries are defined and maintained. The focus is on the social organization of difference or the intergroup processes of differentiation between 'us' and 'them'. Hence, Barth urged a shift away from discussion about the cultural content of ethnic identity towards a consideration of boundary processes between groups. Rather than a classificatory idea of ethnic groups to which the idea of cultural differences leads, he emphasized a relational concept of ethnic groups. 'The critical focus of investigation . . . becomes the ethnic boundary that defines the group, not the cultural stuff that it encloses' (Barth, 1969, p. 15).

Boundaries would be prior to the cultural 'stuff' and cultural practices, and characteristics would primarily be used as diacritical markers. Ethnic identity is almost always linked to the idea of cultural difference and independence. Many studies have shown that a limited number of cultural characteristics is typically put forward as representing the cultural integrity and authenticity of the group. These cultural characteristics and practices symbolize one's history and culture and are used to distinguish oneself from others. In doing so, these characteristics are presented as embodying one's identity, that is as defining what it, for instance, means to be Moluccan, Antillean, Dutch, or Cape Verdean.

Departures of cultural practices are typically defined as a loss or abandonment of one's own culture and a betrayal of one's own people or group. Liang (2004) shows, for example, how overseas Chinese community leaders in European countries construe marriages between Chinese and non-Chinese in terms of cultural loss and assimilation. They use the symbolic value attached to marriage rituals and of marriage within the ethnic in-group to assert ethnic and cultural distinctiveness. Marriage within and across the ethnic boundary is used by leaders to give that boundary a moral dimension in the struggle for cultural maintenance. One's 'own culture' can also be used in discussions about the integration of immigrants and minority groups. For example, following the debate in Germany, there has been, in the Netherlands, a discussion about the 'leitkultur', or dominant culture. It is argued that a clear and precise definition of core aspects of Dutch culture is necessary in order for immigrants to know what to expect and do, and in order to formulate demands and impose sanctions on immigrants, and to break the yoke of political correctness.

Barth's interest was in the social definitions of identities. He argued that ethnic identities are not immutable but transactional and situationally flexible. For him, the management and manipulation of situational identities that result from the disjuncture between ascription and self-ascription is the key aspect. Ethnic identities are examined as pragmatic aspects of the organization of everyday social interactions. This theoretical stance has many similarities with discursive social psychologies that focus on the level of interaction. Barth himself has argued that his original ideas would now be recognized as constructionist (Barth, 1994).

Barth's emphasis on interpersonal transactions has also led to the criticism that both the broader societal and the psychological level of analyses are ignored (see Banks, 1996; Jenkins, 1996). He would neglect power and the role of predominant discourses or discursive regimes, including ideologies of descent. His individualist emphasis would also imply a rather simple form of rational choice voluntarism, which can be severely constrained, however, as for members of racialized minorities, making it necessary to examine the broader context in which situational ethnicity appears. Furthermore, boundaries can be interpreted not only in interactional terms related to the management of identity, but also in terms of what Cohen (1994) calls 'boundaries of consciousness, and consciousness of boundaries'. Ethnic identity can be a fundamental element of self-understanding, rooted in notions of loyalty and a sense of consistency across time and contexts. Hence, the study of ethnicity should also involve the study of ideology and psychological processes. In his later work, Barth (1994) recognizes this and explicitly suggests that ethnicity should be studied on the three interrelated levels of micro, median, and macro analysis.

In addition, it can be argued that Barth, as in most social psychological approaches, does not really examine ethnicity. Rather, he presents a general model of social identity processes. In doing so, he focuses on the social organization of differences and more or less ignores the question of similarities and commonalities. Ethnic identities, however, involve not only group differences but also 'having something in common, whether it be "real" or imagined, trivial or important, strong or weak. Without some commonality there can be no collectivity' (Jenkins, 1996, p. 104). Culture is the aspect of commonality that is typically emphasized in ethnic studies.

Ethnicity and culture

The emphasis on group relations and boundaries has led to the proverbial throwing of the baby out with the bathwater, because there is often little attention to the role of cultural patterns. Culture is more or less reduced to a means of self-definition and an instrument in battles for identity, recognition, and interests. However, the fact that cultural features, such as language and dress, may function as boundary markers does not mean that people do not also take their way of life seriously. Situations of intensive contact between ethnic groups show that actual cultural differences continue to exist. For instance, language, traditions, and religion are not only (arbitrary) means for marking ethnic distinction, but also meaningful cultural aspects as such, both for the in-group and for outsiders. Or as Eriksen (1993, p. 136) puts it, 'Thus, ethnic relations cannot always be fully understood by way of analyses of competition or domination, but may also be regarded as "encounters between cultures".'

Many people from ethnic minority groups, for example, have a cultural background that differs from that of the indigenous inhabitants. Immigrants from Turkey, Morocco, Sudan, Iran, or other places cannot simply choose to do away with their childhood and everything they have learned culturally. When people from different origins live close to each other, the feeling that others have different customs, habits, and ideas is accentuated rather than moderated. After all, people see and experience that a number of supposed differences are not merely stereotypical but have actual implications, related, for example, to gender differences, religious practices, values, norms, and habits. Such differences are not imaginary, as the many misunderstandings and conflicts in intercultural communications show. Cultural differences are often difficult to verbalize, but that does not mean that they are not real. These differences are deduced from very subtle and unspoken signals that are communicated in interactions. Culture is tacit, lived, and physically felt rather than realized and verbalized. It is the unreflexive part of mundane practices. Often people are quite sure of the existence of cultural differences, even though it is difficult to indicate exactly what those difference are.

In cross-cultural psychology and in the field of ethnic psychology, there are numerous studies that examine ethnicity in terms of culture that is transmitted across generations. These studies have provided many interesting and important results. Culture is implicated in acculturation, group relations, and many other psychological processes (e.g. Fiske et al., 1998; Markus & Kitayama, 1991; Triandis, 1989). However, ethnic identity does not have to have a distinct cultural content. For most anthropologists, an equation between ethnicity and culture is simply bad anthropology. Furthermore, there is the danger here of 'culturalization' of ethnicity, and consequently the downplaying of social and material circumstances. For example, research on creolism has clearly shown that the meaning of 'creole' can best be explained by structural and historical conditions rather than by the content of a creole culture (e.g. Henry & Bankston, 1998). Equally, the notion of ethnicity invites thinking about culture and cultural differences in a way that ascribes patterns of behaviour to ethnicity. In contrast, the notion of race leads to questions of social problems, unequal positions, and status differences. Banks (1996) shows that in examining minority populations in the UK, British anthropologists tend to focus on Asians and culture, whereas sociologists tend to examine Britain's black population in terms of social positions. A similar general division of labour tends to exist between cross-cultural psychology and social psychology.

There is another problem with a focus on culture and that is the tendency to underplay the importance of the creation and interactive use of cultural meanings (Holland et al., 2001). The question of human agency, cultural production, and the politics of identity is an important area of debate in which the importance of culture is reclaimed not in a 'culturalist' or culturally deterministic way but by examining the ways that new syncretic cultural forms produce identities and social relations (Solomos & Back, 1994). Here, the emphasis is on everyday practices or the management and negotiation of ethnic identity in interactions. These processes are studied, for example, in metropolitan settings (e.g. Back, 1996; Baumann, 1996; Blokland, 2003; Hewitt, 1991; Mac an Ghaill, 1999), by investigating how wider cultural meanings are appropriated, used, and contested in local situations. The apprehension of culture is viewed 'not as tradition, but rather, as a bricoleur's bag [where] meaning [is] created as much as given' (Hewitt, 1991, p. 15). These cultural processes are understood in the context of global cultural networks and mass culture, that is, media, music, clothing, nonverbal behaviour, speech styles, and symbols. For example, the cultural forms and histories of black Americans form the raw material for the creative process that defines what it means to be black within the Dutch or British setting and within particular localities within these countries (Gilroy, 1993; Mac and Ghaill, 1999; Sansone, 1992).

Another example is the wearing of Lonsdale clothing that has become popular among extreme right-wing skinheads in Germany and the Netherlands. These groups have appropriated this respectable British brand. One reason for Lonsdale's popularity is that it is the middle letters of the brand name *NSDA* that are mainly visible when wearing a Lonsdale sweater under an open jacket. These letters are taken to refer to Hitler's political party the *NSDAP*. And on some Dutch skinheads' websites, *Lonsdale* is treated as an acronym that stands for 'Laat Ons Nederlandse Skinheads De Allogtonen Langzaam Elimineren' ('let us Dutch skinheads slowly eliminate the allochthonous'). Some Dutch schools have forbidden the wearing of Lonsdale clothing because it leads to name-calling and fights between Dutch and ethnic minority pupils.

A focus on actual practices and interactions allows the examination of how individuals and groups creatively define and locate themselves, without ignoring the fact that they are bounded by wider social and material circumstances, cultural meanings, and historical conditions. Ethnographic studies examine how local assertion and assignment processes interrelate with structural and cultural forms of identity. In doing so, these studies are quite similar to those of social psychologists, who, in studying discourse, pay attention to the more global patterns of sense making—interpretative repertoires, subject positions, cultural narratives, and texts of identity—that supply the resources or raw materials with which people build their accounts of themselves (e.g. Billig, 1997a; Wetherell, 1998). Identity is seen here as something that is actively accomplished within particular rhetorical contexts and by mobilizing and interpreting cultural discourses. The focus is on the relational nature of social life and the discursive construction and use of social categories. For ethnicity, this means an emphasis on performing an identity and becoming ethnic rather than on having that identity and being ethnic. However, it is also important to examine the kind of resources that the notion of ethnicity provides. A focus on function and interaction does not mean that the content of the categories by which definitions are established can be neglected. Gramsci (1973) argues that elements of common sense have their own history, so that common sense is situated within a wider context than the actual situated talk. Similarly, it can be argued that the notion of ethnicity brings particular understandings that should be considered.

The genealogical dimension

The Belgian anthropologist Roosens (1994, 1998) recognizes the importance of situated interaction and of Barth's boundary metaphor as it is used by many anthropologists. But he also points out that this metaphor tends to ignore the specific nature of ethnicity. After all, constructing boundaries with cultural markers is not specific to ethnic groups. This occurs with all kinds of groups, from youth cultures and sports clubs to companies and organizations. It is, however, the way in which a group is imagined that makes it an ethnic group; that is, the fact that a group understands itself in a particular way. The reference to a common origin and history makes a sociocultural boundary into an ethnic boundary. 'What, in my view makes an ethnic group specific, is the genealogical dimension, which unavoidably refers to origin, and always involves some form of kinship or family metaphor. To be sure, "origins" do figure in Barth's landmark contribution, but, in our view, has not been elaborated on or given an adequate place in the model, since the distinction between culture and ethnic group has absorbed all attention' (Roosens, 1994, p. 83). An ethnic group is thought to exist whenever the belief in common descent is used to bind people together to some degree. The claim of common ancestry implies continuity through time and makes a group ethnic 'from within'. The definition of what people are is not so much dependent on outsiders as on the (imagined) origin and history of the group itself. The belief in a common origin and shared ancestry prevents the concept of ethnicity from slipping 'away into the enormously diverse mosaic of self-conscious collectivities—sharing varying degrees of history and culture—that any society generates' (Cornell & Hartmann, 1998, p. 18).

Barth's boundary metaphor should be complemented with a kinship or family metaphor; ethnicity is family writ large (Horowitz, 2000).[8] It is the idea of origin and descent that gives a group commonality and a particular social and historical position. The continuity with the past gives an anchor in time, provides a social location in the present, and serves as a starting point for the future (De Vos, 1995).

Social identities have to do with similarities and differences. By drawing boundaries, differences between groups are established. These differences relate to strivings for recognition, esteem, and respect which can develop into 'us and them' thinking, feelings of superiority, and intergroup antagonism and aggression. In contrast, the idea of origin and descent creates similarities and continuities within a group. The emphasis is on that which is shared and on the imagined past. Only a minimal and general reference to those who do not belong is necessary. A situation of 'us and (a vague) not us' is all that is required. To have a sense of being 'a kin group' requires only nonfamily members, and not a strong opposition with neighbouring kin groups. And the idea that people have a common descent and history leads to feelings of belonging, solidarity, and loyalty.

It is clear that Roosens makes an analytic distinction that can be used to identify differences in emphasis between situations. For example, the notion of a shared history and tradition can also evoke feelings of self-esteem and pride, apart from existing group relations. Likewise, most of the time, a reference to one's own origin has an important function towards other groups. It provides a clear and apparently self-evident distinction between groups. An emphasis on origin and kinship stresses the unique and irreplaceable nature of the ethnic group, which can be used to distinguish oneself in a positive way from others (Horowitz, 2000).

Boundaries by themselves do not make groups 'ethnic'. However, in some situations, ethnic group distinctions are much more important than the genealogical dimension, and vice versa. Roosens shows that for children of migrants who have been born and raised in Belgium the boundary or intergroup dynamics are centrally important. However, for first-generation migrants, the continuity in ethnic belonging and roots in the country of origin are central.

Ethnicity is much more a continuous than a dichotomous variable. Notions of common descent and history are present and are invoked to varying degree, depending on the circumstances. Hence, a key question is the extent to which and the reasons for which groups are ethnicized. The term 'ethnicization' is used similarly to racialization, in which, on the basis of certain bodily features or assumed biological characteristics, groups come to be classified as races. Ethnicization is the process 'by which a group of persons comes to see itself as a distinct group linked by bonds of kinship or their equivalents, by a shared history, and by cultural symbols that represent, in Schermerhorn's terms, the "epitome" of their peoplehood' (Cornell & Hartmann, 1998, p. 34).

In this process, the significance attached to an imagined, shared origin varies with context and over time. The fact that in reality people often successfully appeal to a shared origin and kinship does not mean that this appeal is self-evident or simple. It is not self-evident because the idea itself is a contingent human creation. Each society has a notion of kinship and kinship obligations, but there is a large diversity of kinship systems around the world. Who are related, how far should you go back in time and what does kinship entail? These are not questions with fixed answers. Ideas about a common history and references to descent vary. An appeal to origin and kinship can also be problematic. For instance, in Germany, such an appeal often carries the dark shadow of the Second World War (Forsythe,

1989). In addition, such an appeal will be more successful in times of (potential) threat and conflict. The organizational level of an ethnic group, the ideological and political climate, and the relation with other groups—to give a few examples— are all important. Not every ethnic group finds itself in the same circumstances. For some ethnic groups, the idea of origin and kinship can be central, whereas others retain some sense of it but focus more strongly on cultural characteristics —such as religion, tradition, and language—which are used as boundary markers. For some, the question of where one has come from is more important than the question of where one is; for others, it is just the other way around.

The notion of ethnicity emphasizes the historical and continuous dimension of social life. In social psychology, however, there is little concern with a sense of ontological continuity (Condor, 1996) or 'in-group ontogeny' (Lui et al., 1999). The focus is typically on synchronic activity or the fact that a contextually salient identity produces collective behaviour: Individuals acting on the basis of a particular identity display more or less similar behaviour. Social psychology predominantly focuses on the actual situation and is much less concerned with the past.[9] Ethnicity, however, typically involves a sense of endurance over space and time. Ethnic categories are conceived as ontologically continuous, stretching back in time across generations. This subjective understanding will have consequences for the sorts of behaviour people engage in when they act in terms of their ethnic identity. As Condor (1996, p. 306) puts it, 'Once a social category is subjectively understood as being comprised of successive generations of social actors, it then becomes possible for social identity to be experienced not only as a sense of co-evalness (of synchronic co-existence with other ingroup members) but also in terms of serial connectedness with other ingroup members.'

The notion of where we came from and how we have become provides an enduring identity that involves a sense of continuity and connectedness. It often also involves a sense of commitment and obligation towards former and future generations, for example, as a wanting to maintain and protect the symbolic and cultural heritage. The location that ethnic identity provides is not only situational but also historical. The need to avoid problems of reification and essentialism and to link social identity processes to context, should not lead to a neglect of more enduring identities. The group narrative or story about the group's history and the presumed genealogical dimension provides a particular understanding of ethnicity (Kelman, 2001; Tololyan, 1986). To accept this story is to know oneself as part of the group and of a moral community (Margalit, 2002). Furthermore, each ethnic group has its own story which helps to explain why under the same circumstances members of different ethnic groups act differently. It also helps to explain intergroup relations. For example, in some Dutch cities, there have been conflicts and fights between Turkish and Armenian youth. Part of the reason for this is the history of the Armenian genocide by the Turks in 1915–18. Ethnic and national group narratives often include what Eidelson and Eidelson (2003) call dangerous ideas that propel groups toward conflict. In their social psychological organizing framework for collective identity, Ashmore et al. (2004, p. 96) argue that 'more fully exploiting story approaches to group identity will bear considerable fruit'.

This seems certainly true for ethnic and national groups in which (mythical) accounts of the group's history and origin are often central.

Circumstantialism

As mentioned, Barth was primarily concerned with the level of social interaction or the intersection of the claims people make about themselves and those that others make about them.

There are also anthropological approaches that focus more on either a societal or an individual level of analysis. In particular, there is a ongoing debate on the question of whether ethnic identity has a circumstantial or a more primordial character. This debate has many versions and is not very clear. Supporters of both approaches accuse each other of inadequate analyses and misleading inter-pretations.[10] However, both came about as a reaction to assimilationist views which were based on the idea that ethnic-cultural differences are only temporary, and that after some time these differences will disappear, as in the melting pot. In reality, however, ethnic-cultural differences turned out to be more enduring than was thought, not only in the USA but also in other countries. Even after several generations, numerous people still see themselves in ethnic terms and, when given a choice, prefer their own ethnic group. Additionally, ethnic-cultural differences that have virtually vanished can reappear (Roosens, 1989). It was this phenomenon of 'ethnic survival and revival' that demanded an explanation.

Within circumstantial approaches,[11] the emphasis is on structural conditions, political strategies, and ideological determination. The focus is not so much on the groups involved but rather on the external circumstances and conditions that shape ethnic identities. Ethnic groups are studied as the product of political, residential, economic, legal, and historical circumstances. The idea behind this approach is that existing social organizations, ideologies and material conditions create or sustain particular identities and unequal group relations. For example, residential and occupational concentrations structure patterns of interaction and encourage people to see themselves in a distinctly ethnic way. Moreover, as discussed in Chapter 2, receiving societies' classification schemes stimulate and validate particular group definitions. Furthermore, existing power differences reproduce ethnic hierarchies.

Circumstantialism is often closely related to utilitarian and rational choice theories. Ethnicity is seen as an instrumental identity, and ethnic groups are treated as interest groups (Glazer & Moynihan, 1963; Yancey et al., 1976). For example, how ethnic entrepreneurs use existing identities instrumentally in pursuit of their own goals is a major area of examination. A classic example is Cohen's (1969) work on urban ethnicity in Nigeria. He showed how kinship and cultural symbols were manipulated by Hausa traders seeking political gain. Ethnicity is considered a political resource for competing interests.

It is obvious that circumstances and interests often play a central and strate-gic role in ethnic identity processes. Ethnic groups can be studied as interest groups, and the ethnic identity of these groups will remain stable as long as the circumstances remain the same. Changing circumstances alter opportunities and the utility of particular ethnic (self-)definitions. The circumstantialist account argues that people and groups emphasize their ethnicity or present different forms of it when advantageous. It is the circumstances that locate groups in particular situations and encourage them to define themselves in such a way that their interests are met. This perspective is, for example, successfully used in analysing processes of identity politics. Nowadays, an identity that is constructed around the idea of origin and kinship has important political and juridical implications. The rhetoric of descent and origin is, for example, used by extreme right-wing political groups with their 'own people first' slogans. Variations of this slogan, however, are also found among indigenous minority groups that struggle for independence, or among 'first or indigenous peoples' (such as Aboriginal and Native American groups) that demand rights, various forms of compensation, and territory on the basis of their ancestry and history. The right to one's own ethnic identity and culture is a politically accepted argument in many countries, and also internationally. Political and legal opportunities arise as soon as a group can establish that they have their own origin and history (Hodgson, 2002; Morin & Saladin d'Anglure, 1997). For instance, different groups of Native Canadians have successfully made claims on territory. I will discuss this further in Chapter 5.

Circumstantial approaches are important, and in particular cases they provide adequate explanations. However, there are also limitations. For one thing, there is often a tendency to assume that the circumstances do the work and that people react only to that which occurs. The way individuals and groups actively, and in interaction, shape and transform circumstances and identities is not paid much attention. Furthermore, self-interest seems to be the only motive or psychological reason for ethnic identification and affirmation. Hence, these approaches have great difficulty in accounting for those situations in which ethnic identifications persist, even if, from an economic or political point of view, persistence brings disadvantages rather than advantages, as with, for instance, certain groups of Roma, Native Americans, and ethnic separatists that are prepared to lose economically in exchange for autonomy and independence.

Another limitation is that a circumstantial account does not really address ethnicity per se. The focus is on nonethnic circumstances and political and economic interests. Ethnicity is regarded as a mere cipher for (class) interests and has no independent meaning or force in itself. It is seen as a manifestation or by-product of other more basic structural conditions and forces. Ethnicity is viewed either as a screen that hides the real logic of people's position or as an instrument that will disappear when no longer useful. Hence, ethnicity itself is not theorized or accounted for, and the specific meanings, emotions, sentiments, and experiences are neglected or dismissed as irrelevant. However, ethnicity often does have a distinctive meaning and emotional power in people's life.

Constructed primordiality

Ethnic groups and especially ethnonationalist movements frequently appeal to shared origin and kinship. As Connor (1993, p. 373) shows, the rhetoric of such movements is full of terms such as 'fatherland' and 'motherland'. He also points to the 'near universality with which certain images and phrases appear—blood, family, brothers, sisters, mothers, forefathers, home'. In many instances, the reference to origin and kinship turns out to be a useful strategy to convince, mobilize, and appeal to people.

Primordial approaches emphasize the emotional and imperative nature of ethnicity. The focus is on the psychological or internal dimensions of ethnicity or, as discussed in Chapter 2, on the sense of ethnic identity. Primordialism argues that ethnicity is often something deeply meaningful and that ethnic actors tend to perceive themselves and the world through a primordial lens. In this respect, Hutchinson and Smith (1996) talk about 'participant primordialism' and Fearon and Laitin (2000) about 'everyday primordialism', which has been found in many studies (e.g. Blu, 1980; Gil-White, 1999; Weinreich et al., 2003). Independently of actual interactions, the *belief* in common descent and origin can be meaningful psychologically. This belief itself is of course the outcome of social processes, but, depending on the situation, it resonates more or less strongly with psychological dimensions.

Within anthropology, Geertz (1973) is most often identified with a primordial view of ethnicity (see also Epstein, 1978; Isaacs, 1975). Geertz (1973, p. 109) argues that primordial ties are often seen 'to have an ineffable, and at times overpowering, coerciveness in and of themselves. One is bound to one's kinsman, one's neighbor, one's fellow believer, *ipso facto*, as the result not merely of personal affection, practical necessity, common interests or incurred obligation, but at least in great part by virtue of some unaccountable, absolute import attributed to the tie itself.' Geertz does not suggest that ethnicity is primordial, given by birth, fixed, and unchanging. Rather, he emphasizes that it is often seen as such by actors and that the primordialism is in the significance attributed to ethnic identities. Primordiality is bestowed on a relationship and not simply inherent in it. There are at least three reasons why ethnic attachments often persist and are emotionally powerful.[12]

The first reason is related to the discussion of primary identities in Chapter 2. Ethnicity is something we are socialized into. Children develop a sense of ethnic identity and internalize related cultural meanings, in interaction with their parents and other significant others. Children's early identifications with immediate kith and kin generate an affective sense of ethnic belonging (Weinreich et al., 2003). Language, beliefs, norms, and nonverbal behaviours are intertwined with intimate personal relationships between relatives, and children learn to which groups they belong. A process of enculturation takes place: cultural meanings that are related to ethnicity—such as language, history, and values—develop into durable tendencies and an emotional and self-evident frame of reference. Social positions become dispositions, and cultural meanings become personal beliefs. That is how a sense of ethnic identity develops, and people cannot simply do away with the initial attachments and 'habitus' (Bourdieu, 1987) which they have developed at a tender age.

Secondly, Fiske (1992) shows that the ethos of communal sharing and support arises more or less spontaneously among members of a family but is extended to other groups only with the help of ideologies and customs.[13] Throughout history, stories and myths about shared ancestry and common flesh and blood have been used to extend this morally compelling supportive behaviour to mass groups. A symbolic reference to kinship and ancestry tends to create a moral community in which loyalty, trust, and the obligation to mutual aid and support are central, particularly in times of threat, need, and stress. The emotional solidarity with actual relatives and the familiarity with the social environment of the childhood years, are transferred to the larger ethnic community. Ethnic in-group members can appeal to you for help and support, just as you can appeal to them. Relationships are embedded in a community and supported by reciprocity, trust, and a sense of solidarity (Brewer, 2001). The moral community indicates that someone has the right to be part of it, just as other 'family members' have that right. However, the other side of the coin is that outsiders are excluded. The moral obligation towards members of the in-group is frequently accompanied by indifference or feelings of superiority towards others.[14]

Thirdly, anthropologists have argued that ethnicity can provide an answer to the 'perennial problems of life: the question of origins, destiny and, ultimately, the meaning of life' (Cohen, in Eriksen, 1993, p. 45). Humans face existential questions: the inevitable awareness of the certainty of death and decline, the ever-present possibility of suffering and pain for oneself and loved ones. Psychologists and sociologists have argued that this awareness can lead to paralysing terror and that humans have to find basic meanings to assuage this terror (e.g. Becker, 1974; Berger & Luckmann, 1966; Frankl, 1962; Solomon et al., 1991). In most settings, meaningfulness does not have to be individually found but is culturally defined. Cultural world-views can be seen as attempts at providing ultimate meaning to the basic facts of life. These world-views give a description of why the world is as it is, and a prescription of how to live a valuable and good life. They also give some sense of one's own immortality. By living up to the cultural requirements of value and meaning, humans are part of something meaningful that goes beyond their individual existence and extends into the past as well as the future.

Ethnic and national identities can provide a belief that one is a valuable member of a meaningful universe; 'Ethnic identity is ultimately related . . . to the problem of arriving at a mature capacity to tolerate the suffering and death that is the destiny of all' (De Vos, 1995, p. 376). Beliefs about origin and ancestry are often very important for people because they give them a place in time and address existential questions (Cohen, 1974; Grosby, 1994). Rituals, myths, monuments, statues, founding fathers, historical battles, and burial places can all come to represent (part of) this common origin and ancestry. The significance attributed to relations of descent is embodied and made visible in symbolic forms. The symbols reflect the continuing existence of the ethnic or national group in which the ancestors, contemporaries, and future generations are included. These symbols help to sustain and make acceptable the idea of a common origin. Individuals can find meaning-fulness by using these symbolic forms as means to experience the abstract symbolic content (Verkuyten, 1995a).

Primordial approaches try to explain why so many people in so many situations attribute primary qualities to ethnic identity, even when it contradicts their interests. However, the problems of a primordial approach are not difficult to see. For one thing, power differentials and external categorizations, rather than primary socializations and emotional involvement, are often much more important contributors to ethnicity. Furthermore, a primordial understanding tends to leave the changeable, conscious, and dynamic character of ethnicity out of consideration. Individuals' attachments vary across situations, and identity shifts do occur. The primordialist approach has difficulties in accounting for flexibility and variation that appear in all kinds of forms and all kinds of ways in interactions and transactions. The way in which people define, manage, and negotiate their ethnic identity in everyday life is neither explained or ignored.

Circumstantial *and* primordial

The debate between circumstantial and primordial approaches is often conducted in an either/or fashion. Either the one or the other must be true, or be the only adequate one for analysing ethnic identity. The debate, however, is an example of unnecessary polarization (Lange & Westin, 1985). As Scott (1990, p. 149) puts it, 'Hence, these two approaches have been treated *as if* they were mutually exclusive: if ethnic attachments are primordial, they cannot be circumstantial; if they are circumstantial, they cannot be primordial. . . . while they are each *necessary* . . . neither of them alone is *sufficient* . . . a sufficient explanation, in other words, must include *both* approaches' (original italics).

Primordial and circumstantial approaches have their pros and cons and are complementary rather than contradictory. They pose different questions and deliver different answers. According to Banks (1996), the debate offers a contrast between 'ethnicity in the head' and 'ethnicity in the heart'. Circumstantialists would refer to the head or mind and primordialists to the heart or the gut. But there is no choice needed between instrumental manipulation and historical sentiment as contra-dictory aspects of human life. Sentiments and emotions can be manipulated for political gain. And sentiments and interests can go together or conflict, making it necessary to consider both simultaneously. For example, Cohen (1974) argues that ethnic organizations typically both serve political ends and provide a sense of belonging and meaning.[15]

Furthermore, the enormous diversity of ethnic groups and interethnic relations renders the choice for either one or the other approach unnecessary and unhelpful. For some groups and in some situations, primordial aspects can be more salient and important than instrumental ones, and vice versa, or both aspects can be equally important. Using both aspects, McKay (1982) developed a descriptive typology that distinguishes between, for example, ethnic traditionalists, ethnic militants, ethnic manipulators, and pseudoethnics. Hence, there are various authors that have tried to take both the circumstantial and primordial perspective into account (e.g. Cornell, 1996; Epstein, 1978; Esman, 1994). This seems necessary for improving our understanding of ethnic identity issues. Cornell and Hartmann (1998, p. 67) put it as follows, 'Focusing solely on the circumstantial components of ethnicity ignores the personally felt power of many ethnic identities and the socializing process that often produces ethnicities; emphasizing only its primordialist aspects neglects the social and historical conditions that generate, maintain and transform ethnic and racial identities.' And Smaje (1997, p. 310) argues, 'approaches to ethnicity which do not address both its depth of historical meaning and its contemporary functionality are unlikely to be convincing'. Smaje sees the opposition between circumstantial and primordial approaches as a manifestation of the more general distinction between function and meaning that underlies different theoretical approaches. However, the duality of function and meaning and the privileging of one or the other invariably leads to shortcomings.

Approaches that analyse function, such as those taken by many discourse-oriented scholars, generally explore the determinants of what ethnicity or race would be 'really' about. Here ethnic and racial meanings are typically considered to be consequences of oppression, exclusion, and racism. The focus is on patterns of racism and on demonstrating how discrimination and domination are (re-)produced. Ethnicity and race are examined as relational categories of exclusion, and what is ignored is the content of these categories or the questions of ethnic and racial meanings. This leaves us with a 'coat-of-paint theory of racism' which always regards it as the result of other things.

Approaches that focus on meaning—many cognitive ones, for example—examine the content of ethnic and racial categories by which social relations are defined. Ethnicity is important for its own sake, and exclusion and racism are seen as emerging from ethnic and racial meanings. However, an emphasis on meaning faces problems of reification and essentialism, and it often fails to examine how ethnic and racial categories are actually managed and negotiated and have various social and material effects.

A focus on the level of interaction and everyday practices helps to overcome the duality of function and meaning (Bentley, 1987; Eriksen, 1993). It enables us to study the ways in which social categories are understood and experienced in relation to social structures and systems. Ethnicity and ethnic symbols are not only instruments that, explicitly or implicitly, are manipulated strategically for group interests. Ethnicity is also a source and horizon of meaning that provides particular understandings. A sense of the past, of kinship, and of shared culture is a resource that people use to make sense of themselves, others, and their world. The psychological and durable ways of thinking and feeling ethnically contribute to the way that ethnic distinctions are defined, made relevant, and managed in interactions. People express or announce their self-understandings in everyday practices, and it is interactions that these understandings develop and change.

A final word

Anthropological writing on ethnicity has oscillated between a number of polar extremes (Banks, 1996). General theories have been proposed, and the need for contextual understandings has been emphasized. The boundaries of ethnic identity or the importance of particular contents has been stressed. The circumstantial and the instrumental dimension of ethnic identity has been highlighted in contrast to the primordial understanding and emotional meanings. The focus has been on society or on the individual, and on function or on meaning. The debates between these positions have much in common with the distinctions made between different social psychologies. In these debates, adopting one position typically means ignoring or criticizing the other. One's own favoured approach is presented as the good one or the one that addresses the 'real' anthropological or social psychological questions. With this, it becomes virtually impossible to engage with other ideas, and there are few attempts to deal seriously with others' position. In studying ethnic identity, it is possible to ask many questions that can be examined from various perspectives and by a range of different methods. In the ensuing chapters, I will address some of these questions by discussing examples from our empirical research in which a variety of approaches and techniques have been used.

4 Ethnic minority identity: Place, space, and time

This chapter predominantly focuses on the level of social interaction and the ways that ethnic minority group members discursively locate themselves in relation to others. The central argument of this chapter is that ethnic minority identity is dependent on a range of constructive processes. Two points in particular will be addressed. The first one is referent selection or the different forms of comparison. I will argue that ethnic minority identity is more complex than is typically conveyed by mainstream social psychologies. In these psychologies, ethnicity is typically analysed in terms of societal status and power differences in which minorities are defined in comparison to the majority group. This concern with status and power is valuable and has led to many important findings, but it also tends to lead to a dualist or dichotomous model in which it is presupposed that the relationship with the majority group is all that matters. This is a restricted and one-sided view of the process of identity definitions among people from ethnic minority groups. It tends to ignore the centrally important within-group issues and temporal comparisons, as well as the variety of groups in relation to whom people define and locate themselves.

The second argument of this chapter is that the relation between categories can take different forms and therefore should not be seen as unproblematically given. Whereas identity definitions are unavoidably divisive, talking about oneself as a group need not be markedly oppositional. There is a difference between differentiating oneself from others and defining oneself in opposition to others. Furthermore, status and power differences at the societal level can differ from those at work in local situations, in which people are in the process of defining and negotiating relations and positions.

I will develop these arguments by discussing different examples from our research in which we examined how people from different minority groups define themselves and their relationships with others. Our main focus in these studies is on the accomplishment and manifestation of ethnic identity in verbal interactions; that is, on the accounts of the relationships between self and others and of the position of different groups. As I wish to relate these examples to social psychological approaches, I will discuss these briefly first.

Referent selection

Tajfel (1978, 1981) has written about the social psychologies of ethnic minorities. He sees an unfavourable social position as the defining principle of ethnic minority groups, and as the central issue for understanding minority identity. Tajfel distinguishes between numerical and psychological minorities, and defines the latter as a group which feels bound together by common traits that are held in low regard. He focuses on the status and power differential between the majority and the minority group and addresses the question of the psychological effects of minority membership with respect to the threat to social identity that a minority position implies. He describes how, depending on the perceived legitimacy and stability of the social system, individuals can accept or reject a negative social identity, and how minority groups may alter the valuation of their group through creativity or social competition (Tajfel & Turner, 1986). Other theories than Tajfel's social-identity theory have also emphasized the importance of status and power differences in understanding ethnic minority groups. Two examples are social-dominance theory (Sidanius & Pratto, 1999) and system justification theory (Jost & Banaji, 1994). The former theory is concerned with the psychological and ideological mechanisms that contribute to group-based social hierarchies. The focus of the latter theory is particularly on understanding how and why members of low-status groups sometimes develop a sense of collective inferiority and show out-group bias.

Following these conceptualizations, many social psychological studies have investigated ethnic minority identity as an example of the more general effect of status differences between groups. These studies typically use a dualist or dichoto-mous model with a single advantaged (majority) and a disadvantaged (minority) group. Hence, the 'minority' aspect of ethnic minorities is considered central and the 'ethnic' aspect is almost completely ignored. Existing theories see attempts by ethnic minority groups to define an identity as a response to status differences and to the predicaments resulting from negative stereotypes, discrimination, and forms of racism. These conditions are of course crucial for understanding ethnic minority identity, and theories such as social-identity theory and social-dominance theory offer valuable and important frameworks for examining these issues. I will have more to say about this in later chapters.

However, there are also limits to using a perspective that focuses exclusively on social positions. Ethnic identity is not composed simply of a minority status, and treating it as such greatly limits our ability to examine and understand the richness of the meanings and experiences associated with this identity. In focusing on the 'minority' aspect, ethnic minority groups are treated as any low-status or powerless group to which the same social psychological processes are applied. One result is a restriction of the possible comparisons that can be made in defining one's ethnic identity. For example, the majority group is implicitly assumed to be the only really significant other in society.

The question involved here is that of referent selection. To make a social comparison, group members must decide which out-group of the many available should be chosen as the comparison other. Pettigrew (1978a) addresses the referent selection question with respect to groups. He proposes that the range of potential comparisons is very restricted in an intergroup context. He also argues that reference groups tend to be reciprocally paired, as in white–black and native–immigrant. Most studies implicitly follow this dualist model by considering only two groups at a time while regarding third groups as possible comparison alternatives only. However, this model of referent selection seems too simple. Taylor et al. (1989), for example, argue that multiple comparisons are possible, and they show that such comparisons are made by anglophones in Quebec. Gurin et al. (1994) have shown the same for people of Mexican origin living in the USA. And Rothberger and Worchel (1997) found that disadvantaged group members make comparisons with both the advantaged group and with other disadvantaged ones. There is often a variety of groups in relation to whom people locate themselves (Hagendoorn, 1995). The common situation for many ethnic minority groups around the world includes not only a majority group but also one or more other minority groups.

Furthermore, comparisons can be made within the in-group and do not have to involve out-groups directly. Ethnic identity is often strongly shaped by interactions with the members of the ethnic in-group or the co-ethnics. For example, ethnic minority people may feel pressure to adhere to certain norms of behaviour and discourses about ethnic authenticity that come from co-ethnics. And in-group identification has been found to be strongly influenced by in-group support and acceptance (e.g. Ethier & Deaux, 1994; Postmes & Branscombe, 2002). Social-identity theory is essentially a theory of group differentiation. The theory was developed for analysing group behaviours when a comparison out-group is salient. This means that the focus is on situations in which intergroup comparisons are central to the group's existence. However, there are important within-group considerations, and groups can be more autonomous when intergroup comparison is not a primary concern or of little value (Brown et al., 1992).[1]

In addition, following the conceptualization of ethnicity as discussed in the previous chapter, it is to be expected that for ethnic minorities many identity issues have to do with historical narratives and temporal comparisons. Although Albert formulated a temporal comparison theory in 1977, it is only recently that social psychologists have emphasized and examined the importance of temporal comparisons (e.g. Brown & Haeger, 1999; Guimond & Dambrun, 2002). A colonial past or a history of labour migration may have relevance for understanding issues of ethnic minority identity and interethnic relations. Continuities with and obligations to former and future generations probably also have important self-defining meanings. Furthermore, the situation in the country of origin and the emergence of transnational and diaspora communities may influence how people define and locate themselves ethnically. Social psychologies have a tendency to implicitly use the nation state as the unit of analysis. They often fail to consider not only the details of concrete situations but also the wider field of concerns and actions of many minority groups. Hence, it seems necessary to study ethnic minority identity in terms of the diversity of comparisons being made and their relation to each other. Ethnic identity definitions and claims are made in actual interactions and places and in relation to many groups, including the in-group. They are also made in the context of particular histories and in a transnational space.

Category relations

Ethnic self-definitions refer to what people conceive themselves to be in a specific context, or to which category they belong. This intrinsically implies a conception of those to whom one does not belong: to be 'us', we need those who are 'not us'. However, this does not imply a preoccupation with the 'other', as is often derived from the fact that people make a distinction between 'us' and 'them'. The preoccupation may lie entirely within the group to which people belong and the differences that exist within the in-group. Hence, 'us' may be defined in relation to a more or less undefined 'them' or 'not-us', rather than in actual contrast to a specific other. This links with the argument from Chapter 3 that ethnic minority groups are 'ethnic' from the 'inside' because a common imagined origin and culture are used for self-definition. It is also consistent with recent claims by social psychologists that the in-group is psychologically primary (e.g. Brewer, 2001; Yzerbyt et al., 2000). Moreover, it can be argued that a multiple-group setting hinders in-group–out-group identification or an 'us' versus 'them' contrast (Hartstone & Augoustinos, 1995).

Category relations can, thus, take many different forms and therefore should not be seen as a self-evident given. Differentiation may be oppositional whereby the other is used as a negative counter-identity. Oppositional identities are self- and group-affirming identities for stigmatized groups (Ogbu, 1990). Traits and characteristics that are valued and defined as good and worthy are the opposite of those valued by the majority or by other reference groups. This oppositional pattern is predominantly considered reactive because it is seen as a response to racism and discrimination. The emphasis is on 'what we are not and certainly do not want to be'. Waters (1994) has shown among a group of West Indian- and Haitian-Americans in New York City that the perception and understanding of racism and discrimination are related to a self-definition in opposition to the majority group. Saharso (1992) has found a similar pattern among some ethnic minority youth in the Netherlands.[2]

Differentiation, however, does not have to be oppositional. Self-definition in group terms is unavoidably divisive but may also imply a distinction whereby continuity is emphasized. Hence, category relations can take different forms that have different consequences. For example, the existing inequality and discrimination can be used to define an oppositional identity. But for ethnic minorities that do not define themselves in opposition to the majority group, the question of how to account for inequality and discrimination remains.

A dualist majority–minority model, furthermore, tends to turn identities and group relations into existing entities, rather than examining how relations and identities are being locally produced and played out. When examining actual situations and interactions, we cannot unproblematically equate one group with high status and power with others with powerlessness or subordination. There are numerous situations where this equation is valid, but there are also situations where it distorts our understanding of events. The existence of power and dominance at the societal level should not be treated as a priori, or as a backdrop for analysis. In many critical discourse studies, processes of ethnicization, racialization, racism, and identity constructions are seen as flexible, changing, and situationally contingent, whereas the existing power differences (e.g. white–black) are typically treated as an unproblematic given (e.g. Essed, 1991; van Dijk, 1987). The focus is on the discursive processes that reproduce and legitimate inequality and the dominance of the majority group. Power differences appear as an analytic foundation providing direction and coherence to the analysis. For example, van Dijk (1992) analyses the different strategies that Dutch people use to deny their own racism. His starting point for doing so is that the Dutch, as members of the majority group, reproduce the existing racism. Hence, denying racism can be interpreted only as a device to hide racism. As a result, the empirical analysis of discourse tends to produce what is postulated in advance (see van den Berg, 2003; Verkuyten et al., 1994), and the ethnic categories and definitions themselves are not addressed.

However, the issue of identities and of power and status differences should be studied in relation to the wider social situation as well as local circumstances. Identities and power relations can be understood as being actively (re)produced involving global, national, regional, and local circumstances, resources, and boundaries. Individuals and groups may be placed in subordinate or dominant positions by a range of discourses and practices, but there are always competing constructions and challenges possible.

South Moluccans

The first example I want to discuss is a study of third-generation South Moluccans between the ages of 18 and 27 living in different parts of the Netherlands. In total, 40 in-depth interviews were conducted with 21 female and 19 male participants. The transcribed material was analysed in terms of category constructions and ethnic identity.[3] The focus was on the diversity of the discourses that were used to construct and characterize groups and group relations.

In 1945, two days after the end of the Japanese occupation of what was then called the Netherlands East Indies, a group of nationalist leaders proclaimed the independent Republic of Indonesia. The Dutch sent troops to re-establish control over their colony. They also enlisted former soldiers from the Royal Netherlands Indies Army (Koninklijk Nederlands Indies Leger [KNIL]), which had fought during the war and included many soldiers from the Molucca Islands. After Indonesia achieved independence in 1949, the Dutch government wanted to demobilize the KNIL and granted the soldiers the right to choose where they would be demobilized. The Moluccans wanted to go to East Indonesia, where, in 1950, the Republic of Maluku Selatan (RMS [the Republic of South Molucca]) was proclaimed. The leaders of the RMS wanted to be independent of Indonesia.

However, under these circumstances, the Indonesian government would not allow the Moluccan KNIL soldiers to go to East Indonesia. Because the Moluccans were still in the service of the Dutch government and because of the delicate political situation, the Dutch government saw no other solution than to bring the Moluccan soldiers and their families to the Netherlands. Thus, in 1951, around 12,500 Moluccans arrived in the Netherlands. Because it was thought that their stay would be temporary, they were accommodated in more or less isolated camps throughout the country. They lived in cramped conditions, and were not allowed to work. The soldiers were also dismissed from the army, making them feel they had been betrayed and left to their own devices (*'stank voor dank'* [lit. 'stink for thanks']) by a government and a country for which they had risked their lives and which had promised to look after them.

When, in 1963, Soumokil, the leader of the RMS on the Molucca Islands, was arrested by the Indonesian army, the Moluccans established a government in exile in the Netherlands. In the 1970s, some of the younger Moluccans became more radical and started taking violent action by taking hostages and hijacking trains. At first these actions were directed solely at Indonesian interests in the Netherlands. However, when it became apparent that the Dutch government was not going to support the RMS, Dutch people were targeted, and, later still, the leaders of the RMS, because they were perceived as not doing enough to establish a free Republic of South Molucca. These actions left their mark on Moluccans and Dutch alike, and led the Dutch government to take various measures to improve the situation of the Moluccans.[4]

Understandably, this history plays an important role in the way Moluccans locate themselves, make distinctions within the in-group and define their relationship with the Dutch and other ethnic minority groups in the Netherlands. As I will show later, it has affected peoples' ethnic self-definitions and how the nature and legitimacy of ethnic relations in Dutch society are thought about.

Boundaries and the nature of identities are defined by making comparisons and arguing about them. In the interviews, different forms of comparisons with their specific arguments were presented to construct a specific and distinctive ethnic identity. Three comparisons can be considered: comparisons within the Moluccan group, with the Dutch, and with 'foreigners'.

Moluccans

Almost all participants defined themselves (in part) as Moluccans and indicated that they were proud of being Moluccan. This feeling of pride was related not only to the Moluccan culture but also to Moluccan political history. Being Moluccan was said to be important, and considered as something valuable and emotionally positive because of the unique Moluccan culture and the history of political struggle and endurance.

For all participants, the RMS was an unavoidable topic (Steijlen, 1996). It is so much part of Moluccan history that everyone has to face the question of what it means to them and to Moluccans as a whole. Three participants indicated that the

RMS played a central role in their lives, and that they fully supported the idea of a Moluccan state and were prepared to fight for it. The other participants argued that they no longer believed in the old political RMS ideal of a return to an independent South Moluccan state. For them, the RMS and the annual commemoration of the 1950 declaration of independence, held on 25 April in The Hague, had no strong political significance. It did, however, engender a strong feeling of unity and belonging to one's people. In accounting for their views on the RMS, these participants made a distinction between generations and also drew on the principle/practice dichotomy (Wetherell et al., 1987). The following excerpts are examples of this:

> On the one hand it is very important because my grandma and grandad strongly believed in it and my parents probably still believe in it somehow. They were very much in favour of it and would probably have wanted to die for it, but looking at it from a rational viewpoint now I don't think it's feasible, really. It just isn't possible, it just isn't realistic. No, I can't imagine how anyone could make it happen. No, for the moment I'm not really for it.

> The RMS is a lost cause. As far as I'm concerned, I don't think it's of any use. Of course you should show respect for what your parents fought for, but I don't think you should start fighting for it again. It's no longer realistic to do so.

> Looking back at what happened in The Hague on April 25, it seems they always need to demolish something, and then they blame the RMS. Or they parrot their grandma and grandad, and say things like, 'Yes, the Dutch have deceived us.' I think that's a bit short-sighted, really. Of course that's the case but on the other hand people don't go on about the role of the Germans [in the Second World War], either. We are here now and we should either stay here or go back, and no more bullshit.

I am concerned with two things in these excerpts. First, the person speaking makes a distinction between the first and second generations, and uses this 'generation gap' as a justification for the view that is then given. The RMS as an ideal is presented as something particular to the previous generations. As one participant put it, 'Of course I'm a third-generation Moluccan, and I feel differently about it. I don't really feel the need to go back, for instance.' Most participants defined their situation within the Dutch context (see the third excerpt above). They emphasized that they live in the Netherlands and that their future lies in the Netherlands. Although they acknowledged the importance of the RMS, this definition implies a different stance towards the ideal of the RMS than the one maintained by previous generations. However, the political struggle and hardships of these generations clearly provide a sense of continuity and an important means with which to affirm a close connection.

Second, as can be seen in the first two extracts, the argumentation is structured around the principle/practice dichotomy. Considerations of principle can always be countered by practical ones, and vice versa. All participants agreed that their groups' past history is one of injustices perpetrated against them; nevertheless, most moderated the conclusions they drew from these past wrongs. They argued that it may be justified and good in principle to maintain the ideal of the RMS, but it also has to be feasible and useful in the Netherlands. In this rhetorical construction, the principle of the RMS is acknowledged but at the same time defined as unworkable and emotional. Hence, this construction formulates a continuity but also provides a justification for differentiation.

The distinction being made within the group evolved not only in relation to politics and generations but also from the question of what it really means to be Moluccan and how this group should be characterized. The participants talked about 'real' Moluccans, thus defining the essence of the category and, by implication, constructing a group of 'less real' Moluccans. Three closely related discourses, referring to issues of race, culture, and Malay language, were used to authenticate a Moluccan identity and make a distinction between categories of Moluccans.[5] One discourse involved claims about biological descent, which had implications for making a distinction between what were referred to as 'full-blooded' as opposed to 'half-caste' Moluccans. Thus, the essence of the category 'Moluccan' was defined in racial and biological terms. Real Moluccans are born to two Moluccan parents and were clearly evaluated more positively than those who are only 'half'-Moluccan.

Most participants, although talking in terms of 'half-breeds', rejected traditional concerns about racial purity, invoking instead a discourse of cultural identity and maintenance. That is, racial crossing and 'mixed-race' children were discussed not as threatening the 'Moluccan race' but as threatening Moluccan culture and the continuity of traditions:

> Too many Moluccan youngsters marry Dutch boys and girls, which will increase the number of half-castes. I'm afraid this will mean that we'll be left with totally Dutch children with a Moluccan surname. That's what you'll get. But I think these youngsters should be told where their name comes from. This is what we should get into their heads. So that they, too, will understand that they should pass on their culture.

The cultural narrative used for making distinctions within the Moluccan group revolved around several oppositional dichotomies such as traditional versus modern, and changing versus unchanging. These oppositions were used to make a distinction between those who are more traditional and those whom the participants referred to as 'Westernized or Dutchified'. This distinction was partly related to the different generations living in the Netherlands, but it also applies to the third generation for defining 'real' and 'less real' Moluccans.

Two different meanings of Westernization were identifiable in the interviews: a continuous and a discontinuous formulation. In the continuous formulation,

Westernization was presented as an inevitable process of change in which Moluccan culture will disappear, or rather, aspects of it will intermingle with modern Dutch cultural practices. The inevitability of these changes was, again, maintained with the help of the principle/practice dichotomy. It was argued that although it may be all right to keep one's culture in principle, it also has to be useful in the current Dutch and international context.

However, practical considerations can always be countered by ones of principle. Among our interviewees arguing for cultural maintenance, practical considerations were secondary to the moral obligation of preserving the unique Moluccan culture. They argued that they had an obligation to the first generation in particular but also to Moluccans in general. They presented Westernization not as a change but as a loss of and a break with Moluccan culture. They used the notion of incompatible cultures and cultural integration as an impossibility. The participants who described themselves as 'real' Moluccans used an essentialist and 'modern racist' ideal of Moluccan culture by presenting it as a precious inheritance that should be transmitted uncontaminated and undiminished (Balibar, 1991).

The idea of cultural maintenance was closely related to the Malay language. Language was considered the key to Moluccan culture. The issue of the Malay language was brought up by most participants and was used independently of race and culture to define who and what real Moluccans are:

> It's all right for you to say that you're a real Moluccan, but if you don't have a good command of the language, if you don't speak the language, you're not a real Moluccan to me.

> If you can't speak Malay, you're not a real Moluccan.

Here language is used as a crucial marker of identity that defines what it means to be a real Moluccan and that, therefore, can be used to authenticate a Moluccan identity. The importance of language was also accepted by 'mixed-race' participants, who all said they very much regretted the fact that they could not speak the Malay language properly. For them, not speaking Malay was related to patterns of exclusion from the Moluccan community.

The Dutch

Biological and cultural distinctions have meaning not only within the Moluccan group but also in relation to other groups. The ties of common descent and the idea of cultural purity provided a vessel for the cultivation of a distinct identity in relation to others in general, and to the Dutch in particular. The participants differentiated themselves from the Dutch, but they did not define themselves in opposition to this group. There were similarities and continuities with the Dutch that had relevance to self- and group definitions. I will discuss the construction of continuities first and then the construction of differences.

With the exception of two participants, who said that they wanted to live on the Moluccan Islands, all others defined their situation and future as one within the Netherlands. For them, a move to the Moluccas was no longer an option because they had settled in the Netherlands and had adapted themselves to the Western way of life and standard of living. They also argued that third-generation Moluccans are born and bred in the Netherlands, speak Dutch, have Dutch friends, and are Dutch nationals. Hence Moluccan identity was defined in the context of the Netherlands and in relation to the Dutch. There were objective characteristics, such as the passport and the language, which not only had instrumental value in society but were also presented as indicative of similarities and points of contact. Most participants said that they were Dutch although they felt Moluccan.[6]

However, it is not only the present but also the past that can be used to argue for a relationship. History can be used to define continuities between the Moluccans and the Dutch. The following excerpt provides an example:

> I'm very proud of being a Moluccan, looking at what has happened since the time of the United East Indies Company, considering the long-standing relationship we've had with the Dutch, considering that I'm now living in the Netherlands. . . . On the one hand, it may be rotten for us to be here. On the other hand, it can be an asset; there certainly are advantages, especially considering how badly off the other Moluccans back in the Moluccas are. I always say, 'Us, Moluccans, we are the history of the Netherlands. We are your history, and you should know about your own history.'

This participant is arguing that the history of the Moluccans is inextricably linked with that of the Dutch. There is a very old relationship between the two groups, dating back to the seventeenth century. Stressing this historical relationship constructs a continuity with the Dutch and with the present situation in the Netherlands. This historical discourse also implies rights and claims. After all, the Dutch bear great responsibility for the fate of the South Moluccans and the way they were treated both in Indonesia and after their arrival in the Netherlands. This can be used to justify a claim, or claims, to a special position and treatment, in particular in comparison with other minority groups (see below).

The participants used two kinds of discourse to argue that Moluccans differ from the Dutch: a cultural one and a racial one. Differences between the ethnic Dutch and the Moluccans were presented predominantly in terms of culture. In their talk, culture was turned into a self-evident object linked to ethnicity. Both groups were said to have their own typical culture that determines people's understandings and practices. It was argued that Moluccans differ from the Dutch, and there are self-defining cultural differences that should be preserved. 'We shouldn't allow our culture to be forgotten because if we do, the children, for instance those of the fourth generation, will be totally ignorant of our culture, and it will eventually die out here in the Netherlands. If that happens, we might just as well . . . we would just be like any-old Dutch person, basically.' Dutch culture was discussed in relation to Moluccan culture, which functioned as the standard of comparison and the frame of reference. More specifically, in those instances where the notion of culture was specified and elaborated on, Dutch culture was defined as *lacking* typically Moluccan cultural elements. The Dutch were said to lack the Moluccan values of respect for the elderly as well as close and supportive relationships with (extended) family members and other Moluccans in general. They were also said to lack typical Moluccan hospitality, generosity, and inter-personal warmth. Thus, the participants created a normative image of their group by using a set of cultural values to construct the Dutch as different.

Second, a racial discourse was used to emphasize the differences between the Moluccans and the Dutch. It was stressed that Moluccans have darker skin than the Dutch and therefore are always visibly different. In the following excerpts, two other participants talk about their experiences of being of a different skin colour and hence being treated differently:

> I'm not Dutch. I may live in the Netherlands, but the colour of my skin is different. This is something I can't ignore.

> It's because I have a dark skin, you know. Yes, it's certainly true that we're discriminated against. Although they say that we are Dutch, we don't really notice that that's the case.

What sets them apart is the colour of their skin, which forms an unbridgeable gap. Thus, the boundary delineating Moluccan identity is, at least in part, racial and thereby closely linked to issues of power. In the second excerpt, this link is made explicit by the participant by his talking in the same breath about being dark-skinned and experiencing discrimination. The participants argued that the existence of discrimination played an important role in defining them and in constructing a clear boundary between the Moluccans and the Dutch. Hence, issues of power and dominance were used to understand the position of the Moluccans. However, the participants indicated that they also experienced discrim-ination *as* foreigners rather than as people with a darker skin or as Moluccans per se.

Foreigners

Most participants argued that the Dutch categorize Moluccans as foreigners. The Dutch were said to use one broad category for all ethnic minority groups, ignoring historical and cultural differences, and discriminating against them all without distinction. Or, as one participant put it, 'I have always noticed that for Dutch people, from early on, all foreigners are the same, they're birds of a feather.'

The participants, however, rejected the label 'foreigner' as an option for self-definition. They made a clear and consistent distinction between themselves and other ethnic minority groups in the Netherlands. Foreigners were negatively described in terms such as 'dirty', 'lazy', and 'bums', and were used as an oppo-sitional identity. Although shared experiences of discrimination and stigmatization were acknowledged, no common identity or common political agenda was accepted. On the contrary, foreigners were held partially responsible for the discrimination Moluccans experienced. Their maladjusted behaviour was said to diminish the Moluccans' opportunities in society because the Dutch see them all as foreigners:

> Moluccans are treated as any other foreigners. Almost all Moluccans will say, 'We're not foreigners, we're not immigrants', for if you look back properly, if you read the history books, you will see that the Moluccans didn't come here to work or anything like that. They didn't come here of their own accord. On the contrary, they were brought here by the Dutch government. Well, that's the difference between them and the foreigners. The foreigners came here to work and they all came here of their own free will.

> They can't send us away just like that. The others came here voluntarily, but the Dutch brought us here, promising that we would go back at some time. We can't help being here. And I always defend the Moluccans. I don't want to be compared with the Turks and the Moroccans, I don't want to be considered an immigrant, because that's not what we were.

> Asylum seekers who arrive in the Netherlands, refugees who arrive in the Netherlands are immediately given a house of their own, a television set, a fridge, the lot. That's unfair. My grandad and my father and mother were born in the Moluccans and were put into barracks here, where they slept with 20 people in one room which also served as a living room and a kitchen. It makes me wonder. That also plays a role and those asylum seekers . . . they've only been in the Netherlands for two days and they start protesting against the bad treatment they've been receiving. It makes me wonder. . . . We've been here for almost 47 years and we're still treated badly, and we don't even have the right to become angry. At a certain moment you acquire a little . . . you start getting a bit angry. Even my mother, whenever she sees a Moroccan or a Turk complaining on television, says, 'Why don't you go back to your own country?' Things were a lot harder for her, and these people have only been here for two days and they organize a campaign without even knowing the language. Look, we've adjusted ourselves. Why can't they? And at a certain moment they'll do strange things and who will be held accountable? We will. I'm also seen as 'a darkie' and I think that's quite difficult, for we're in-between. I think so, yes, there are too many of them. I don't mean to discriminate against anyone—there are good people among the Turks and Moroccans, too—but that's the way I feel. I just think we've not been done justice. Life is made difficult for us Moluccans, even though we've been here for 47 years. This is why I don't agree when a Moroccan person says to me, 'Us foreigners'. I'm not a foreigner, I don't feel I'm an immigrant. I'm a Moluccan in the Netherlands.

In all three excerpts, the participants clearly do not wish to be considered foreigners and in particular do not wish to be defined as similar to other minority groups. The participants claimed a distinct position for themselves and their group. As can be seen in the first two of these excerpts, the distinction between Moluccans and foreigners was predominantly presented and justified in an immigrant narrative. In this narrative, the notion of freedom and choice played a central role.[7] Freedom implies not only self-determination but also responsibility. If people determine for themselves what they want to do they are also responsible for themselves.[8] The argument put forward by the participants that foreigners should integrate was mainly based on this notion of responsibility. They have chosen to come to the Netherlands and, as a corollary, have to accept the responsibility of their own choice—integration. But in contrast to the Moluccans, who know the language and would have adapted to society despite the fact that they were brought here, foreigners are said to not (want to) integrate.

It was argued that the Moluccans were brought to the country by the Dutch government or, as some participants put it, they were ordered or commanded to come, and they came on a political basis. Thus, for the participants, it was the government's decision and the government made promises that were not kept. Therefore, the Dutch have a moral responsibility for and duty to the Moluccans, who were presented as a separate group that has unique claims and rights. The historical and political situation justifies the Moluccans' specific position and challenges the dominant group's definition of foreigner.

The immigrant narrative involves not only the reasons for migration but also the actual arrival in the country. As can be seen in the third excerpt, the participants invoked an immigrant history in which the first generation had a hard life, full of toil and sacrifice, and after many years were still confronted with bad treatment. This narrative of the hardship and struggle after arrival in the Netherlands was used to draw a clear contrast with foreigners who had come to the country only recently but were already making claims. This was considered unfair because it means unequal treatment. Foreigners are making claims and are immediately taken care of, whereas Moluccans not only had to endure hardship but have been in the country much longer.

In the second and third of these excerpts, the category of foreigners is also specified by referring to Turks and Moroccans. As is common in the Netherlands, the participants considered these two Islamic groups as virtually paradigmatic examples of foreigners. However, the difference with these Islamic groups was not presented in an immigration narrative but in cultural and religious terms, as it is in the following excerpt.

I think that, in general, Moluccans have adjusted themselves. I think that's partly because they have the same religion. After all, most Moluccans are Christians. They've taken over lots of things from Dutch culture. Moluccan and Dutch values are comparable, which cannot be said about Moroccan and Turkish groups. As Turks and Moroccans have an entirely different religion, their values are very different from those of Dutch people and Moluccan people. I think there's a bigger difference between them. I think that Dutch people and Turks or Moroccans have more difficulties understanding each other than Dutch people and Moluccans because Turkish and Moroccan religion and culture are so different from Moluccan and Dutch religion and culture.

As can be seen in the excerpt, the opposition to the Islamic groups was also used to define a similarity with the Dutch. Turks and Moroccans are presented in contrast to Moluccans and the Dutch, making the Moluccans similar to the Dutch and different from other ethnic minorities. We also see here the flexibility of a cultural discourse. It can be used for making a contrast between the Dutch and Moluccans, but in this context it is used for defining a similarity between these two groups.

Problematic constructions

The examples given above cover the main distinctions that participants made. However, arguments over categories and definitions are potentially inexhaustible because competing constructions are always possible (Billig, 1987). For example, we saw that considerations of principle can be challenged by practical ones, that some participants argued that past injustices should not be righted by differential policies, and that the present situation cannot bear the brunt of historical wrongs. Moreover, a discussion about ethnicity and cultural differences can be criticized, as in the next excerpt:

> Most people take as their starting point, ah, how shall I put it, an ethnic identity: 'I am Moluccan, I am a Turk, I am a Moroccan', etc. But I feel—I've thought about this a lot, but what's essential for every human being is the fact that they're human. And it's the different customs that create the differences between people. But I feel I should no longer think about that all the time, saying to myself, 'I cannot yet do this or that very well so I'm not a good Moluccan.' As for a purely Moluccan culture, I don't think there is such a thing. After all, we've been in contact with other nations through commerce and we've taken on things from them.

This participant criticizes ethnic distinctions and the notion of cultural purity by using the idea of a common humanity and the history of cultural diffusion. Earlier in the interview, the same participant indicated that she felt personally addressed when others said something negative about Moluccans. And she also talked in terms of 'we, the Moluccans' when she said, 'I have to say that among us the ties are closer, more close than among the Dutch, the family ties, and we also have other close ties beside family.' However, in the excerpt above, she draws upon other interpretative resources for questioning the distinctions and reification she uses herself.

Although these examples do not represent the dominant pattern in the interviews, they show that there are always alternative discourses available for challenging ethnic constructions, just as there are discourses that produce situationally accept-able distinctions.

Second-generation Turks

A second empirical example is taken from our focus-group research. In these studies, a total of 168 people (between 15 and 70 years of age) have participated. Seventy-one participants were of ethnic Dutch origin, and 97 were ethnic minorities, mostly Turkish, Moroccan, and Hindustani people. Fifty-seven per cent were female, and 43% were male. The participants lived predominantly in inner-city Rotterdam. In total, there were 21 focus groups that met for at least 45 minutes, some sessions lasting as long as two and a half hours. Fifteen groups met only once, but the other groups met up to five times. In total, there were 41 meetings. In most groups (18), the participants were either ethnic Dutch or ethnic minorities. The meetings were held at local schools and at two local community centres.

The following example is based on a group of nine second-generation Turkish residents that met one evening a week for five consecutive weeks (Verkuyten, 1997a).[9] In analysing these discussions, it became clear that ethnic self-definition is a complex and flexible process. To discuss this, I will refer to Figure 4.1, which is based on the discussions. The figure is not meant to present a static picture of ethnic self-definitions but rather to raise and illustrate four points.

First, Figure 4.1 shows a much more complicated process of self-definition than a majority–minority dualist model would assume. Many different distinctions are made and many categories are relevant. For example, major distinctions are *within* the Turkish community and do not involve the Dutch directly. Much of the discussion was on differences and relations within the group of Turkish immigrants. For example, major parts of the discussion were about differences and relationships between first- and second-generation Turks living in the Netherlands. The first generation was related to what they saw as traditional culture and they would also be more connected to the situation in Turkey. Turkey was also an important point of reference for the participants but in a less emotional way.

The participants also drew a contrast between moderate and more segregated Turks. They distinguished themselves from the latter category, who were said to emphasize their Turkish origin and Islamic background, to be traditional and rigid, and to be opposed to Dutch culture and society. In contrast, they defined for themselves a position and future within the Dutch context, which implied adaptation to Dutch culture and a more moderate position in relation to it.

In addition to these distinctions, within the Turkish 'in-group' comparisons were made with other ethnic minority groups and with the Dutch. The way the participants defined and positioned themselves cannot be understood without taking these comparisons into consideration. As Figure 4.1 indicates, the participants tried to define, carve out, and account for a distinctive Turkish identity in relation to other Turks, to other ethnic minority groups, and to the Dutch. These comparisons act together in defining categories and in giving an account of the position

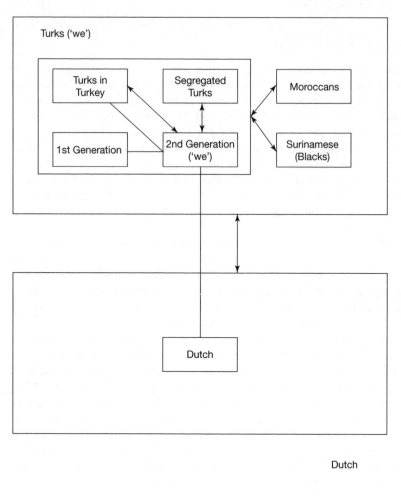

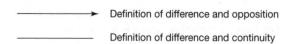

Figure 4.1 Self-definitions and social comparisons of Turkish participants.

constructed. In other words, the participants construct and cross the borders of various categories in order to define themselves.

The second point is that the participants defined themselves on different levels in relation to different groups. In Figure 4.1, this is indicated by the term 'we'. Sometimes they defined themselves as 'we' second-generation Turks; sometimes as 'we' Turks, in contrast, for example, to Moroccans; and sometimes as 'we' foreigners in comparison to the Dutch. Hence, there was a level of indeterminacy in the dimensions and features of comparison used for self-definition. Social psychological theories stress that comparisons are always made against the background of a common identity. For example, self-categorization theory (Turner et al., 1987) argues that categorization and comparison depend upon each other because things can be compared only 'in so far as they have already been categorized as identical, alike, or equivalent at some higher level of abstraction, which in turn presupposes a prior process of comparison' (p. 46). However, the issue of comparative framework tends to be left unspecified, although it is acknowledged that categories define social reality as well as vice versa. The dimensions of comparison and the framework of comparison are open to debate and therefore can be examined as discursive constructions. Tying the determination of categorization to dimensions and levels of comparison raises the question of how these dimensions and levels come to be defined. In analysing the discussions, we found that the higher-order categorical frame within which comparisons are made is not always clear. For example, the inclusive self-category in terms of which Dutch and Turks were compared, was implicit, and a common identity was not mentioned. In contrast, the participants made a distinction between first- and second-generation immigrants in terms of the higher-level category of Turks, and the Islamic Moroccan immigrants were distinguished from the Islamic Turkish immigrants.

Furthermore, there are always many criteria that can be used for defining categories, and this is significant for self-definitions. The participants used different features for constituting social categories and used the same category labels on different levels. The use of different dimensions has consequences for the level of comparison. The Dutch as a comparison group were used in the discussions both on the level of Dutch versus foreigners and on the level of specific ethnic groups: Dutch versus Turks. And the category of 'foreigners' was interpreted in different ways (as non-Dutch and as maladjusted minorities) and therefore used within different higher-level categories. Hence, in their discussions, the participants did not use fixed categories with a clear hierarchy of abstractions, in which, for example, the self-category of 'foreigners' contains the category of 'Turks'. Different comparisons were made, indicating that categories are a matter of interpretation and definition.

Moreover depending on the level of comparison, other stereotypical features were used for description and definition. For example, in relation to the traditional Moroccans, a European and modern outlook was presented as typically Turkish, whereas, in contrast, to the Dutch the distinction focused on traditions and culture as being typically Turkish. Hence, how the participants defined themselves depended on the frame within which the comparison was being made (e.g. Biernat & Thompson, 2002; Hopkins et al., 1997; Hopkins & Murdoch, 1999). This variability shows the difficulty in defining ethnic groups in terms of fixed sets of attributes or stereotypical traits.

The third point is that category *relations* can take many different forms and therefore should not be seen as self-evidently given. As argued earlier, self-definition in group terms is unavoidably divisive but may imply a distinction whereby continuity is emphasized. In Figure 4.1, we see different category relations. Some relations are more oppositional (arrowed lines) whereby the other is used as a negative counter-identity. Moroccans, 'maladjusted' foreigners, and segregationist Turks were used as an oppositional identity. These groups were described in negative terms, and the distancing from them led to the use of many of society's negative stereotypes for portraying these groups and for blaming them for diminishing one's own chances in society.

However, although the participants differentiated themselves from the first-generation Turks and Turks in Turkey, they did not define themselves in opposition to these groups. There are continuities with other Turkish people that have relevance to self-definition, such as Turkish history and culture, the parents' immigration and their sacrifices and hard work from the day they arrived, and the existence of discrimination.

Further, the relationship with the same group (in this case, the Dutch) may in one context be presented as more oppositional—Dutch versus foreigners—than in another context, such as Dutch and second-generation Turks. In the latter context, the participants presented themselves as culturally different but not as opposed to Dutch people, although the perception of discrimination played a significant role in identity construction (see Verkuyten, 1997a). The participants defined their situation within the Netherlands, and they situated their future in this country. However, they also rejected the idea of becoming Dutch.

The fourth and final point is that the different comparisons and self-definitions are by no means self-evident. They have clear connotations and can be a major topic of debate. There are always different criteria available with which to make distinctions, making definitions potentially open to debate. The participants predominantly used categories in a self-evident way. Labels such as 'foreigners' and 'Turks' were used for self-definition. But in the discussions there are also instances in which the dimensions of identity become topics of debate, and the participants show their knowledge of the fact that terms such as 'migrants', 'foreigners', and 'allochthonous' have different meanings and connotations (see Verkuyten, 1997a).

Accounting for discrimination

In the Moluccan and Turkish example, it was indicated that discrimination plays a role in ethnic self-definitions. Discrimination and racism are pervasive and highly problematic phenomena. They exist on the institutional and structural levels of society, they are communicated through the media and by politicians, and they are a feature of many everyday situations. The fact that ethnic minorities are sometimes discriminated against in Dutch society is a recurrent and important topic in discussions and interactions. The distinction between majority and minority, which is used as a standard scheme or a social representation in interpreting relations in society, is present and evident in concrete situations. The scheme in which the majority group is dominant and discriminates, and in which minority groups are subordinate and discriminated against, is, for example, used in multicultural education and schools (Leeman, 1994; Verkuyten, 1999) and plays a role in everyday talk. For example, in one of our studies in a multiethnic school, I asked a Cape Verdean boy whether there was discrimination at his school. His answer was, 'No, I do not experience it, but of course there are only foreigners here.'

Here the word 'but' is interesting because it introduces an explanation and defines the Dutch as the discriminating group. Because there are very few Dutch, there would be little discrimination. Another example is as follows. During a physical education lesson, a Dutch teacher became annoyed with the slowness of a Surinamese boy and almost let his tongue run away with him, saying, 'Come on, blac . . . '. Afterwards, the class spoke about the incident. Both the Dutch and the minority group students were angry, but the minority students were inclined to place this event in the context of a pattern of racism and as evidence that the Dutch cannot be trusted. The Dutch students on the other hand were more likely to see it as specific to the teacher. So societal definitions of majority–minority relations (discriminating and discriminated at) are used to interpret local situations.

In social psychology, discrimination is predominantly examined in terms of intergroup differentiation and minority group members' perception of discrimination. Many studies have focused on the differential evaluation of, and behaviour towards, in-group and out-group members. There are also an increasing number of studies on the perceptions of and reactions to discrimination (see Major et al., 2002; Schmitt & Branscombe, 2002; Taylor et al., 1994, for reviews). I will discuss some of these in Chapter 7.

Although there are many differences between these studies, they are similar in their focus on cognitive and affective reactions and processes. Shelton (2000) notes that this emphasis on perception and evaluation is quite ironic, because discrimination is fundamentally an interactive phenomenon. It is in social interactions that discrimination typically occurs. Further, interpretations in terms of discrimination have social costs and consequences, such as being labelled as oversensitive or racist (Kaiser & Miller, 2001). In everyday life, issues of discrimination and racism involve blaming and accusations, making them a sensitive topic of debate. The seriousness and omnipresence of discrimination, the causes of discrimination, the responsibilities for discrimination, and the consequences of discrimination are all topics of debate. Assessments and interpretations of discrimination are not self-evident, but involve arguments and explanations. Discrimination is part of daily life, and our understanding of it is shaped and argued over in conversation. Taking a discursive analytic stance makes it possible to examine how ethnic discrimination is presented and the ways that people account for discrimination.

Using focus-group discussions and 127 in-depth interviews, we have examined how ethnic majority and minority group members describe and explain ethnic discrimination (Verkuyten, 1997a, 1997b, 2004a). In these studies, members of *both* groups were found to use similar discursive strategies questioning the omnipresence of discrimination and problematizing its causes, while other members of *both* groups were found to employ devices that made discrimination appear factual, with the Dutch as its sole agents.

One way to make sense of this is in terms of subject positions. Positioning theory, as propounded by Davies and Harré (1990) and van Langenhove and Harré (1994), proposes that when talking about social issues, people are involved in the discursive construction through which statements and actions are made intelligible and coherent. People actively employ discourses that provide particular possibilities and limitations for making claims and building accounts. As Burr (2002, p. 113) has put it, 'The concept of positioning recognizes both the power of culturally available discourses to frame our experience and constrain our behaviour while allowing room for the person to actively engage with those discourses and employ them in social situations.'

Positioning theory locates subject positions within the wider discourses of social life (Edley, 2001a; Törrönen, 2001; Wetherell, 1998). Talk therefore reflects discourses and narrative forms that already exist in society. People draw on different discourses in the positioning of themselves and others by, for example, adopting a humanitarian or nationalist narrative, or by referring to individualistic and Protestant ethical values. These discourses can be expected to affect the way the existence of discrimination and racism is accounted for. For example, positioning oneself within a nationalist discourse raises the question of how discrimination against ethnic minorities in society can be accounted for. Further, ethnic minorities may find talk about discrimination that defines them as victims difficult to reconcile with claims of personal responsibility and opportunities for social improvement.

We have various examples of Dutch participants stressing the reality of discrimination and blaming the Dutch. The next two excerpts are examples.

Interviewer: Do foreigners ever get discriminated against in the Netherlands?
Dick: Yeah, they certainly do.
Tineke: I know for sure, yeah.
Dick: They certainly do.

Interviewer: Do you think that foreigners ever get discriminated against in the Netherlands?
Henny: I don't think they do, *I know they do*.

In both excerpts, the participants do not hesitate to respond to the interviewer's direct question. These participants define the existence of discrimination as a reality that is beyond discussion. Discrimination exists; that is the way things are. However, in doing so, they seem to attend to or orientate themselves towards the idea that discrimination is only a possibility and rather uncommon. This idea is indicated by the mere fact of asking the question and by the interviewer's use of the term 'ever get'. Both features suggest that discrimination is not an obvious and regular phenomenon. In the first excerpt, the response to the factual and difficult-to-contradict question is a strong affirmative answer in which the reality of discrimination is emphasized by modalizing terms (Pomerantz, 1986). In the second excerpt, the interviewer asks a more personal question, whether the participant thinks that discrimination exists. In her answer, Henny explicitly and with emphasis rejects the idea that her assessment can be discounted or undermined as an opinion that is not supported by reality. That discrimination exists is not something that she thinks might be the case, but a thing that she definitely knows to be true.

These factual accounts of discrimination can be made sense of in terms of the subject positions that were taken up. On a broad level, most of these participants took up and developed particular discourses. They tended to position themselves in moral discourses of humanitarian and Christian ideals in which ideas of justice, care, and concern for others were emphasized. These discourses tended to structure questions of immigration and ethnic minorities in particular. That is to say, the talk about 'foreigners' was grounded in these discourses that provided the meanings and values within which the participants positioned themselves. They presented a framework for the description and explanation of ethnic discrimination in society (see Verkuyten, 2004a).

Interestingly, in some of the interviews with ethnic minority members, the accounts of discrimination had clear similarities to those of these Dutch participants. However, although similar discursive strategies were used, a different subject position was adopted, and the strategies were related to this. It is worthwhile to look at an excerpt in more detail. The excerpt is taken from an interview with a Surinamese man, Lloyd.

Interviewer: Does discrimination occur?
Lloyd: Do you mean towards us?
Interviewer: Yes.
Lloyd: Of course, there most certainly is discrimination against us. It isn't necessarily, er, a conscious thing. But if you are in a shop or a pub or suchlike, then there's certain Dutch people that, er, be it consciously or not, avoid you in one way or another. They'll look at you, in a discotheque or whatever, like, who's this guy? You can feel, if you're in the streets and you meet somebody Dutch, they will look down or avoid you. They act like they don't want to know.
Interviewer: So it happens a lot?
Lloyd: Yeah, sure thing, it really does, yeah. It happens all the time, also in school and stuff. There's so much prejudice and racism among the Dutch, er, and that's why they discriminate, without knowing.

In his response, Lloyd gives a clear assessment of both the existence and cause of discrimination. Similar to some of the Dutch participants, discrimination is described by him as a self-evident reality, or an obvious fact of life. It is something that certainly does happen often, and it is not restricted to particular spheres of life. Furthermore, in the last two lines discrimination is explicitly explained by referring to the negative attitudes of the Dutch. Because of their racism, ethnic minorities are discriminated against.

However, although the assessment is similar to that of some of the Dutch participants, it is fabricated in another way. Lloyd, in particular, adopts the position of an insider who is knowledgeable about discrimination against minorities. He begins by asking whether the interviewer means discrimination towards 'us' (lines 2 and 4). Subsequently, the concrete and detailed examples and the modalizing terms (e.g. 'all the time') help to make his claim factual (Edwards & Potter, 1992). They suggest a careful observation and a good understanding of discrimination, and define discrimination as something that exists in actual fact, independently of his own concerns and preoccupations.[10]

Thus, in explaining discrimination, Lloyd takes up the position of ethnic minority group members who are victims of discrimination. He positions himself within a discourse of victimization that locates minorities as victims of (nonintentional) Dutch racism. This was certainly not a unique example. Several participants in parts of the interview took up the victim position and defined themselves as standing apart from Dutch culture and society. In doing so, they also emphasized their ethnic identity and stressed characteristics as being self-defining that differed from those typically valued by the Dutch. Studies in other countries have come to a similar conclusion (e.g. Ogbu, 1993; Waters, 1994).

In our studies, we found that Dutch and ethnic minority participants sometimes also use various discursive strategies—e.g. questioning the omnipresence of discrimination, problematizing its causes, and defining minorities as (somewhat) oversensitive, exaggerating, and (in part) responsible themselves—to challenge or undermine the reality and explanation of discrimination (Verkuyten, 2004a).

Among the *Dutch* participants, the use of these strategies was related to strong national self-definitions. To the Dutch, discrimination against ethnic minorities poses a potential difficulty for the Dutch self-image of tolerance and openness. Discrimination against ethnic minorities that reflects negatively on the Dutch raises interactional difficulties. Using discursive devices to question the reality and causes of discrimination is a way of dealing with this difficulty.

Some of the *ethnic minority* participants rejected the one-sided role of victim implied by discriminatory practices and claimed an active and responsible position for themselves. They located themselves within a discourse of social opportunities and Protestant ethics. They argued that there were real opportunities for upward social mobility in the Netherlands, depending on one's own efforts and perseverance.

In accounting for discrimination, they used—like some of the Dutch—several strategies that questioned the omnipresence of discrimination and problematized its causes. For example, discrimination was also accounted for in terms of being a general human phenomenon and the result of an interaction in which both parties have a responsibility. Furthermore, claims of discrimination were attributed to the (over-)sensitive feelings of ethnic minorities themselves and disqualified as easy excuses for not doing well and lack of personal effort. These strategies supported these participants' claims of an active and constructive role for themselves and their group, and avoided an interpretation in terms of being determined only by, or as a victim of, the majority group.

Els (Hindustani-Surinamese woman):   In my opinion, Hindustanis tend to look for a scapegoat straight off, for someone to blame.
Interviewer: And who would that be?
Els: Well, the Dutch of course.
Interviewer: Is that right?
Els: I think so. They do something wrong and, er, pass the buck to the Dutch straightaway. I think there's no point. If somebody can't find a job, well, then, of course they are never to blame, no, it's the Dutch because they discriminate. Well, er, look, sorry, you should try hard yourself first and er, learn to be critical of yourself.

Interviewer: Yeah, but surely there are a lot more unemployed foreigners than unemployed Dutch people?
Kadir (Turkish man):   Yes that's right, but er, it's their own fault.
Interviewer: Do you think so?
Kadir: Yeah, sure thing. Look, I've never been to school here in the Netherlands, but if I really want a job, I get job offers, like, everywhere. It's got nothing to do with discrimination—those people have, like, themselves to blame, sure thing. If a person wants, like, something, then he will get ahead.

In both excerpts, the speakers draw upon two contrasting accounts for the lack of social success of ethnic minorities. The one is discrimination with its victim position and the other is one's own efforts and perseverance. In doing so, the former account is rejected in favour of the latter. Discrimination would be an easy excuse for lack of personal effort and self-reflection. Hence, the drawing of this distinction allows them to downplay the importance of discrimination and to cast ethnic minorities as blameworthy. In contrast, these participants differentiate themselves from the role of victim and define minorities as being in charge of and responsible for their own lives.

Hence, discursive strategies that are used to challenge the existence, omnipresence, and seriousness of discrimination and to problematize its causes can function in different ways in different contexts. They can function to sustain and legitimize the position and interests of the dominant group, but they can also function to uphold the idea of possibilities for social improvement and change.

An emphasis on subject positions makes it possible to go beyond the simple dichotomy between dominant and subordinate or majority and minority identities. Such a dichotomy tends to ignore the diversity within majority and minority groups. Members of both groups are not 'locked' inside their group or incapable of shifting positions, but, rather, are competent discursive agents. With a dominant–subordinate dichotomy, it is sometimes difficult to make sense of discourses in which people are in the process of arguing about discrimination, exclusion, and self-definition, and in doing so use various discursive strategies. This dichotomy tends to turn identities and group relations into relatively fixed and homogeneous entities, rather than examining how group relations and identities are being produced and acted out. There are a range of discourses and practices that place individuals and groups in particular subject positions. Competing constructions and challenges are always possible.

Examining the actual use of discursive practices also offers scope for acknowledging personal agency. Studies of discrimination carry the danger of portraying majority group individuals as more or less passive recipients of socially oppressive practices and ideas, and minority members as rather helpless victims (Oyserman & Swim, 2001; Shelton, 2000). However, majority group members can position themselves within various discourses, including humanitarian and Christian ones, and ethnic minority group members are able to reject the victim position and to claim an active, constructive, and responsible role for themselves.

Power and identity in local context

In our more ethnographic work in Rotterdam, we have found the usefulness of studying issues of power and status differences in relation to the wider social situation as well as local circumstances. Power relations are being actively (re)produced and negotiated, involving global, national, and local circumstances, resources, and boundaries. There are multiple forms and sources of social power.

For example, the standard scheme defining majority–minority relations can have power implications because it places *ethnic minorities* in an advantageous position compared to the Dutch. The charge of racism is one of the strongest moral condemnations that can be levelled today. For example, the taboo on racism and its strong moral meaning tend to make teachers very sensitive to possible manifestations of racism. In the schools we studied, it was clear that ethnic minority students were sometimes able to interpret their experiences in terms of racism and discrimination and to get these interpretations accepted by teachers. For Dutch students, such an interpretation is less obvious. After all, the Dutch are typically seen as the perpetrators and the Dutch students had much more difficulty in convincing teachers that they sometimes faced discrimination. Therefore, the taboo on racism and the dualist majority–minority model can work as a power resource for ethnic minorities.

Language is another example of such a resource. Many schools have a policy that only the Dutch language is to be used in school. This has practical reasons because the lack of a common language hampers interactions and causes misunderstandings and conflicts. It limits the possibility of shared understandings, making it very hard to develop a modus vivendi in schools. But there are also other aspects involved. For example, the obligation to speak Dutch can be interpreted as an act of majority group domination that ignores diversity and ethnic identities. Furthermore, stressing a lack of command of the Dutch language is a strong argument because it can be used as a socially acceptable and understandable reason for expressing negative feelings and arguing for assimilation (Verkuyten, 1997b). Teachers sometimes use the topic of language in this way.

However, using one's own language also plays a role in group relations among youths. It gives ethnic minorities a position of power whereby they can exclude others, in particular the Dutch. Not being able to understand what others are talking about means being defenceless and unable to have influence, and it leads to suspicions and feelings of exclusion. In schools we encountered various examples of ethnic minorities using their own language to make the Dutch feel excluded. The Dutch themselves are not able to use their language as a power resource in this way because ethnic minority students speak Dutch.

Although asymmetrical power relations in favour of the ethnic Dutch are often assumed, in many local situations the Dutch have lost much of their power (see De Jong & Verkuyten, 1996). Power relations of subordination and resistance are actively (re)produced in relation to shifting identity definitions and alliances. Within particular sites or places, there are a range of contextually based discourses and ideologies that assign people to particular positions and that are also used to resist assignments and to assert and articulate other categories of social difference. Younger people, in particular, are in the process of negotiating forms of identity and belonging, and this process is marked by a plurality of differences, cultural syncretism, and the appropriation of social representations. Studies in other cities and countries have presented similar findings and arguments (e.g. Back, 1996; Conquergood, 1994; Hewitt, 1986; Mac an Ghaill, 1999; Marshall et al., 1999). Working in the UK, Modood et al. (1994, p. 218), for example, conclude: 'Our research . . . challenges those who think in terms of simplistic oppositions of British–alien or black–white. A significant population on the ground is living in ways that refute these dualisms. It is time for social analysts and policy-makers to catch up.'

A dichotomy between domination (ethnic Dutch) and subordination (ethnic minorities) is of limited value for interpreting and analysing many local situations. These studies show that it is necessary to have a more detailed understanding of how people define and negotiate themselves and their everyday life. With the common-sense dichotomy of majority–minority or perpetrator–victim, it is difficult to make contact with the experiences of people who are in the process of arguing about belonging, exclusion and self-definition, and in doing so are making all kinds of comparisons and distinctions.

Local situations are affected by existing social representations and group relations in society. However, localities also have their own characteristics and dynamics that should be taken into account. Failing to do so and applying the dualist model to local situations may in part be responsible for the often limited success of anti-racism (Bonnett, 2000). This model is the implicit frame of reference in different forms of anti-racism, making it practically not very adequate for changing local situations. A frequently observed risk is that strategies aimed at reducing racism are not effective because they aim either at goals that are too restricted or at areas that are too generic (Goldberg, 1993). That is, a too generic theory or 'solution' may prevent one from grasping the specific nature of and answers to racism in concrete settings, whereas the understanding of a very specific aspect, expression, or condition of racism may lose sight of the wider implications. Using local analyses to criticize structural racism is an example of the latter, whereas simply applying the common-sense dichotomy to a local situation is an example of the former.

The stress on situation and interaction should, however, not lead to ignoring the importance of group differences at the level of society and the related differences in experience and sources of moral asymmetry (Blum, 2002). In contrast to the majority group, minority members often have to 'explain' themselves, are held responsible for the misconduct of a few in-group members, have to fight for acceptance, and have to prove that they are a 'good foreigner' or 'the exception to the rule'. Furthermore, the experience of discrimination can be painful for both majority and minority group members but will most likely have different meanings and implications for both. Being a target of prejudice and discrimination is apt to be quite different for members of ethnic majority and minority groups (Schmitt & Branscombe, 2002). There are differences in the probability, prevalence, and severity of discriminatory events experienced and in coping resources. Furthermore, there is a moral asymmetry, because a discriminatory act against a member of a minority group often carries the weight of historical, political, and social meanings. Ethnic name-calling and denigrating slurs, for example, reflect social positions and invoke negative cultural stereotypes. People are often very aware of this. In one of our studies among early adolescents, a boy related how his peers always called him 'Turk or Turkey'. He found this upsetting 'because it is as if they say to me that I don't belong here, that I should go home, to Turkey'. The situation of a Dutch person's calling a Hindustani a coolie is also clearly different from a Dutch person's being called 'cheese head' (Verkuyten, 1999). The latter does not have the historical legacy of low-paid Hindustani labourers working for the Dutch in the former colony of Surinam. Similarly, calling Moroccan youths 'Osama' (bin Laden) or 'terrorist' and referring to refugees as 'cowards' and 'losers' carry the weight of international politics. These examples show that history and the global penetrate the local and are appropriated and used in the process of identity negotiations. Actual places are connected to previous times and to global spaces. This spatial connection is also obvious in transnationalism and diaspora.

Transnationalism and diaspora

The examples of our research among Moluccans and Turks show the importance of the (imagined) homeland. The country of one's own or parents' origin provides a source of self-understanding and location in the world. It is a horizon of meaning that is used for self-definition and self-presentation. In addition, there are often homeland-focused activities, particularly in times of political and economic crises.

For example, the riots and killings that broke out in 1999 on the Moluccan Islands between Christian and Muslim groups had a strong influence on Moluccans living in the Netherlands. There have always been contacts with the Moluccan Islands, but these were intensified after 1999. The Moluccan community in the Netherlands was in favour of a UN intervention in the Islands, and tried to persuade the Dutch government to raise the issue at the Security Council. Demonstrations were held, and groups with names such as 'Free Moluccan Youth' and 'Maluku Warchild' threatened violent action if the Dutch government failed to act. The Dutch government discussed the situation on the Moluccan Islands at a special meeting of the UN in September 2000.

However, not only crises are stimuli for homeland-focused orientations and activities. For example, in the Netherlands, some 75% of young Turkish and Moroccan people choose a marriage partner from Turkey or Morocco, often from the area from which their parents migrated.[11] And in his study on illegal Turkish migrants in the Netherlands, Staring (2001) shows that contacts between immigrants and those remaining in Turkey are crucial for the travel and reception of new migrants and refers to these as transnational support networks.[12]

In the latter part of the 1990s, 'transnationalism' became a key field of study in migration research (e.g. Basch et al., 1994; Faist, 2000; Portes et al., 1999). The focus is on transnational social spaces in which activities and affiliations are maintained that cut across national boundaries. Initially, this literature was developed around experiences in the USA, particularly the labour-market experiences of Central and South American migrants. However, the literature on transnationalism has expanded and become increasingly diverse in approach and scope (Kivisto, 2001). For example, Vertovec (1999) identifies six distinct uses of the term, including transnational corporations, sites of political engagement, and diasporic consciousness. Furthermore, the concepts of transnationalism and diaspora have become closely connected. At the heart of 'diaspora' is the notion of a group's dispersal from the original homeland to which ties of allegiance are maintained. Traditionally, the term is associated with the historical dispersal of the Jews from Palestine but is now used to describe large-scale diasporas, such as Turks and Moroccans in Western Europe, Cubans and Vietnamese in the USA, and Chinese and Greeks across the world.

The concepts of transnationalism and diaspora shift attention away from a concern with ethnic relations at the national and local level, to a focus on affective and instrumental social relationships and identities spanning borders (Cohen, 1997). Migrant communities maintain continuing material, social, and sentimental links with their country of origin. This certainly is not a recent or new phenomenon, but improved communication technologies and facilities to travel have increased the possibilities (Basch et al., 1994).[13]

There are two related consequences of sustaining a diaspora community and a transnational orientation (Clifford, 1997). The first is a shift from the 'here' to the 'there' or from the question, 'where are you?' to 'where are you from?'. By focusing on the imagined community with others elsewhere, the diaspora concept tends to de-emphasize the import of living in a particular location.[14] On the one hand, this is useful in rejecting and redefining the unfavourable position of 'ethnic minority' in the country in which one lives. Diaspora offers a positive sense of being 'a people' outside the time and place of the host nation in which one can feel excluded or as not really belonging. On the other hand, attention can become deflected from local circumstances, structural inequalities, accommodation processes, and the actual living together of different ethnic groups. After all, places people find themselves in continue to count even in transnational social spaces.

The second aspect is that the concept of diaspora does not replace a concern with ethnicity but is crucially dependent on it (Anthias, 1998). The emphasis is on sameness-in-dispersal (Ang, 2001). There is a tendency to emphasize internal coherence, unity and essentialist and absolutist notions of being that originate from the (imagined) history and homeland. The focus on the homeland and the idea of being part of 'a people' or one big 'family' prioritizes ethnic identity. It provides a sense of connectedness and belonging which can form a solution to the feelings of dislocation and uprooting that many migrants experience. And a visit to the country of origin can give a sense of homecoming. William Yang (in Ang, 2001, p. 49) describes it as follows: 'I've been back to China and I've had the experience that the expatriate American writer Amy Tan describes; when she first set foot in China, she immediately became Chinese. Although it didn't quite happen like that for me I know what Amy's talking about. The experience is very powerful and specific, it has to do with land, with standing on the soil of the ancestors and feeling the blood of China run through your veins.'

Diaspora communities tend to promote a sense of historical continuity, kinship, and tradition that counters the numerous and inevitable changes resulting from migration and spatial scattering. The signifiers 'Turk', 'Chinese', 'Jew', 'Kurd', and 'Greek' alone are considered sufficient to differentiate between groups of people, independently of the particular histories and situations people find themselves in and the variety of meanings that have developed. These signifiers are also used for defining obligations, reciprocity, and claims to solidarity. For example, Ang (2001), who was raised in the Netherlands and now lives in Australia, describes how an appeal was made to her Chineseness during the anti-Chinese riots in 1998 in Indonesia. The initiators of the Huaren ('Chinese people') website asked her as a diaspora Chinese intellectual to speak up and operate as a representative.

The increasing importance of transnational and disapora communities raises many interesting questions and issues. Although much of the writing is theoretical, there are a growing number of empirical studies in the social sciences (e.g. Al-Ali et al., 2001; Griffiths, 2002; Procter, 2000; Pryke, 2003). Social psychology, however, has not paid much attention to these developments despite the fact that there are clear social psychological issues involved. For example, Kivisto (2001) argues that the anthropological and sociological literature has undertheorized the affective element of transnational ties, such as emotions related to longing, the sorrow of absence, and the desire to remain bounded and rooted.

It is also unclear to what extent migrants actually identify with their homeland and with ethnic group members dispersed in other countries. Identification processes will vary situationally and depend on many circumstances, such as international politics, the situation in the country of origin, the opportunity structure in the host country, and the material, social, cultural, and organizational resources available to communities. In addition, diasporas differ in terms of the different forms of leaving and dispersal, as in slavery, labour migration, or refugee flight (Brah, 1996).

In a study conducted at the beginning of 2002, we examined identification processes among two groups of labour migrants to the Netherlands (Moroccans and Antilleans) and two groups of asylum seekers (Yugoslavs and Iraqis).[15] From each group, 50 people were interviewed and in the interviews some standard questions on group identification were asked. The participants were asked to indicate how strongly they identified with 1) ethnic in-group members living in the Netherlands; 2) ethnic in-group members in the country of origin; and 3) ethnic in-group members in other countries.[16] Table 4.1 shows the results.

The row results in Table 4.1 indicate that participants identified with in-group members in all three situations. The scores for in-group members in the Netherlands and in the homeland are quite similar, with the scores for 'other countries' being somewhat lower, but not significantly so. The participants in these four groups made it clear that they felt emotionally connected and committed to in-group members in the Netherlands and in the homeland, and to a lesser degree to members living in other countries. They argued that the homeland was an important point of reference for them and that they were interested in or concerned about the situation there. Most of them were also involved in transnational activities, and their ethnic identity provided a historical and political location in a globalizing world. In fact, the participants made practically no distinction between identification with in-group members in the three situations. The lowest correlation between two situations was .82. Hence, the focus was on a common ethnic identity rather than on situational differences—ethnic identity was prioritized.

However, there were also differences between the four groups of participants. In general, ethnic identification was stronger among the two groups of asylum seekers than among the labour migrants. Analysis of variance indicated significant differences for all three measures, and post-hoc tests showed that the Iraqis scored higher than the other groups. In addition, the Iraqis and Yugoslavs, on the one hand, and the Moroccans and Antilleans, on the other hand, tended to form homogeneous

Table 4.1 In-group identification for three situations and four groups of participants. Mean scores (5-point scale) and standard deviations (in parentheses)

	In-group members in Netherlands	In-group members in the homeland	In-group members in other countries
Participants			
Antilleans	3.26 (.90)	3.27 (.90)	3.17 (.87)
Moroccans	3.46 (.83)	3.20 (.85)	3.10 (.71)
Yugoslavs	3.53 (.79)	3.63 (.81)	3.46 (.82)
Iraqis	4.15 (.82)	4.06 (.88)	3.81 (.79)

subsets.[17] There are several possible reasons for this difference, such as the more recent arrival of Iraqis and Yugoslavs and the political, economic, and social crises in their countries of origin.

Conclusions

The empirical examples in this chapter were used to make two related theoretical points. These points have to do with the majority–minority dualist model that is typically used in mainstream social psychological research on ethnic minority identity. This model has been used successfully in many empirical studies and theories (e.g. Tajfel & Turner, 1986; Sidanius & Pratto, 1999), and it stresses societal group differences in status and power. However, in focusing on the level of interaction, there are clear limits to this model. For one thing, there is the danger of confounding a critical position with an analytic explanation that perpetuates racial and ethnic dualism (Cameron, 1998; Reicher, 2001). Furthermore, the predominant concern with status and power leads to the presupposition that the relationship with the majority group is all that matters. This is a restricted and one-sided view of the ways that people from ethnic minority groups define and locate themselves in interactions.

   This view ignores or underestimates the importance of continuity or the imagined history, culture, and homeland of many of these groups. In our studies, the participants were involved in discussions on differences and relations within their own ethnic group and in relation to the situation in the homeland. Different characteristics and discourses were used to authenticate an ethnic identity in relation to the in-group. Ethnic identity is fundamentally shaped by interactions with co-ethnics and by discourses about ethnic authenticity. Individuals negotiate their ethnic self-definitions in relation to in-group members and by using various characteristics, such as language, race, and cultural practices. Our studies point to the important role of co-ethnics. The same has been found in ethnographic work (see Song, 2003). An example is a study by Clay (2003) on how African-American youths use hip-hop culture, particularly rap music, to form and negotiate their black identity in everyday interactions with other African-Americans. She shows how in-group acceptance as authentically black depends on one's ability to master the tools of hip-hop performance, that is, the right language, clothes, posture, attitude, and bodily gestures. These examples indicate that ethnic group membership involves crucial issues of in-group acceptance and support as well as in-group obligations and pressures. These intragroup processes should not be ignored, and the need to take them into account is increasingly being emphasized by social psychologists (e.g. Deaux & Martin, 2003; Postmes & Branscombe, 2002).

   A majority–minority dualist model is also limited because it tends to ignore the many different group comparisons that are made. The ways the participants in our studies defined and positioned themselves cannot be understood without taking these comparisons into consideration. They tried to define, carve out, and account for a distinctive ethnic identity not only in relation to the Dutch but also in relation to various other ethnic minority groups and to subgroups within their own ethnic category. These comparisons acted together in defining categories and in giving an account of the position that was constructed and taken up.

A dualist model also implies a tendency to place ethnic minority members in the position of helpless victims (Shelton, 2000). However, many participants in our studies typically claim an active and constructive role. They make it clear that their identity is not derived from that of the majority group that is doing the defining. The participants presented themselves not only as victims but also as agents who have their own responsibilities, and who can draw upon a rich culture, tradition, and homeland in defining themselves in relation to the Dutch. There is an active and reflective part to situational self-definitions. The participants argued about categories, and in claiming an active and constructive role for themselves and their group, they rejected the idea of being subject to and determined by existing group relations, discourses, or discriminatory practices.

However, issues of dominance and inequality are not absent from our studies and some ethnic minority participants did emphasize the defining role of inequalities and discrimination. Furthermore, the differences between Moluccans or Turks and Dutch were presented not only in historical and cultural terms but also in terms of power. Participants argued that the existence of discrimination and racism plays an important role in defining them as outsiders or foreigners and in constructing a clear boundary. The way the existence of ethnic discrimination is described and accounted for depends, however, on the subject positions taken up. Ethnic minority members do not have to interpret discrimination from a victim perspective but can take up different ideological subject positions.

The second point of this chapter is that the relation between categories can take different forms and therefore should not be seen as unproblematically given. There is a difference between differentiating oneself from others and defining oneself in opposition to others. Whereas self-definition in group terms is unavoidably divisive, talking about oneself as a group need not be markedly oppositional. Some comparisons can be in clear contrast to other groups that are used as adversaries. Moroccans, foreigners in general, 'maladjusted' foreigners, and segregationist Turks are examples. These groups were described in negative terms, and the distancing from them led to the use of many of society's negative stereotypes for portraying these groups and for blaming them for diminishing one's own chances in society.

However, although participants in our studies differentiated themselves from former generations, they did not define themselves in opposition to them. There are continuities with these generations that have relevance for self-definition, such as the parents' immigration narrative, and the group's history and culture. Self-definition does not have to be in opposition to the Dutch either, although this occurs. In general, participants presented themselves as culturally, historically, and ethnically different from, but not as opposed to, Dutch people. However, inclusive self-categories or superordinate identities were seldom used explicitly.

In this chapter, I have tried to argue that social psychology must broaden its scope. A problem with theories that focus on status differences between majority and minority groups is that, implicitly, the unit of analysis is the nation state. Again, for many situations and questions, this is adequate but there are also drawbacks. It means, on the one hand, that there is no adequate basis for comprehending particular localities or places, and, on the other hand, that there is no room for the wider field of action or transnational spaces in which many immigrant groups operate. Both the local and the global can be seen as challenging the dualist model that predominates in social psychology.

The way people in everyday and localized interactions define themselves and others is complex. In many situations, diversified and changing ethnic maps of identities and relations are being negotiated in which institutional features and dominant discourses and representations are both used and challenged, appropriated, and ignored. There are shifting ethnic tensions and alliances, and there are many ways in which individuals can locate and position themselves in relation to various others, and in trying to establish a 'togetherness-in-difference' in a particular place.

At the same time, increasingly, transnational social spaces and diasporic communities challenge national boundaries. These spaces provide senses of identity that go beyond the majority–minority dualist model. The emphasis is on long-distance relationships with communities elsewhere, with the concomitant promotion of historical continuity, kinship, and ethnic unity. The focus is on 'sameness-in-dispersal' across global space. What happens elsewhere can have consequences for how people define and present themselves here. People live not only in the 'here and now' but also in the 'there and then'. Ethnic minority groups have a (imagined and often mythologized) history, culture, and homeland that provide important sources for situational identity definitions in relation to both in-group and out-group members in a multitude of contexts.

5   Ethnic group essentialism

In 1999, a nationwide survey was conducted among a representative sample of 2000 ethnically Dutch people.[1] The survey contained many questions on 'contemporary social issues', including ones on stereotypes of Turks and Moroccans. In answering these, a considerable number of participants agreed with the statements that Turkish and Moroccan people are selfish (30%), violent (28%), complainers (28%), and slackers (22%). Strikingly, 8% agreed that most Turks and Moroccans are by nature inferior to Dutch people, while as few as 12% disagreed only somewhat with this statement.[2] The participants' endorsement of these stereotypes was significantly related to anti-Muslim attitudes and to support for exclusionary measures.[3]

The next excerpt is from the focus-group research we carried out among our Dutch participants. One participant is responding to another who has just argued that it is difficult for ethnic minority groups to integrate because they do not always have the same opportunities and are often discriminated against. To substantiate this claim, the participant had referred to a newspaper article which stated that Hindu people in the UK have yet to integrate into British society and that there are no Hindus in the House of Commons. The responding participant accounts for social disparities and exclusion in terms of culture, presenting a direct link between ethnicity and culture as self-evident and inevitable.[4]

> But it's as easy as anything—if you give somebody an English passport that doesn't make him an Englishman, and if you give somebody a Dutch passport that doesn't make him a Dutchman, and that's what it's all about. It's just like when you take any 6-year-old kid—or these days you start going to school when you're 5—whatever your parents are, doesn't matter, if he's going to a Dutch school but he's entirely brought up in a different culture, he's never going to be a Dutchman and that's the problem.

In our focus-group discussions, there were many such examples in which ethnicity was presented as an obvious and more or less natural way of categorizing people. The resulting ethnic groups were defined in terms of relatively fixed cultural characteristics that have changed little throughout history. This involved a view in which culture is seen as a mould that determines people's lives, understanding, and behaviour. It also presents people as inevitably marked by their culture, making them easy to identify and exclude from other groups. Speakers putting this view used a discourse of early socialization to make people's cultural determination plausible and acceptable. They stressed that all those born into a cultural community inevitably absorb and internalize the customary ways of thinking and feeling of the ethnic group in question. This was typically presented as factual and as nothing out of the ordinary. People simply are marked by their culture through enculturation, whatever subsequent layers of other meanings they may absorb or have absorbed. Culture is quasi-biological, a second nature that inevitably makes people who and what they are. Characteristics and actions were presented as the fixed outcomes of environmental cultural inputs.

Many authors have argued that essentialist group beliefs are central to racism (e.g. Brah, 1992; Hirschfeld, 1996; Jones, 1997; Mason, 1994; Solomos & Back, 1994). In different forms of racism, racial and ethnic categories are presented as natural, inevitable, and therefore unchangeable. These categories are taken to represent human types, specifying that an individual is fundamentally a certain sort of person. Racism attempts to fix social groups in terms of essential, quasi-natural properties of belonging within particular political and social contexts. Certain traits of mind, character, and temperament are considered to be an intrinsic part of an ethnic or racial group's 'nature' and hence to define its ethnic or racial fate. Although the survey results and the example of the Moluccans in the previous chapter show that there are still traces of biological forms of essentialism, contemporary discourses focus on culture. Blum (2002, p. 134) describes the belief in cultural inherentism as follows: 'These people (Jews, whites, Asians) just are that way (stringy, racist, studious); it's part of their culture.' And studies on 'new' or 'cultural racism' have shown that the idea of fundamental and inherent cultural differences is used to exclude and abnormalize ethnic minority groups (e.g. Barker, 1981; Hopkins et al., 1997; Rapley, 1998; Taguieff, 1988; Wieviorka, 1995).

A critique of essentialism lies at the heart of critical social theories and discourse analyses of racism and ethnocentrism. In particular, critical discourse analyses of racism have shown how various linguistic devices and discursive constructions are used to essentialize, legitimize and disseminate patterns of social power and racial dominance (e.g. Brown, 1999; Essed, 1991; Rapley, 1998; van Dijk, 1987; Wetherell & Potter, 1992). Problems of racism are understood to be problems of essentialism, and the concepts of race, ethnicity, and culture have become suspect as essentializing categories. Theories that claim invariable and fundamental differences between social groups are defined as in need of deconstruction. Similar analyses are presented in mainstream social psychological studies of essentialism. Here the focus is on lay theories or concepts which posit that category members have a property or attribute (essence) that determines their identity. Yzerbyt et al. (1997) argue that essentialist explanations best account for the way things are or justify the existing social system. They emphasize the role of essentialist beliefs in stereotypes and argue that these beliefs serve to rationalize existing social arrangements or the status quo (Jost & Banaji, 1994).

Hence, within the social sciences and social psychology, the term 'essentialism' is seen as reactionary and is increasingly employed as a term of criticism. Instead of essentialist beliefs, the socially constructed and changeable nature of identities is emphasized. Ethnicity is seen as first and foremost a form of organizing and maintaining social relations rather than a question of essential or inherent characteristics. Anti-essentialism has emerged as an emancipatory or progressive discourse that challenges hegemonic representations, the fixity of identities, and oppressive relations.

However, anti-essentialism has itself become the target of recent critiques by academics and, in anthropology, also by those who are the subject of analysis. Some academics distance themselves from classic essentialism but also point to the complex and multifaceted nature of essentialist thinking and the various contexts of its use. For example, anti-racism has often relied on notions of fixed essence (Dominguez, 1994). Bonnett (2000, p. 133) gives a historical and international analysis of the development of anti-racism, arguing that 'essentialism is not some marginal current within anti-racism, but weaves through almost every aspect of its historical and contemporary practices. It is anti-racists who have called for indigenous peoples' racial identity to be "respected". It is anti-racists who have tried to identify and celebrate racial struggles against dominant groups. And it is anti-racists who have mobilized terms such as "white people", "black people", and so on, in the service of equality.'

Furthermore, members of ethnic and racial minority groups often resist stigmatization by taking pride in their 'essential' or authentic group identity. In doing so, they tend to adopt the racial or cultural thinking that is at the root of their exclusion and oppression. Verdery (1994) argues that what she calls 'new essentialism' is a central aspect of contemporary constructions of difference that are posited as inherent and imperative. Ethnic minority identities are celebrated, and one stands up for the particular rights of one's group, but these rights are restricted to the person who is a genuine group member.

In the context of current debates about identity politics and multiculturalism, 'identity' and 'culture' are obviously the right categories on which to rest a claim for group rights and group pride. Gitlin (1995, p. 164) argues that 'many exponents of identity politics are fundamentalists—in the language of the academy, "essentialists"'. And Wrong (1997, p. 298) argues that 'in basing itself on relatively permanent groups . . . [multiculturalism] mirror[s] the very prejudices it opposes'.

Multiculturalism is about groups and group identities. It is a 'social-intellectual movement that promotes the value of diversity as a core principle and insists that all cultural groups be treated with respect and as equals' (Flowers & Richardson, 1996, p. 609). Multiculturalism is defined differently and takes different forms in, for example, schools, organizations, and countries. However, underlying these differences are common arguments. Multiculturalism promotes the value of diversity as a core principle, and insists that all ethnic groups have a right to their own culture. It tends to prioritize group identity and requires a conception of groups as internally homogeneous, bounded, and having unique and inherent characteristics (e.g. Barry, 2001). It is interesting to note that biological and organic metaphors are often used when arguing in favour of multiculturalism. Cultures are talked about as species threatened with 'extinction' and that are in need of 'preservation' or 'conservation'. The clearest example of this is Tully (1995), who uses the metaphor of a black canoe occupied by various animals.

In the literature, terms such as 'anti-anti-essentialism' (Fischer, 1999; Gilroy, 1993; Modood, 1998) have started to appear. It is pointed out that anti-essentialism is far from progressive because it makes all political mobilization rest on a fictive unity. To solve this problem, a distinction between essentialist and political group identification is proposed. Hall (1988, p. 45), for example, analyses racial identity as a necessary fiction in order to make 'both politics and identity possible'. Others talk about 'strategic essentialism' to indicate that in a political context one acts as if essentialism were true. Essentialism is needed for cultural empowering and political mobilization and would differ from racist reifications that are used for exclusion (Werbner, 1997).

In this chapter, I focus on ethnic group (de-)essentialism in relation to notions of multiculturalism. Ethnic group essentialism will be examined at both the level of social interaction and the level of individual perception. I will discuss various examples in trying to show that essentialism is not by definition oppressive and that de-essentialism is not by definition progressive. The political and discursive power of (de-)essentialist group beliefs depends on the way they are used and the group context in which they appear (Hopkins et al., 2003). I will begin by elaborating on social psychological approaches to essentialist thinking.[5]

Essentialist thinking

In social psychology, systematic interest in essentialist beliefs about social groups is rather recent, even though the concept of essentialism was used by Sherif in 1948 and Allport in 1954. Allport emphasized the role of essentialist beliefs in prejudicial thinking and took these beliefs to result from a particular cognitive style. In addition, the work of Campbell (1958) on entativity is very closely related to essentialist beliefs. The perception of a coherent and unified entity is linked to a belief in an underlying essence, and essentialist beliefs encourage the perception of coherence and unity (McGarty et al., 1995; Yzerbyt et al., 2001).

Interest in essentialist thinking has been growing in recent years. In cognitive psychology, Medin (1989) has investigated the common-sense belief that many categories have essences. Categories are assumed to be held together by theories—'essence placeholders'—that individuals develop about the nature of each category. Medin (1989) claims that people hold implicitly essentialist theories because it gives them a firm understanding of the social world. In a theoretical paper, Rothbart and Taylor (1992) have argued that people are inclined to treat many social categories as natural kinds, assuming these to have an underlying essence that is responsible for the many observable differences in appearance and behaviour. Hence, these categories are rich sources of inference about their members. Yzerbyt et al. (1997) have extended and empirically investigated these ideas. An essentialist view of social groups would provide an acceptable and justified account of the status quo.

Yzerbyt et al. (1997, p. 37) state that 'the critical question really is to understand why it is that people adopt a subjective essentialistic approach about social categories'. There are several answers to this question. For example, in his research on the development of children's racial thinking, Hirschfeld (1996) argues for the existence of a specific 'human kind module' that, as a conceptual system, organizes knowledge of social groups along essentialist lines (Gil-White, 2001). Others have attributed the essentializing of social categories to more general cognitive processes (Allport, 1954; Rothbart & Taylor, 1992). Yzerbyt et al. (1997) propose a syndrome of essentialist categorization that serves to rationalize the social order. Their functional analysis takes social conditions into account but remains a clearly psychological approach to essentialism. People are presented as inclined to rely on inherent features which they use to characterize social groups. Conceived in this way, essentialist beliefs are thought to function as causal attributions by providing explanations and rationalizations for the differential treatment of social groups.

In examining the diverse literature on essentialism, Haslam et al. (2000) conclude that the concept has several discernible elements or criteria such as ideas about inductive potential, exclusivity, and necessary features. Haslam and colleagues found in two questionnaire studies of lay persons' beliefs about social categories that the notion of essentialism can be divided into two independent dimensions (Haslam et al., 2000, 2002). The first is the extent to which categories are understood as natural kinds, and the second is the extent to which categories are reified or perceived as coherent and unified entities or 'real things'. The first dimension combines ideas of naturalness, immutability of group membership, discreteness, and historical stability. The second dimension combines the elements of informativeness or inductive potential, uniformity, inherence or underlying similarity, and identity determination. However, they found that there are social categories that were relatively essentialized on both dimensions, such as ethnic and racial groups (Yzerbyt et al., 2001). Thus, essentialism can be examined in terms of category differences that are presented as discrete, necessary, historically stable, and personally unalterable, and which allow many inferences about category members to be made, when, 'underneath', these members would be basically the same.

Although there are differences between these social psychological explanations, they are similar in their focus on inner psychological processes. Psychological essentialism is a claim about human perception and reasoning. However, essentialist ideas about social groups can also be examined as social practices. In this case, not cognition and perception but action and interaction are the focus of research. Taking a discourse-analytic stance, one can examine conversations to see how groups are essentialized and group membership is presented as quasi-natural and unchangeable. In doing so, essentialist group beliefs are not studied as perceptual and (socio-)cognitive activities but as social acts performed within discourse. The act of essentializing groups can be treated as a discursive one that

can perform a variety of social functions, each with different ideological consequences. Such an analysis does not replace a social-cognitive one, but provides an
important addition. A focus on talk in interaction is important in itself, and such
an examination gives an action-oriented rather than a cognitive answer to Yzerbyt
et al.'s critical question, that is, why people adopt a subjective, essentialist
approach.

In addition, a focus on talk in interactions raises a further critical question,
namely, why is it that essentialist presentations and arguments are effective in
social interactions? Why do these presentations have either reactionary and racist,
or progressive and emancipatory effects? This is a complex question, but one way
of answering it is to consider broader political and ideological ideas. For example,
ethnic and cultural identity has become an important political tool for the thousands
of groups classified as or considered to be indigenous or aboriginal peoples, such
as the Inuit and the First Peoples in Canada, the Aboriginals in Australia, and the
Maoris in New Zealand (Morin & Saladin d'Anglure, 1997; Roosens, 1998; Tully,
1995). These groups argue that they are '*a* people' rather than a population, and
they put forward essentialist arguments for the legitimation of their ethnicity and
the authenticity of their cultures. It has become increasingly difficult to ignore their
claims because these relate to dominant political and moral ideas about cultural
and group rights. The UN General Assembly proclaimed 1991 the International
Year for Indigenous People, and the UN's decade for indigenous peoples has come
to a close in 2004. A UN permanent forum on indigenous issues was set up in 2000,
and there is a UN draft declaration on the rights of indigenous peoples. The rights
specified in the draft declaration are premised on a notion of indigenous culture
that is quite reified and essentialist (see Hodgson, 2002). Furthermore, in order to
be heard, indigenous delegates have learned to speak an essentialist language
(Karlsson, 2003).

Similar types of essentialism can be found in multicultural approaches that
equate ethnicity with culture and emphasize authentic and inherent cultural
differences that should be recognized and respected.[6] The deconstruction of
ethnicity, culture, and race is not very useful for those who want to mobilize around
notions of ethnic exclusion, cultural rights, or racial oppression. Anthropologists
have shown that ethnic activists base many of their claims on a legitimacy rooted
in essential notions of culture and identity underlying diverse forms (e.g. Fischer,
1999; Karlsson, 2003; Lentz, 1997). However, extreme right-wing groups do
the same. For example, Alain de Benoist of the French National Front has said
that they feel a strong bond with Taylor's (1992) politics of recognition, and they
have claimed their 'droit de différence' (Birnbaum, 1996). In short, an essentialist
argument is not in itself liberating, as it can just as easily be used in a racist way.

I turn now to two examples of the political and legal power that essentialist ideas
about group identities can have for minority groups. Both examples illustrate that
these ideas are not simply oppressive but are also important political tools. In
addition, I will examine how ethnic Dutch and ethnic minority people define and
use essentialist notions about ethnic groups when discussing these in a focus group.
Here, my focus will be on the actual use and manifestation of these notions in

conversations and the way they are related to claims and justifications. I use this example to show that essentialism can be examined as a flexible conversational resource that is variously defined and deployed, depending on the interactional task at hand. Subsequently, I will discuss a research example that focuses on the perceptual aspects of essentialist thinking. In this study among ethnic minority and Dutch participants, the perception of in- and out-group essentialism was examined in relation to ethnic identification and the endorsement of multiculturalism.

Two examples: The Amish and the Arab European League (AEL)

The Amish

The Amish trace their roots back to the Anabaptists of sixteenth-century Europe and were one of the first groups to settle in Pennsylvania.[7] Once settled, they spread to the Midwestern states of the USA and to Canada. At present, there are some 150,000 Amish people living in various states of the USA. The Amish form an orthodox Christian community that has retained much of its original, rural, farming ways. They have also retained their own particular style of hair and clothing, as well as their language—Pennsylvania Dutch—which is a dialect of High German with many English loanwords. They form a tightly knit community in which religion predominates. The Amish see themselves as a chosen people in a sinful world.

They live by two major principles: 'ordnung' (order) and 'meidung' (avoidance). 'Ordnung' refers to the behavioural guidelines and rules that prescribe a simple, humble, and sober life in which potential threats to their way of life and the community should be avoided ('meidung'). These threats include modern technologies such as electricity, cars, self-powered machines, and the telephone, which are rejected or restricted accordingly. Individuals who do not behave according to the 'ordnung' are also avoided and shunned. The Amish rules define clear group boundaries and help to sustain the cohesion of the community.

The Amish educational system reflects that of the nineteenth century. Children complete eight grades at an Amish school and do not go on to any form of secondary education. The Amish consider secondary education unnecessary for future life within their community. Pursuing secondary education would also require unwanted contact with the outside world—a world that endorses values, such as intellectual accomplishments, self-distinction, and competitiveness. Such values contradict those of informal learning-through-doing, wisdom, and community welfare that are considered central to Amish identity. Secondary education would also lead and keep children away from their family and community, and would in the end result in the disintegration of Amish society. For the Amish, secondary education threatens both the inherent character of their culture and their way of life.

These were the arguments put before the US Supreme Court by the Amish in the famous case of *Wisconsin* v. *Yoder* (1972). The case arose because three fathers had been arrested for refusing to send their children to high school. The central question of the case was whether secondary education can be enforced on a group that has religious and cultural objections to it. The state of Wisconsin argued that its interest in the system of compulsory secondary education was so compelling that established practices must give way. The Supreme Court ruled that the Amish were right and that compulsory secondary education does not apply to them.

Here I am interested in the Supreme Court's argumentation, which defined the Amish as 'a separate, sharply identifiable and highly self-sufficient community' with some culturally inherent characteristics:[8]

> Aided by a history of three centuries as an identifiable religious sect and a long history as a successful and self-sufficient segment of American society, the Amish in this case have convincingly demonstrated the sincerity of their religious beliefs, the interrelationship of belief with their mode of life, the vital role that belief and daily conduct play in the continued survival of Old Order Amish communities and their religious organization, and the hazards presented by the State's enforcement of a statute generally valid as to others.

> There can be no assumption that today's majority is 'right' and the Amish and others like them are 'wrong'. A way of life that is odd or even erratic but interferes with no rights or interests of others is not to be condemned because it is different. . . . Even their idiosyncratic separateness exemplifies the diversity we profess to admire and encourage.

The Amish were presented as a clearly identifiable and traditional community and their noninterference with others and the sincerity of their belief, along with diversity for its own sake, were given as arguments for the decision. Most of these arguments have been criticized since, and some critical points were made at the time by Justice Douglas in his dissenting opinion.

He challenged the Amish claim to be a traditional and identifiable community on the grounds that among the Amish there had been a process leading from 'plows to profits' (Kraybill & Nolt, 1995), and that there was considerable internal differentiation within the presumed homogeneity of the Amish community. Justice Douglas also argued that the verdict of the Supreme Court had a political meaning within the community because it supported the more orthodox factions, silenced the liberal voices, and ignored the interests and opinions of the children. Douglas further argued that the Amish identity is mythical and idyllic, and that 'the point is that the Amish are not people set apart and different'.

A second criticism disputed the idea that a long-standing tradition, cultural inherentism, and sincerity of beliefs and practices were valid arguments for the Amish claim (Barry, 2001). The fact that something is traditional or considered an authentic and constitutive part of one's cultural identity was in itself not seen as a sufficiently justifiable argument. In other words, the reasoning that 'we have always done it this way and it represents the core of who we are' was seen to support conservatism and fundamentalism, potentially harmful practices, illiberal internal rules, and in-group oppression.

The Arab European League (AEL)

In the spring of 2003, the Dutch branch of the Arab European League (AEL) was founded. The AEL is a Belgian-based organization that is active in defining and defending the civil and religious rights of Arabs and Muslims in Europe as well as the Arab and Muslim cause in the world. Under the leadership of the charismatic Dyab Abou Jahjah, a Belgian citizen of Lebanese origin, the organization has attracted much media attention and considerable support, mainly among young Moroccans. The notions of exclusion, racism, discrimination, and group autonomy are central for Abou Jahjah, who is strongly influenced by Malcolm X and the black power movement in the USA. He calls himself an Arabic nationalist, after Malcolm X, who argued that he was a black nationalist.

At first, the AEL operated as a movement predominantly in inner-city Antwerp. Gradually, it became involved in national debates, and when the Dutch branch was formed, it was founded as a political party. Opinion polls conducted in the beginning of 2003 found that some 25% of young Moroccans and 5% of young Turks indicated that they would vote for the AEL in the Dutch elections.

The conceptual programme of the AEL-Netherlands contains an analysis of Dutch society and the party's vision, philosophy, and priorities. The analysis focuses on the growing intolerance and increasing disadvantages faced by Arabs and Muslims in many spheres of life, and on the fact that these groups are here to stay and want to participate as equal citizens in Dutch society.

> We do not intend to go to countries we only know from vacations. We do not intend to live as second-rate citizens and to be offended and intimidated. We do not intend to give up our identity, to cut our bond with our countries of origin and to let down our [Muslim] brothers. We will stay in this country, say what we think, and defend our rights.

> We want to remain who we are, participate in the broader society while keeping our own cultural identity.

The AEL is in favour of a 'real' multicultural Dutch society in which groups are recognizable, recognized, and respected, and are able to develop sovereignty and autonomy within their own circle. Identity and culture are central concepts for the AEL.[9] Assimilation is considered a form of ethnic cleansing without deportation, and defending and promoting the Arab-Islamic identity is presented as an obligation to God, the Arab community, and future generations.

The conceptual programme lists four leading principles: empowerment, self-responsibility, identity, and positive self-concept. The last emphasizes that 'our children should know who they are and should be proud of who they are. Being lost between identities only leads to a dysfunctional self-image and emotional insecurity.' Such a self-image is seen to lead to social problems and antisocial behaviour. On 'identity', the programme states, 'We want to keep our identity and culture while acting as responsible citizens *who* respect the laws of the country. To do so, it is necessary to educate our children in the Arabic language and history, and the Islamic belief. We will resist all attempts to deny our right to our own culture and identity because we are convinced that this is one of the most fundamental human rights.' Claim is laid to an identifiable culture and an identity that should be preserved and transmitted to future generations. This identity should not be neglected, diluted, or lost.[10] Importantly, the appeal to 'culture' and 'identity' seems to constitute a justification in itself. Having a 'culture' or an 'identity' is presented as a basic right, justifying recognition and protection. The AEL's conceptual programme argues that cultural identities should be respected and supported, in accord with the European Charter for the Protection of Minorities.

The establishment of the AEL-Netherlands led to much public debate. Some politicians immediately said that such a party should not be allowed and that legal steps should be taken to forbid it. Other commentators argued that the AEL would give a public and political voice to Islamic youth and thereby canalize their feelings of frustration, dissatisfaction, and anger. There were also points of criticism raised within the Moroccan group. Some objected to the 'A' of *Arabic* because most Moroccans in the Netherlands are not Arabs, but Berbers (Amazigh). Hence, the AEL could never represent the Moroccans. It was argued that the AEL was against the assimilation of Islamic groups but in turn tried to 'Arabify' the Amazigh. Others said that there is no such thing as an Arab culture or identity because there are many ethnic and religious differences within the Arab world. The AEL was accused of fundamentalism in that it takes group identity seriously as a reality rather than as a political necessity and tactic.

Clearly, essentialist group beliefs can be used in various ways and with clearly political implications. Essentialism is useful not only for excluding and oppressing minority groups but also for making claims and challenging group relations. All kinds of groups put forward arguments about their authentic identity and inherent culture, and these arguments have become difficult to challenge or ignore. The 'essence' or 'nature' of one's ethnic group has become a powerful weapon in the social and political arena. Ideas about ethnic-group essentialism also feature in everyday interactions.

Essentialism and de-essentialism in interactions

In our focus-group research among members of ethnic minorities and the Dutch, we have come across many examples of ethnic-group essentialism. These examples can be analysed in terms of the actual use and manifestation of these notions in conversations and the way they are related to claims and justifications (see Verkuyten, 2003). Essentialism can be examined as a flexible conversational resource that is variously defined and deployed, depending on the debate's context and the interactional task at hand. In doing so, the analytic focus is on the question of how people use cultural essentialist presentations and how these presentations are discursively effective.

In our research, not only the Dutch but also ethnic minority members deployed a discourse about cultural essentialism. In the following example, Turkish participants are discussing the differences between ethnic groups and the possibilities of cultural change. One participant has argued that there are many similarities between people because of their shared humanity. Another participant reacted to this by emphasizing group differences: 'Of course, we are all humans but we also have our own history and culture. The Turks, the Dutch, they just have their own ideas, own tradition, own culture, erm, with every race you have those kinds of things. It's just the way things are, and it's something that will not change easily.' A clear link between ethnicity and culture is made that is presented as obvious and inevitable. By using the Dutch word 'gewoon' ('just' or 'simply'), the differences are described in such a way that they appear ordinary and are therefore beyond discussion (Lee, 1987). Different groups have different cultures; that is just the way things are.

In all of our focus-group discussions, there are examples of ethnicity being presented as an obvious and more or less natural way of categorizing people. The resulting ethnic groups are defined in terms of relatively fixed cultural characteristics that have not changed much throughout history. Furthermore, the members of ethnic minority groups presented culture as determining people's lives, understandings, and behaviour (see Verkuyten, 2003). Those born into a cultural community would inevitably absorb and internalize the customary ways of thinking and feeling of the ethnic group in question. This, again, was presented as factual and as nothing out of the ordinary. The use of cultural essentialism by ethnic minority groups can be related to the conversation's context.

In some focus-group discussions, the moderator used statements to elicit and direct the discussion. One statement attributed to 'people in society' was, 'To be able to get ahead in Dutch society, you have to adapt as much as possible and forget your own culture as much as possible.' Reactions to this statement ranged from laughter to disbelief, but in all 10 ethnic minority discussion groups where this statement was used, the participants disagreed outright. Their disagreement focused on the aspect of 'having to forget one's own culture'. This was considered virtually impossible. Below are two examples taken from the discussions. In the first excerpt, the participants in the group initially reacted with laughter:

Excerpt 1

1	*10C*:	No, no, no. No way, Just no way.
	10D:	You've got to adapt, but you can't forget your own culture. How on earth could you?
	10A:	Of course you can't. How can you forget your own culture?
5		That's not normal.

	Moderator:	So, if we take out the last bit, it does make sense? To be able to get ahead in Dutch society, you've got to adapt as much as possible?'
	10C:	Yes, yeah, it would then.
10	*10A*:	Yeah, that's right.
	10C:	You are living in their country, but this is it, in Holland and you will adapt.
	10A:	Of course you've got to adapt, but not in every way. You are who you are. Whether you are in Holland or in France, you are
15		who you are, you can't change that, you can't just adapt like that.
	Moderator:	So the second bit. The last bit isn't correct?
	10A:	No. It's nothing but discrimination.
	Moderator:	Nothing but discrimination?
20	*10A*:	Yeah.
	10B:	Yes, but you will forget it of course, your culture's gonna change. Everyone goes about with everyone else and it'll all change.
	10D:	Yes, Moroccans, Turks, and the Dutch as well and foreigners,
25		and it'll all change.

Excerpt 2

1	*8F*:	Cor! Shit, man, no.
	8B:	No, you've gotta adapt to Dutch society, but you can't forget your own culture.
	8C:	You don't forget your own culture, there's no way, you can learn Dutch
5		or something but . . .
	8F:	No, that's how you've grown up.
	8C:	Yes.
	8F:	You just don't forget.

In both excerpts, the impossibility of forgetting your own culture is stressed because culture determines who you are: you are your culture. In these parts of the discussions and collectively, the participants presented cultural identity as an unalterable and integral part of themselves that should not and could not be forgotten even if they wanted to. You cannot deny your 'roots', as it were, unless you deny yourself and ignore who you are (but see lines 21–25 in excerpt 1, and see below).

The notable thing here is that this discourse is deployed in response to an assimilationist statement. This discourse is very effective in challenging the idea that adaptation to Dutch society implies cultural assimilation. Assimilation is presented as impossible and discriminatory. It is impossible because people are inevitably moulded by their culture and discriminatory because it denies an ethnic minority's culture. Furthermore, the participants reject a one-dimensional or bipolar perspective that pits adaptation against cultural maintenance. Adaptation without assimilation is presented as feasible, preferable, and, considering the importance of culture, the only viable option.

The equation of culture with ethnicity implies an us–them distinction involving the issue of adaptation. When there are different groups with differing cultures, the question of adaptation becomes relevant. As can be seen in the two excerpts above, the participants agreed that one should adapt to Dutch society. There are two strands to this argument. The more pragmatic of the two is that one should adapt to give oneself the most opportunity to advance in Dutch society. In this strand of the argument, adaptation is considered necessary for finding a good job later in life. To do this, one must be able to speak Dutch and know the rules: As one student said, 'Although I am a Turk, I still have to talk Dutch.' The other strand views adaptation almost as a moral obligation, entered into by virtue of living in the Netherlands. For instance, in lines 11–12 of excerpt 1, the speaker argues that one should adapt because 'you live in their country'.

However, in lines 13–15 of this excerpt, the speaker argues that adaptation has clear limits because of the essentialist nature of identity; one must adapt but not forget one's own culture. Presenting culture as inevitably shaping members of a group makes it more difficult for the majority group to expect assimilation or to attribute the blame to minorities for failing to adapt. Here, the emphasis rests more on the inability or impossibility to adapt than on unwillingness to do so. At other points in the discussion, the speakers clearly argue that one cannot be personally responsible for how one is shaped culturally during early socialization. Therefore, within this discourse, adhering to one's culture is not so much a moral issue as an inevitable and necessary fact of life. The participants talked about culture and ethnicity and stated that their typical in-group culture was important to them. They defined themselves as living in the Netherlands, but not as being Dutch or wanting to become Dutch. They argued that they should adapt to Dutch society but, at the same time, they rejected and protested against any demand for adaptation by the Dutch. The Dutch conceived of adaptation as assimilation, meaning a denial and rejection of ethnic minorities' own rich traditions and culture, that is, denying who they have become during early childhood. Additionally, assimilation was seen as discriminatory and a denial of a group's cultural rights (excerpt 1, lines 18–20). Excerpt 3 gives an example of this. It is also from a discussion about culture and the need for adaptation to Dutch society.

Excerpt 3

1	*Moderator*:	What can the Dutch and, erm, migrants expect from each other?
	5B:	Nothing, nothing.
	5C:	Each to his own.
	5G:	Yeah, you can't, you can't turn a Turk into a Dutchman, or a
5		Dutchman into a Turk. You simply can't—it's very difficult.
	5C:	Yes, that's true—there'll be always a difference.

5B:	You can't expect Turks to change and become just like the Dutch.
5C:	And why should we change? We've got as much as a right to
10	our culture, just like everybody else.
5B:	Yeah, exactly. Our culture's really important to us.

In lines 4–8, a similar line of essentialist argumentation is used as in the statement from the Dutch speaker at the beginning of this chapter. However, here cultural essentialism is not used for explaining social disparity between majority and minority groups but to argue for separation. Each ethnic group is different, and therefore each group has the right to live in its own way. The use of this culturalist discourse has consequences because it involves accounts and claims that are being related to multiculturalism. Acknowledgement of and respect for different cultures implies that a cultural-identity argument can be used to justify claims and to make accusations. Multicultural notions such as these were common in the ethnic minorities' discussions. For instance, in excerpt 1, lines 18–20 the speaker argues that having to forget one's culture amounts to discrimination. The negative reactions to the statement presented by the moderator were strongly related to the verb 'have to'. The participants argued that they were under no obligation to do anything of the sort. A more explicit use of an essentialist discourse combined with multicultural notions can be seen in the last three lines in excerpt 3.

Hence, in the discussions, ethnic minorities did use a culturally essentialist discourse and deployed the recognized right to cultural identity to make claims and justify their behaviour. Acknowledgement of and respect for other cultures implies that 'one's own culture' can function as an acceptable argument and explanation. In the discussions, there were different examples of ethnic minorities claiming social recognition and the implementation of actual provisions for the uniqueness of their culturally distinct practices and beliefs. These claims were made in relation to education, the workplace, religion, and the law. It was argued that one's own culture should be taken into account and that it constitutes a legitimate basis for wanting to have, for example, Islamic schools, multicultural work units, and changes in the legal system. These claims were also made in relation to social work and health care. The next excerpt is taken from a discussion in which the participants were arguing about the need for changes in existing care provisions. It was argued, particularly, that a great many more ethnic minority members should be employed in these sectors and that culturally sensitive approaches were needed to provide adequate care.

My doctor also knows a lot about our culture, you know—it makes you feel like, um, well, he understands what you're about, but if you go to somebody who doesn't understand your culture, then . . . I've also got a social worker—she works here now—but she gives me nothing. It makes me feel like there's no point in coming. It's very important to understand. I mean if I've got to explain, you've got to explain all about your culture, if people don't under-stand, it doesn't work. His or her culture is very different from mine. A Turkish social worker will understand straightaway, but if you tell a Dutch, or a Surinamese person or whatever, he or she will have to take in your culture first before she can help you. And that plays a really big part.

In this excerpt, deep cultural differences are emphasized by using extreme case formulations (Pomerantz, 1986). People are presented as *having* their own culture which has shaped their feelings, understanding, and problems. Ethnicity is equated with culture, making ethnic group members basically the same and group membership inductively potent. To provide adequate help and care, it is necessary to 'take in' (Dutch 'innemen') the culture. There are several examples in the discussions where it is argued that psychological, medical, and social problems are culturally specific, making separate provisions necessary.

Cultural de-essentialism

Equating ethnicity and culture was clearly the participants' preferred discourse. It was the one they engaged in most often and most self-evidently. However, there were also various points in the discussion when cultural essentialism was explicitly criticized and rejected. The speakers used not only a discourse about cultural determination and being, but also questioned their own reifications. The conversation below between two girls is an example of this. In talking about school, they argued—as many other students did—that at the beginning of the new school year, they always immediately noticed and wanted to know the ethnocultural background of their classmates (see Verkuyten, 1999). They explained this as follows:

13A: Of course you notice. I mean you want to know what a fellow student is like and all—you just want to know how somebody is.

Here, ethnicity is presented as an inductively potent category: you want to know someone's ethnocultural background because you want to know what someone is like. Ethnic categories were presented as highly informative because they allow one to make many judgements about category members. However, in the same discussion, these girls also used another line of argumentation stressing the unimportance of ethnicity and culture.

13A: Every human being is the same, I think, whether you're Moroccan, whether you're Turkish.
13B: Yeah, culture isn't what counts, it doesn't come into it. They're all just people—we're all just teenagers.
13A: It's not like it's colour, black or white. You are who you are and that's the end of it—everyone's different.

In this excerpt, the importance of ethnicity and culture is denied by stressing a common humanity, another social category ('teenagers'), and unique personal differences. Thus, in contrast to culture, there are concepts available that deny the relevance of cultural groups. The distinctions and reifications that are used are also questioned and problematized. The equation between culture and ethnicity is also dissolved and the relevance of culture denied. Although this questioning was not the dominant pattern in the discussions, it shows that there are always alternative discourses available to challenge dominant definitions. Cultural (de-)essentialism can be examined as a flexible conversational resource that is variously deployed in talk, depending on the issues at hand.

In some contexts, cultural essentialism was criticized and denied by ethnic minority participants. The interesting thing about this talk is that the question of adaptation becomes more problematic. In a discourse about cross-cutting ties, cultural changes, and mixings, the ethnic us–them distinction breaks down and with it the question of cultural adaptation. Similarly, emphasizing human similarities or unique personal differences makes questions of culture differences both less relevant and more problematic. For ethnic minorities, discourses that are available for situated purposes also stress personal determination and responsibility.

The former discourse may be used to challenge homogeneous and often negative majority group representations and behaviour. The next excerpt stems from a discussion about the way ethnic Dutch people treat all ethnic minorities as though they were the same. The first speaker tells a long story about some Dutch people she had met who did not differentiate between Turkish and Moroccan people. She ends her story as follows:

Excerpt 4

1   *8D*:   So I said no, Turkish people's culture's very different, and they didn't even know stuff like that, and, like them, a lot of people just don't know the difference between foreigners.

    8E: 'Cos we're Muslim, right, they think we're all the same.

5   *8I*:   But there are lots of differences among the Turks themselves.

    8D: Yeah, a lot.

    8B: A lot, indeed.

    8D: But it is difficult for Dutch people to differentiate between a Turk and a Turk.

10   *8F*:   Yeah, they'll say, like, you're a Turk, why aren't you wearing a headscarf?

    8G: If they aren't wearing headscarves, they think they're not Turks.

    8D: Yeah, they act like we're all the same, but people from the city, for instance, you can't compare with those coming from the country. It really

15   is a completely different thing.

Modalizing terms such as 'a lot', 'really', and 'completely' (Pomerantz, 1986) are used to argue that there are differences among Turkish people (lines 5–15), and that some groups of Turks are actually incomparable (lines 14–15). Dissolving the equation between ethnicity and culture is useful here to challenge uniform conceptions and treatment by the Dutch. Turks are presented as people who differ greatly from one another. Furthermore, presenting in-group differences as factual and contrasting these to the false beliefs and ignorance of the Dutch acts to substantiate the challenge further.

Crucially, not only was a discourse used about cultural determination and being, but also one about personal determination and doing. There are several examples where speakers distance themselves from their ethnic minority group. In an essentialist discourse, culture is presented as inevitably determining people's understanding and behaviour, making them easy to identify. It entails a concomitant loss of individuality. People are pictured as more or less passive carriers of their culture, and their attitudes, beliefs, and achievements are supposed to reflect typical cultural patterns. It is difficult to reconcile this discourse with the idea of personal agency and responsibility, whereby attitudes and beliefs are seen as resulting from personal experiences and interpretations, and achievements as depending on one's own efforts and perseverance.

Particularly among student participants, there are several examples where it is argued that one's ethnic identity is based on personal experiences and individual choices and less so on culture and tradition. By stressing personal choices and responsibilities, culture is presented as something that may or may not be maintained, rather than as something somebody happens to 'have'. The next excerpt stems from a discussion about the participants' future in the Netherlands and the inevitable cultural and religious changes. When talking about their future, the speakers deployed a liberal individualist conception of the person in which personal choice and responsibilities were emphasized. In this discourse, people are not inevitably moulded by their culture, but it is up to them to maintain their culture or distance themselves from it.

Moderator:	Should you maintain your own culture?
14B:	That's your own choice, erm, it's your own future, you know.
14C:	Yeah, if you don't want to, you don't.
14B:	It's up to you to decide or to do.

A discourse that presents culture as inevitably moulding people is difficult to reconcile with ideas of personal agency. Cultural essentialism presents people as personifications of the ethnic group. This implies a form of social control (Widdicombe & Wooffitt, 1995) and tends to ignore individuality. However, in discussing their future, ethnic minority members also stressed their personal experiences and efforts, deploying a discourse about self-determination and cultural choice. They claimed an active and constructive role and presented themselves as agents with a future, plans, and responsibilities of their own.

From the *Dutch* discussion groups, there were various examples in which essentialist cultural differences were presented as incompatible, and the cultural 'other' was held to constitute a threat to the Dutch way of life. The mixing or coexistence of different cultures was presented as leading to social conflict and the dissolution of Dutch identity. The next excerpt is an example of this.

19A: I think they should adopt our values and norms. They simply have to adapt.
If that doesn't happen, not a single country will have its own identity—you'll
end up with a messy mixture of all kinds of different cultures and all.

19B: Yeah, definitely. I, well, I think that they should adapt to Dutch culture.
They've got to, erm, integrate and if they don't stick to our norms and values,
then erm, it'll become a mess and, erm, well, you'll get criminality and
suchlike, and well, they've got to adapt.

In this excerpt, a case is made for assimilation; 'they' should take on 'our' norms
and values. The interesting thing here is that such a claim rests on the idea that
cultural change is possible and thus that culture does not inevitably mould people.
Cultural essentialism is useful in talking about segregation and deportation but
less so in arguing for assimilation. For this, a more de-essentialist notion of culture
is needed in which change is stressed. As one might expect, for de-essentialism, a
variety of different claims, arguments, and stories emerged during discussions. For
example, ethnic Dutch participants dealt with minority group cultural claims by
arguing about the meaning of culture itself, questioning whether particular kinds
of behaviours are instances of minority group culture, and restricting these claims
to the private sphere (Verkuyten, 2001a). In addition to these strategies, giving
examples of 'good' minorities and emphasizing out-group differences are useful
strategies.

On several occasions, references were made to minority group members who
had fully adapted to the Dutch way of life:

My children also play with a Turkish boy from, erm, what I could call a Dutch
family. They are Turkish people, but they've just become Westernized, turned
into Dutch people. They don't go to the mosque any more, they've just turned
into Dutch people. That kid also likes to play indoors, erm, that kid is also
working hard at his homework, erm, working hard at his homework, and at
least they keep an eye on him all right.

There is not only a condemnation of different customs here but also the message
that as long as foreigners behave like Dutch people, it is all right, and then they
can even be categorized as Dutch. The equation between ethnicity and culture is
dissolved. The ethnic origin of the family is Turkish, but culturally they are Dutch.
Examples of 'good' minorities prove that adaptation is possible if people are
willing. Additionally, the 'good' minorities were said to disapprove just as much
as the Dutch of the behaviour of members of their ethnic group. These 'good'
minorities are entitled to judge because of their insider knowledge, thus justifying and validating the speaker's opinion about the possibility of and need for
adaptation.

The examples of 'good' minorities demonstrate that the participants implicitly
used the notion of change and also referred to the idea of self-determination. Giving
examples of ethnic minorities who are said to have integrated in Dutch society
is a way of implying that culture does not determine people's understanding

completely. People may distance themselves from their culture and their own immediate contexts. They are able to consider alternatives, to plan their actions, and to determine what they themselves think, say, or do. This notion of self-determination is necessary when claiming that ethnic minorities should adapt and that they should bear responsibility for (not) doing so. Such a claim would be unrealistic and reproaches would become difficult if people are presented as completely determined by their culture.

A case was also made for the possibility of and need for cultural change and adaptation by pointing out the inevitable differences that arise between ethnic minorities' first and later generations as well as other differences within ethnic groups. These presentations are also useful for criticizing differential treatment of and actual provisions for ethnic minority groups. The following excerpt was taken from a discussion about the growing number of Islamic primary schools. One Dutch participant is in favour of these schools, as opposed to his fellow participants, who present Islamic schools as a fairly futile attempt by the parents to control their children, because in reality changes are already taking place.

4C: There's conflicts as it is in those families between children and parents—once the children start growing up they'll Dutchify anyway.
4B: Yeah, that's true.
4C: It's happening now, those children just go on Dutchifying. It's a process that can't be stopped. So once those kids grow a little older, they'll rebel against the limiting side of their parents' culture.

Here, the first speaker presents cultural change among ethnic minorities as inevitable and normal. The older generation may stick to their culture, but the 'Dutchification' (in Dutch, 'vernederlandsing') of their children is a fact. This claim is made factual by using an empiricist discourse that presents the changes as law-like (Edwards & Potter, 1992). The problems that the children are thought to face are seen as mainly related to their parents.

There also is an implicit equation between ethnicity and culture. The children are said to distance themselves from their parents' culture and to become like the Dutch. Furthermore, the two cultures are presented as incompatible in that quarrels and conflicts between parents and children are bound to appear. Hence, children are not inevitably moulded by their parents' culture. Rather, change, and particularly, becoming increasingly Dutch are presented as the normal and natural process, calling into question the need for separate Islamic schools.

Our focus-group research concentrated on the level of social interaction and showed that participants engaged in a culturally essentialist discourse in which an intrinsic link between culture and ethnicity was made. People's 'own' culture was thereby as readily essentialized as 'other' cultures. Furthermore, participants used a mechanistic model of early socialization in order to present people as inevitably moulded and marked by their culture, supposedly making them easy to identify. However, the discursive competence of the participants also included a de- or un-essentialist discourse that challenged and denied the equation between culture and ethnicity. This availability and the use of both discourses are not specific to the present study but have also been found in ethnographic research on, for example, neighbourhoods in the London area (Back, 1996; Baumann, 1996; Mac an Ghaill, 1999). Baumann (1996), for instance, found that residents of Southall make a distinction between a dominant and a demotic discourse. The former envisages homogeneous communities defined by an inherited culture that is based on ethnic identity, whereas the latter counteracts this discourse by stressing change, hetero-geneity, and the making of culture. Cultural essentialism and de-essentialism are discourses that are available for situated purposes. They are used and work in different ways and are not by definition oppressive or emancipatory.

Using survey data, Haslam et al. (2002) came to a similar conclusion. They found that individual differences in sexism and racism were not consistently associated with essentialist beliefs about these categories. Furthermore, they found that anti-gay prejudice was related to a mixture of essentialist *and* anti-essentialist beliefs. In the next section, I will discuss another of our studies among Dutch and ethnic minority group participants in which survey data were used to examine perceived essentialism and its relationship to ethnic identification and the endorse-ment of multiculturalism.

Perceived essentialism

We examined perceptions of in-group and out-group essentialism in a majority–minority context. That is to say, the research was framed in terms of a study on opinions about social issues, including multiculturalism, and the analytic focus was on the comparison between both groups of participants.[11] We examined to what extent, in the context of the survey, Dutch and minority group participants agreed with statements of group essentialism, multiculturalism, and ethnic identification. The sample for the study contained 758 students: 649 were ethnically Dutch and 109 belonged to an ethnic minority group (34 Turkish, 35 Moroccan, and 40 Surinamese).[12] Of the sample, 49% were females and 51% males, and participants were between 15 and 18 years of age.

In general, in-group essentialism is seen as a positive feature of the in-group (Sherman et al., 1999). Empirical results showing a positive relation between essentialism and identification support this idea (e.g. Lickel et al., 2000; Yzerbyt et al., 2000). People who identify strongly with a group are inclined to perceive the group as a real entity with fundamental and inherent features, and in-group essentialism may contribute to a secure sense of identity. Hence, a positive asso-ciation between ethnic identification and in-group essentialism can be expected. Moreover, being in a minority position increases people's need to see their group as a unique, coherent, and homogeneous whole. Hence, in-group essentialism can be expected to be higher for the minority group participants than for the Dutch.

The results supported these expectations. Compared to the Dutch, the minority group participants had significantly higher scores for ethnic identification and in-group essentialism, but a lower score for out-group essentialism. The score for in-group essentialism for the majority group equalled the minority group's score for out-group essentialism. Furthermore, the out-group essentialism score for the former was equal to the in-group essentialism score for the latter. It follows that the Dutch as well as the ethnic minorities in the Netherlands were perceived as equally essentialist by both the high- and low-status groups. Furthermore, both groups perceived the Dutch as being less essentialist than the ethnic minorities.

In addition, for both groups, there was a statistically significant and positive correlation (.30, $p < .01$) between ethnic identification and in-group essentialism. A higher level of ethnic identification was related to a higher perception of in-group essentialism. In addition, there was a significant positive association between ethnic identification and perceived out-group essentialism (.31, $p < .01$), but only for the majority group. Dutch participants perceived ethnic minority groups in more essentialist terms when they identified strongly with their in-group. For the minority group, there was no association between identification and out-group essentialism.[13]

In general, multiculturalism is more important for ethnic minority groups than for the majority group. Multiculturalism is about groups and requires groups to be conceptualized as being to a certain extent bounded and having their own fundamental and authentic cultural characteristics (Barry, 2001; Parekh, 2000). Multicultural approaches tend to equate ethnicity with culture and to use essentialist arguments to present cultures as precious inheritances that should be transmitted uncontaminated and unweakened, while essentialist views of ethnic minority groups provide a justification for multiculturalism. Multiculturalism is morally and intellectually more acceptable when ethnic minorities are considered to be real, already-existing groups with basic and inherent cultural characteristics. Such groups can more easily argue for the need for cultural diversity.

Hence, for ethnic minority groups, *in*-group essentialism can be expected to be related positively to an endorsement of multiculturalism. Ideas about the importance of cultural identity and group representation will become more relevant when the in-group is perceived as more essentialist and entity-like. Multiculturalism has much to offer to ethnic minority groups, and it serves an essentialist in-group better than a non-essentialist in-group. In contrast, for the majority group, perceived essentialist minority groups are more threatening. This perception can easily lead to a pattern of cultural racism, leading in turn to the rejection of multiculturalism in favour of the assimilation of minority groups. Hence, for the majority group, ethnic *out*-group essentialism can be expected to relate negatively to multi-culturalism.

Stepwise hierarchical regression analysis was used to determine which variables predicted the endorsement of multiculturalism. For these analyses, a dummy variable for ethnic group was constructed. In the analysis, ethnic group together with ethnic identification, in-group essentialism, and out-group essentialism were used as (centred) continuous variables. In the second step, the three interaction terms between ethnic group and the four continuous variables were included in the regression equation.

As expected, the majority group participants were significantly less in favour of multiculturalism than the minority group participants.[14] The analysis yielded no

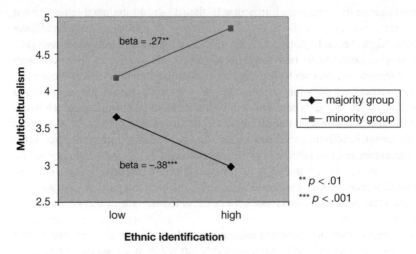

Figure 5.1 Multiculturalism by ethnic identification for ethnic majority and minority
        groups.

significant main effect for ethnic identification. However, the results showed a
significant interaction effect between ethnic identification and ethnic group. This
interaction was as expected and is shown in Figure 5.1. For the majority group,
simple slope analysis indicated that higher ethnic identification was associated with
lower endorsement of multiculturalism. In contrast, for the minority groups, ethnic
identification was related positively to multiculturalism.

In the regression analysis, significant main effects were found for in-group
essentialism, and for out-group essentialism. The effect of the former was positive,
whereas that of the latter was negative. However, both these effects were qualified
by significant interaction effects with ethnic group in step 2. The nature of these
interaction effects was examined by simple slope analyses. For the majority group,
higher perceived *out*-group essentialism was associated with weaker endorsement of multiculturalism (beta = –40, $p < .01$), whereas in-group essentialism
showed no effect (beta = .06, $p > .05$). In contrast, for the minority groups, higher
perceived *in*-group essentialism was associated with stronger endorsement
of multiculturalism (beta = .32, $p < .01$); out-group essentialism showed no such
effect (beta = –.08, $p > .10$). Hence, when minority groups are perceived more in
essentialist terms, the majority group is less in favour of multiculturalism, whereas
minority groups are more in favour of multiculturalism. This result is shown in
Figure 5.2.

The perceived essentialism of the majority group had no effects on multicultural
attitudes. There was no relation between whether or not the majority group
was seen as having fundamental, inherent, and homogeneous characteristics and
the endorsement of multiculturalism by either the Dutch or the ethnic minorities.
This suggests that, at least in the Netherlands, the emphasis, when discussing
multiculturalism, lies not on the majority group but on ethnic minorities, an

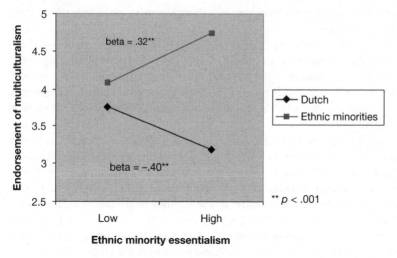

Figure 5.2 Perceived ethnic minority group essentialism and multiculturalism.

emphasis which has been noted by various observers. Dutch research has shown that people tend to interpret multiculturalism in terms of assimilation of ethnic minority groups (Arends-Tóth & van de Vijver, 2000; van Oudenhoven et al., 1998).

Conclusions

Social psychologists argue that people are inclined to treat many social categories, such as ethnicity, as reified and as natural kinds by assuming that these have an underlying essence (e.g. Haslam et al., 2000, 2002; Yzerbyt et al., 1997, 2001). Essentialist beliefs are thought to rationalize social hierarchies and existing social arrangements (Jost & Banaji, 1994; Yzerbyt et al., 1997). They provide an acceptable and justified account for the status quo. However, most of these studies focus predominantly on majority group members and tend to neglect the possible emancipatory effects of essence-related beliefs.

Social psychology can make an important contribution to our understanding of essentialist reasoning and to current debates on, for example, multiculturalism, (anti-)racism, and identity politics, within which essentialism and anti-essentialism are central but contested notions (e.g. Modood, 1998; Sampson, 1993; Werbner, 1997).[15] The stance known as 'strategic essentialism', for instance, has been proposed as a solution to the question of how the political power of essentialism may be salvaged from the logic of anti-essentialism. Anti-racism and critical social analyses have also been criticized for subverting their own anti-essentialist project by defining majority group members as essentially oppressive and racist (Bonnett, 2000). Similarly, some critiques of forms of multiculturalism ultimately rationalize and justify segregation and separation by merging the concept of culture with that of ethnic identity, and by reifying cultures as separate entities (e.g. Turner, 1993).

These are all important and lively debates in which social psychologists can and should be involved.

In this chapter, I have tried to show that some of these issues can be examined at the level of social interaction as well as that of individual perception. The former emphasizes the complexity and variability of interactive processes, whereas the latter focuses on the perceptual aspects of group essentialism. Despite the differences between these levels of analysis, the results of the two studies point in a similar direction.

The Dutch participants used essential cultural differences in an exclusionary discourse which presented the mixing and coexistence of different cultures as inherently problematic. In the survey research, essentialist perceptions of minority groups were also negatively related to the endorsement of multiculturalism. Hence, for the Dutch essentialist, beliefs about ethnic minority groups are related to the rejection of cultural diversity and minority group rights. This pattern fits a 'new racist' discourse which presents the mixing and coexistence of fundamentally and intrinsically different cultures as inherently problematic (e.g. Barker, 1981; Hopkins et al., 1997).

There were, however, many examples where ethnic minority groups engaged in a culturally essentialist discourse. Furthermore, on examination of perceptions of essentialism, a positive association with multiculturalism was found. For the ethnic minority group participants, a more essentialist view of the in-group was related to a stronger endorsement of multiculturalism. Cultural essentialism is very useful for challenging assimilationist ideas. It allows multicultural notions to be used to claim the right to cultural identity and the recognition of fundamental differences. It allows ethnic minorities to argue for provisions and measures that accommodate the uniqueness of their culturally distinct practices and beliefs. In short, cultural essentialism is an important political tool for ethnic minorities, especially as essentialist arguments that legitimize one's identity are increasingly difficult to challenge or ignore.

It follows that cultural essentialism is not just oppressive, just as de-essentialism can have limiting and legitimizing effects. Various Dutch participants argued for the assimilation of ethnic minorities. To do so, a more de-essentialist notion of culture must be employed in which differences among ethnic minority members are emphasized as well as the possibility for change. Providing examples of 'good' or assimilated minorities and stressing inevitable differences between generations were strategies used to argue for the possibility of change and for minorities' own responsibilities in relation to this. When people are presented as completely determined by their culture, arguments for assimilation become unrealistic and reproaches more difficult. The notion of self-determination allows the majority to make minorities themselves responsible and accountable for their position in society. Furthermore, it can be used to challenge claims for ethnically or culturally sensitive measures.

In contrast, ethnic minorities can present culture as inevitably having shaped them. In a culturally essentialist discourse, the emphasis is on the inability or impossibility to adapt, thus turning questions of adaptation or of keeping one's culture into factual issues instead of moral ones. In other words, cultural essentialism can be used by ethnic minorities to counter assimilationist ideas and to claim group rights. On the other hand, cultural de-essentialism can also be a useful strategy for ethnic minorities. Stressing in-group differences, for example, was used to challenge homogeneous and often negative majority group representations and behaviour.

Psychological essentialism is a key aspect of social identities. People tend to infuse an essence into social groups in order to explain group differences, and a discourse about ethnic group essentialism has important interactive and perceptual consequences. Through attributing an essence to a group, the very nature of it is defined. The essence is used to explain the observable properties of group members and to argue about rights and responsibilities. Social categories and ethnic identities, however, can be essentialized to different degrees and in different ways. Classic racial thought locates the inherent nature in the group's race or biology. Traces of this kind of thinking still become visible in times of conflict. This racial reasoning typically has a qualified form because the characteristics attributed to the group are viewed to be present in most group members, but not all; that is, there are exceptions, but they are not considered prototypical cases and therefore can be ignored.

Cultural essentialism is socially and intellectually much more acceptable than racial thinking. It has become the dominant discourse in many societies, but there are also challenges and criticisms. The idea of fundamental and inherent cultural differences makes groups incompatible and provides convincing explanations for the observable practices of ethnic group members. Culture is typically thought of as more than skin deep and therefore as something that really makes a difference. People are defined as being just the way they are because it is part of their culture. However, cultural essentialism is not a coherent form of essentialism because cultural characteristics can change and have interactive, reflexive, and conflicting features. Cultures are interactive because norms and practices are adjusted and (re)confirmed in daily life. That is, people are not merely passive carriers of culture; they are also involved in the continuous construction of new meanings. Furthermore, cultures have numerous rules, convictions, and values permitting divergent and conflicting interpretations.

In many countries, including the Netherlands, the discussion about the need for and merits of multiculturalism is far from settled.[16] In general, multiculturalism is about groups and group identities. Multiculturalism tends to prioritize group identity and requires a conception of groups as—to a certain extent—internally homogeneous and bounded, and as having unique and inherent characteristics (e.g. Barry, 2001; Kymlicka, 1995; Taylor, 1992). These features have been used to criticize multiculturalism. Brewer (1997, p. 208), for example, has suggested that multiculturalism can lead to reified group distinctions that become 'fault lines for conflict and separatism'. Similarly, others have argued that multiculturalism stresses and justifies essentialist group identities and endangers social unity and cohesion. Multiculturalism is also considered by some to contradict the ideals of individualism and meritocracy (e.g. Barry, 2001; Schlesinger, 1992). Thus, although multiculturalism has been recommended as an effective intervention at societal and local levels, many concerns have been expressed.

These concerns have led some social scientists to argue for a distinction between two forms of multiculturalism for which various terms are used, such as 'critical' versus 'difference' multiculturalism (Turner, 1993), 'liberal' versus 'illiberal' multiculturalism (Appiah, 1997), and 'cosmopolitan' multiculturalism versus 'pluralist' multiculturalism (Hollinger, 2000). These scholars recognize the dangers of essentialist group thinking and argue for a multiculturalism in which cultural diversity is used 'as a basis for challenging, revising, and revitalizing basic notions and principles common to dominant and minority cultures alike' (Turner, 1993, p. 413). Anthropologists and sociologists have also claimed that it is necessary to rethink and rehabilitate assimilation theory as an alternative to multiculturalism (e.g. Alba & Nee, 1997; Gans, 1999; Morawska, 1994). They do so by emphasizing acculturation, which allows for the persistence of ethnic retention, and by stressing that immigrants and minorities do not assimilate into societies that are fixed and given but, rather, into ones that are fluid and subject to constant change and alteration.

These discussions are important for social psychology because they show that ideas about multiculturalism and assimilation can be developed and used in different ways. For example, social-dominance theory (Sidanius & Pratto, 1999) suggests that legitimizing ideologies fall into one of two categories: hierarchy-attenuating legitimizing ideologies and hierarchy-enhancing legitimizing ideologies. Multi-culturalism is considered an example of the former because it would provide intellectual and moral support for greater levels of group equality. In contrast, assimilationist thinking would provide intellectual and moral justification for the superior and unchanging character of the dominant culture. This distinction between enhancing and attenuating ideologies is useful to a certain extent, but tends to ignore how these ideologies are differently understood and variably deployed in social reality.

Blum (2002) argues that in addition to racial and cultural essentialism some current essentialism has something like a metaphysical form. He mentions that philosophers such as Hegel and Herder developed a form of protoracial thought involving 'the spirit of a people' (*Volksgeist* in German). Herder, for example, took a more relativistic position, arguing that each people has a distinct spirit with its own intrinsic value and worth.[17] For Herder, every culture was uniquely associated with the experiences of a *Volk* and the product or expression of its deepest and mysterious yearnings and spirit (Parekh, 2000). This metaphysical essentialism is assumed to have no actual instantiation in the world but is symbolized in different observable forms. Attributing essential characteristics to something like the spirit of a people, race, or ethnicity is not uncommon. This can be part, for example, of a myth of ethnic election in which the belief in being a 'chosen people' is central, as among the Amish (Smith, 1992). Another example is that of the Polish Tatars, to be discussed in Chapter 6.

6   Hyphenated identities and hybridity

> I am often confronted by the necessity of standing by one of my empirical selves and relinquishing the rest. Not that I would not, if I could, be both handsome and fat and well dressed, and a great athlete, and make a million a year, be a wit, a *bon-vivant*, and a lady killer as well as a philosopher, a philanthropist, statesman, warrior, and African explorer, as well as a 'tone-poet' and saint. But the thing is simply impossible. The millionaire's work would run counter to the saint's; the *bon-vivant* and the philanthropist would trip each other up; the philosopher and the lady killer could not well keep house in the same tenement of clay. Such different characters may conceivably at the outset of life be alike *possible* to be a man. But to make one of them actual, the rest must more or less be suppressed.

This quotation from William James (1890, pp. 309–310) emphasizes the impossibility of being several things at the same time. James is speaking about the different characters which one might, in theory, develop. Yet, the expectations and meanings of some characters compete with each other and simply cannot coexist. James seems to suggest that they cannot be developed simultaneously and that there are few possibilities for mixing and blending. Making one actual requires the suppression of the others. This incompatibility is an example of the possible 'rivalry and conflict of different selves' (p. 309) that make up the empirical me. In differentiating various aspects of the self, including the multiplicity of social selves, James anticipated current discussions on multiple identities. However, his emphasis on the impossibility of combinations seems less adequate for our globalizing world, in which, increasingly, interconnections and mixings of all kinds take place. In contrast to James, I can quote Gloria Anzaldua (1987, p. 9) on 'mestizaje consciousness', a consciousness that could be taken as typical of individuals living in borderlands, that is, places where people of different cultures intermingle.

> The new *mestiza* (person of mixed ancestry) copes by developing a tolerance for contradiction, a tolerance for ambiguity. She learns to be Indian in Mexican culture; to be Mexican from an Anglo point of view. She learns to juggle cultures. She has a plural personality, she operates in a pluralistic

mode—nothing is thrust out, the good the bad and the ugly, nothing rejected, nothing abandoned. Not only does she survive contradictions, she turns the ambivalence into something else.

Although James and Anzaldua are not talking about exactly the same thing, the difference is striking. Whereas James stresses the impossibility of different characters, Anzaldua is speaking about a plural personality. In cultural and global-ization theories and in post-structural approaches terms such as 'hyphenated and dual identities', 'hybridity', 'syncretism', 'mongrelization', and 'creolization' have become fashionable and common tropes. These terms draw attention to cases where various meanings and identities converge or are blended, thereby forming new ways of being and challenging existing category conceptions.

Social psychologists as a whole are not very interested in the messier categories of human affairs. As a result, social psychological approaches are not well equipped for the difficult task of describing and understanding complex identities. Social identities are predominantly studied as unitary categories with relatively clear-cut boundaries and a reciprocally and mutually exclusive structure, such as male–female, black–white, and majority–minority. Most studies consider two groups at one time and pay no attention to more 'problematic' positions and definitions that are intermediate and at the boundaries or borders. In cognitive-oriented approaches, the focus typically is on the consequences of categorization or what happens when self and others are defined in particular group terms. Perceived homogeneity and forms of in-group favouritism are studied in terms of social identity processes. In these studies, group memberships form the starting-point for analysis, and in that sense social categories are taken for granted.

Hence, in general, social psychological theories propose explanations that suppose clear identities. Self-categorization theory (SCT) (Turner et al., 1987) is a good example because it offers a dynamic and context-sensitive account of social categorization processes. In SCT, the emphasis is on consistency in identity definitions. A central claim of SCT is that identity salience depends on context. Thus, for example, in some situations, it is one's identity as a national of a country that is salient, and in others it is one's ethnicity or race. There is no inconsistency in this because the identities in question are not mixed and are not mutually exclusive, but contextually and alternately salient. But what should we make of the champion golfer Tiger Woods, who describes himself as 'Cablinasian', a blend of Caucasian, black, Indian, and Asian. And how should social psychologists make sense of self-definitions such as 'Neder-Turk' and 'Eurasian', or understand the social identity of a Palestinian Christian Arab with Israeli citizenship (Horenczyk & Munayer, 2003). In addition, how should we understand individuals who are defined by others and themselves as 'half-breeds', 'biracial', or 'mixed ethnic'? The claiming of a bicultural, biracial, mixed-race, and multiethnic identity is an important and growing phenomenon in many countries. For example, the year 2000 census was the first in which Americans could identify themselves as multiracial, and seven million did so. And, in Britain's 2001 census, one of the five main categories available was Mixed Race, under which were four further subheadings:

White and Black Caribbean, White and Black African, White and Asian, and any other mixed background.

SCT also distinguishes between self-definitions at different levels of abstraction. For instance, people may define themselves as discrete individuals in contrast to other individuals or in-group members, or as members of a particular social category in contrast to other social categories, and as human beings in contrast to animals. These different levels of identity are seen as highly dependent upon each other. But as long as they exist at different levels of abstraction, there is no real inconsistency. The possibility of movement and mixing of categories within a given level of abstraction is ignored. Furthermore, for SCT, the central mechanism producing group behaviour is self-stereotyping. The necessary condition here is that there are stereotypical characteristics which define the social category. However, there are many situations where social categories are less clear-cut, and the blending and mixing of meanings that occur require continuous negotiation.

Discourse analytic studies focus more on the antecedents of categorization and investigate how categories are constructed and defined. These studies show that social categories should not be taken for granted but fulfil a number of localized and ideological functions. However, although the variable meaning of categories is examined, these studies sometimes also tend to start from predetermined categories in their research design and analysis. Wetherell and Potter (1992), for example, investigate the flexible and racist way in which white New Zealanders, or pakehas talk about Maoris and immigrants. And Dixon and Reicher (1997) examine how white South Africans construct local race relations in different ways. That is, in examining how categories and category relations are constructed and the racist functions these serve, the starting point is distinctive categories. Here also there is little attention to the more messy categories of social life or the mixed and borderland positions that people can inhabit.

Hybridity

Much of the theoretical literature in the social sciences claims that globalization has led to the fragmentation and hybridization of identities. Theories of hybridity emphasize the mixing and fusion of meanings and reject the notion of homogeneous, uniformly defined identities. Increasingly, notions of heterogeneity and multiple identities are being advanced (e.g. Ang, 2001; Nederveen Pieterse, 1995; Werbner & Modood, 1997). Hybridity is seen as an argument against homogeneity, essentialism, and absolutism, and as one which entails empirical, theoretical, and normative claims (Nederveen Pieterse, 2001).

Empirically, it is argued that forms of mixing are historically far from new or recent, but contemporary times show an acceleration of mixing of all kinds. There is a proliferation of cultural, structural, institutional, organizational, linguistic, and artistic, as well as ethnic and racial forms of hybridity. Globalization has led to the hybridization of many practices and meanings. This is most evident in popular music styles, such as rap, and in many other artistic genres, and in the increased use of 'ethnically ambiguous' persons and pictures in advertisements and commercials. It also appears in everyday life. In December 2002, the Amsterdam Regional Centre of Education produced a book as a Christmas gift. In the book, each page was made by a student and a Moroccan girl chose pictures of her idols: the actor Brad Pitt, the singer Justin Timberlake, the rapper Puff Daddy, and 'the fighter' Osama Bin Laden. Hybridity has become common and continues to increase in all spheres of life.

Theoretically, the recent thematization of hybridity dates from the 1980s. However, *hybridity* is a nineteenth-century word that was used to refer to physiological phenomena and played a prominent role in the racialized formulations about miscegenation and 'racial mixture' (see Young, 1995). Some of these formulations appear in contemporary language and concepts, as for example, when a distinction between pure and mixed race is (covertly) made. Currently, hybridity is predominantly used to describe cultural phenomena. Furthermore, the term is applied to the different lifestyles, behaviours, practices, and orientations that result in multiple identities. And for Hall (1988), hybridity is linked to the idea of 'new ethnicities', an approach which attempts to provide a nonstatic and nonessentialized perspective on ethnic culture. Hybridity, used in this way, breaks down the whole notion of belonging to *an* ethnic group.

The term 'hybridity' is used in two ways (Werbner, 1997; Young, 1995). One is in analysing phenomena in which elements, meanings, and forms are combined, blended, and mixed. Two or more meanings merge into a new mode, and pidgin and creolized languages constitute clear examples and metaphors of this process. Hybridization as creolization or syncretism involves fusion in which new forms are created that are partly made up of the old ones. This analytic understanding of 'liberal hybridity' (Ang, 2001) is meaningful in relation to the prior assumption of existing old differences and clear (ethnic, racial or national) categories.

The second way in which the term is used is as a process of intervention and subversion in which, through dialogical means, a space of discontinuities is constructed. Here, no stable new form is produced but rather a 'third space': 'For me the importance of hybridity is not to be able to trace two original moments from which the third emerges; rather hybridity to me is the "third space" which enables other positions to emerge. This third space displaces the histories that constitute it, and sets up new structures of authority, new political initiatives, which are inadequately understood through received wisdom' (Bhaba, 1990, p. 211). It is from this space of liminality or 'in-betweenness' that it is possible to interrupt, to interrogate, to challenge, to unsettle, and to intervene tactically in the dominant discourses and categorical constructions. 'Critical hybridity' (Ang, 2001) is used here to transcend dualism and binary thinking. It refers to trans-ethnic and trans-racial cultural syncretism. Gilroy's (1993) concept of 'Black Atlantic' is an example of an attempt to go beyond existing boundaries. In his study on the African diaspora, he develops W. E. B. Du Bois's double consciousness by trying to delineate a space that is both inside and outside modernity.

Normatively, 'hybridity' and related terms are used to criticize ethnic boundaries and essentialisms, and to valorize mixture and change. The space of the hybrid would be transgressive, and hybridity is celebrated as an innovative and creative

power. Hybridity would constitute an emancipatory and liberating human condition and a political alternative to the exclusionary and racist consequences of
social categorizations. By emphasizing cultural syncretism, hybridity would also
challenge forms of multiculturalism that solidify cultural differences and lead to
virtual apartheid. Hybridity is preferred because it emphasizes 'togetherness-in-
difference' rather than the 'living-apart-together' of multiculturalism (Ang, 2001).

Criticisms

Several critical points have been raised in relation to hybridity.[1] It has been argued
that hybridity ignores questions of power and inequality, that it is meaningful only
as a critique of essentialism, that it depends on a notion of purity, and that it is an
elitist posture promoted by privileged postcolonial and diasporic intellectuals
located in the West (e.g. Ahmad, 1995; Anthias, 2001; Friedman, 1997; Hutnyk,
1997). Nederveen Pieterse (2001) has responded to most of these criticisms, and
others have argued that people in many parts of the world face questions of
hybridity and multiple identities (e.g. Ang, 2001; Niranjana, 1992). Still others
have argued that hybridity matters to the extent that it affects self-definitions (e.g.
Friedman, 1999).

In the social sciences, the theoretical studies on hybridity and related notions
greatly outnumber the empirical works. In short, it is unclear whether the 'new'
identities are really as multiple and fragmented as the discussions would indicate.
For example, theories of hybridity emphasize the apparently unlimited sources of
identity, such as ethnicity, race, class, religion, gender, nation, and so on, but
provide few clues as to whether these positions are actually taken up and how their
relationships are negotiated and managed.

What is needed are empirical analyses of hyphenated and hybrid identities.
Research in different contexts can assess the normative aspects of different theories
and can provide the much needed empirical material for evaluating the many
fashionable theoretical claims about hybridity, intersections, and new ethnicities
(Modood, 1998). These claims need further investigation and more grounding
in empirical analysis of diverse cases. This will allow us to understand the ways
that multiple identities are actually managed—psychologically and in social
interactions.

An added difficulty when it comes to evaluating and interpreting empirical
studies is that different concepts are used and various phenomena are studied.
Terms such as 'dual', 'multiple', 'hyphenated', and 'hybrid identities' are used,
and questions on acculturation, 'mixed race' and 'double consciousness' are
examined.

In the literature on hybridity, there is much talk of 'multiple identities'. It is not
always clear what is meant by this term, but it often seems to refer to what in
Chapter 2 I discussed as partial identities—the fact that social identities are always
'among other' identities. Every individual simultaneously belongs to a great
number of social categories and can thus be flexibly categorized in a multitude of
ways. These identities do not have to contradict each other or get in each other's

way because they are of different kinds, are differently defined, or are situated on different levels of abstraction. One can be a member of an ethnic and national group as well as a superordinate category—it is quite possible to be Frisian,[2] Dutch, and European at the same time. There is little problem as long as these identities are not defined on the same level of abstraction and in contrasting or competing terms. Depending on the situation, one or the other is relevant and becomes salient.

These processes are extensively studied by social psychologists who examine categorizations and social identities. Social psychological studies on cross-categorization effects have also examined situations in which more than one social category is salient—such as ethnicity and gender—and participants share category membership on no, one, or two dimensions of categorization. Different models of cross-categorization effects have been delineated (see Hewstone et al., 1993; Migdal et al., 1998; Urban & Miller, 1998). For example, in a hierarchical model, differences on one dimension depend on how the person is classified on the other dimension. In a category-dominance model, one dimension dominates and the other is ignored. A category-conjunction model assumes that only individuals who are similar on both categorization dimensions are classified as an in-group member, and all other combinations are classified as out-group. In addition, recent work on cross-categorization has focused not only on patterns of responses predicted by these models, but also on factors that moderate crossed-categorization effects (see Crisp & Hewstone, 2000; Urban & Miller, 1998).

Multiple identities understood as partial identities and cross-categorization studies are important for several reasons (see Chapter 2), but they do not seem to capture the central issue of hybridity. Multiple identities do not have to involve a mixing and blending of meanings that result in new forms. And the acquisition of a new identity may not be transgressive or interfere with an original or old one. In relation to migration, Bauböck (1998) talks about additive identities and additive assimilation, that is, 'retaining a previous cultural membership while acquiring a new one' (Bauböck, 1998, p. 43). The notion of additive identities and the idea that multiple identifications can be compatible are increasingly becoming common-place. Hybrid self-identification or hyphenated identities proliferate and are proudly claimed. However, as indicated, these kinds of identities also raise questions of management and reconciliation. Psychologically, it is not always simple to combine or mix different identities, and this may require particular coping strategies. And in social interactions, hyphenated identities require negotiation, validation, and accounting.

The possibility of hyphenated identities depends on the ways that these identities are defined. For example, in contrast to a civic conception of nationality, an ethnic one makes it very difficult for immigrants to adopt a hyphenated position. In Germany, a self-definition in terms of Turkish-German is much more problematic than is a definition as Irish-American or Italian-American in the USA. In the USA, these hyphenated identities are common and emphasize different ways of being an American. They combine the notion of national identity with that of a distinctive ethnic identity, and one is not an alternative to the other. However, in the context of US history, 'multiracial' and 'biracial' individuals have more difficulties with dealing with the volatile and shifting racial divide in the country. These individuals often have little choice about their racial identity because whiteness and blackness are typically considered competing definitions.

Anthropologists following Mary Douglas have come to use the terms 'ethnic' or 'racial anomalies or ambiguities' (Eriksen, 1993). These terms indicate people who do not fit into existing categories. They refer to irregularities in a regular pattern, of which children from racially and ethnically mixed marriages[3] are a prime example. Such children belong to two ethnic or racial groups at the same time. Because of this, they transgress the dichotomous scheme of belonging and thereby challenge the criteria on which social categorizations are constructed. After all, what is a child who has a Moluccan father and a Dutch mother, or one Turkish and one Greek parent? The apparently clear criteria on which ethnic and racial distinctions are made do not suffice to categorize these children. Anomalies disturb the pattern of clear categories and can, therefore, serve to blur boundaries and to challenge and break through existing categorizations. However, in the name of purity, they also can be used to define boundaries more strictly and to reject exceptions. Examples are not only limited to those plentiful in colonial history (Young, 1995). The British National Party (BNP) uses the value of diversity to argue against mixed relationships on its website.[4]

> We are against mixed-raced relationships because we believe that all species and races of life on this planet are beautiful and must be preserved. When whites take partners from other ethnic groups, a white family line that stretches back into deep pre-history is destroyed. And, of course, the same is true of the non-white side. We want generations that spring from us to be the same as us, look like us, and be moved by the same things as us. We feel that to preserve the rich tapestry of mankind, we must preserve ethnic differences, not 'mish-mash' them together.

Throughout history, many different classification systems have been used, but most of them categorize people only in one ethnic or racial category. This categorization can be based on visible characteristics and supposed descent, but in the case of children of mixed marriages, it can also depend on the parents' actions. For example, in many colonial systems the official 'race' of a child born to a colonial father and a native mother depended upon acknowledgement by the father (Stoler, 1995). People do not necessarily belong to the same 'race' as their parents or forefathers. Processes of racialization and changes in racial status are well known. For example, the English considered the Irish a distinctly inferior race during the eighteenth and (for a part of the) nineteenth century. And the racial status of early Irish immigrants to the USA was a matter of debate. As Ignatiev (in Cornell & Hartmann, 1998, p. 32) writes, 'In the early years, Irish were frequently referred to as "niggers turned inside out"; the Negroes, for their part, were sometimes called "smoked Irish", an appellation they must have found no more flattering than it was intended to be.'

In other words, ethnic and racial hybrids may well be recognized conceptually without needing to be recognized categorically as belonging to a distinctive and new category (Hirschfeld, 1996). That is, although hybrids may be recognized, they can, nonetheless, be counted categorically as, for example, black, Turkish, or Moroccan. It is also possible, however, that a separate intermediate category is established, as for example when a group is sufficiently large enough numerically to form a community with boundaries and symbols that indicate its uniqueness. The coloureds in South Africa, the mestizos in Mexico, and the Metis in Canada are examples of a new racial or ethnic status. The Metis are also acknowledged to be a people with a unique culture and identity (Roosens, 1998). These descendants of Native Canadians and colonial rulers define themselves explicitly on the basis of their mixed descent, and in some areas they even have developed their own language, Michif.

These mixed categories make up a separate social identity, in which the original plurality becomes a new singularity. Another example is the mulattos, who up to the end of the nineteenth century constituted a separate mixed category in the USA, alongside blacks and whites. This categorization was related to the mulattos' specific socioeconomic position between black slaves and free white men. However, when the socioeconomic necessity for a third category disappeared, so did their separate position. The children of these mixed marriages were thereafter considered and treated as blacks. After the abolition of slavery, the 'one drop of black blood' rule was put into practice, meaning that every person with one black parent or ancestor was classified as black. Originally, this rule was used by whites to keep the 'white race' pure and to protect their own dominant position. In the 1960s, however, the leaders of the black movement used this rule in their own way. People from mixed marriages were urged to consider themselves black, and other identifications were seen as a rejection and betrayal of the black community. Black identity can be considered a means of maintaining the black heritage and a unified fight against racial discrimination and oppression. For example, Spencer (1997, p. 52) argues that 'all black people (of "race" and "mixed race") have come this far together and absolutely must stay together until we are all free'.

In the remaining part of this chapter, I will discuss three examples of our empirical work. The first focuses on hyphenated identities in relation to research on psychological acculturation. This research has proposed useful models for describing and explaining acculturation processes but is not without its problems. The next example is the case of 'mixed race' within the South Moluccan community in the Netherlands. This example is used to examine some of the meanings involved and some of the ways in which 'biracial' individuals can position themselves. The third example focuses on the question of how the categories of ethnicity, religion, and nation are combined and the ways in which their potential contradictions are managed. Here, the interest is in the discursive strategies used for publicly explaining and accommodating these senses of belonging and membership. This issue is examined among a specific minority group, the Polish Tatars.

Acculturation and identification

Acculturation research is a growing field of study. Questions of behaviours, attitudes, values, and identifications that change with contacts between cultures are considered key issues in understanding immigration and cultural diversity (e.g. Liebkind, 2001). Thinking about acculturation can follow a unidimensional or a bidimensional approach. The former is based on an assimilation perspective and sees heritage culture maintenance and mainstream contacts as bipolar phenomena. In contrast, a bidimensional approach assumes that cultural maintenance and contacts are not necessarily bipolar or mutually exclusive. It is possible that these are two relatively independent dimensions that might result in bicultural positions. A bidimensional framework makes a combination of culture maintenance and mainstream contacts possible, resulting in four different acculturation positions[5] (Berry, 1997; Bochner, 1982). Assimilation, or one-sided adaptation to the dominant culture without preservation of the heritage culture, is one of these positions. The opposite of assimilation is separation, or the one-sided maintenance of the heritage culture without a focus on the dominant culture. In addition to these two positions, integration refers to that form of acculturation which favours both culture maintenance and cultural contacts, whereas marginalization refers to the rejection of both cultures.

In three empirical studies, Ryder et al. (2000) explicitly compared the unidimensional and bidimensional models of acculturation. They concluded that the latter constitutes a broader and more valid framework than the former. Other studies have reached a similar conclusion (e.g. Berry & Sam, 1996; Horenczyk, 1996; Laroche et al., 1996; Piontkowski et al., 2000; Taylor & Lambert, 1996; Ward & Rana-Deuba, 1999). Thus, there are both theoretical and empirical reasons to use a bidimensional perspective instead of a unidimensional one in acculturation research.

Ethnic identity becomes salient as part of the acculturation process. The concepts of ethnic identity and acculturation are often used interchangeably, but it seems better to consider the latter to be a broader construct that encompasses a wide range of changes. A sense of ethnic identity can be considered a central aspect of acculturation. By analogy with a two-dimensional model of acculturation, ethnic identification and identification as a member of the new society can be thought of as two dimensions that vary independently (Hutnik, 1991).

Traditionally, identification with one's own ethnic group was considered to be inversely related to identification with other groups, in particular the majority group. Research presented participants with a forced-choice test to measure ethnic identification, such as in studies using black and white dolls or questions such as, 'Do you feel Dutch *or* Turkish?' As a result, identification was studied as an either/or phenomenon and the possibility of a hyphenated identity was disregarded. The result was, for example, a conceptualization of positive ethnic self-esteem and majority group orientation as mutually exclusive attitudes. The more strongly people identified with their own minority group, the more they would distance themselves from others. Identification with the one would indicate dis-identification with the other.

However, in a situation where people are free to describe themselves, they do not always use this dichotomous scheme of ethnic identification (e.g. Hutnik, 1991; Sánchez & Fernández, 1993). Findings from cross-cultural studies suggest that ethnic identification is not necessarily a singular given but may be constituted of hyphenated identities that indicate varying degrees of identification with *both* the ethnic minority group and the majority group simultaneously. For example, for many young Turks living in the Netherlands, it is often not a question of being Turkish or Dutch but a question of the extent to which they feel Turkish as well as the degree to which they feel Dutch (Verkuyten, 1999). Among the first generation of migrants, the use of a singular ethnic label for self-definition is common, but later generations may reject such a label. For example, first-generation Turks and Moroccans strongly focus on their country of origin, whereas many youths consider themselves members of their ethnic in-group but also as having to relate to, if not quite be members of, the majority group.

Similar to Berry's model, Hutnik (1991)[6] makes a distinction between four identity positions: separation, where the identification is predominantly with one's own ethnic group; assimilation, where identification with the majority group predominates; integration (or hyphenated identity), where there is identification both with one's ethnic minority group and with the majority group; and marginality, where one identifies with neither the in-group nor the majority group.

These four positions have been found to exist among different ethnic minority groups in the USA (e.g. Sánchez & Fernández, 1993), the UK (e.g. Hutnik, 1991; Modood et al., 1997), Australia (e.g. Nesdale & Mak, 2000), and the Netherlands (Kemper, 1996; Phalet et al., 2000; van Heelsum, 1997; Vollebergh & Huiberts, 1996).

In several studies, we have examined ethnic self-definitions among minority members of different groups and different ages. In these studies, we asked participants how they see themselves, and we used four response categories representing Hutnik's four identity positions: predominantly ethnic minority group member (segregation), hyphenated position (minority-Dutch; integration), predominantly Dutch (assimilation), and 'neither' (marginality). The results of these studies are presented in Table 6.1, which shows that the about half of the participants of each ethnic and age group claimed to have a separate identity. In addition, around a third opted for an integrative position or hyphenated identity. In all samples, there were few participants that took an assimilative or marginal position. In short, different studies have shown that the four forms of identification do exist, but not all to the same extent. Defining oneself in terms of one's own ethnic group or in terms of a hyphenated position is more frequent, whereas adopting an assimilative and/or marginal position is rather exceptional. The same has been found in other countries, such as the UK (Modood et al., 1997) and Belgium (Snauwaert et al., 2003).

It is obvious that the four forms of identification are affected by many factors and conditions. There are structural limitations that have to do with socioeconomic positions, there are dominant discourses and ideologies, there are more or less visible characteristics, there are stereotypes and discrimination in society, there are

Table 6.1 Percentages of ethnic self-definitions for four identity positions

	Separation	Integration	Assimilation	Marginality
Middle adolescents				
Chinese (N = 119)	45%	41%	5%	9%
Turks (N = 122)	64%	20%	10%	6%
Late adolescents				
Chinese (N = 151)	43%	39%	10%	8%
Turks (N = 134)	56%	34%	4%	6%
Adults				
Iranians (N = 68)	44%	34%	9%	13%
Turks (N = 104)	54%	40%	2%	4%
Kurds (N = 103)	58%	31%	8%	3%

cultural characteristics and traditions, and there are geographical circumstances (Berry, 1990). For instance, the fact that in our research Chinese middle adolescents were more likely than their Turkish contemporaries to indicate that they had a hyphenated identity could have to do with the higher socioeconomic position and/or greater geographic dispersal of the Chinese group. Furthermore, discrimination and exclusion can lead to a segregated identification. Rumbaut (1994) found that among immigrant youths in the USA, the experience of discrimination was related to lower assimilative identification and higher segregated identification (Portes & MacLeod, 1996). We found the same among the group of Turkish late adolescents.[7]

There are clear indications that not all ethnic groups are equally accepted in society. In the Netherlands, the Turks, together with the Moroccans, belong to the least accepted ethnic groups, as research on the ethnic hierarchy shows (see Hagendoorn, 1995). The low appreciation of the Turks appears not only among the Dutch but also among young people from other ethnic minority groups (Verkuyten et al., 1996). One of our studies found that more than 50% of Dutch young people think that the Turks as a group are among the most discriminated against and 39% think that Turks belong to the groups that live under the worst socioeconomic circumstances (Verkuyten, 1992). For the Chinese, these percentages were respectively 4% and 19%. The Turks and Chinese themselves also perceive this difference in social position, and this may partially explain the higher percentage of segregated identification among Turkish young people.

However, it is not only socioeconomic conditions that are important for identification processes. The characteristics of the ethnic minority groups themselves, such as ethnic networks, are also important, as are forms of in-group social control and cultural values that emphasize the group and group loyalty. For example, people from cultures with a more collectivist orientation are assumed to feel more connected to the own group and to define themselves more strongly in terms of the in-group. Thus, in the study among the Chinese late adolescents, there was a significant association ($p < .01$) between identity position and individual collectivism (allocentrism). Post-hoc analyses indicated that the Chinese participants with a segregated identity were more collectivist oriented than the other three identity groups, which did not differ from each other.[8] Hence, differences between one group's orientation and another's may also be (partially) responsible for the observed difference in identification between the Chinese and Turkish participants.

There are various conditions that can influence ethnic identification. However, these conditions do not determine people's positions: there is always room for choice and negotiation. Assimilation, segregation, and integration are to a certain extent the result of people's own choices and orientations. For marginalization, this is generally different. People seldom choose to marginalize themselves, but are usually marginalized. In that case, access to the majority group is denied and, at the same time, contact and solidarity with co-ethnics are lost. This does not mean that choice is completely impossible, but it demands an autonomous stance in which the importance of ethnic-group ties is minimized. This can happen in at least two ways. Firstly, a superordinate self-definition or 'pan-ethnic identification' can be involved. In the Dutch context, people can think of themselves in terms of citizens, allochthonous, (im)migrants, or Europeans. Secondly, the rejection of a definition along group lines can be the outcome of an emphasis on personal characteristics and qualities. The rejection then does not happen on the basis of a feeling of marginalization but from an individualist position in which there is little room for self-definitions in terms of group membership (Bourhis et al., 1997). The straitjacket of group memberships is exchanged for an emphasis on individual capacities and personal goals. Similarly, the importance of ethnic identity can be minimized by emphasizing other social identities. Since there always are more social identities available, other ways of being can be put forward.

Restrictions and characteristics

The popular two-dimensional model of group identification offers a more elaborate approach to identification among ethnic minorities than a unidimensional one. It shows that ethnic-minority and majority-group identifications must be considered in conjunction with each other. However, in Chapter 4, we saw that ethnic self-identification is often more complex than this and involves a greater diversity of comparisons than this model allows. Yet, the implicit assumption behind the two-dimensional model is that ethnic minorities define their identity in comparison to only two groups. This clearly imposes a restriction on the possible comparisons that can be made and on our understanding of ethnic identity. To be able to account for diversity and to enable an evaluation of the two-dimensional model, four other restrictions and characteristics need to be taken into account (see also Rudmin, 2003).

Firstly, language is not innocent and labels often reflect a particular perspective. Multiethnic societies are sensitive to the terms used because these guide thinking about positions and responsibilities and imply a specific understanding and implicit political stance. Hence, various labels have been proposed for the same acculturation position, such as 'separation', 'segregation', or 'dissociation' for the one, and 'integration', 'bicultural', 'dual', or 'hyphenated' for the other. Furthermore, the well-known labels in Berry's model seem to reflect the perspective of the majority group. From a minority perspective, other terms may be more adequate. For example, instead of talking about 'separation' or 'dissociation', minority groups may talk of 'exclusion' or 'loyalty', and 'disloyalty' instead of 'integration'. This diversity of terms does not invalidate the two-dimensional model itself, but it does indicate that results and implications can be evaluated and interpreted in different ways.

Most research focuses on the acculturation attitudes of immigrants and minority groups and does not involve majority group members.[9] However, it is important to examine the views and reactions of the majority group because these play an important role in how open and inclusive society's orientation is towards diversity. For example, van Oudenhoven et al. (1998), found that both Moroccans and Turks preferred integration, whereas the Dutch had positive attitudes towards assimilation and integration. Furthermore, the Dutch liked separation least but believed this to be the position most frequently chosen by immigrants. Similarly, Arends-Tóah and van de Vijver (2003) found that views on acculturation and multiculturalism differ substantially between Dutch and Turkish adults. The Dutch preferred assimilation in all domains of life, whereas the Turks preferred integration in public domains and separation in private domains. Such a lack of 'fit' between majority and immigrant preferences of acculturation strategy has been found to be related to negative intergroup relations (Zagefka & Brown, 2002).

Secondly, ethnic identification may be relatively independent of cultural changes and adaptations. In an acculturation framework, ethnic identity is considered to be an aspect of psychological acculturation. However, acculturation is not a homogeneous process but differs for various cultural elements and spheres of life, such as the public and private domain. Enduring contacts with another culture do not lead to uniform changes in behaviours, contacts, attitudes, beliefs, and values. Furthermore, ethnic identity has been found to be relatively independent of other aspects of acculturation. In the UK, Hutnik (1991), for example, found that ethnic in-group identification does not necessarily coincide with ethnic-specific preferences and behaviour. Research among Mexicans living in the USA has concluded that identification is not strongly related to cultural adjustments (Hurtado et al., 1994). And, using Liebkind's (2001) distinction, Snauwaert et al. (2003) compared three conceptualizations of acculturation orientations: 1) preferred social contacts with the majority and one's own minority group; 2) preference for cultural maintenance and cultural adoption; and 3) majority and minority group identification. They found that among Turkish and Moroccan young people living in Belgium, these three conceptualizations yielded substantially different distributions of the participants across the four different acculturation positions. For example, in relation to social interaction and contacts, integration was the most popular position, whereas most participants chose separation when asked about their identifications.

People from ethnic groups may become socially and culturally assimilated to a great extent while still maintaining a strong sense of ethnic belonging. Therefore, the process of self-identification need not necessarily undergo a change similar to that undergone in relation to social and cultural features. An individual can still identify herself predominantly as Turkish, although she has made important cultural adaptations for effective living in the host country. Ethnic self-identification may be resistant to change and relatively independent of styles of cultural adaptation and social contacts. Moreover, increased social contacts and cultural changes can lead to the affirmation of in-group identity. From social identity theory (Tajfel & Turner, 1986), it can be argued that cultural adoption is an identity threat and that contact with an out-group makes a particular group membership more salient. Kosmitzki (1996) found support for this idea in her study among samples of Germans and Americans living in Germany and in the USA.

One of the advantages of stressing the independence of ethnic self-identification is that it makes it possible to study second- and third-generation immigrants to a greater degree. Their expressed attitudes and overt manifestations of lifestyle may be quite identical with that of the majority of young people, but they can maintain varying senses of ethnic belonging. Another advantage is that it allows us to put political discussion in perspective. For example, Dutch politicians are often worried by the lack of Dutch identification among minority groups. But a lack of such identification does not imply a lack of interest in Dutch culture, or that regular and supportive relationships with Dutch people are not being developed. Social contacts, cultural adaptations, and group identifications do not have to correspond closely. They are psychologically not equally demanding and sociologically not equally necessary for the effective functioning of society.

Thirdly, the model focuses on how strongly people identify with a group or on quantitative differences. The four identification positions are distinguished on the basis of low and high identification with one's own group and the majority group. However, as Cameron and Lalonde (1994) found, differences in identity positions are not only a matter of decline of identification, but also of a transformation and change in what it means to be part of an ethnic minority group. Often it is tacitly assumed that the degree of identification is crucial, and little attention is paid to the divergent meanings that identification can have for individuals and groups. If the degree of identification with both groups corresponds, it is implicitly assumed that the meanings and consequences are also corresponding. But this is not necessarily the case. There can be important qualitative differences in identification. For example, young people with Moluccan parents often characterize themselves as both Moluccan and Dutch. However, to them, being Dutch is more a neutral and objective fact, and this self-definition is primarily based on an acknowledgement of objective characteristics such as having a Dutch passport and the fact that they have been born in the Netherlands. That these young people view themselves as Dutch does not mean that they also feel Dutch. On the other hand, they do feel Moluccan, and this has an emotional value for many of them. Moreover, people of Turkish origin can identify as strongly with the Turks as with the Dutch, but the meaning of these identifications may differ substantially. They may consider themselves Turkish by descent, but culturally more Dutch. Moreover, identification with the Turks involves stereotypical expectations different from identification with the Dutch. Therefore, an equally strong identification with one's in-group and the majority group does not imply similar meanings. These meanings, however, should be considered in relation to the strength of identification. In particular, the *intensity* of behaviour may be predicted by the strength of identification, but the *sort* of behaviour is likely to be determined by the stereotypical or normative content of identities (Turner et al., 1987).

Three interpretations

And fourthly, there is the question of how to interpret the different identification and acculturation positions. There are various possibilities that will be discussed more fully in Chapter 7. Here I want to draw attention to three of these. The first two are more on the psychological level, and the third one focuses on the level of social interaction.

In the first interpretation, most studies examine psychological acculturation in terms of the mental and behavioural changes that an individual experiences. The focus is on relatively stable or enduring changes in internal dispositions and characteristics. This does not have to imply a permanent or fixed classification of people into one of four 'types' of being as, for example, assimilationists or separatists. We could take a long-term developmental perspective, in which we would examine whether any gradual changes occur over time and in what sequence change is most likely. Schuyt (1995), for example, argues that a development from marginalization through segregation into integration is more likely than that of marginalization into integration. The fact that people consistently define themselves in a certain way does not mean that this self-definition always has or will be there. There are also psychological developments and these do not exclude momentarily more stable self-understanding. Psychologically, people can adopt a more consistent acculturation position that affects their well-being and behaviour (see Berry & Sam, 1996).

For example, there are indications that from a psychological point of view the least desirable positions are the marginal and assimilative ones. Both positions imply a certain denial of one's own complex reality, although acceptance of this is considered a prerequisite for effective coping. A marginal orientation is traditionally associated with psychological problems and stress. One way to deal with this is by adopting a segregative or assimilative position. The first of these options offers the individual or group a renewed sense of security and is linked to a strong emphasis on a person's own identity and culture, and this can involve group militancy. The second of the two implies other psychological costs, such as those detailed in, for example, Fordham and Ogbu's (1986) concept of 'racelessness' (Fordham, 1988). They use this concept for African-American students who are motivated to do well in school and thereby distance themselves from the African-American community. These students believe that educational achievement offers an increased chance for success in society. They can (partially) accept the negative stereotypes about blacks because they do not apply these to themselves. Other African-Americans criticize them, and, at the same time, they are not completely accepted by their white fellow students. They are criticized because they do not comply with a group norm that views educational success as useless in a white supremacist society. Other African-American young people see failing in school as a sign of their rejection of society and as self-defining. From their perspective, striving for success in school is a form of acting white or selling out. Added to which fellow white students will not accept them, because they are and remain visibly different. Thus, those African-American students who choose to strive for success become 'raceless' and are likely to be characterized by a strong degree of self-confidence and educational commitment. However, at the same time, they are likely to suffer from psychological costs such as cultural alienation, depression, fear, and loneliness (Arroyo & Zigler, 1995).

In contrast to marginalization and assimilation, the psychological correlates of integration and segregation appear to be more positive. Our research among Turkish and Chinese middle adolescents (Verkuyten & Kwa, 1994) found that those with a marginal or predominantly assimilative position scored lower on a diverse range of psychological well-being measures (such as self-esteem, and life satisfaction) than did young people with an integrative identification (Turkish-Dutch, Dutch-Chinese) or with a segregated identification (Turk, Chinese). These results are similar to findings reported in the international literature, and they indicate that preserving a tie with one's own group and culture has a positive influence on well-being. Crucially, these results are a correction to the traditional view that relates a bicultural, dual, or hyphenated identification to feelings of insecurity, fear, and denial. This idea rests mainly on assumptions that such identities would necessarily lead to a conflict of cultures within an individual or group and thus to a 'life between two cultures'. More recently, however, the beneficial aspects of a dual identification have been pointed to, such as flexibility and the ability to adjust to and function within two different groups (LaFromboise et al., 1993). Furthermore, identifying with two groups and living within (rather than between) two cultures is thought to lead to a reflexive attitude that enables a critical and innovative view of groups and cultures. A hyphenated and bicultural position can result in a broader horizon, a sharper view of social relationships, and the ability to act as an intermediary in attempts to bridge the gap between different ethnic and cultural groups.

The second interpretation emphasizes situational perceptions and evaluations. A developmental approach with a focus on more stable psychological correlates does not imply that momentary and situational identifications are unimportant. People can differ in their current preference for an assimilative, integrative, or other position, and this preference influences their thoughts, feelings, and behaviours. In other words, acculturation attitudes, for example, can be examined as context-sensitive responses to questions of heritage-culture maintenance and change. Categorization, stereotyping, and related phenomena can be seen as context-dependent processes rather than expressions of enduring and stable psychological characteristics (Turner et al., 1987). Thus, depending on the comparative context, ethnic minorities may evaluate cultural maintenance and mainstream contacts differently. For example, in relation to the majority group, arguing for maintenance of the heritage culture may be an assertion or reaffirmation of identity (Kosmitzki, 1996), whereas, in relation to the ethnic in-group, it may indicate commitment and loyalty (Verkuyten, 1999). In short, issues of cultural maintenance and change may have different meanings in intragroup and in intergroup situations.

In an experimental questionnaire study undertaken among 151 Chinese participants between 17 and 28 years of age living in the Netherlands, we found evidence that the meanings attributed to instances or examples of cultural maintenance and change do indeed differ situationally (Verkuyten & De Wolf, 2002b). In a between-subjects design, participants' attention was focused on either an intragroup (Chinese in the Netherlands) or an intergroup (Chinese versus Dutch) context. The attitude towards cultural maintenance was examined in terms of the extent to which it was considered important by the Chinese to maintain their own culture as well as close ties with Chinese people. In addition, cultural contact with the mainstream was examined in terms of the importance attached to adopting Dutch culture and having close ties with the Dutch. Both dependent measures were moderately associated (r = .24, p < .01), and pairwise comparison of means showed that cultural maintenance was favoured significantly more than cultural contacts. In addition, the analysis showed that participants in the intergroup condition were more strongly in favour of maintenance of the heritage culture than those in the intragroup condition.

Subsequently, classification of the participants in the four acculturation positions was achieved by a bipartite split of the two acculturation measures. The four acculturation positions were found: separation, integration, assimilation, and marginalization. In agreement with other studies, separation and integration predominated. However, in the intergroup context, a third of the participants indicated a separated position, whereas in the intragroup condition, less than one-fifth opted for this position. Thus, in the intergroup condition, separation was stronger than in the intragroup condition, in which assimilation was more frequent. In both conditions, an equal percentage of participants (around 55%) indicated an integrative position of acculturation.

These results are important for interpreting existing research on acculturation, which typically investigates acculturation attitudes in relation to the majority group. Hence, implicitly, the studies use an intergroup context to examine questions of cultural maintenance and change, without paying attention to the distinctions and relationships within the subject's own group. We have found similar context-sensitive responses for identification and self-stereotyping, as I will explain in Chapter 7.

The third interpretation is to see the different acculturation and identification positions as discursive actions. Here the focus is not on relatively stable inner dispositions or on situational perceptions and evaluations, but on the flexible expression of appraisals in social interactions. The object of investigation is the ways that immigrants and minorities define and negotiate their identity. Ethnic self-definitions are seen as interactional accomplishments that are sensitive to potential criticisms and justifications (Bhatia, 2002; Bhatia & Ram, 2001; Ullah, 1990). Hyphenated identities are considered to involve a constant process of dialogue, struggle, and mediation that is connected to a larger set of political and historical conditions and practices. Acculturation and identity positions can be treated as contextual stances or arguments concerning ethnic self-definitions. That is to say, the ways in which discourses on ethnic identity are actually used, negotiated, managed, and accounted for in interactions can be examined.

One of our focus-group studies provides an example of how the uses to which and the methods by which discourse is used can be studied. For this study, we approached students of Chinese descent (17–29 years). In total, 22 students (13 women and 9 men) participated in six small focus groups (Verkuyten & De Wolf, 2002a). In the groups, the moderator's introduction focused on the question of 'what it means to be Chinese'. At the start of each session, the moderator used this question for eliciting ethnic self-definitions. Thus, by the introduction and by posing a direct question, the moderator rendered the very act of self-definition relevant and accountable. The expected response was an explanation for the participants' sense of ethnic identity, and that is what was given.

Following acculturation research, we used the four acculturation positions to categorize the participants' answers. Nine participants indicated an integration mode and thus defined themselves as both Chinese and Dutch. Six participants defined themselves as only Chinese (separation), three as Dutch (assimilation), and four as neither Chinese nor Dutch (marginal). While no doubt helpful for some purposes, such a categorization has its limitations. To start with, although most participants settled for a particular self-definition, which one was by no means self-evident, unproblematic, and consistent. Added to which, a classification in acculturation positions ignores the social context of accountability and argumentation. These two points are illustrated by the following extract from the start of a discussion:

1	*Sven*:	Erm, let's see, what does it mean to be Chinese? Yes, in principle, in principle, erm, I do not really feel, erm, 100% Chinese, or 100% Dutch.
	Wailing:	Yes, yes.
5	*Sven*:	I am who I am, so you know, in fact, erm.
	Wailing:	Yes, I know what you mean, but I feel 100% Chinese.
	Sven:	You do?
	Wailing:	Yes, I did grow up in the Netherlands, but yes.
	Sven:	Hm.
10	*Aizhen*:	Were you born in the Netherlands?
	Wailing:	I wasn't born in the Netherlands, I was born in Hong Kong, but, erm, there are quite a lot of things you pick up from your parents and the like, and, erm, at school you pick up other things.
15	*Sven*:	Yes, yes.
	Wailing:	Nevertheless I feel 100% Chinese.
	Chun-Kin:	Yes, perhaps, 100% is perhaps a bit, erm, too extreme, I think.
	Sven:	Yes.

In lines 1–3, Sven pauses, delays answering, and repeats the question before he starts to give an explanation about feeling neither completely Chinese nor Dutch. In the discussions, there were several of these pauses, hesitations, self-corrections, and false starts. These are typical of talk about difficult and sensitive topics (Condor, 2000; van Dijk, 1984). Interestingly, in giving an answer, Sven frames it as an answer 'in principle' (lines 1 and 2), a phrase which he repeats. This also suggests that giving a particular self-definition is not a simple thing to do because there are always many different circumstances and situations that may affect one's self-understanding. In addition, the use of the phrase 'in principle' allows the presentation of a different self-definition in relation to specific practical and situational considerations.

Further, in line 6 Sven is interrupted by Wailing, who, in contrast, shows his ethnic commitment by arguing that he feels 100% Chinese. Subsequently, Wailing is criticized by Chun-Kin, whose criticism (in line 17) is mild. He suggests that 'perhaps 100% is a bit too extreme', and does not go as far as to say, for example, 'that is extreme', but the idea is expressed and explanations are offered. This shows that ethnic self-definitions are not self-evident, but are discussed and accounted for, not only in response to the moderator, but particularly in relation to the other participants. Ethnic self-definitions can be seen as accomplishments that are sensitive to justifications and criticisms. To express their views and to persuade others, the participants orient themselves to the possibility that their definitions are discounted or undermined.

In the discussions, biological references and related issues of being a victim of racism and discrimination, as well as the language of early socialization, were clearly treated as acceptable ways to account for ethnic identity. I will discuss this in Chapter 7. However, such accounts offer deterministic explanations. The emphasis is on the inevitable way that people are marked biologically or 'moulded' culturally, leaving little room for personal agency. In these explanations, a sense of ethnic identity is not a matter of one's own choice and responsibility. You are what you are, and you personally cannot be criticized for that. Hence, these deterministic explanations enable the normative issues involved to be avoided; but they are also problematic because they deny agency and the possibility of change.

In the discussions, there were several instances in which the participants claimed an active and constructive role for themselves. For example, they talked about personal decisions and motivations and presented themselves as responsible persons who make their own decisions without denying their ethnic background. The next three extracts are examples of the way in which the language of personal choice and preference was deployed.

Loeng: What I'm doing is, erm, combining the positive sides of Western culture with Chinese culture, because, erm, yes, that's always better than just one culture.

Yi Yen: Yes, it is a lot of fun, yes, to know something of two cultures.

Moderator: So you don't perceive the fact that you are in between two languages and cultures as a problem?

Kee: No, no problem.

Yun-Shan: You simply take what you need, or what you think you will need.

Huan: You simply pick the good things.

Jenny: Yes.

Huan: It's an advantage, you have a choice. In principle, you choose what you want. You look at things from two sides, what you can and what you can't, and you simply determine your own way.

Qiao Wei: In a way I do like being a Chinese who grew up in the Netherlands, and not a Dutchman who, erm.

Sidney: Yes.

Wing: Me, too.

Qiao Wei: You know both cultures. That's always a good thing.

Wing: Yes, then you can take your pick from both cultures.

Here the participants present themselves as agents who make their own combinations and choices. Interestingly, in these extracts and in the discussions in general, references to personal choices were particularly evident in those instances where participants talked about different cultural influences. It is here that choices became relevant and justifications were provided. In the talk about these different influences, there is the familiar reification of culture and an equation between ethnicity and culture. The Chinese and the Dutch are presented as two groups with their own particular cultures. However, culture is here not presented as something that inevitably shapes people. Rather, it is argued that personal choices and combinations are possible *because* they grew up in both cultures and know them well. Thus, in these instances, learning and socialization are not presented as determining people, but as enabling them to develop their own lives. An emphasis on personal choice and self-determination is difficult to reconcile with the idea that people are moulded by their culture, but it is also problematic when people do not have intimate knowledge of what they can choose from or want to combine.

A combination of cultures or a multicultural influence is also presented as a positive thing. It is not only very nice (first and last of the three extracts) and better (first extract) but also 'always' advantageous (second and third extracts). Here the participants seem to draw upon a progressive discourse about multiculturalism in which monoculturalism is presented as one-sided and restricted. Furthermore, the combination of different cultures is not presented as psychologically problematic, as is the case in popular notions about 'living between two cultures'. The speakers do not present themselves as experiencing cultural clashes and as being forced to deal with the worst of both worlds. Instead, they argue that they can combine and choose the best of both.

What this shows is that the different identification and acculturation positions can be interpreted in various ways and on different levels. Interpretations of a more psychological or a social-interactive character are possible. Furthermore, acculturation positions and identity options are also defined at the societal level, as for example, in migration and integration policies. I will return to some of these interpretations in Chapter 7.

Mixed ethnic people

The lives of children from ethnically and racially mixed marriages are often described as being full of uncertainty, confusion, and tragedy. They face all kinds of social and psychological tensions and conflicts—identity problems in particular. According to Stonequist (1935), their position is typically marginal and problematic. These children do not really belong to their mother or father's ethnic or racial group, and neither community is prepared to fully accept them. They live in a situation of permanent conflict and remain insecure in their ethnic or racial identity. The (older) clinical literature offers many descriptions of children who, because of their marginal position, suffer from feelings of isolation, not belonging to anything, and confusion. A singular identity is seen as the only healthy response for these children. The solution that this literature suggests is that such individuals should choose one of their two group identities, which in reality comes down to a committed choice for the minority or low-status identity.

Researchers have increasingly been arguing, however, that a racial or ethnically mixed identity is not by definition a burden and might even be the psychologically more healthy ideal for children of mixed marriages. Empirical research shows that in some cases these children can develop a positive ethnic or racial identity and can reject a choice in terms of either the one or the other (e.g. Pinderhughes, 1995; Tizard & Phoenix, 1993; Wilson, 1987). According to these studies, children from ethnically mixed marriages would be better equipped to function in different situations and to take the demands and requirements of both groups into consideration. They would be able to develop a bicultural or integrative orientation in which they identify with both groups. This approach is reminiscent of Park (1928), who introduced the marginal man concept and recognized the positive or bicultural aspects of it.

Particular outcomes and developments depend on many things, such as local and broader social conditions (Mark, 2001; Parker & Song, 2001). For example, when one is of white Jewish and African-American heritage, identity negotiation is not simple in the context of antagonism between Jewish and black groups (Zack, 1996). Moreover, in her study in the UK, Wilson (1987) found that a secure mixed-race identity was associated with living in a multiracial area. She suggests that this is because there are sufficient numbers of mixed-race people to make 'mixed race' a viable option. Furthermore, sociocultural changes in many societies have expanded the identity options and self-understandings of 'mixed' individuals. For example, there are now mixed-race movements and foundations, as well as associations of multiethnic people,[10] as well as national conferences on the mixed-race experience. Books, magazines, and brochures are being produced, and there is a proliferation of autobiographical literature exploring the experiences of 'mixed' individuals. The aim of all these efforts is to try to create a sense of identity, to claim the right to choose one's ethnic affiliations, and to celebrate mixed race and ethnic people and families. In addition, it is claimed that the unique mixed perspective would offer new and much-needed ideas on how people can live together and prosper in a multicultural world (Nakashima, 1996). Others see the acknowledgement of the multiracial category as a step towards the elimination of racial thinking. For example, in a speech at the 1997 Multiracial Solidarity March, Michael Byrd said, 'Mixed-race is a repudiation of the notion of racial purity. This discussion of racial identity is already blowing the lid off most people's perceptions of race, and that's good. Eventually, we would scrap all racial classifications. Until that day comes, a multiracial category would be a good first step along the way to racial sanity.'[11]

In our research among South Moluccans in the Netherlands, we interviewed people whose parents were Moluccan and those who had a Moluccan and a Dutch parent. In the interviews, a major distinction that was made within the Moluccan group revolved around the question of what it really means to be Moluccan and how this group should be characterized. The participants talked about 'real' Moluccans, thus defining the essence of the category and, by implication, constructing a group of 'less real' Moluccans. To make this distinction, a racial discourse as well as one about culture and language was used (see Chapter 4). All participants made a distinction at one time or another between what they called 'full-blooded' or 'real' Moluccans and 'half-breeds'. Real Moluccans are born to two Moluccan parents, and the labels of 'full-blooded' and 'half-breeds' were used by both groups of Moluccans. For instance, one of the participants said at the beginning of the interview that only his father is Moluccan, and then he concluded, 'So I am a half-breed.' Real Moluccans were clearly evaluated more positively than those who were only 'half'-Moluccan. Participants with only one Moluccan parent said that they felt inferior or had felt inferior in the past. In the words of one of them, 'I used to feel a bit inferior, because they were real Moluccans, and I was part Moluccan and part Dutch.' Another remarked, 'You are not a real Moluccan, you're just a half-caste', and yet another said, 'Sometimes you notice that they [other Moluccans] think, you're not really Moluccan.' For most participants, being 'half-breed' had a negative connotation, and the participants did not speak in terms of double or mixed blood. A 'half-breed' was defined not by what they were but by what they were not, and, although they applied the concept to others and to themselves, they did not attach any new specific characteristics to it. The term indicated no separate racial status with its own meanings, but stipulated what was lacking (Verkuyten et al., 1999).

In the interviews, the emphasis was on being 'half'-Moluccan, and not on being 'half'-Dutch, which was not considered a very positive thing. This evaluative distinction is different from what has been described in the USA and the UK in terms of desired whiteness, whereby 'mixed-race' people try to increase the distance between themselves and blackness (e.g. Gordon, 1995; Tizard & Phoenix, 1993). However, these reactions should be understood in their historical and political context. Using the particular history and political position of the Moluccans to define the group in a positive way (see Chapter 4) had an influence on the position and status of 'mixed-race' people.

Much of the theoretical and research literature depicts the racial identity options available to 'mixed' people as falling into one of two binary categories: black or biracial. Rockquemore (1999), however, takes a social interaction approach and argues that 'mixed' individuals can construct various understanding of their racial or ethnic identity. These variations are negotiated in relation to the legitimate racial and ethnic identities available in the social environment. The racial and ethnic self-understandings are interactionally presented and validated. Rockquemore synthesizes the growing literature on multiracial identity by presenting a typology of four different racial identity options. These four options have some similarities with the four acculturation positions discussed previously.

The first one is the singular identity option in which racial identity is either exclusively black or exclusively white. The former position is of course the most common because biracial people are typically assumed to choose, or normatively forced to adopt, a black identity. In our research, one-quarter of the 'mixed-race' participants took this position. The following extract gives an example of this, as the participant indicated later in the interview that he does not feel Dutch.[12] 'I don't think in terms of, am I Moluccan or am I not? I just am Moluccan, I just know it. Am I Moluccan or Dutch? No, I'm just Moluccan. My friends always call me a light-coloured full-blood. They see me just as a Moluccan, and not as Dutch.' What this example shows is that some participants took an exclusively Moluccan position and that the acceptance and validation of a significant other is important in this. In the interviews, a singular self-definition in terms of Moluccan was linked to a political stance in which the importance of maintaining the Moluccan culture and the struggle for the RMS (the Republic of South Molucca) was emphasized. These participants indicated that they are very proud to be Moluccan; for them, being Moluccan entailed that 'you don't let yourself be suppressed'.

The second option identified by Rockquemore is the border or blended identity that is conceptualized as a separate and new racial category that is neither exclusively white or black but a blending or mixing of the two. There are two different possibilities here. The first is that 'others in the actor's social network accept and *validate* the category biracial as an identity option' (Rockquemore & Brunsma, 2002, p. 344, their italics). The other possibility is that the biracial self-understanding is neither validated nor considered a legitimate new identity option. In our research, the latter situation predominated. About half of the participants[13] indicated that they felt both Moluccan and Dutch because they simply *are* both Moluccan and Dutch. The next two extracts are examples.

If you are a full-blood, you're just a Moluccan. You are that way or you're not. For half-breeds, even if you really feel like a Moluccan, you're just not, although you may want to be it. There are half-breeds who say that they are Moluccan and 'away with the Netherlands'. I think that is strange—you just are half-Dutch. I think it's strange if you deny that. Then you just neglect your other origin, if you're a half-breed. I used to be a bit like, you know, you just wanted to be something, either Dutch or Moluccan. And then I wanted to be a real Moluccan. I thought like, if I could only speak the language. I wish I were a full-breed. But not now anymore. It is not more important than my Dutch side.

When I have a real argument with particular people, they say: 'You're not really Dutch, you're not really Moluccan.' Then I really think like, what's that got to do with anything? I am a Moluccan and I am also Dutch. I really don't feel like I am less Moluccan or more Dutch.

These participants rejected an exclusive self-definition of Moluccan. They pointed out that they are also Dutch, were born in the Netherlands, have Dutch friends, and have been raised partly within Dutch culture. Several of these participants stated that in the past they had struggled with the question of who they were (as can be seen in the first extract above), and have had the feeling that they had to make a choice, which, for them, was impossible because each choice entailed a denial of one of the two backgrounds.

In the interviews, a blended self-understanding predominated. These participants indicated that they did not really or completely belong to one of the two groups. After all, they are both Moluccan and Dutch, but other Moluccans see and treat them as 'half-breeds', and the Dutch see and treat them as Moluccans. However, this intermediate position does not have to be seen as problematic but can also be evaluated positively, as the next extract indicates. 'Yes, I am a half-Moluccan, so I feel both Moluccan and Dutch, but, to say so, neither really. I always say to myself that I am a bit of both, but neither of them fully. And actually that is something I really like, that I have something of two cultures. Because I see that each culture has its positive and negative sides. I am just both, but neither really, you know.'

A third racial identity option identified by Rockquemore is a protean one. This involves the more or less fluid movement between black, white, and biracial identities, depending on the interactional setting and situational requirements.[14] This movement can be interpreted in terms of capacities and skills, as in the following extract. 'You've got half of things from here [the Netherlands]. But I see that as something positive. I can take positive things out of both cultures. I think that I have less problems with the things here and with adapting to different situations. I know both settings and I feel equally comfortable in both.'

However, most participants argued that their movement between identities was related to context-dependent saliency. It was pointed out that the actual situation is important for whether one feels Moluccan or Dutch. In some situations, such as among Moluccans, one feels Moluccan; in other situations, such as among Dutch people, one feels Dutch. However, the presence of Moluccan or Dutch people can also work the other way round. Or, as one of the participants put it, 'I feel Moluccan if I am with Dutch people, and I feel Dutch when I am around Moluccans.' A Moluccan girl gave the following answer to the question of when she really feels Moluccan: 'Yes, especially if you're just among Moluccans you know. And sometimes also when you are somewhere where there are no Moluccans at all, then you also feel like, yes, still different.'

This quotation indicates that the Moluccan identity can play a role in different situations. But this does not mean that this identity has the same meaning in divergent situations. Feeling Moluccan among Moluccans is probably not the same as feeling Moluccan among Dutch people. Similarly, feeling Dutch among Dutch people is probably not the same as feeling Dutch among Moluccans.

Rockquemore's fourth option is the transcendent identity whereby biracial people refuse to define themselves in any racial terms but prefer a self-understanding as individual, human, or a social category other than race. Their intermediate position leads to a discounting of racial categorizations and a challenging and disrupting of racial definitions. These people typically argue that race is meaningless and that they do not believe in racial identities. There were a few participants who took up this position at various points of the interview. However, at other points, they defined themselves in terms of one of the other three options. I have indicated this in Chapter 4 in discussing 'problematic constructions'.

Rockquemore's four biracial identity options can be interpreted in terms of negotiations and interactional accomplishments.[15] Her focus is on the various understandings of their mixed identity that people define and construct in social interactions. However, the discussion of the four options does not tell us much about how people actually manage mixed identities. That is to say, it does not address the question of the discursive devices and strategies that are used to account for hybridity. I will have more to say about this question in Chapter 7 in relation to our focus-group study among Chinese students. Here, I will give a brief discussion of another case of interactional strategies related not to race but to the blending of ethnicity, nationality, and religion.

Managing hybridity: The case of the Polish Tatars

As indicated earlier, questions of hybridity and the intersection of multiple identities are overtheorized and understudied. 'Hybridity' has become something of a catchword, but the number of empirical studies is limited. Theories of inter-section emphasize the many sources of identity but tend to neglect the empirical issue about the ways that these are actually managed. The notion that people occupy potentially competing identity positions raises the important question of how these positions are negotiated and dealt with.

We have examined this question in a study[16] among the Polish Tatars, a numerically small (at present around 6000 people) Islamic group that has lived for more than 600 years in Poland, a country where the national identity is largely based on being Roman Catholic. The situation of the Polish Tatars is an interesting one because of their long historical presence in Poland together with their Oriental and Islamic background. For the Polish Tatars, being a Tatar, a Muslim, and a Pole at the same time is not only possible but central to their self-understanding (Warminska, 1997). Tatars constantly stress the integration of these aspects without limiting the importance of any of them. This raises the question of how these different, seemingly contradictory, identities are combined or managed. How do Polish Tatars reconcile their Tatar, Polish, and Muslim identities?

In addressing this question, we focused on group narratives. A growing number of theorists have argued that an important way in which identities and self-understandings are given shape is through narrative (e.g. Ashmore et al., 2004; Bhabha, 1990; Hermans & Kempen, 1993; Holland et al., 2001). As indicated in Chapter 3, ethnic and national narratives provide accounts of the group's origin, its history, and its relationship to others. Identities involve continuing stories that individuals and groups construct and tell about themselves and which locate them in society. However, the stories available to tell are not unrestricted. Different groups have different narrative opportunities and face different narrative constraints. Historical, social, and political patterns limit and shape the possible group narratives or the available narrative space through which groups can manage and negotiate their multiple identities. Particularly minority groups with a history in a society that has a clearly dominant group are faced with the task of dealing with the tensions and contradictions between the various identitites. The Polish Tatars are an example.[17]

Hybridity, in any real sense, implies that one is able to claim desired images, positions, and self-understandings in a variety of contexts and especially in public spaces. Being a Polish Tatar is often a more 'problematic' or accountable issue in public than in private life. Hence, we investigated how different identities intersect at the level of societal, public discourse. Apart from visits to Tatar communities and villages and informal interviews with Tatars, two Tatar cultural magazines were collected.[18] The media is a powerful ideological institution that affects identities, and the magazines offer an accessible and systematic source for studying this. In total, 27 issues published between 1988 and 2001 were examined.

Being a Tatar, a Muslim, and a Pole

For the Polish Tatars, being simultaneously a Tatar, a Muslim, and a Pole is central to their self-understanding. In the interviews and the magazines, there are many stories that deal with their origin, religious background, and their presence in and connection to Poland.

One narrative refers to the idea that the Tatars have of themselves as being descendants of Mongols that lived under Genghis Khan in their first motherland, the steppe. The time of the conquests made by the Mongolian Empire is presented as the glorious past of the Tatar warriors riding from their storied homeland. The Tatar ancestors are presented as a warrior people living on the wild steppe. These forefathers are depicted as being courageous, powerful, and full of dignity. This image has been carried with them through the centuries and is used to describe the identity of the present-day Tatars.

Another main narrative is that of religion. In the interviews and in many articles, aspects of Islam are discussed and described in various ways, connecting the Tatars with different communities. For example, Islam is the religion of the ancestors and is presented as a source of solidarity with the Tatar past. Further, the fact that Islam has survived in a Roman Catholic surrounding bears witness to the strength of this religion. In addition, Islam links the Tatars with Muslims all over the world. Thanks to Islam, the Tatars can see themselves as part of a larger community of the Muslim 'umma'.

A third narrative is that of the Tatars in Poland. This includes events and situations since their settling in this country, as well as biographies of important figures from the past (war heroes, writers, political leaders, etc.), and Tatar involvement in the struggle for Polish independence. The fact that in various wars, Tatars did fight and gave their lives for Poland is presented as decisive proof of their patriotism and true Polishness. Within the framework of this Polish narrative, Poland is the new motherland, or, as it is often referred to, the 'adopted motherland'. Polish territory and landscape have become their land. It is argued that the territory has great significance, as Tatar ancestors are buried in Polish soil. The Polish narrative portrays the Tatars as the adopted sons of Poland. Ties with Poland are presented as deep and sincere because of the Tatars' presence in Poland for many centuries. Polishness is seen as an indissoluble and chosen feature of their identity. It has not been imposed by anyone, and the fact of being *Polish* Tatars is stressed as distinguishing them from Tatars elsewhere.

For the Polish Tatars, there is no inconsistency in being Tatar and Muslim as well as Polish simultaneously. Thus, the question for us was how were these elements or narratives combined or reconciled. In the analysis, we identified discursive strategies that relate to differences in identity definitions and strategies that emphasize identity connections. By the defining of identities in different ways, a conceptual space is created in which the three narratives can coexist. A focus on connections, in turn, brings the elements together by mutual diffusion or by stressing the similarities.

Identity definitions

There are clear differences in the ways that the different stories are presented in the magazines. In general, the Polish narrative was historical and factual, whereas the narratives about the Tatar past and about Islam had a mythical and symbolic form.

For example, most of the articles using the Polish narrative were written in a historically factual way and covered events from the fourteenth century up to the present. The articles were often written by specialists in the field, such as historians and social scientists. They contained many references to primary and secondary sources as well as vivid and detailed descriptions with concrete examples that were used to illustrate and substantiate the argumentation. These were stories with all kinds of details, including exact period, time of day, place, circumstances, and actual behaviour, all suggesting a careful recording of the events (Edwards & Potter, 1992). Old photographs added a documentary aspect to the writing.

In contrast, the Tatar narrative was mythologized. The main device used in the Oriental narrative was symbolism (Verkuyten, 1995a). Symbolism can be found in the poetic metaphors and images used. The prevalent message is nostalgia for the Eastern world, its beauty and mystery, or the glorious past of Tatar warriors. The exoticism of the Middle East, its vivid symbolism, and the images of tall minarets or of the rising sun, are reflected in Tatar poems. Similarly, Oriental motifs, such as Tatar warriors on horseback in the steppe, and beautiful girls with dark eyes and black hair, are also poeticized in the lyrics.[19]

The result of the ways in which the narratives are told is that they are presented at different levels of 'reality' so that the potential contradictions between them are avoided. The Tatars can see themselves as Polish and Oriental at the same time. The former refers to historical reality, whereas the latter is the symbolic expression of the spiritual nature or metaphysical essence (Blum, 2002) of the Tatars. On the one hand, there is the factual story about the Tatars being Polish heroes who participated in many Polish wars, and the detailed accounts and photographs prove this. On the other hand, the Tatars are presented as having a spiritual connection to the Oriental and Muslim world, and the beauty of minarets is an expression of this. The stories provide different understandings of Polish Tatars that do not contradict each other. They can exist side by side in the discursive space in which Polish Tatarness is defined.

Connections and similarities

For the Tatars, Islam not only has a symbolic meaning but is also central to their everyday life. Islam as practised by the Polish Tatars is the main character-istic distinguishing them from the Roman Catholic Poles. The Tatars perceive themselves as authentic Muslims even though their religion developed as a specialized local variant of Islam. Furthermore, the social and cultural aspects of their religious life are central to maintaining Tatar ethnic solidarity. In contrast, Roman Catholicism is strongly connected with the idea of the Polish nation and is a central aspect of 'being Polish' (Warminska, 1997). Polish national identity is largely based on being Catholic and includes negative stereotypes of other religions, particularly Islam.

Hence, the Tatars' claim to Polishness can be problematic when their religious background is emphasized too much. It is difficult to find the right balance between being Polish and Muslim at the same time. There is a potential conflict between the two aspects, raising the question of how these two identities can be accom-modated or reconciled.[20]

One of the ways in which the two are brought together is by emphasizing religious similarities rather than differences. The potential conflict between Tatar and Polish identity can be accommodated by presenting Islam and Christianity as similar monotheistic religions and by emphasizing the general importance of religious commitment. In the magazines, Islam and Christianity are often presented as resembling each other closely. Islamic values are depicted as corresponding with Catholic ones, and the religious commitment is presented as a clearly common feature. Furthermore, the Old Testament, as a book common to Muslims and Catholics, represents the link between the two communities.

Another way in which in the magazines accommodate being a Muslim and a

Pole is the idea that the Tatars have a unique role in linking Poland and countries to the East, or Christianity and Islam. This idea gives the religious background of the Tatars a particular and positive significance. The Tatars have long claimed the position of an intermediary or negotiator between Christian Poland and the Islamic world. Historically, they did indeed play a role in the relations between Poland and the Mongolian and Turkish empires.[21] Between 1918 and 1939, the messianic ideology of the Polish Tatars was often articulated. At that time, one of the Tatar activists, Olgierd Kryczynski (1932), wrote, 'In the great ideological movement, which looks for the synthesis of the East and the West, the Lithuanian Tatars are called upon to play a role. The Tatar community is somehow a miniature of that synthesis. The aim is to create a new civilization, which will initiate a new era in human history.' The idea of the Tatars as representing a link between Poland and countries of the East has been undergoing a renaissance, and in the magazines it was repeatedly brought to the fore. The Tatars see themselves as having a role to play in religious reconciliation. In an editorial for *The World of Islam* (February 1994), one of the purposes of the magazine is defined as follows: 'We hope that our magazine will contribute to a better mutual understanding; to deepening of friendship between the world of Islam and the world of Christianity.'

The magazine emphasizes the possibility of integrating Christianity and Islam. Here Tatar survival in Poland illustrates that Muslims and Christians can live together by offering a prime example of the possibility and viability of a multiple or hybrid identity. Their ethos of 'having a role as mediators' turns their connection and spiritual belonging to the world of Islam from a disadvantage to an advantage. The fact that they are Muslims who have lived for centuries in their adopted Christian motherland becomes a favourable characteristic that can be utilized in the service of Poland as well as in the present-day conflicts between the Orient and the Occident. In that way, both their Polish and Muslim identities are affirmed, and neither of them is denied. They can coexist, since they are made to be complementary and useful to each other. Thus, the Tatars confirm their spiritual link with Islam, their Eastern heritage, but they present it as an asset that can make them even better servants of Poland, their adopted motherland, and, perhaps, of the world at large.

The Polish Tatars use various strategies in trying to manage their different identities in such a way that there is no contradiction between their ethnic, national, and religious orientations. However, identities are never finished, and the Tatars' attempts at reconciliation and creating the idea of complementarity can be challenged by global and more local developments. For example, the increased global tensions and divergences between the Orient and the Occident may also force Polish Tatars into a position of having to make local choices of loyalty. Furthermore, the increased mobility of people can have an effect. The Tatars are not the only Muslims in Poland. For some time now, students and immigrants, mostly from Arab countries, have come to Poland. These people have established new associations such as the Islamic Circle of Poland and the Muslim Students of Poland. These associations want to explain and introduce Islam to the Polish people, but they also want to reinforce the Islamic faith and practices in Muslims.

The Polish Tatars, particularly, are considered to have a very limited and often inaccurate knowledge of Islam. The particular local and cultural character given to Islam by the Polish Tatars is rejected by these new groups in favour of the 'real' Islam and the need for increased Islamic activity. This development may raise new questions and tensions in the way that the Polish Tatars understand and define themselves. The current ways of being a Tatar, a Muslim, and a Pole at the same time may change. Narrative opportunities and constraints are not fixed, particularly not for those identities that are currently among the most contested ones, such as ethnicity, religion, and nationhood. New developments can create new commonalities and discrepancies. This is also true for minority groups with a long historical and traditional role within a particular country, such as the Polish Tatars.

Conclusions

This chapter has focused on the messier categories of social life that are typically ignored or excluded in social psychological theories and research. Social psychology has shown that categorization is key to understanding identity processes and group relations. An extensive literature has described and explained the self-defining consequences of categorizations and the divisive consequences of group distinctions. However, this research is liable to present a rather oversimplified and restricted account of the actual self-understandings that people can develop and the subject positions they can take up. Questions of mixing, blending, and combining that are indicated by concepts such as multiple, hyphenated, and hybrid identities, and creolization and syncretism, are increasingly common in many localities and spheres of life.

Mainstream psychological theories not only tend to ignore such issues, but in many cases these theories are formulated in ways that would seem to exclude the very possibility of hybridity. Group identity typically tends to be taken as a unitary given. The focus is, for example, on identity salience, which makes people think and act in terms of their common understanding of their identity. The majority of social psychological studies work within the parameters built on 'pure' categories and analyse category members' perceptions and discursive constructions. Notions of combination, syncretism, and hybridity open up a series of new ways of social psychological thinking. These notions all emphasize and allow the complexities of identities and cultures rather than ignoring or limiting them by the assumption and imposition of clear boundaries and categories. In addition, social psychology can make a valuable contribution to our understanding of some of the questions of multiple, hyphenated, and hybrid identities. In the social sciences, these terms have become fashionable tropes, but their meaning is not always very clear. There are at least three modalities of hybridity or ways in which the notion is used.

Firstly, many scholars emphasize the importance of multiple identities. The idea that people have multiple identities or occupy different intersecting social positions raises the important question of how these positions are dealt with and negotiated. There are many possibilities here. For example, the various identities may interact according to a situational hierarchy whereby one position becomes the main distinction along which other sources of identity are ranked and periodically subsumed. Cross-categorization studies have identified and examined many different 'intersecting' models, and factors that moderate crossed-categorization effects (e.g. Crisp & Hewstone, 2000; Urban & Miller, 1998). These studies have their limitations but they do provide theoretical models and the necessary empirical data with which the theoretical claims on hybridity and intersection can be examined.

Multiple identities may also imply a kind of rivalry or psychological conflict between different understandings and loyalties. Potential tensions and conflicts between different identities may require strategies of coping and reconciliation, and different models have been proposed (see LaFromboise et al., 1993). In social psychology, an example of this is Roccas and Brewer's (2002) concept of social identity complexity that refers to the nature of the subjective representation of the interrelationship between multiple group identities. They propose four alternative forms of identity structure that increase in complexity and that have similarities to ideas about acculturation and biculturalism. Hyphenated identities would correspond to their intersection model in which a compound combination of two categories is self-defining. Assimilation or separation positions would correspond to the situation in which one identity dominates or overrides others. Cultural alternation (LaFromboise et al., 1993) or 'ambidextrousness' would correspond to cognitive compartmentalization of social identities that are considered incompatible and situation specific. And the acculturative integration position would correspond to a representation of merger or an intercultural identity (Sussman, 2000) in which memberships in different groups are combined and integrated.

Secondly, in the social sciences, the notion of hybridity is used to analyse phenomena of cultural creolization and syncretism in which elements and meanings are combined and mixed, and new consensual forms emerge. The mongrel, 'half-breed', and 'mixed ethnic' are typical examples of this process. These examples depend on the notion of pre-existing and clear categories or elements that are being mixed. Hybridity is meaningful here in relation to ideas of purity and fixed boundaries. Mixed identities question pure categories and revalorize the half-castes. Social psychology has largely neglected the ongoing processes of mixing and moving through which immigrants and ethnic minorities constitute and negotiate their identity. The ways in which the multiple and often contrasting histories and positions are managed and used to challenge dominant discourses and distinctions are, however, important topics to consider.

Mixed identities raise many interesting social psychological questions that in a way are the mirror image of schisms, which are also a neglected topic in social psychology (e.g. Sani & Reicher, 1998). A schism occurs when opposed subgroups have differing understandings of their common identity, whereas, in mixing, separate groups come together in a new collective self-understanding. Both are complex processes that involve consensualization in which discussion and negotiation can emerge in collective agreement and shared understandings. New forms of identity can develop, expanding the identity options available to 'mixed' people. However, this very much depends on the legitimate and validated identities in the local and broader sociocultural conditions and the groups concerned. Ethnic self-understanding can be seen as a matter of identity options, but these options exist within structural, cultural, and historical parameters. Society can refuse to validate the identity of people who wish to be designated as 'mixed race' or multiethnic. The conceptualization of these positions does not have to lead to a separate category or ethnic status. Ethnic and racial self-understandings are interactionally presented and validated, and the 'mixed ethnic' or 'mixed race' option is not always available, as our example of the South Moluccans shows. The formation and management of mixed identities can be problematic when there are contrasting and competing meanings and claims. This requires negotiations and strategies of reconciliation, and some of these were examined among the Polish Tatars. Furthermore, psychologically, it can be difficult to combine different loyalties and to feel accepted and comfortable in various cultural settings. The integrative acculturation position can be more functional than psychologically synthesized (Daniel, 1996).

Thirdly, in the social sciences, the notion of hybridity is used to define a 'third space', 'in-betweenness' or liminality, that transgresses binary thinking and is used to destabilize, interrogate, and intervene tactically in the dominant constructions. This critical hybridity involves no consensual fusion or amalgamation. It is argued that consensual definitions do not come out of hybridity because the ideological closure on which such consensus depends will always be subject to debate and change. Social psychologically interesting questions can be asked here. For example, it can be asked to what extent it is psychologically and interactionally possible to take a subject position of 'in-betweenness'. What is involved here and what is required in terms of skills, resources, discursive strategies, and sociocultural conditions? And is liminality or 'in-betweenness' also not a particular *place*, subject position, or shared discursive territory comparable to other identities, or is it more accurate to talk about a liminal or 'in-between' *phase*?

Furthermore, in the social sciences, there is a tendency to celebrate and romanticize hybridity. This is mainly based on the belief that all categories and boundaries are reactionary and crippling, and that transgression symbolizes creativity and freedom. However, categories structure everyday life, give a sense of being and belonging, and provide a point of reference. The need to challenge and question categories and boundaries does not have to imply a rejection of them altogether. Without relative, coherent, stable categories that have a history and cultural content, there are few points of reference with which to define ourselves and others, and there is 'no basis to decide which boundaries to transgress, why, what new world to build out of such acts of transgression, and which differences do really make a difference' (Parekh, 2000, p. 151).

Hybridity does not necessarily lead to transgressivity or empowerment. Colonial history is full of examples where mixing fuels racism and forms of othering. Furthermore, hybridity questions forms of essentialism that—as discussed in Chapter 5—can have important political and strategic functions for minority groups. Hybridity can stand for ethnic or racial disappearance that undermines resistance and ethnic affirmation. Ang (2001) gives the example of Anderson, who as a Tasmanian Aboriginal descendant of Truganini, strongly refuses to call himself a 'hybrid'. He resists the disempowerment ensuing from such a category in order to counter the dominant definition of Truganini's descendants as the 'hybrid children of a dead race'.

With this chapter and the empirical examples discussed, I have tried to take some first steps into a landscape that is largely unexplored by social psychologists. There is much to be discovered here, and the present efforts give by no means an adequate mapping of the whole area. I have tried to indicate a few striking landmarks and to put up some signposts that may be useful in developing and exploring the terrain. Social psychology should not ignore the questions of hybridity and related phenomena that are becoming more common. The discipline should stay in touch with the rapid social changes of our globalizing world and should try to make a contribution to important debates in communities, societies, and other disciplines. Furthermore, such a contribution can be an important impetus to social psychology itself because it may require a reconceptualization of key concepts, such as group identity, stereotypes, and group consensus.

7 Self-descriptions and the ethnic self

> I sure feel Turkish. Like Ahmed says, we really feel Turkish and that's very important to us. Our culture should be maintained and we are proud of it.

> Of course I am Turkish, but I do not mind much. I mean, I can hardly speak Turkish, and I do not go to the mosque. I have lived here almost all my life and will stay here, so I have become more Dutch than Turkish.

Both these quotations are from the same person, Selçuk, a 15-year-old Turkish boy in the third form of a class we examined in our research in multiethnic schools. The first quotation is taken from a lesson in which there was a discussion about cultural diversity and discrimination in society. The discussion covered many aspects, including the issue of self-definition. Selçuk argues that he really feels Turkish, like other Turkish classmates, and that their Turkish identity is very important to them. He also argues that their Turkish culture is important and should be maintained.

The second quotation is a statement that Selçuk made in the canteen of his school while discussing with some Turkish friends their future in the Netherlands. Here he seems to argue that his Turkish identity is not very important to him and that he has become more Dutch than Turkish. He explains his self-definition by referring to his lack of language abilities and religious practices. Later in this discussion, he also argued that their future is in the Netherlands and therefore that they should adapt as much as possible to Dutch society.

This is not a unique example. The apparent inconsistency between the two self-definitions is not particular for Selçuk. In our research, we regularly came across examples where the same person emphasizes his or her ethnic identity in one context and de-emphasizes it in another, albeit not always so clearly.

In what way should this apparent inconsistency be interpreted? Can we consider Selçuk as having a Turkish orientation, or is he more oriented towards Dutch society; does he feel Turkish or not, or even Dutch? There are at least three possible interpretations.

The first interpretation is that one of the two statements represents Selçuk's true views or real sense of identity and the other feelings such as his desire to comply or the social desirability of responding in this way. Such an interpretation implies that we should try to assess his true self because only this will explain Selçuk's thinking and behaviour. In practice, this means devising and asking questions to elicit his sense of identity in the most neutral way independently of situations and interactions. What people really think or how they really feel about themselves should be assessed across different points in time, and independently of context. The assumption here is that individuals develop an internal, relatively stable, structured ethnic self that is affective and to a certain degree secure. This interpretation brings us to questions of the organization of the self-concept and the development of a sense of ethnic identity throughout the life course.

The second interpretation is that there is no inconsistency because Selçuk's statements are not similar. The idea of inconsistency presupposes similarity because otherwise a comparison of the specific utterances is not appropriate. It is quite possible, however, that Selçuk is not talking about the same thing in the two situations. His statement that he really feels Turkish can refer to quite different things than his statement that he is more Dutch. The implication here is that we should try to examine what exactly Selçuk is talking about and whether his statements are indeed inconsistent.

The third interpretation is that Selçuk's utterances should be understood in their context. This is the idea that meaning is always contextual and variable and that situational self-conception, rather than the organized self-concept, should be examined. What people say reflects more than an underlying, relatively stable predisposition, because we are always trying to make sense of ourselves and others in context. Different theories emphasize the importance of social context. For example, self-categorization theory (Turner et al., 1987) argues extensively that people define their identity in relation to other relevant groups. Social identity involves comparison processes. This means that self-descriptions should be understood within group situations. Discursive psychologists also stress the importance of context by emphasizing that talking is a social activity and that self-definition is inherently controversial because one definition can always be challenged by an alternative. Therefore, the choice of a category for self- or group definition belongs to an argument that may be defended—actually or potentially—against alternative constructions (Billig, 1987; Edwards, 1991). The consequence of these interpretations is that we should examine utterances and statements not so much in terms of inner beliefs as in their perceptual or rhetorical context.

I will discuss these three interpretations in reverse order. The reason for doing so is that in my view the pendulum has swung from a previous emphasis on the idea of stable predispositions to a focus on contextual interpretations. The tendency to treat the sense of ethnic identity in stable and fixed ways has increasingly given way to an emphasis on flexibility and situational dependency. However, there is always the danger of throwing out the baby with the bathwater. The emphasis on change and variability can easily lead to ignoring the development of more stable and secure meanings, relatively enduring commitments, and cross-situational tendencies. A sense of ethnic identity can be flexible, changing, and situational, but that does not mean that no more stable individual differences will develop. In discussing these interpretations, references to the Selçuk example will be made. This is for illustrative purposes only and is not to suggest that this particular example is adequately explained by any of these alternative interpretations.

The role of context

The apparent inconsistency between Selçuk's two statements can be understood in terms of the social context. In the classroom with a teacher and students from all kinds of ethnic groups, talk about cultural diversity and discrimination is quite a different thing from talking informally in the canteen with co-ethnic peers about one's future in the Netherlands. The idea that the context is important seems obvious, and in social psychology more and more attention is being paid to the role of context. However, this leads to recurrent problems of conceptualization, both in mainstream and discursive psychology. Not only does context mean quite different things within different approaches but also these approaches entail a different stance towards the role context should play in analyses. The notion of context is used in different ways across psychological approaches. For example, context is taken to refer to the particular task or activity people are engaged in, such as the comparative context in eliciting group evaluations, the public and private expression of these evaluations, or the conversational and rhetorical context. Furthermore, the notion of context is used for historical, cultural and ideological circumstances, and immigration conditions, but also for actual local situations, such as in schools, neighbourhoods, and workplaces (Ashmore et al., 2004).

These different notions of context raise different questions. For example, for ethnic minorities, actual local conditions are important because of the differential experiences with racism, stereotyping, and discrimination, and the opportunities for friendship and social support. Garcia Coll et al. (1996) argue that many existing psychological models are not specific enough for the study of racial and ethnic minority populations. An understanding of ethnic identification among minority groups would require explicit attention to negative social circumstances, such as racism and discrimination, in relation to concrete environmental influences, such as school and neighbourhood variables.

Using multilevel analysis, we have found in several studies that spontaneous ethnic self-definitions depend on the classroom context. For example, in one study among Dutch and Turkish early adolescents, we found that as much as 44% of the variance in ethnic self-descriptions was explained by the grouping structure (Kinket & Verkuyten, 1997). Hence, independently of individual differences, early adolescents were far more likely in some classes than in others to refer to their ethnicity in their self-descriptions. The salience of ethnicity was highly sensitive to the context of the classroom situation. The definition of who one is depended on who was present and on the way the context was defined. In this and other studies, we found not only ethnic self-description but also the evaluation of ethnic identity to be dependent on the classroom context, (e.g. Verkuyten & Thijs, 2004). In some classes, students evaluated their ethnic identity more positively than in others. However, the percentage of the variance explained by the grouping structure was low (around 7.5%). Therefore, individual factors clearly explained more variance in the evaluation of ethnic identity than did classroom features.

In reality, it is often very difficult to know which aspects of the context or situation have an influence on what people say. The situations in the classroom and the canteen differ in many ways, making it quite impossible to know what exactly made Selçuk take up different positions. It is also highly unlikely that only one factor or contextual aspect is responsible for the difference in self-definition. There are many things involved, and the actual situation is much more complex than an experimental setting. However, this does not mean that we cannot examine the role of particular contextual factors in a more controlled way. Such an examination can tell us at least whether and which contextual factors do influence ethnic self-definitions. The existence of such influences brings into question approaches that treat the ethnic self solely as an enduring and relatively stable set of attitudes, and argues for more context-sensitive approaches. It would indicate that ethnic self-identifications are not absolute, but that they depend on the context in which they are grounded. I will discuss three examples of our empirical work. These are on self-perceptions and focus on the importance of the ideological context, the role of the comparative group context, and the cultural context, respectively. In addition, I will indicate the importance of the discursive and rhetorical context in social interactions.

Ideological context

Selçuk's statement in the classroom that he really feels Turkish is perhaps related to the fact that the class was discussing the importance of cultural diversity and discrimination. In contrast, in the canteen with his Turkish friends, the issue was about the need to adapt to Dutch society. There seem to be two ideological ideas involved here. On the one hand, multiculturalism tries to foster understanding and appreciation of ethnic diversity by acknowledging and respecting group identities and promoting positive interethnic relations. However, in contrast to multicultural notions, there are socially shared beliefs that argue for assimilation whereby members of ethnic minority groups abandon their heritage culture and adopt mainstream society's way of life.

There is an ongoing debate about these two conflicting ideological positions. Both are widely endorsed by many people in Western societies and are used to legitimize or question ethnic identities and group relations. Although these ideologies are adhered to by individuals, they may be thought of as discourses in society, or collective representations (Moscovici, 1984). That is, they are socially shared beliefs about key aspects of society that affect people's perceptions and interpretations. Both ideologies are argued over and used to make sense of changes in society. Consequently, whether multiculturalism or assimilationism is used as a framework for group identification may depend on aspects of the situation that make either multiculturalism or assimilationism more salient.

In social psychology, the idea that people use ideological beliefs to question or support the legitimacy of identities and group relations is examined from different theoretical perspectives, such as system-justification theory (Jost & Banaji, 1994) and social-dominance theory (Sidanius & Pratto, 1999). Both these theories draw on social identity principles that were first developed in social-identity theory (SIT) (Tajfel & Turner, 1986). From the start, this theory emphasized the issue of legitimacy also in relation to ethnic minority groups (Tajfel, 1978, 1981). Writing about the social psychology of minorities and anticipating current debates, Tajfel (1981, p. 317) argues that 'the new claims of the minorities are based on their right to decide to be different (preserve their separateness) as defined *in their own terms* and not in terms implicitly adopted or explicitly dictated by the majorities . . . the wish to preserve their right to take their own decisions and keep their own "identity"' (original italics).

However, the issue of legitimacy has been rather neglected in social-identity research. Moreover, existing research tends to limit it to questions of status and power and ignores what Tajfel (1981, p. 316) calls the 'world-wide push towards differentiation originating from minorities'.

Because group members derive their social identity from membership of social groups, it can be assumed that people prefer their in-group to be socially recognized, accepted, and valued. This confers a meaningful and positive social identity on them that they will try to maintain and protect. In contrast, a lack of distinctiveness and a devalued social identity represent identity threats that are likely to lead to the deployment of a wide range of identity-management strategies (e.g., Ellemers, 1993; Tajfel & Turner, 1986; van Knippenberg, 1989). The strategy adopted depends on the stability, permeability and legitimacy of the intergroup relations.

SIT argues that the effect of group relations on in-group identification is moderated by legitimacy. Experimental research seems to support this prediction. In their meta-analytic examination of this research, Bettencourt et al. (2001) conclude that, under legitimate conditions, majority group members tend to show higher in-group identification than minority group members, whereas under nonlegitimate conditions, minority and majority group members tend to express more similar levels of in-group identification.

Changes in the stability and legitimacy of group differences have been found to be related to group identification, not only in experimental research but also in field studies with natural groups (e.g. Jackson, 2002; Mummendey et al., 1999). For example, using samples from the USA and Israel, Levin et al. (1998) found a positive correlation for minority groups between in-group identification and ideologies that challenge the legitimacy of the status hierarchy, whereas they found a negative association for the majority groups (see also Sidanius & Pratto, 1999; Sinclair et al., 1998). However, these correlation studies were not concerned with multiculturalism and they do not allow for causal interpretations.

In emphasizing the value of cultural diversity and identity maintenance of ethnic minority groups, multiculturalism challenges the perceived legitimacy of the overall standing of groups in society. In the Netherlands, multiculturalism is typically seen as identity threatening for the majority group and identity supporting for minority groups (van Oudenhoven et al., 1998). Berry and Kalin (1995) argue that groups are more in favour of multiculturalism when they see gains for themselves. Hence, it is likely that multiculturalism appeals more to ethnic minority groups than to majority group members who may in turn endorse assimilation more strongly. There is some empirical evidence supporting this assumption (see Chapter 6, and Arends-Tóth & van de Vijver, 2003; Berry & Kalin, 1995; Verkuyten & Thijs, 1999). Furthermore, whereas assimilationist thinking provides intellectual and moral justification for the identity of the majority group, multiculturalism challenges the legitimacy of the dominant position. Multiculturalism provides majority group members with less justifiable grounds for strong in-group identification. In contrast, multiculturalism supports the identity and improvement of the position of ethnic minority groups, and justifies minority group members' identification with their in-group. A multicultural perspective provides the ideological justification for affirming one's ethnic minority identity and to value ethnic differentiation positively.

In our research, we conducted four studies to examine multiculturalism in relation to ethnic group identification among Dutch and Turkish participants (see Verkuyten, 2004b). In these studies, Turkish participants were expected to endorse multiculturalism more strongly than the Dutch. In addition, it was expected that the more Turkish participants endorsed the ideology of multiculturalism, the more likely they would be to identify with their ethnic in-group. In contrast, it was expected that the more Dutch participants endorsed the ideology of multiculturalism, the less likely they would be to identify with their in-group. Hence, positive associations between multiculturalism and in-group identification were predicted for the Turkish participants, whereas negative associations were predicted for the Dutch.

In the first two studies, surveys were conducted among Turkish (N = 129) and Dutch (N = 329) middle adolescents, and among Turkish (N = 48) and Dutch (N =50) late adolescents. The results of both studies supported the expectations. The Turks endorsed multiculturalism significantly more than the Dutch. Furthermore, the effect for ethnic group on identification was moderated by individual differences in the endorsement of multiculturalism. It was found that the more strongly the Turkish participants endorsed the ideology of multiculturalism, the more likely they were to identify with their ethnic in-group. In contrast, the more the Dutch participants endorsed multiculturalism, the less likely they tended to be to identify with their ethnic group. Figure 7.1 shows the results of this significant interaction effect for study 2.

Although the results of both studies were supportive of SIT, the focus was on multiculturalism only, and the methodology of these studies leaves room for alternative explanations. Accordingly, two additional studies were conducted, in which the endorsement of both multiculturalism and assimilationism was assessed. Furthermore, these studies had an experimental character in order to investigate the causal effects of these ideologies. The first two studies examined correlations, and the participants may have, for example, endorsed multiculturalism because they identified with their ethnic group rather than vice versa. Hence, the results of these studies do not show that the ideology of multiculturalism actually affects in-group identification.

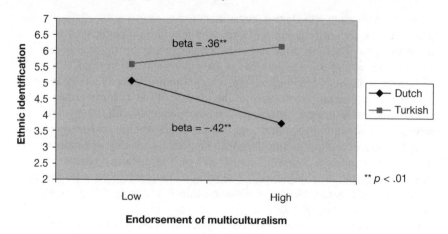

Figure 7.1 Ethnic identification by multiculturalism for Dutch and Turkish participants.

In the third and fourth study, multicultural and assimilation ideology were made salient in separate conditions. In both studies, the Turks (N = 110, and N = 46) endorsed multiculturalism more strongly in the multicultural experimental condition, whereas the Dutch (N = 110, and N = 47) had a significantly higher score on assimilation attitude than the Turks in the assimilation condition. In addition, in predicting ethnic identification, there were significant interaction effects between ethnic group and both ideologies. Hence, the results show that multi-cultural and assimilation ideologies had causal effects on ethnic identification and that these effects were moderated by ethnic group. Figure 7.2 shows the results of

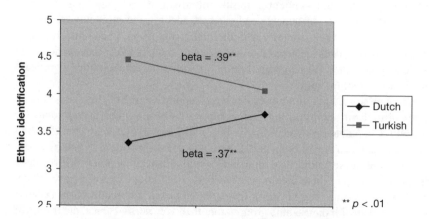

Figure 7.2 Ethnic identification by experimental condition for Dutch and Turkish participants.

study 4. As was expected, the Dutch, showed the most in-group identification in the assimilation experimental condition, whereas the Turks showed the most in-group identification in the multicultural condition.

This research shows the impact of general, legitimizing ideologies on ethnic group identification. Ethnic identification appeared to depend on the ethnic groups together with the specific nature of the legitimizing ideologies involved. This interaction between ethnic group ideology was reliable and consistent across the four studies, which were based on different methodologies (survey versus experimental), and different age and educational groups, as well as various measures (see Verkuyten, 2004b).

So, the difference between Selçuk's statements in the classroom and in the canteen may be due to the different ideological frameworks that were salient in both situations. The emphasis on the value of cultural diversity and the need to treat all groups with respect and as equals provides a different ideological setting for self-identification than a setting in which adaptation and assimilation are stressed and required.

Ethnic self-stereotyping and group context

The example of Selçuk can also be interpreted in a different way. A situation in which students from different ethnic groups are talking about cultural diversity and discrimination in Dutch society can be considered an intergroup situation. This can be seen in Selçuk's first statement where he starts talking about 'we' and 'us'. In contrast, in the canteen with his Turkish friends, the situation is an intragroup one, and here Selçuk stresses his personal identity by using several times the pronoun 'I'.

In Chapter 4, I argued that social psychological research typically investigates ethnic identity in relation to the majority group. However, issues of ethnic identity are not only of relevance in relation to this group, but also in relation to one's own group or co-ethnics. In that chapter, I maintained that not only intergroup but also intragroup comparisons are frequent and important in describing oneself and defining one's place in society, and in group attitudes. Thus, it seems important to study ethnic minority issues in different group contexts. What it means to be Turkish may be one thing in relation to other Turks, and quite another in relation to the Dutch or other groups.

We examined this issue in a study among 151 Chinese students living in the Netherlands (see Verkuyten & De Wolf, 2002b). According to self-categorization theory (SCT) (Turner et al., 1987), both a personal and social sense of identity involve comparison processes. The difference between the two is the level of inclusiveness at which similarities and differences are described. Self-descriptions are not defined by specific traits but by the level of categorization and comparison. Hence, depending on the social context, traits such as modesty, patience, or a sense of duty can meaningfully define personal identity as well as social identities. According to SCT, personal identity is particularly related to intragroup comparisons, whereas social self-definition is more likely to occur in an intergroup context (e.g. Hogg & Turner, 1987). Thus, self-definition on the individual level is pre-dominantly based on and constrained by intragroup comparisons. The content of personal identity depends on the in-group within which distinctions and differentiations are made. In contrast, when social identity is salient, group members self-stereotype themselves in terms of what characterizes the in-group in relation to a relevant out-group. Thus, the same Chinese person may describe herself differently in relation to her ethnic in-group than in relation to the Dutch. Changes in identity from the personal to the social level may affect self-descriptions.

We examined this idea by investigating self-stereotyping in both an intragroup and an intergroup context. In a between-subjects design and using a variant of Markus's (1977) self-rating paradigm as adapted by Turner and Onorato (1999), participants were asked to rate themselves in comparison to their ethnic in-group (Chinese) or in comparison to the majority out-group (Dutch). It was expected that self-descriptions would differ between the two experimental conditions. What was particularly expected to be used in the intergroup context were the stereotypical traits which maximize perceived differences between the Chinese and the Dutch (Oakes et al., 1994). Hence, it was predicted that, for self-description, familiar and commonly used stereotypes about the Chinese (Bond & Hwang, 1986; Geense & Pels, 1998) would be used more in the intergroup than the intragroup condition. That is, participants would define themselves, for example, as being more reserved, emotionally controlled, obedient, modest, and dutiful in relation to the Dutch than in relation to the Chinese.

The results indicated that participants in the intergroup condition, as opposed to the intragroup condition, did indeed describe themselves as more 'emotionally controlled', more 'reserved', more 'obedient', and, to a marginally significant degree, more 'modest'. Hence, participants described themselves more strongly in stereotypical terms when compared to the Dutch than when compared to other Chinese.

Thus, the social comparative context affected ethnic self-description. This shows that ethnic self-stereotypes depend on the comparative group context in which they are made sense of. The self-ratings on trait adjectives differ between an intragroup and intergroup context. How participants described themselves varied according to the level of self-definition. In relation to the Dutch, the Chinese participants described themselves more in in-group stereotypical terms than they did in relation to other Chinese. Importantly, the differences in self-ratings were in agreement with the relevance of particular dimensions for defining categories in relation to each other. That is, familiar and commonly used stereotypes about the Chinese were used more often for self-description in the intergroup than in the intragroup context.[1]

Thus, Selçuk's statements may be understood in terms of the comparative group context. In the intergroup context of the classroom, he stressed his Turkish identity, whereas in the intragroup context of the canteen he played down this identity and tried to distinguish himself from his Turkish peers. In the former context, ethnic identities and group differences are relevant, whereas in the latter context individual differences and personal identities become more meaningful.

This interpretation focuses on the distinction between personal and ethnic identity and the principles of distinctiveness and perceived differences. But inter- and intragroup situations also differ, for example, in terms of contextually appropriate utterances, accountability, and power of sanction. The social identity model of de-individuation effects (e.g. Reicher et al., 1995) suggests that identity expressions involve a strategic component in addition to a cognitive one. These expressions are affected by contextual constraints and opportunities, such as the likelihood that others will question or challenge one's self-definition. Hence, the cognitive salience of particular identities alone is not sufficient to understand contextually changing self-definitions. Both cognitive and self-presentation processes are likely to be involved in identity expressions. For example, for ethnic minority groups, statements of identification can be strategic coping responses in relation to in-group and out-group threats.

In their study among ethnic minority members in the Netherlands, Barreto et al. (2003) found evidence for this idea. Turkish participants expressed stronger identification with both the in-group and the Dutch when addressing a Dutch audience than when addressing a Turkish audience. Hence, towards the Dutch, who tend to favour assimilation (e.g. Arends-Tóth & van de Vijver, 2003), they presented an integrationist or dual sense of identity, whereas towards the Turks separation was more favoured. Interestingly, no audience effect was found for Iranian participants. Barreto et al. explain this by arguing that Iranians are less visible in society and experience less threat from the majority group. In a second study among Portuguese participants living in the Netherlands, Barreto et al. showed that personal accountability affected expressed identifications. The participants were found to moderate their expression of Portuguese and Dutch identity when the audience was in a position to scrutinize the credibility of these identity claims. These results show that for ethnic minority members, minority and majority group identifications are sensitive to social consideration and open to strategic presentations.

Hence, the difference between Selçuk's statements can reflect communicative and strategic considerations. Claims to a Turkish identity can be more problematic among his friends in the canteen than in the classroom situation. His friends probably know the limits of such a claim and could more easily challenge the validity and credibility of it. In contrast, such a claim is more difficult to challenge in a classroom where the value and importance of cultural and ethnic differences is discussed. This interpretation in terms of self-presentation and strategic concerns brings us close to the level of social interaction and discursive strategies. However, before going into this, I will discuss a third interpretation in terms of self-perception.

Cultural context

In the first part of the previous section, the apparent inconsistency in Selçuk's statements was made sense of in terms of self-categorization theory. A framework quite similar to this theory but developed in cross-cultural psychology is the perspective of cultural frame-switching. Hong et al. (2000) present a dynamic constructivist model for understanding what they call frame-switching in bicultural individuals. The first premise of the model is that culture is not internalized in the form of an integrated structure but rather as domain-specific knowledge, such as implicit social theories. Furthermore, individuals are thought to be able to acquire more than one cultural frame even if these contain conflicting elements. However, these frames are not thought to guide thinking simultaneously. Cognitive accessibility of constructs and contextual salience are the concepts used to explain how different cultural knowledge becomes operative in particular situations.

In their experimental research, Hong et al. (2000) examined cultural frame-switching in response to contextual cues that make different ethnocultural identities salient. Particularly, when using attribution tasks, they found that Westernized Chinese students in Hong Kong were more likely to give situational explanations when their Chinese identity was activated than when an American cultural priming condition was activated. The same results were found among Chinese-American students in California. Their findings indicate that cultural frame-switching occurs in response to contextual cues that make different cultural identities salient. When a given cultural identity is salient, beliefs, theories, and standards that define the salient identity govern people's thinking and acting.

In one of our studies, we examined biculturalism in relation to self-identification (see Verkuyten & Pouliasi, 2002). Existing research on cross-cultural differences in the conception of self is extensive (see Fiske et al., 1998; Markus et al., 1996).[2] In general, people in individualistic cultures are more likely than those in collectivist cultures to give personal and independent self-descriptions, and they are less likely to give interdependent self-descriptions in which relatedness and the importance of close relationships are emphasized. Furthermore, in collectivist cultures, people have been found to make fewer self-enhancing statements (e.g. Heine et al., 1999). By priming different cultural identities, we tried to replicate these cross-cultural differences on the level of bicultural individuals (see Hong et al., 2000). In doing so, we focused on identification with friends and on the evaluation of personal and social identity among bicultural early adolescents of Greek descent living in the Netherlands.

Greek culture has been found to be more collectivist than Dutch culture (Hofstede, 1980, 1991; Triandis et al., 1986). Traditionally, in Greece, there is a relatively stronger emphasis on collectivist values than in the Netherlands. Although Greek society has undergone extensive individualization (Georgas, 1989), important differences remain. This is especially evident in relation to extended family life and family values (Georgas et al., 1996, 1997). Furthermore, compared to students and adults, who increasingly adopt individualistic views, Greek children are thought to be more influenced by traditional values.

High in-group identification is a defining attribute of collectivism (Triandis, 1989). Identification with friends is particularly important for children and adolescents (Harter, 1999). Among ethnic minority and majority adolescents in the Netherlands, we found a positive association between personal collectivism (or allocentrism) and identification with friends (Verkuyten & Masson, 1996). Hence, in the present study, bicultural children were expected to consider their relation-ships with friends as closer whenever their Greek identity was activated rather than their Dutch identity.

Although few self-enhancing statements are made in collectivist cultures, self-evaluation motives are not necessarily absent in these cultures. Members of these cultures are more likely to evaluate their social identities favourably, whereas, in individualist cultures, it is personal identities that tend to be evaluated positively (Hetts et al., 1999; Pelham & Hetts, 1999). Furthermore, Hetts and colleagues have both argued and found that among ethnic minority groups these tendencies are most evident for more indirect or implicit measures of self-evaluation. These measures are thought to reflect people's subconscious feelings about the self that are related to the normative beliefs and values learned in early childhood. Explicit self-evaluations are more transparent and are thought to be more dependent on the current social and cultural context (Greenwald & Banaji, 1995). Hence, we measured personal and social identity indirectly. Bicultural participants were expected to evaluate themselves and their group differently depending on the salient identity: Greek or Dutch. Whenever Greek identity was salient, a more positive implicit evaluation of social identity was expected, whereas personal identity was expected to be rated more positively whenever Dutch identity was salient.

When we tested these predictions for cultural frame-switching among bicultural early adolescents living in the Netherlands, a group of monocultural Dutch contemporaries and a group of monocultural Greek participants in Greece were included. There were two reasons for doing so, the first one being that differences in, for example, self-evaluations between Greek and Dutch identity priming conditions do not necessarily have to reflect cultural frame-switching. One alter-native interpretation for a more positive social identity evaluation in the Greek condition may be that the minority position of the in-group in the Netherlands becomes salient. When this happens, people may respond by emphasizing their social identity and accentuating positive in-group distinctiveness (Tajfel & Turner, 1986). A cultural interpretation is more convincing if the result for Greek identity activation among biculturals is similar to that of Greek early adolescents in Greece, and the result for Dutch identity activation is similar to that of Dutch contem-poraries. The second reason is that it makes it possible to examine whether there are indeed cultural differences between the early adolescents of both societies.

An experimental questionnaire study was carried out. There were two versions of the questionnaire. For priming Dutch and Greek cultural identity, iconic cultural symbols and language were used. That is, in keeping our procedure consistent with that used by Hong et al. (2000), we presented the participants with pictures of either Dutch icons (the National flag, a windmill, and a person in traditional clothing) or Greek icons (the National flag, the Acropolis, and a person in traditional clothing). In addition, the questionnaires were presented in the Dutch and Greek languages, respectively. That is, the whole study was introduced and conducted in one or the other language. The combination of icons and language (see Krauss & Chiu, 1998) was considered an effective means of activating the two different cultural identities.

The children were given three self-identification questions. With the Inclusion of Other in the Self Scale (Tropp & Wright, 2001; Verkuyten & Masson, 1996), the participants were asked to indicate the level of connectedness between themselves and their friends. In addition, two identification questions assessed personal and social self-evaluation, respectively. In order to attain more implicit or indirect measures of self-evaluations, the participants were asked about their feelings towards the personal pronouns 'I' and 'we'. Experiments have demonstrated that these pronouns carry evaluative significance that is activated automatically and subconsciously (Hetts et al., 1999; Perdue et al., 1990). The results are presented in Table 7.1.

As expected, the Dutch-Greek participants (biculturals, primed for Dutch) identified less strongly with their friends than did the Greek-Dutch (biculturals, primed for Greek) and Greek participants. Furthermore, the Dutch and Dutch-Greek early adolescents evaluated their social identity less positively than the Greek and Greek-Dutch early adolescents. Also as expected, compared to the Greek-Dutch participants, the Dutch-Greek participants evaluated their personal identity more positively. Hence, when Greek identity was activated, bicultural early adolescents tended to identify more strongly with their friends, and evaluate their social identity more positively and their personal identity less positively to a greater degree than when Dutch identity was activated.

In addition, the participants in Greece and those in the Greek-Dutch condition scored similarly, but their scores differed from those of the Dutch participants and the participants in the Dutch-Greek condition. The scores of the latter two groups were again similar. These results suggest that the differences between the two experimental groups of bicultural early adolescents are related to cultural frame-switching (Hong et al., 2000), and not, for example, to a higher salience of the in-group minority position in the Greek-Dutch condition. In response to cultural identity cues, biculturals seem to shift between interpretive frames rooted in different cultures. Other studies have reported similar findings (e.g, Ambady et al., 2001; Benet-Martínez et al., 2002).

Table 7.1 Mean scores and standard deviations (in parentheses) for self-identification for four groups of participants. Univariate analyses

	Dutch (N=51)	Dutch–Greek (N=37)	Greek–Dutch (N=37)	Greek (N=58)	F-value
Identification friends	5.41[ab] (1.76)	5.02[a] (1.84)	5.76[b] (1.67)	5.88[b] (1.28)	2.38*
Evaluation social identity	5.90[a] (1.06)	5.91[a] (0.99)	6.43[b] (0.90)	6.45[b] (0.75)	5.27**
Evaluation personal identity	4.98[a] (1.23)	6.30[b] (1.01)	5.67[c] (1.75)	5.96[bc] (1.08)	9.09***

*$p < .07$, **$p < .01$, ***$p < .001$.
Row means with different superscripts represent significant differences.

The idea of cultural frame-switching proposes that individuals can possess dual cultural identities and move between different cultural meaning systems in response to situational cues. Biculturals would have access to different systems of meaning and switch between different culturally appropriate behaviours, depending on the context. This idea has many similarities with self-categorization theory. These theories argue that when social identity is salient, the norms and values attached to this identity will guide group members' behaviour, perception, and evaluation. In the words of Turner (1991, p. 3), 'Group norms arise from interaction between group members and they express a generally accepted way of thinking, feeling or behaving that is endorsed and expected because it is perceived as the right and proper thing to do.' A contextual shift in identity salience involves a shift in the related group norms with the concomitant changes in perceptions and behaviour. This would be the case for individuals who identify highly with the relevant identity in particular. For example, Jetten et al. (2002) show that high identifiers are more likely than low identifiers to incorporate salient group norms prescribing either individualism or collectivism into their self-descriptions.

Social-identity and self-categorization theory, however, are less interested in the relationships between various identities and the ways in which different meaning systems are experienced and internalized. For example, in Chapter 6, we saw that there are various ways that people manage and experience multiple or dual identities. Biculturalism can take many different forms. People can feel equally comfortable in different cultural settings or can be able to identify and function in both settings but feel a stronger orientation to and comfort within a particular setting. Furthermore, some individuals can see their cultural identities as additive and compatible, whereas others may describe and experience them as oppositional and contradictory. Benet-Martínez et al. (2002) found that cultural frame-switching is moderated by perceived compatibility in contrast to opposition between two cultural orientations. Chinese-American biculturals who perceived their cultural identities as compatible responded in culturally congruent ways when explaining social events. However, Chinese-American biculturals who perceived their cultural identities as oppositional showed a reverse priming effect. That is, they responded in a more American way when exposed to Chinese primes and in a more Chinese way when exposed to American primes. Hence, individual differences in biculturalism were found to affect how cultural knowledge is used to interpret social events.

Conversational and rhetorical context

The previous examples were concerned with perception and cognition. Selçuk's statements can be understood in terms of the cognitive processes involved in making sense of oneself and others in context. However, his statement among his friends that he does not feel very Turkish can also be seen as meaningful in the context of the topic being discussed and the possible positions that his friends (may) take. Discursive psychologists see it as being part of a debate or as a positioning against counterpositions, as for example, against those arguing in favour of opposition to Dutch society and of (over-)communicating their Turkish identity. However, in the context of a class discussion on cultural diversity and discrimination, similar statements can have different meanings and should be understood within that particular rhetorical context. Hence, Selçuk's statements can be understood in terms of social interactions. In the classroom discussion about multiculturalism, he stressed his Turkish identity and the importance of the unique Turkish culture. In discussing his future in the Netherlands in the canteen, he questioned the relevance of Turkish identity and culture and emphasized his personal responsibility and choice. The positions he took are related to those of the others present.

People manage and negotiate their identities in social interactions, and they use different discourses and discursive strategies for doing so. Ethnic self-definitions can be seen as something people do, instead of being the result of perception. They can be treated as discursive actions that perform a variety of interpersonal and interactional functions, such as blaming and excusing, and wider social functions, such as reifying and legitimatizing patterns of social dominance (e.g. Antaki & Widdicombe, 1998; Billig, 1997b; Edwards, 1997; Edwards & Potter, 1992; Hopkins et al., 1997; Rapley, 2001). Discursive psychologists argue that it is important to examine the actual use of ethnic self-definitions in argument and debate. Such an examination gives an action-oriented rather than a cognitive answer to the question of the context dependency of self-definitions.

In the previous chapters, I have discussed several empirical examples of this approach. For example, in Chapter 6, some of the ways in which multiple identities are publicly managed and negotiated were examined. In Chapter 5, I examined essentialism as a flexible resource which is variously defined and deployed by both ethnic minority and majority members, depending on the debate's context and the interactional task at hand. And in Chapter 4, identity constructions of South Moluccans and second-generation Turks were discussed as well as the accounting for discrimination. In the next section, another example of this approach will be discussed.

Differences in meaning

In the previous sections, I have discussed how the apparent inconsistency in Selçuk's statements can be understood in terms of contextual and situational variation. There are different approaches to taking context or situation into account, such as in terms of cognitive, strategic or discursive processes, but they share an emphasis on the importance of context.

However, there is another possible interpretation of Selçuk's statements. This interpretation is not necessarily contradictory to a contextual one but raises other questions. The idea of inconsistency presupposes similarity because otherwise a comparison of the specific utterances is not appropriate. It is quite possible, however, that Selçuk is not talking about the same thing in the two situations. His statement that he feels really Turkish can refer to different things than his statement that he does not consider himself very Turkish. His sense of

Turkish identity may be multifaceted or multidimensional, and his two utterances may refer to different facets or dimensions.[3] The implication is that we should try to examine what exactly Selçuk is talking about and to what his statements refer.

In social psychology, a mass of empirical work has been devoted to the causes and consequences of social identification and the sense of social identity. In contrast, the concept of social identity has received relatively little theoretical and empirical attention (Simon, 2004). However, there are some recent empirical studies on the ethnic and racial self (e.g. De la Garza et al., 1995; Sellers et al., 1998), and the social self in general (e.g. Ellemers et al., 1999; Jackson, 2002; Jackson & Smith, 1999; Smith et al., 1999). These studies have argued and found that different aspects of the social self can be distinguished. Tajfel (1981) postulated a tridimensional conceptualization of the sense of social identity, consisting of a cognitive, an evaluative, and an affective component. In general, there is a reasonable degree of agreement about the usefulness of Tajfel's distinction (see Jackson, 2002). Other authors, however, have added and proposed other components, such as perceived common fate, social embeddedness, and behavioural involvement (see Ashmore et al., 2004, for a review).

In studies on ethnic and racial identity, there is the additional issue of describing the unique cultural, structural, and historical experiences of specific ethnic and racial groups. Particular frameworks and dimensions have been proposed for this. For example, Sellers et al. (1998) provide a framework for examining the political and cultural influences on the sense of African-American identity, whereas De la Garza et al. (1995) are concerned with Latino identity. In contrast to these group-specific models, the focus can be on the more general dimensions of the ethnic and racial self. More common dimensions are, for example, the importance attached to ethnic identity, the evaluation of and feelings about group membership, interest in and knowledge of group features, and ethnic behaviours and practices. Dimensions such as group consciousness, commitment, and public regard are less commonly used.

Hence, various dimensions or aspects have been proposed, and it is possible that these components are relatively independent in a psychological sense and are used discursively in relation to each other. Relative independence would imply that the same statement, such as a Turkish self-definition, can have different meanings and that different statements, such as the two made by Selçuk, can refer to different aspects and therefore do not have to be inconsistent.

The sociologist Fishman (1980) discusses ethnicity in terms of 'being', 'doing', and 'knowing'. He argues that ethnicity is often and partly experienced as 'being' or as a kinship phenomenon expressed in biological or quasi-biological metaphors. The heritage of ethnicity also creates obligations and opportunities for 'doing' or behaving in such a way that ethnicity is preserved and confirmed. He notes that this 'doing' is ultimately more negotiable than 'being' since behaviour is subject to change. This does not mean that any change is possible, however, because changes are subject to processes of authentication and validation by others. Ethnicity can also be experienced as 'knowing'; that is, the beliefs, ideas, ideologies, and history of an ethnic group. In addition to this tripartite distinction, social psychologists like to add the 'feeling' of ethnicity or what it feels like to be member of an ethnic group. Thus, and as shown in Figure 7.3, ethnic identity can be conceptualized as that which you 'are', as that which you 'do', as that which you 'know', and as that which you 'feel'. These four 'ways of ethnicity' can be examined as dimensions or aspects of the sense of ethnic identity, but also as accounts that people use in social interactions. I will discuss both types of investigation.

Sense of ethnic identity

In her review of the theory and research, Phinney (1990, p. 503; her italics) discusses 'components related to what might be called the *state* of ethnic identity— that is, a person's identification at a given time'. She discusses four components that have some overlap with those of Figure 7.3. The first one is self-definition or self-labelling, and this refers to the ethnic label that people use for themselves. An ethnic label may be chosen or imposed, asserted or assigned, and a single label may also be seen as inaccurate. The kind of ethnic label people select, however, is typically considered in categorical terms or as a zero-sum choice rather than a dimension of variation. The label describes what one is or the ethnic identity one has, in contrast to how one feels about oneself and what one does and knows. However, what individuals ethnically are is not always simple and can be assessed in different ways. For example, participants can be asked about 'what they actually are', about their parents' ethnicity, or about the attribution of an ethnic label by outsiders based on some observable characteristics. The type of assessment can affect the results obtained.

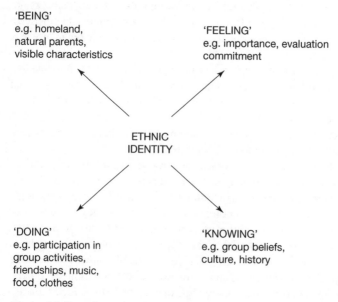

'BEING'
e.g. homeland,
natural parents,
visible characteristics

'FEELING'
e.g. importance, evaluation
commitment

ETHNIC
IDENTITY

'DOING'
e.g. participation in
group activities,
friendships, music,
food, clothes

'KNOWING'
e.g. group beliefs,
culture, history

Figure 7.3 Four dimensions of ethnic identity.

The second dimension refers to the feelings related to one's ethnic identity. People may use an ethnic label for describing themselves, but this does not tell us much about whether they have a strong sense of belonging and positive feelings towards their ethnic identity and whether they consider this identity personally important. Individuals who describe themselves as belonging to the same ethnic group may differ in their sense of belonging, commitment, and importance. For example, being Turkish, Moroccan, or Dutch does not mean that one feels that way or considers it personally important. Furthermore, there are individual differences in the degree to which people accept their ethnic identity and feel positively about it. In addition, individuals may differ in the emotional meanings, pleasures, and satisfaction that their ethnic identity brings. Researchers have devised a number of approaches and measures for assessing ethnic feelings (Phinney, 1990). Moreover, different terms have been used such as 'ethnic identi-fication', 'ethnic importance', and 'ethnic self-esteem as a form of collective self-esteem' (Luhtanen & Crocker, 1992).

The third dimension concerns ethnic involvement. According to Phinney (1990), this is the most widely used indicator of ethnic identity, but also the most problematic one. The individual's actual involvement in the social life and cultural practices of the ethnic in-group is assessed by various indicators, such as language use, friendship patterns, cultural traditions and symbols (such as celebrations, music, dress, food, and newspapers), membership of ethnic organizations, and participation in political activities and religious practices. The focus is on the ethnic activities and practices people are involved in, and these can be quite specific for each group. The importance of the different 'doings' clearly varies with the group and particular situations, making comparisons across groups and situations difficult. Furthermore, the use of such measures presupposes that specific ethnic and cultural practices and customs define ethnic identity. For example, participation in ethnic organizations or a preference for in-group friends is taken to indicate or reflect a strong sense of ethnic identity. But there is always the possibility that other factors or processes underlie these activities. Ethnic identity salience leads to behaviour and practices consistent with that identity, but a sense of ethnic identity does not have to underlie ethnic cultural practices (Deaux, 1993).

Fishman discusses also the 'knowing' of ethnicity. This is the fourth dimension in Figure 7.3, which is not addressed separately by Phinney. The emphasis here is on the extent to which people are interested in and knowledgeable about the culture and history of their ethnic group. Ethnicity helps to explain origins and social locations. It offers an understanding of where one is and where one is from. Knowledge of the history and culture of the in-group allows you to explore the different meanings and experiences involved and to situate oneself in relation to others. This dimension also involves ideological notions about experiences, entitlements, and the ways in which in-group members should live and interact with other groups and society (Sellers et al., 1998).

These four dimensions can be used to conceptualize and assess different aspects of an individual's sense of ethnic identity. However, although a distinction in dimensions and aspects is important, it also raises the important question of interrelationships. How should these dimensions be understood and how are they related? The relationship between what people say they are does not have to correspond to what they feel, know, and actually do. And what they do does not have to correspond to what they feel and so on. The different aspects can combine in various and unexpected ways and can form unique profiles. There are often complex relationships between these aspects, and existing relationships do not have to be very strong.

However, whatever the approach and whatever dimensions are considered necessary to include, there is always the important question of construct validity. Ashmore et al. (2001, pp. 239–240) explain this question as follows:

> In the simplest terms, where does collective social identity end and related variables (causes, correlates, and consequences) begin? For example, is 'interest in and knowledge about' one's ethnic group part of one's social identity, or is it best seen as an outcome predictable from identification? This question becomes even more difficult regarding behavior: are ethnic behaviors part of social identity or an outcome that can be used to assess the construct validity of social identity measures?

This is a key question, and scholars have taken different and not always consistent positions or approaches to it. Ethnic involvement and friendship patterns, for example, are taken as aspects of ethnic identity but also as the outcome of a strong sense of ethnic identity. In-group and out-group attitudes are sometimes also taken as indicators or aspects of ethnic identity (LaFromboise et al., 1993). In contrast, intergroup theories make a clear distinction between group identification and intergroup relations. The latter is typically considered a consequence of the former.

The book *Ethnic Minorities in Britain* (Modood et al., 1997b) presents the results of a major survey on the experiences and views of Caribbean, Indian, African-Asian, Pakistani, Bangladeshi, and Chinese people. One chapter of the book is on culture and identity. The results show that ethnicity is of considerable importance for self-understanding and that there is a strong sense of ethnic identity among these minority groups. In each group, around 90% of the participants agreed that they thought of themselves in terms of their ethnic group. However, among all groups, ethnic self-identification correlated only weakly with ethnic behaviours, practices, and knowledge, such as clothing, marriage preferences, and the use of ethnic language (< .23). These low correlations bring into question the idea that we are dealing with different aspects of a common construct, ethnic identity. From this research, Modood et al. (1997b, p. 385) conclude, 'Ethnic identification is no longer necessarily connected to personal participation in distinctive cultural practices, such as those of language, religion or dress.'

The implications of this finding are not limited to the British situation. Similar developments have been noted in other countries, such as the USA and the Netherlands. For example, in one study among Chinese adolescents, we found an association of .36 between ethnic practices and ethnic self-definition (Verkuyten & Kwa, 1996).

Ethnic identification can persist while increasingly becoming drained of cultural content. Hence, it is possible to claim that one is Turkish because of one's ethnic background and also to argue that one is not really Turkish because one does not speak the language or does not follow ethnically Turkish practices. Hence, Selçuk's two statements do not have to be inconsistent because in the first one he is talking about his feelings, and in the second one about ethnic practices and behaviour. In Chapter 4, in which we discussed our research with South Moluccans, we saw other examples of how these distinctions can work. Depending on the questions asked, different responses are elicited which lead to different conclusions about people's sense of ethnic identity. It is possible to feel Turkish without knowing much of Turkish culture or doing Turkish things. And it is possible to become Dutch culturally and to stay Turkish, Moroccan, or Surinamese ethnically (e.g. van Niekerk, 2001). As anthropologists stress, a distinction between ethnicity and culture should be made. For example, Gans (1979) talks about symbolic ethnicity to indicate that people may resort to adopting ethnic symbols in cases where little remains of their former ethnic culture. And Vermeulen (2001) argues that with 'old' ethnicity, groups are so obviously different that they do not feel the need to distinguish themselves from others. In contrast, with 'new' ethnicity, the fading away of cultural differences causes people to place new emphasis on being different as part of their identity. It is often the most acculturated individuals who are apt to stress their ethnic belonging.[4]

Accounts

The four aspects in Figure 7.3 can not only be seen as dimensions of a sense of ethnic identity but can also be examined as accounts or repertoires that people use in negotiating ethnic self-definitions in interactions. Ethnic self-definitions are also accomplishments that are sensitive to justifications and criticisms. To express their views and persuade others, people orient themselves to the possibility that their self-definitions are discounted or undermined. We have seen several examples of this in previous chapters. One example, discussed in Chapter 6, was our focus-group study among Chinese participants. There I indicated that, for these participants, ethnic self-definitions were not self-evident, but were discussed and accounted for in relation to each other. Hence, we can examine how the participants made their self-definitions acceptable (see Verkuyten & De Wolf, 2002a).

In the discussions, there were four different ways of talking about ethnic identity—'being', 'feeling', 'doing', and 'knowing' Chinese. All four offer an account that can be used for ethnic self-definitions, but differ in the degree of determinism that is involved. A distinction between 'being' a member of a group and 'doing' activities associated with membership is a pervasive and general one through which people have been found to argue about themselves and their social world (e.g. Watson & Weinberg, 1982; Widdicombe & Wooffitt, 1990). The distinction is a recurrent resource for differentiating between groups and members and was also apparent in our discussion groups. In addition, the importance of 'feeling' and 'knowing' Chinese was stressed in the discussions—references to knowledge and feelings are also common interpretative resources (e.g. Edwards, 1997).

'Being Chinese' was predominantly interpreted in terms of biological notions and visible differences. Several participants pointed out that they simply were Chinese by birth. Thereby, the category of Chinese was defined in biological terms. They looked Chinese, and 'real' Chinese were considered those born of two Chinese parents. Hence, being Chinese was defined in biological terms and presented as a coincidental but inevitable and fixed characteristic. It is not a personal choice but a fact of life that is objectively known and cannot be changed. This account places the issue of ethnic identity beyond discussion and makes people not responsible for their ethnic identity. It is just biology, and that cannot be helped.

The participants used the language of 'feeling' to explain their sense of ethnicity. In the discussions, they frequently talked about feeling Chinese or feeling Dutch, and these feelings were predominantly explained in terms of early socialization. The participants presented 'being' and 'feeling' Chinese as different and sometimes used the two accounts in opposition to each other. References to 'feelings' provide an interesting account of the sense of identity. Firstly, such references can give an 'account for not accounting'. That is, a reference to feelings can be one way of avoiding having to provide explanations for difficult or sensitive issues. 'Irrationality' is useful for dealing with problematic questions.

Secondly, references to feelings make a clear distinction between the 'outer' and the 'inner'. A description of what one looks like physically is contrasted with how one is psychologically. Contrasting structures can have a range of interactional functions, such as to distance oneself from certain assigned categories and to position oneself favourably (e.g. Dickerson, 2000). In general, contrasts are not symmetrical because one side is presented as more favourable, genuine, important, or relevant than the other. In the discussions, 'feeling' Chinese or Dutch was presented as more important or 'real' than 'being' or looking Chinese. Compared to the 'outer', the 'inner' was treated as the true self.

Thirdly, this contrast provides an account of one's sense of ethnic identity that is difficult to challenge. The 'inner' is by definition private, unknown to others. A claim that one feels Chinese or Dutch cannot be challenged without questioning the sincerity or integrity of the speaker. Furthermore, the term 'feeling' suggests an emotional or affective state, and not so much a way of thinking. In general, a feeling is typically presented as something that should be respected and that is difficult to change, whereas the concept of thinking does not include these suggestions to the same degree (Edwards, 1997). One's thinking can be changed and corrected, whereas one's feelings are just that: one just feels Chinese. Hence, using the term 'feeling' makes it more difficult to make people responsible or to criticize their ethnic self-definition.

'Being' and 'feeling' Chinese are different ways of talking about ethnic identity. Both offer an account of ethnic self-definitions and both can be used in opposition to each other. However, there is also 'doing Chinese', in which self-definitions are substantiated by references to category-bound activities. Claiming possession or nonpossession of an attribute that is defined as critical or typical of an ethnic group is an important way of accounting for one's sense of ethnic identity. In the second quotation at the beginning of this chapter, Selçuk argues that he does not mind much being Turkish because he hardly speaks Turkish and does not go to the mosque. So he explains his lack of commitment by the fact that he is not involved in activities that are implicitly defined as critical for Turkish identity.

In the discussions among the Chinese, there were similar examples, as when it was argued that one cannot really be Chinese if one can hardly speak or write the Chinese language. The issue of language was frequently brought up and used to define who and what 'real' Chinese are. In a manner similar to that used by the South Moluccans discussed in Chapter 4, language functioned as a central marker of ethnic identity. Being raised as Chinese means being able to speak the language. For example, in one group, it was argued that people are 'fake' (in Dutch *nep*) Chinese if they cannot speak and understand the Chinese language. And, writing about her own experiences, Ang (2001, p. 23) says, 'Throughout my life, I have been implicitly or explicitly categorized, willy-nilly, as an "overseas Chinese" (*hua qiao*). I look Chinese. Why, then, don't I speak Chinese? I have had to explain this embarrassment countless times.' In the discussions, there were various examples where language and other cultural characteristics were presented as prototypical or group-defining features. The category-boundedness of attributes can be used to define an acceptable sense of ethnic identity (e.g. Widdicombe & Wooffitt, 1995). Accounts about Chinese, but also Dutch, identity were closely related to Chinese and Dutch practices, having Chinese and Dutch friends, and language ability.

In the discussions, the Chinese language was referred to in terms of being able to speak, read, and write, but also as evidence of knowledge of or as a gateway to Chinese culture. The Chinese language was presented and discussed in terms of being aware of and familiar with Chinese culture, history, and subtle Chinese sensitivities. 'Knowing' Chinese was used to substantiate claims to an authentic and committed sense of Chinese identity. It was argued that 'real' Chinese people know their history and culture, think alike, and understand each other. Knowledge was presented as intimate or 'insider' knowledge in which there is a lived understanding of Chinese subtleties and history. 'Knowing Chinese' can, however, also provide an acceptable account of not 'feeling' and 'doing' Chinese. When people know Chinese culture and history, they know what they are talking about, making their lack of commitment a considered and conscious choice. In that case, knowledge is intellectual understanding or 'outsider' knowledge which can be acquired by anyone studying sinology and does not necessarily indicate an identification as Chinese.

'Being', 'feeling', 'doing', and 'knowing' can all offer an account of ethnic identity, but involve different degrees of determinism. These are familiar, socially shared understandings or interpretative resources used to account for ethnic self-definitions. Explanations in terms of appearance, early socialization, and critical group attributes are used in many different situations and for different purposes. For example, Watson and Weinberg (1982) indicate that different studies have found a distinction in people's accounts similar to the one between 'being' and 'doing'. In the discussions, the participants oriented themselves to these discourses in ways that sometimes complemented each other but were also sometimes in opposition to each other. They could complement and support each other, for example, when Chinese self-definition is explained in terms of Chinese appearance, Chinese early socialization, involvement in critical activities specifically Chinese, and possession of Chinese knowledge. However, these discourses can also be used in contrasting ways. For example, the claim to a sense of Chinese-Dutch or Dutch identity has to deal with the facts of birth and appearance. Furthermore, such a claim may be interpreted as distancing oneself from one's Chinese parents and Chinese people in general, and rejecting one's cultural background. As explained in Chapter 4, accounts of ethnic minority identity often encapsulate issues that present dilemmas of continuity and change, solidarity and diffusion, and determinism and agency. The next extract from our research is an example.

Kent: I absolutely don't feel Chinese; only the fact is that my parents are Chinese. For the rest, no, absolutely not. If I felt really Chinese, I would, for example, talk Chinese, this and that, yes, perhaps I do possess, um, what it takes, I mean I might be able to say a few words in Chinese now and then, but I mean I absolutely haven't got the motivation to do so. I have Chinese friends, not because they *are Chinese*, but simply because they are, yes, because I like them or whatever, yes, and for the rest, I simply try to, I'm not saying that, um, I don't want anything to do with it, after all, my parents are Chinese, I know they are Chinese, and I do respect that, I don't mind that they are, you know, but, um, I consider myself more as a Dutchman and I'm also not into Chinese culture anymore. But I don't forget that my parents are Chinese.

Here, the claim to feeling Dutch and not feeling Chinese is accounted for in different ways, such as strong formulations (line 1, 'absolutely don't feel Chinese') that make the claim factual and difficult to challenge (Pomerantz, 1986). Furthermore, the issue of being Chinese by birth is played down in describing it as 'a fact', and as only the visible outside. In addition, the fact that he does not talk Chinese although he probably could to some extent, and is no longer interested in Chinese culture, presents him as lacking attributes critical for being Chinese, a conclusion he draws himself later in his account (see Verkuyten & De Wolf, 2002a).

The extract is also a clear example of some of the dilemmas that ethnic minority group members face in claiming a particular sense of identity. For example, in giving a particular self-definition, Kent orients himself to the possible interpretations of 'being' and 'feeling'. A claim to feeling Dutch has to deal with the facts of birth and physical appearance.

Furthermore, arguing that one does not feel Chinese but rather Dutch may be interpreted as rejecting one's Chinese background and distancing oneself from one's parents. Kent is clearly orienting himself to this interpretation. He deals with it by stating explicitly that he values his parents' being Chinese and that he will not forget that. Thus, he not only differentiates himself from his Chinese parents, but also defines a link and continuation. Hence, he tries to carve out and account for a sense of ethnic identity in relation to his parents and his own Chinese background, and to the Dutch and his present situation in the Netherlands.

The ethnic self

Discursive and critical psychologists focus on the discourses that define particular subject positions and examine the linguistic strategies and accounts whereby participants achieve particular definitions of themselves and others. The emphasis is on the kinds of resources available in a culture for constructing identities and the discursive strategies of negotiation and management in actual social interactions. We have seen examples of this in the previous section and in other chapters. These approaches, however, do not tell us much about why particular identity positions are taken up in a specific situation but also habitually and predictably across situations. That is to say, discourse studies do not explain why an individual adopts a particular position out of a range of identity options or why there are individual differences in the identity positions adopted. Within ethnic groups, individuals may experience and respond differently to the forms of ethnic assignment they encounter. The inner life or personal subjectivity should not be ignored or neglected but is needed to understand each subject's abilities, investments, and creativity in identity negotiations. Several theorists sympathetic to discourse analyses have pointed out that an emphasis on discourse and discursive strategies runs the risk of overlooking the psychological or subjective dimension (e.g. Burr, 1995). For example, some writers have incorporated psychoanalytic ideas in order to complement discourse analysis (e.g. Billig, 1997a; Frosh et al., 2003; Parker, 1997), and others emphasize personal experiences and life histories (e.g. Hollway, 1989; Stapleton & Wilson, 2003).

Ethnic minority individuals are agents who actively negotiate their situational ethnic identity in relation to various others in a multitude of contexts. For these negotiations, the inner life or more private, interiorized sense of identity is important. Individual agency regarding the assertion and management of ethnic identity is constrained and influenced not only by discursive regimes and the politics of recognition, but also by personal resources such as feelings, capacities, abilities, and the structured mental representations of one's experiences and self. Situated self-conceptions are also dependent on the self-concept or on ongoing self-understandings and sets of commitments. Furthermore, this inner life is an important topic in itself. For one thing, it relates to the subjective human experience of self-continuity and singularity, which is obscured by discursive psychology (Craig, 1997). In addition, it is relevant to know what it actually feels like to be treated as an 'outsider', face discrimination and racism, or be defined as an asylum seeker or given refugee status. Discriminatory treatment, for example, can have serious cognitive and emotional consequences, such as feelings of helplessness, anxiety, and depression (see Major et al., 2002). Discursive approaches argue that these psychological consequences themselves are not separate from discourse but intrinsically social, constituted within shared patterns of understanding and interactions (e.g. Edwards, 1997; Harré & Gillett, 1994). However, this does not mean that these consequences can be reduced to discourses, and that we can ignore how positions or experiences become personal or part of people's psychology. The psychological realm may play a role in (habitually) taking up particular positions and in understanding the disturbing effects of negative experiences on human functioning and well-being. For example, members of ethnic minority groups may feel insecure and preoccupied with their ethnic identity or develop a clear and achieved sense of what their ethnicity means to them. There can be important tensions between identity assignments, or what people are socially taken to be, and the way they typically see and experience themselves.

Selçuk's two statements are perhaps related to being unclear, confused, or insecure about what his ethnic identity means to him. He might be going through the typical adolescent process of searching and exploring alternative positions and meanings. This process of exploration and choosing may not have evolved yet into a formed and secure ethnic self-understanding and commitment. This can make him volatile and more susceptible to situational pressures, resulting, for example, in his responding in a socially desirable way. Selçuk may also consider his ethnic identity as a not very central part of what he considers himself to be and therefore may not have very strong views about it. Or his feelings about his ethnicity may not be very stable; on a more unconscious level, he may be less positive about his ethnic identity than he claims.

These possible interpretations focus on Selçuk's inner life or the development of his ethnic self. In the literature, there are various approaches and models that try to account for the more psychological dimension of ethnic identity. There are cognitive-structural approaches that focus on the extent to which ethnicity is a central part of the self-concept and how ethnic identity is related to other aspects of the self. There are approaches that examine the evaluative and affective meanings, such as ethnic self-esteem. And there are studies that examine the process of becoming Turkish, Chinese, Dutch, or black in terms of a developmental progression involving various stages. I will discuss these three approaches in the following sections by considering the relevant literature.

Cognitive centrality

Using a structural approach, many social psychologists have investigated different components of the self-concept and the way they are organized (e.g. Byrne & Shavelson, 1996; Greenwald & Pratkanis, 1984; Higgins, 1996; Markus, 1977; Marsh & Shavelson, 1976). This body of work is quite influential and has led to some well-established findings. These studies examine the self as a relatively stable, enduring cognitive-affective structure that reflects personal experiences and circumstances and determines the processing of information. In this 'personality' model of the self-concept (Turner & Onorato, 1999), the unique characteristics of the individual are emphasized. The focus is on personal meanings and on the self as a separate schema or stored mental structure of self-knowledge that organizes experiences.

The idea of the differential importance of aspects or dimensions is proposed by various models of the self, using terms such as 'self-schema' (Markus, 1977), 'psychological centrality' (Rosenberg, 1979), and 'identity prominence' (McCall & Simmons, 1978). The general assumption here is that social identities vary in the degree to which they are part of the self relative to other identities. Cognitively, certain self-categories or constructs stand out, are at the forefront of attention, and are close to one's core definition of self. These categories strongly organize knowledge about the self, whereas others are more peripheral or secondary. In Chapter 2, the example of 'race man' and 'race woman' was given.

The concept of centrality features in many approaches to ethnic and racial minority identity. Typically, it is assumed that these identities are quite central to how minority members see themselves. Furthermore, studying the structure of the self is considered essential in multicultural societies because of the interplay of multiple identifications (e.g. Chryssochoou, 2000).

Sellers et al. (1998) have developed a multidimensional model of ethnic and racial identity. The model tries to offer a synthesis of the strengths of approaches that focus on general properties associated with ethnic and racial identities and approaches that emphasize the unique cultural and historical experiences of minority groups (in their case, African-Americans). One dimension in their model is racial centrality, which refers to the significance that individuals attach to race in defining themselves. It is described as 'the extent to which a person normatively defines himself or herself with regard to race. . . . Centrality is, by definition, relatively stable across situations' (Sellers et al., 1998, p. 25). In combination with contextual cues, centrality or perceiver readiness (Turner, 1999) would result in momentary, situated racial identity salience. Centrality would also explain individual differences in salience within the same event.

The conceptualization of centrality relies on a phenomenological perspective in determining whether ethnicity or race is important to a person's self-concept. The focus is on individual differences in the importance of these categories in people's mental lives. Researchers have proposed various measures to assess the centrality of identity dimensions of the self. For example, the 'identity' subscale of Luhtanen and Crocker's (1992) measure of collective self-esteem focuses on the perceived importance of one's membership in a particular group. Sellers et al. (1998) propose a 'centrality subscale'. In our own studies in the Netherlands, we have assessed ethnic centrality by similar scales. These studies show that, in general, ethnic identity is a more central dimension of the self-concept for minority than majority group members (see Verkuyten, 1999). An example is a large-scale study among early adolescents in which items of the 'identity' subscale were used. Table 7.2 presents the results. Analysis of variance indicated a significant and clealy ethnic group difference. Post-hoc analysis showed that the Dutch participants had a lower score than the three minority groups. In addition, the Surinamese scored signifi- cantly lower than the two Islamic groups.

However, there are also differences within the minority and majority groups. For some members of these groups, ethnicity is quite pivotal, standing at the centre of their self-understanding, whereas for others it is more secondary. The former

Table 7.2 Perceived importance of ethnic identity (5-point scale) for four ethnic groups: mean scores and standard deviations (in parentheses)

	Dutch (N = 1525)	Surinamese (N = 123)	Moroccans (N = 409)	Turks (N = 529)
Importance of ethnic identity	2.67[a] (.86)	3.20[b] (.88)	3.43[c] (.73)	3.44[c] (.81)

Row means with different superscripts represent significant differences.

tend to define and present themselves ethnically in a relatively consistent and committed way, and change and inconsistencies tend to produce cognitive disruptions and emotional tensions. For the latter, change and inconsistencies are less problematic, and Selçuk is perhaps an example.

The fact that ethnicity is generally cognitively more central among minority groups does not mean that ethnicity predominates in the self-concept. Implicit in the conceptualization of centrality is a hierarchical ranking of different identities (e.g. Banaji & Prentice, 1994; Stryker, 1987). Measuring the perceived importance of a particular identity does not tell us much about how this identity is ranked and related to other dimensions of the self. People can consider their ethnicity important but define themselves more in terms of gender, age, religion, or nationality. For example, gender is often found to be a more central dimension of the self than ethnicity. In one of our large-scale studies using an open-ended elicitation technique,[5] we asked participants to rank-order their five most important self-definitions (Verkuyten, 1988). The results showed that Turkish and Moroccan adolescents ranked ethnic identity third, after religion and gender (see also Phinney & Alipuria, 1990).

Theories of self-knowledge structure argue that it is not just the various aspects of the self but also the relationships among the aspects that constitute the whole. Hence, it is important to theorize the structure of the self. As Deaux (1993, p. 8) observes, 'knowing which identities a person claims is not enough. Information about the position of an identity within the overall structure may be an important predictor of an affective state, behavioral choice and response to interventions.' The idea of the multiplicity of the self raises issues of rank-ordering and, in general, the question of how multiple identities are organized within the individual's overall self-concept. For example, Roccas and Brewer (2002) introduce the concept of social identity complexity to refer to people's subjective representation of the interrelationships among their multiple group memberships. They argue that the degree of complexity depends on the degree of overlap perceived to exist between multiple identities. Cognitively, ethnic identity can be close to or connected and enmeshed with other social identities, and various identity clusters can exist. That is to say, some identities can be perceived to be more similar than others, whereby each identity within a particular cluster tends to become more relevant when one identity within it is invoked in consciousness (Linville, 1985). Thus, when religion and ethnicity are cognitively clustered together, the one is likely to inform the content of the other.[6]

Relatively little is known about the structure of multiple social identities within the self, and the existing work uses a wide range of distinct theoretical and methodological approaches. Freeman (2003) gives a review of this literature and also presents his own research on the self-concept structure of 11 social identities among a representative sample of Sinhala adults in Sri Lanka. His analysis identified four identity clusters. One of which, 'conflictual' identities, is implicated in intergroup tensions in Sri Lanka, namely, religion, race, nation, and caste. The other clusters are 'geographic' identities (town of residence and political party), 'socioeconomic' identities (class, education, and occupations), and 'demographic' identities (age and gender). In addition, hierarchical clustering analysis indicated two higher-order identity clusters that combined, respectively, the first two and the last two clusters.

In our own research among Dutch and Turkish young people, we identified three identity clusters (Verkuyten, 1990). The first one contained religion, gender, and ethnicity; the second one combined age and appearance; and the third one included kinship and educational status. The clusters were very similar for both groups, with the exception of religion, which was not clustered by the Dutch, and place of residence, which for the Turks was included in the second cluster.

Freeman (2003) also found strong consistency in the structure of the self-concept across a wide range of distinct Sinhala subpopulations. These results raise the question of interpretation because the structures found may reflect culturally shared forms of social representation rather than private self-understandings (Deaux et al., 1995). However, the structures in these studies have been derived from self-descriptions, suggesting a connection to the self-concept at the individual level. Social representations are considered part of social reality but also of a person's cognition. The shared ideas and assumptions about the world are used to make sense of the self. There is, typically, a correspondence between social representations and personal understandings. However, personal meanings, needs, and experiences will inevitably also colour the internalization of the identity positions and options as defined in society.

Ethnicity and self-esteem

For several decades now, the self-esteem of ethnic and racial minorities has been a subject of great interest. There is a substantial body of research on various minority groups in different countries. A global feeling of self-esteem is widely recognized as a central aspect of the self-concept, of psychological functioning and well-being (Greenwald et al., 1988; Taylor & Brown, 1988; Wells & Marwell, 1976), and is strongly related to many other variables (Kaplan, 1982; Rosenberg, 1985), including general satisfaction with one's life (Veenhoven, 1984). Hence, many theorists agree that 'self-esteem is a crucial and pivotal concept in analysing race-relations' (Bagley, 1979, p. 127).

In their meta-analysis of the relationship between ethnic identity and global personal self-esteem, Bat-Chava and Steen (1997) classified the existing literature into three generations. The first generation saw members of ethnic minority groups as more or less passive recipients of the existing prejudice and stigmatization to which they are subject. The core idea was that minority group members would come to internalize society's negative view about their group and therefore show the 'mark of oppression' (Kardiner & Ovesey, 1951). This literature was predominantly theoretical and clinical in nature, and drew on insights from symbolic interaction theory and psychodynamics.

The second generation of this literature examined the assumption of low self-esteem empirically. Despite the existence of prejudice and stigmatization, many of these studies found that minority group membership was not systematically related to low personal self-esteem. The first empirical findings pointing in this direction triggered quite a debate (e.g. Adam, 1978; Pettigrew, 1978a), and this counterintuitive finding has been called the puzzle of high self-esteem (Simmons, 1978). However, since then, numerous studies in various Western countries and among diverse minority groups have found that in general, ethnic minorities do not have lower self-esteem (for reviews see Gray-Little & Hafdahl, 2000; Twenge & Crocker, 2002; Verkuyten, 1994).

In attempting to solve this puzzle, third-generation researchers have put forward several explanations. There are (sub)cultural explanations which stress the development of in-group values that allow a favourable interpretation of the self (McCarthy & Yancey, 1971). There are also more sociological explanations, which stress the importance of social networks in providing emotional and practical support in the face of negative group evaluations. Especially microsocial relations within family and community would insulate self-esteem from systems of inequality and derogation (Hughes & Demo, 1989). And there are more social psychological explanations that focus on how minorities themselves perceive and interpret their situation, and value their ethnic identity (Crocker & Major, 1989; Verkuyten, 1994). For example, Crocker and Major (1989) discuss three mechanisms by which stigmatized people may protect their self-esteem. Firstly, negative feedback can be attributed to prejudice against their group. Secondly, outcomes can be selectively compared with those of the members of one's own group. Thirdly, those attributes on which one's group typically fares poorly can be selectively devalued, and at the same time those attributes at which one's group excels can be emphasized and valued.

The notion of self-esteem can refer to the overall evaluation of oneself as a person, or how one feels about oneself in a comprehensive sense, and also to the evaluation of specific aspects of the self such as ethnic identity, global personal self-esteem, and ethnic self-esteem. Although global personal self-esteem is often inferred from measures of ethnic identity, several studies have shown that personal self-esteem is not the same as ethnic self-esteem (see Bat-Chava & Steen, 1997; Cross, 1991; Phinney, 1991, for reviews). How people feel about themselves in general is something different from how they feel about being a member of a specific ethnic group.[7]

Individuals' feelings about their ethnic or racial group membership are considered an important aspect of the ethnic or racial self. Terms such as 'ethnic and racial self-hatred' and 'negative identity', but also 'ethnic regard and pride' have been used to describe the identity of minority group members. Positive feelings and a positive evaluation of one's ethnicity are considered important components of a healthy and strong ethnic identity. In the literature, there are, however, differences in conceptualizing ethnic self-esteem. One difference relates to the question of stability as opposed to variability, and the other to the dual structure of (self-)attitudes.

Ethnic self-esteem is conceptualized as a more situational or state-like phenomenon and also as being more stable or trait-like. The former refers to a person's self-affect and self-evaluation in a particular situation, whereas the latter is the person's long-term, typical way of self-feeling. The former is assessed by asking how one feels about oneself right here and now (Heatherton & Polivy, 1991), whereas the latter assesses how one feels about oneself on average or generally (Rosenberg, 1965). These approaches are often discussed and presented in an either/or form: self-esteem is either stable or situational. However, in phenomenological terms, both are important and real. All of us are familiar with temporary increases or decreases in self-esteem due to, for example, a compliment or a criticism. But most of us have also developed a more habitual and characteristic form of self-esteem. Empirically, Savin-Williams and Demo (1983, p. 131) found that 'Self-feelings are apparently global and context dependent. The largest number of our adolescents had a baseline of self-evaluation from which fluctuations rose or fell mildly, most likely dependent on features of the context.' Following William James, Rosenberg (1986) makes a distinction between the barometric self-concept and the baseline self-concept. The barometric self refers to whether the person experiences a rapid shift and fluctuation of self-feelings from situation to situation. The baseline self, in contrast, refers to self-concept changes that take place slowly and over an extended period of time. It is against the baseline that there are situational fluctuations.

Empirically, studies on minority groups have provided evidence for the importance of both types of self-esteem, although the studies on trait-like self-esteem far outnumber those that examine situational self-feelings.

Several studies have examined situational or state-dependent self-esteem. For example, Brown (1998) shows that ethnic stigma is a contextual experience that leads to a negative self-image in the context of certain relationships. Crocker (1999) has argued and shown that self-esteem is constructed in the situation and depends on the shared meanings, or collective representations that are made contextually relevant. She concludes that self-esteem may change from situation to situation.

In one of our studies among 106 Turkish early adolescents, we elicited self-reports on experiences of either personal or ethnic peer victimization (Verkuyten & Thijs, 2001). Personal victimization refers to those situations where negative peer experiences are related to individual characteristics, such as acting 'strange' and stuttering. Ethnic group victimization occurs when children's negative experiences are connected to their ethnic group membership. To examine the causal effects of victimization, we assessed momentary self-feelings directly after self-reported peer victimization. It was expected that peer victimization had a negative effect on momentary self-feelings, independently of the level of trait-like personal and ethnic self-esteem. Furthermore, in order to examine the possible different effects of personal and ethnic victimization, we used a between-subjects design with two conditions.[8] For one group of Turkish participants, experiences with personal victimizations were elicited, whereas for the other group ethnic victimization was made salient. We explored whether personal and ethnic victimization differ in their negative impact on momentary self-feelings. In contrast to personal victimization, ethnic victimization is more specific for ethnic minority early adolescents than for majority group contemporaries. Hence, compared to personal victimization, ethnic victimization may be more strongly related to negative self-feelings. Stepwise multiple-regression analysis was performed to predict momentary self-feelings. The results are presented in Table 7.3.

Table 7.3 shows that peer victimization had a negative causal effect on momentary self-feelings, independently of the level of trait-like self-esteem. This effect for peer victimization was qualified by a significant interaction effect with the experimental condition (step 3). In the ethnic condition, the association between peer victimization and momentary self-feelings was marginally significant ($-.27$, $p = .062$), whereas in the personal condition the correlation was $-.13$ ($p > .10$). Hence, peer victimization based on ethnic background tended to have a stronger negative effect on momentary self-feelings of Turkish children than peer victimization based on personal characteristics.

Various studies have examined trait-like ethnic and racial self-esteem among minority group members. The idea here is that ethnic group memberships will develop into a more stable emotional and evaluative self-understanding. Research on the stability of self-esteem has found substantial continuity over time, comparable to the stability found for personality traits (see Trzesniewski et al., 2003).[9]

Underlying much of the design and interpretation of early identity research among African-Americans was the thesis of self-hatred. Literature on the development of racial identity dates back to the 1930s. These studies, typified by the work of the Clarks on colour and doll preferences among children, had a major

Table 7.3 Stepwise multiple regression analysis predicting momentary self-feelings (betas)

	Step 1	*Step 2*	*Step 3*
Contrast	−.08	−.07	−.08
Personal self-esteem	.43***	.37***	.40***
Ethnic self-esteem	.04	.05	.01
Peer victimization		−.19*	−.20*
Contrast			−.20*
Multiple r	.44	.47	.51
R square change	.17	.03	.04
F-change	7.79***	3.98*	4.86*

Contrast = ethnic − personal.
* $p < .05$; ** $p < .01$; *** $p < .001$.

impact on clinicians, theorists, and policy makers. The self-hatred thesis held that out-group preferences expressed by blacks reflected the damaging effects of racism. However, within the context of the social changes coinciding with the Civil Rights Movement in the 1960s, this thesis was replaced by an emphasis on a more assertive black identity. Subsequently, a more balanced perspective has developed in social psychology in which both vulnerability and resilience are seen as common responses to negative stereotypes and discrimination. The focus has shifted to the diversity and variability in responses and the factors that can explain this diversity and variability (see Major et al., 2002). It is recognized that individuals are not passive victims of others' opinions and beliefs but active agents who try to develop and maintain a positive sense of themselves and their ethnic or racial identity. There is increasing attention to the target's perspective (e.g. Celious & Oyserman, 2001).

Our research has consistently found that, compared to the Dutch, ethnic minority group members perceive more discrimination directed at themselves and their group, but also that they have a more positive sense of ethnic self-esteem (see Verkuyten, 1999). One explanation for this result focuses on the 'minority' aspect of ethnic minorities. For example, social-identity theory (Tajfel & Turner, 1986) argues that being a member of a minority group poses a threat to one's self-concept and that threat can be counteracted by accentuating positive distinctiveness. Based on social-identity theory, the 'rejection-identification model' (Branscombe et al., 1999) argues that members of minority groups increase group identification in response to perceived prejudice and discrimination. This model has received empirical support in studies of African-Americans and Mexican-Americans (Schmitt & Branscombe, 2002). In our own studies, we have also found evidence for this model. For example, in a study among Turkish and Kurdish adults, we found a significant and positive association ($r = .26$, $p < .01$) between perceived group discrimination and ethnic identification. This association was similar for both ethnic groups.

Another explanation emphasizes the 'ethnic' aspect. Hutnik (1991) argues that ethnic self-esteem is related to characteristics particular to the ethnic minority groups themselves. Most ethnic minority groups are endowed with a rich culture, tradition and structure of their own, which provides members with a sense of identity and dignity. Therefore, ethnic minority members do not have to look elsewhere for the construction of a positive ethnic identity. Furthermore, parental approval, support, and acceptance, as well as family harmony, are highly predictive indicators for self-esteem, at least during adolescence (Harter, 1999). The importance of parental nurturing and family harmony to self-esteem is found in various (Western and Eastern) countries (e.g. Herz & Gullone, 1999; Scott et al., 1991; Shek, 1999), and among both ethnic majority and minority group members (e.g. Greenberger & Chen, 1996; Hughes & Demo, 1989). Early childhood socialization leads to the development of a greater or lesser positive self-evaluation. Furthermore, ethnic minority families are sometimes able to filter out racist and discriminatory messages from the dominant community and provide positive feedback that enhances self-esteem (Barnes, 1980; Yabiku et al., 1999). Studies in the Netherlands have found that Turkish and Moroccan minority (early) adolescents endorse the value of family integrity more strongly than do Dutch adolescents, and that among the former group family integrity is more strongly related to ethnic self-esteem (e.g. Huiberts et al., 1999; Verkuyten, 2001b).[10]

Conceptualizations of ethnic self-esteem differ not only in their emphasis on stability as opposed to variability, but also in terms of explicitness. In writing about racial identity, Erikson (1966) argues that a sense of identity has conscious as well as unconscious aspects. He points out that there are aspects that are accessible only at moments of special awareness or not at all. In line with psychoanalytic ideas, he talks about repression and resistance. Recently, in social psychology, the distinction between conscious and unconscious has been conceptualized as one of dual attitudes (Wilson et al., 2000). The central idea here is that people can have different evaluations of the same attitude object: an implicit attitude and an explicit attitude. The former tend to be relatively stable and habitual evaluations that are formed early in life and are difficult to access through introspection. The latter are more context-sensitive and self-presentational responses that often change on the basis of the situation and available information. The attitude that people endorse at a particular moment depends on whether they have the time, capacity, and motivation to consider the situation. Sometimes people's evaluations are quick and spontaneous, and sometimes they are more thoughtful. Furthermore, implicit attitudes are thought to influence implicit or spontaneous behaviours, whereas explicit attitudes are related to more deliberative behaviour, such as when the person sees a link between attitude and behaviour. There is increasing empirical support for the implicit–explicit distinction, particularly in relation to stereotypes, prejudice, and self-esteem (for reviews, see Greenwald & Banaji, 1995; Greenwald et al., 2002; Wilson et al., 2000).

Implicit self-esteem refers to 'the introspectively unidentified . . . effect of the self-attitude on evaluation of self-associated and self-dissociated objects' (Greenwald & Banaji, 1995, p. 11). Assessing implicit self-esteem requires indirect or unobtrusive measures that do not use explicit self-report questions, which predominate in studies on self-esteem.[11] There can be a difference in implicit and explicit self-esteem. Hetts et al. (1999), for example, found an interesting discrepancy in implicit and explicit self-evaluations in Asian immigrants to the USA. They argued that groups with greater exposure to individualistic cultures would exhibit more favourable evaluations of the personal self and less favourable evaluations of the social self. However, this was expected only for implicit measures, and not for explicit ones. Responses on the latter measure would be influenced by the normative individualistic demands of the US cultural context that are quickly learned. In contrast, implicit measures would reflect the long-term influence of the immigrants' cultural collectivist upbringing that resists immediate change. Hence, acculturation would occur first at a conscious, explicit level and then more slowly at a habitual, implicit level. The results showed that compared to Anglos, these immigrants exhibited relatively low levels of personal self-esteem and high levels of social self-esteem on implicit measures, whereas there were no differences on the explicit measures. Hetts et al. also found that implicit and explicit measures were generally uncorrelated, supporting other research that finds dissociations between implicit and explicit belief systems (Greenwald & Banaji, 1995; Greenwald et al., 2002).[12]

In another study, Pelham and Hetts (1999) examined the puzzle of high self-esteem among minority groups. As indicated, this puzzle refers to the fact that despite the negative stereotypes, prejudice, and discrimination, the self-esteem of minority group members is at least as high as, and often higher than, the self-esteem of majority group members. Pelham and Hetts suggest that this puzzle may involve the explicit self-esteem of minority groups, and that on an implicit level minority members may feel less positive about their group membership. They found that, relative to Anglos, minority group members were lower in implicit ethnic self-esteem but higher in implicit personal self-esteem. Furthermore, participants' responses on the explicit and implicit measures again bore little resemblance to each other.

We found similar results when examining explicit and implicit personal and ethnic self-esteem among three groups of early adolescents: Dutch, Turks born and living in the Netherlands (Turkish-Dutch), and Turks in Turkey. We used different scales for measuring explicit and implicit self-esteem, including the name-letter technique.[13] The main results of this study are shown in Table 7.4.

Table 7.4 shows that for personal self-esteem, there is no significant difference between the three groups on the implicit measures. However, on the explicit measure, the Dutch score lower, and post-hoc analysis showed that only the difference between the Dutch and the Turkish-Dutch was significant. In ethnic self-esteem, the Turkish-Dutch and the Turks scored significantly higher than the Dutch. However, on the implicit measure, the Turkish-Dutch scored significantly lower

Table 7.4 Mean scores and standard deviations (in parentheses) on explicit and implicit measures of personal and ethnic self-esteem among three groups of participants

	Dutch (N=56)	*Turkish-Dutch* (N=47)	*Turks in Turkey* (N=49)	*F-value*
Personal self-esteem				
Explicit	3.41^a (.59)	3.78^b (.61)	3.57^{ab} (.56)	3.95*
Implicit				
'I/me'	5.05 (.99)	5.31 (1.37)	5.49 (1.45)	1.48
Name letter	0.56 (1.23)	0.89 (1.48)	0.69 (1.27)	0.54
Ethnic self-esteem				
Explicit	3.90^a (.70)	4.39^b (.68)	4.51^b (.72)	10.23***
Implicit				
'We/us'	5.33^a (.98)	4.58^b (1.14)	5.88^c (1.15)	14.39***

*$p < .05$, ***$p < .01$.
Row means with different superscripts represent significant differences.
For name letter evaluation: Dutch, N=37; Turkish-Dutch, N = 28; Turks in Turkey, N = 32.
Implicit self-esteem was measured on 7-point scales, and explicit self-esteem was measured on 5-point scales.

than the other two groups. Hence, on a conscious level, the Turkish-Dutch present a positive evaluation of their ethnic selves, but at a more unconscious level they are less positive about their ethnicity. Their minority position in the Netherlands seems to have a negative effect on their more implicit ethnic self-feelings. An additional finding supporting this interpretation is that for this group, perceived discrimination was negatively associated only with implicit ethnic self-esteem ($r = -.31, p < .01$), and not with the other self-esteem measures.

The fact that for personal self-esteem there is no difference in the implicit measure may indicate the importance of parental nurturing and family harmony for the development of early positive self-esteem. However, the Turkish-Dutch have higher explicit personal self-esteem than the Dutch. One reason could be that they tend more strongly to present a favourable conception of themselves.

Furthermore, as in other studies, there was a clear dissociation between explicit and implicit self-evaluations. The explicit personal and ethnic self-esteem measures were positively correlated ($.33, p < .01$). However, there were no associations between the implicit measures, nor between the explicit and implicit measures. This result is similar to what is found in many other studies (see Bosson et al., 2000; Fazio & Olson, 2003) and suggests that different measures do not tap into the same underlying construct.

The relative length of this section reflects the great amount of work that has been done on self-esteem among ethnic minority groups (for reviews, see Gray-Little & Hafdahl, 2000; Twenge & Crocker, 2002). Numerous studies have been conducted and many variables and conditions have been examined. I have not tried to give an overview of this research, but I have, rather, focused on the issue of stability and variability of self-esteem and on the distinction between explicit and implicit self-evaluations. To return to Selçuk, there are various possible inter-pretations of his two statements. On the more implicit level, he may be less positive about his ethnic identity than he claims to be in the classroom. There can be a difference between his implicit and explicit ethnic self-esteem. Or he may momentarily feel very positive about his ethnicity in the context of the class discussion and rather indifferent about it in the situation of the canteen.

The development of the ethnic self

From a developmental perspective, Selçuk's statements might indicate or reflect insecurity, confusion, or an 'identity crisis' about his ethnicity. He may be involved in a search for a meaningful and coherent sense of identity and have not yet made a clear commitment. Developmental models assume that the sense of ethnic and racial identity develops over the lifespan and that a period of exploration into the meanings of ethnicity is central to ethnic identity development. The ethnic self is taken to be a developmental process moving from a lack of awareness to acceptance and internalization of ethnic identity.[14]

Different developmental models have been proposed to describe the unique cultural and structural experiences associated with the position of African-Americans (e.g. Cross, 1991; Helms, 1995; Parham, 1989).[15] These models describe the process of 'becoming black' or racial self-actualization. One of the first formal and most influential of these is Cross's model of nigrescence (Cross, 1991). The model describes the social-developmental sequence through which African-Americans come to terms with their race and the society in which they live.[16] The original model describes four distinct racial identity stages: 1) The pre-encounter stage is marked by nonracial identification in which a white frame of reference rather than a black one is used. 2) Next comes the encounter stage in which typically negative experiences with racial prejudice and discrimination raise racial consciousness and encourage the (re)examination of racial identity. 3) The immersion-emersion stage indicates high racial identity involvement in thought, feeling, and behaviour. Here an African-American frame of reference predominates, and pro-black and anti-white attitudes develop. 4) Finally, we have the internalization stage in which the individual's racial identity 'matures' into a secure, comfortable, stable, and yet more flexible orientation, and a less idealized view of black identity.

Some of the assumptions of this original model have been revised and extended (Cross, 1991; Parham, 1989), but the model remains an important framework for examining racial identity. However, the fact that the Cross model focuses on the experiential and cultural influences on African-American identity is both its strength and a weakness. On the one hand, the model examines the qualitative aspects of racial identity development in detail. However, on the other hand, the model is specific to African-Americans; that is, the model does not simply apply to other ethnic minority groups in and outside the USA (e.g. Atkinson et al., 1990).[17]

Other proposed models focus more on general developments of racial and ethnic identity.[18] The emphasis here is on common psychological processes related to ethnic identities, and not on the unique experiences of each group. An example of this is 'identity structure analysis', as developed by Weinreich (1986, 2003). Weinreich has developed a complex conceptual framework that consists of a synthesis of concepts derived from aspects of Erikson's psychodynamic work on identity development, Kelly's personal construct theory, and symbolic inter-actionism. He stresses that individuals are all subject to the same psychological pressures which produce their changing self-conceptions, but that there are also special pressures faced by ethnic minorities, such as negative group images and discrimination. In addition, there are the unique biographical histories of individuals. Weinreich examines ethnic identity as that part of the totality of one's self-construal that is made up of one's interpretation of ancestral heritage and future aspirations for progeny. Based on identification patterns, identity-structure analysis makes a distinction among 'identity variants' such as identity diffusion, defensive high self-regard, indeterminate identity, and confident identity.

Another example is offered by Phinney (1990, 1992), who argues that ethnic identity entails general phenomena that are relevant and comparable across groups. Her starting point is Erikson's (1968) developmental theory of ego identity formation and the related identity statuses proposed and studied by Marcia (1966). As in the ego-identity statuses of diffusion, foreclosure, moratorium, and achievement, individuals are thought to form their ethnic or racial identity by exploring and making decisions about the role of race and ethnicity in their lives. Phinney (1989) proposes a three-stage progression from an unexamined ethnic identity (diffusion and foreclosure) through a period of exploration (moratorium) to an achieved or committed ethnic identity. The process of ethnic identity formation involves the exploration of the meanings and implications of one's ethnicity that leads to a secure or more diffuse sense of one's ethnic group membership. Ethnic identity achievement refers to the extent to which people have developed a secure sense of themselves as members of an ethnic group, and a clear understanding and confident acceptance of their ethnicity. Phinney has conducted several studies that provide empirical evidence for these three distinct stages of ethnic identity (e.g. Phinney, 1989; Phinney & Tarver, 1988). She has also developed a measure for assessing ethnic identity achievement that can be applied across groups (Phinney, 1992), and that has been used among minority groups in the USA, including African-Americans (e.g. Goodstein & Ponterotto, 1997; Phinney, 1989), and outside the USA (e.g. Jasinskaja-Lahti & Liebkind, 1999).

We have also used this measure in different studies. Age has been defined as a key variable affecting the ethnic identity status of adolescents and young adults. As Phinney (1992, p. 162) argues, 'Ethnic identity achievement, by analogy with ego identity formation, has been assumed to be a central developmental process during adolescence, and there is some longitudinal data showing the expected change with age.' The early stages of development are seen as typical of early adolescents, with an achieved ethnic identity developing in late adolescence or young adulthood. However, empirical studies have not always found an age effect in ethnic identity achievement (e.g. Branch et al., 2000), and we have also not been able to find clear evidence for increased ethnic identity achievement in adolescence. In general, the scores for ethnic minority groups on Phinney's ethnic achievement scale tend to be quite high, and the results suggest that ethnic group membership is a much more powerful contributor to achievement scores than age. Furthermore, in a study among 94 Surinamese participants between the ages of 14 and 17 (Verkuyten & Brug, 2002), we found that the evaluation of ethnic identity mediated the relationship between ethnic identity achievement and global self-esteem. Exploration and resolution of identity issues and a clear understanding of the role of ethnicity for oneself were related to a positive attitude towards one's ethnic identity, which in turn was related to a more positive self-esteem. Hence, ethnic identity achievement affected global self-esteem insofar as the evaluation of ethnic group membership was affected and to the degree that self-esteem was derived from ethnic group aspects of the self.

Ethnic identity exploration and development might be the result of significant experiences that force one to consider one's ethnicity. These experiences will often include discrimination and negative stereotypes from the majority group or at least an increased awareness that one's group is seen and treated differently. Most models of racial and ethnic identity suggest that experiences of ethnic prejudice and discrimination serve as an 'encounter'. In the first, early stage of development, ethnic identity would not clearly be related to discrimination but would be predominantly influenced by the positive ethnic attitudes of family and other adults. In the second stage, negative experiences would stimulate explorations into the meaning of one's ethnicity. In two studies among Turkish, Moroccan, and Surinamese early adolescents, we found that the importance attached to one's ethnic identity was not related to the perception of discrimination (Verkuyten, 2002). Thus, those who attached great importance to their ethnic group membership did not perceive more discrimination than did those who had a more diffused ethnic self. Studies in the USA as well in the Netherlands also found no relationship between ethnic identity achievement and perceived discrimination in middle adolescence (e.g. Phinney et al., 1998; Verkuyten & Brug, 2002). Such a relationship may be more characteristic of late adolescence. In a study among Turkish middle adolescents, we found no significant association between ethnic identity achievement and perceived discrimination (.09, $p > .05$), whereas there was a positive association for Turkish late adolescents and young adults (.31, $p < .05$).

However, in the previous paragraph, we discussed our finding for Turkish early adolescents of a significant negative correlation between perceived discrimination and implicit ethnic self-esteem. The distinction between explicit and implicit self-esteem can be used to define qualitatively different forms of self-esteem that are related to defensiveness. Particularly, it has been suggested that high self-esteem can be secure and adaptive or rather defensive and maladaptive. Secure high self-esteem is confidently held and would involve positive explicit and implicit self-esteem. Defensive high self-esteem is characterized by fragility and vulnerability to threat and would involve high explicit and low implicit self-esteem (see Jordan et al., 2003; Kernis & Paradise, 2002).

In our study, a split around the neutral midpoint of the scales was used to construct two categories of high ethnic self-esteem participants: defensive and secure high ethnic self-esteem. Of all participants, 77.3% had secure high ethnic self-esteem, and 22.7% were categorized as having defensive high ethnic self-esteem. There was, however, a clear and significant difference between the three groups of participants. As shown in Figure 7.4, a much higher percentage of the Turkish-Dutch participants (44.4%) had defensive high ethnic self-esteem.[19] These results indicate more defensive ethnic self-esteem among the ethnic minority group (44.4%). A substantial proportion of Turkish adolescents seem to have defensive high self-esteem, and Selçuk might be one of them.

However, it is unclear whether a similar pattern exists for older minority group members and for different ethnic minority groups. Examining stages of ethnic identity development is not without difficulties. There are theoretical and conceptual problems related to stage models in general and with respect to ethnic and racial identity in particular. There are also methodological difficulties, and there is a lack of longitudinal and cross-sectional data. A developmental perspective, however, offers a way of thinking about gradual changes in the ethnic self as individuals develop and resolve issues and feelings about their ethnicity. There is an extensive literature on ego identity development that can be used to examine the psychological correlates of ethnicity which influence an individual's inner life and well-being. However, it is important to note that this literature is

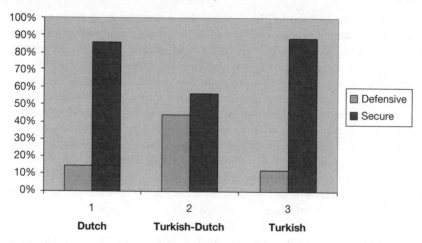

Figure 7.4 Percentages of participants with defensive and secure ethnic self-esteem: three groups of early adolescents.

moving away from general, rather simple conceptions of human development toward more ecological conceptions that depict variable pathways. There is no one pathway of development, and there is no single pathway for the development of a sense of ethnic identity. Rather, there are many ways to become ethnic. Not all people will go through the different stages or experience them in the proposed order. Much more work is needed to portray and examine the diversity of the ethnic and racial trajectories in relation to sociocultural circumstances.

Conclusions

In this chapter, I have discussed a number of different empirical studies. I started with Selçuk and used his example throughout the chapter to illustrate the kind of questions and issues that the various empirical approaches address. My aim was to show what is involved in these approaches and to identify the main points of difference. The discussion focused on three different interpretations of Selçuk's apparently inconsistent statements.

The first one emphasizes the key role of context in what people say and do. Context can mean quite different things within different approaches, and the problem of context is a recurrent one, both in mainstream and discursive social psychology.

The notion that features of the self are activated and constructed in response to different environments is a central tenet of various approaches within mainstream social psychology. Work on 'multiple selves' and on the situated self-concept have emphasized this. For example, McGuire and colleagues have shown that the salience of ethnicity in 'spontaneous' self-descriptions is a function of one's ethnic distinctiveness in the social environment (McGuire et al., 1978).[20] People tend to describe themselves in ethnic terms when ethnic characteristics are distinctive in relation to others in the situation. Furthermore, work using social-identity theory has convincingly shown that individual perception, evaluation, and behaviour are determined by a variety of contextual features, including social norms and the nature of the intergroup situation. For example, in self-categorization theory, the focus is on the self as a set of comparative, relational judgements rather than as subsets of mental structures (Turner & Onorato, 1999). This line of work strongly emphasizes the changing and situational character of social-identity processes. People describe themselves in relation to specific social contexts, meaning that their self-descriptions can differ across situations. In these approaches, variations in self-descriptions are predominantly interpreted in terms of cognitive processes. The focus is on individuals' sense-making in context or the processes of self-conception rather than on the structured self-concept.

In discourse studies, an emphasis on context is also central to understanding and interpreting how people define and describe themselves and others. These studies are concerned with social interactions and examine discourses in relation to action and accountability. The way people define and describe themselves is examined as accomplishments of interactive tasks. Variability in self-descriptions is related to identity management and negotiation in context. However, in discourse studies, the problem of context is not a simple one (see Auer & Di Luzio, 1992; Goodwin & Duranti, 1992). Not only does context mean quite different things within different discourse approaches, but these approaches also have a different stance towards the role context should play in analyses. Context is often seen as a frame—which is itself constituted in discourse—that provides resources for the appropriate interpretation of the talk being examined. Discursive psychologists that use a more conversational analytic procedure focus on the sequential organization of interactions and tend to restrict context to the text or discourse itself. Other discursive oriented psychologists are less interested in the sequencing of activities in talk and examine talk as embedded within a wider social context (Billig, 1987; Wetherell, 1998).

A second interpretation of Selçuk's statements discussed in this chapter focused on the multifaceted nature of the sense of ethnic identity. Most researchers regard self-understanding in terms of ethnic, racial, and other social identities as multi-dimensional. Various dimensions have been proposed, and these can be relatively independent. Hence, a self-definition in ethnic terms can have different meanings, and therefore inconsistencies may be more apparent than real.

In this chapter, I have discussed four more general dimensions that refer to being, feeling, doing, and knowing. These four dimensions can be used to conceptualize and assess different aspects of the sense of ethnic identity. These dimensions can be relatively independent, but the often low interrelations raise questions about whether these are indeed aspects of a common construct. In studies on social identities, there is the much neglected but key question of construct validity (Ashmore et al., 2001). In the literature, different dimensions and aspects are being proposed as part of the sense of ethnicity, but some of these are also treated as causes, correlates, and consequences of identification. For example, contacts, friendships, and all kinds of preferences are taken as indicators of a sense of ethnic identity but also as consequences and causes. Depending on the researcher's often implicit understanding of what defines (a particular) ethnic identity, various dimensions and measures are used and different correlates are examined.

The four aspects of being, feeling, doing, and knowing can be treated not only as dimensions of the ethnic self but also as accounts or cultural discourses used interactionally for managing and negotiating ethnic self-definitions. The example of the Chinese participants showed that being, feeling, doing, and knowing Chinese offers particular accounts that involve different degrees of determinism. These are familiar and socially shared understandings that were used by the participants to criticize and justify their own self-definitions and those of others. For example, the ability to speak and read Chinese was used to define 'real', or authentic, and 'fake' Chinese people. Claims made as to the possession or nonpossession of these and/or other prototypical or group-defining attributes can be a useful strategy in accounting for ethnic self-definitions. Studies into the complex, diverse, and interactive accounts of identity definitions can tell us something about the ways that people negotiate about how they themselves and others are positioned and understood. The focus is on the kind of resources available in society for constructing identity positions and the positions that are actually taken up in interactions. These studies, however, do not show that underlying mental tendencies, attitudes, or personal subjectivity do not exist or are secondary. An emphasis on discourse and discursive strategies does not mean that the psychological or subjective dimension can be ignored.

The third interpretation of Selçuk's example focused on the inner life or sense of ethnic identity. People can be unclear or confused about what their ethnic identity means to them. They may have yet to form a secure ethnic self-understanding and commitment. They may also consider their ethnic identity as either a central or a rather secondary part of what they consider themselves to be. And self-feelings about one's ethnicity may not be very stable, or, on a more unconscious level, they may be less positive than how one presents oneself. In the literature, there are various approaches and models that focus on the psychological dimension or the ethnic self. I have discussed three of them.

Firstly, cognitive structural approaches focus on the extent to which ethnicity or race is a central part of the self-concept and how these social identities are related to other aspects of the self. The idea of differential importance of aspects of the self is proposed in various models, and the notion of centrality features in most approaches to the ethnic and racial self. Cognitively, certain self-categories are assumed to strongly influence the organization of knowledge about the self, whereas others are more peripheral. Cognitive centrality would mean relative stability across situations and a person's high readiness to use the category for situational self-definition (e.g. Sellers et al., 1998).

Secondly, numerous studies have examined the evaluative and affective meanings of ethnic identity and ethnic self-esteem in particular (see Gray-Little & Hafdahl, 2000; Twenge & Crocker, 2002). Feelings about one's ethnic identity are considered important aspects of the ethnic self. Positive feelings are typically considered as essential for a healthy and strong sense of identity, and concepts such as self-hatred and negative identity have been used to describe the psychological predicaments of a stigmatized minority position. In the context of this chapter, I have not tried to give an overview of this extensive field but have, rather, focused on two points of debate: stability versus variability, and implicit and explicit self-esteem. These debates are often conducted in an either/or way, but I have tried to show that the different positions can coexist and be used alongside each other.

Thirdly, there are studies that examine the process of becoming ethnic in terms of a developmental progression involving various stages (see Phinney, 1990). Similar to Erikson's (1968) work on ego identity development, ethnic identification is considered a developmental process moving from a lack of awareness to acceptance and internalization of ethnic identity. Developmental models assume that the sense of ethnic and racial identity develops over the lifespan and that a period of exploration into the meaning of ethnicity is central to ethnic identity development. Different models have been proposed, but these are not without problems and there is also a lack of empirical data.

These three approaches offer a particular understanding of the ethnic self. Such an understanding is important in itself because it allows an examination of the subjective meanings and correlates of ethnicity. Ethnic assignments can differ from the sense of ethnic identity that develops over the lifespan and which may involve complex self-understandings and feelings, such as pride, belonging, and security, but also distress, self-rejection, and disruption. It is also important because, as an internal point of reference, the ethnic self plays a role in each subject's abilities and investments in managing and negotiating identities in social interactions. Coté and Levine (2002, p. 157) talk about 'identity capital' to denote the psychological investments individuals make and have in 'who they are'. This notion describes 'how the individual invests in a certain identity (or identities) and engages in a series of exchanges with other actors aimed at the validation of personal and social identities'. Concepts and perspectives that model psychological processes and structures are necessary. Without these, the individual is undertheorized, and as a result so is the structure–agency relationship (Jenkins, 2001).

8 Conclusion: Towards a better understanding

Questions of ethnicity, international migration, integration, and multiculturalism are hotly debated in many countries. There is growing popular attention to and concern about the meanings, experiences, and politics surrounding ethnic identity. Ethnicity is a main axis of differentiation and identification for many people and in various contexts. It structures relationships at the global, national, and local level, in institutions and everyday interactions, and it has become centrally important to many people's sense of themselves. No single Western nation can resist or reverse the developments of ethnic pluralism and migration. And no nation can control processes of globalization that challenge old boundaries and produce a new framework within which identities are shaped in relation to diaspora, trans-nationalism, and hybridity. These developments produce uncertainty because they challenge existing frames of reference, including people's sense of who they are. Politicians, institutions, and ordinary people struggle with the associated questions and problems. Increasing xenophobia and racism, but also multicultural programmes and anti-racism initiatives, are but some of the ways in which these quite different groups have responded. A politics of identity or one of assimilation, is another. Immigration and the presence of ethnic minority groups can be conceived as a valuable addition to society, leading to multicultural notions, or as posing threats to the majority group and hampering the upward social mobility of minorities, leading to assimilationist thinking. Ethnicity, migration, and notions of cultural diversity are key social issues and have led to a proliferation of theoretical and empirical studies in the social sciences.

Ethnicity and social psychology

In the past decades, the number of popular and academic writings on ethnic identity has increased enormously. Social psychologists, however, have been rather slow in making a contribution to this area. This is somewhat surprising because social psychology has much to offer with its central interest in social categories, identities, and intergroup relations. In the different chapters of this book, I have shown that social psychological concepts and theories can improve our understanding of questions and issues surrounding ethnic identity and cultural diversity. For example, social-identity theory and self-categorization theory provide valuable frameworks. Furthermore, research on stereotypes, group essentialism, cross-categorization, acculturation, and self-concepts raises important questions and offers useful perspectives. Scholars in sociology, anthropology, and cultural studies have stressed the close relationship between ethnicity and essentialist group beliefs, but little is known about the psychological processes involved and about the rhetorical ways in which essentialist notions are used and challenged in social interactions. In addition, there is the often important role of emotions and the diffuse sense of belonging that tends to give ethnic groups a primordial character. In popular discourse, ethnic attachments and identities are seen typically as part of the realm of sentiments, passions, and belonging. Social psychologists can make an important contribution to understanding the role, nature, and types of affect involved in relation to category constructions and how emotional discourses feature in social interactions. In addition, social psychology can make a contribution by empirically examining the many fashionable claims in the social sciences about syncretism, creolization, and hyphenated and hybrid identities. The theoretical writing on these issues greatly exceeds the empirical work. Hence, it is unclear whether identities are really as multiple, mixed, and fragmented as they are claimed to be in some discussions. It is also unclear what is involved here in terms of skills, competences, feelings, self-concept structures, and discursive strategies in producing social accountability.

The diversity within social psychology allows us to examine ethnic identity from different perspectives, at different levels, and with various methods. Critical and discursive social psychologists have moved the field beyond a focus on mental processes in the direction of sociological social psychology with its interest in social structure and social interactions. Attention to structural and cultural conditions that define particular subject positions and identity options is critically important for understanding issues of ethnic identity. And it is centrally important to examine exactly how these positions actually are taken up in interactions and the ways that identity choices are managed and negotiated. It is the level of interaction that mediates between society and the individual. It is in social interactions that beliefs, images, and definitions are (re-)produced and changed, validated, and challenged, and it is in interactions that a sense of identity develops. A focus on interaction and discursive action is necessary to understand how ethnicity structures people's lives and the ways in which ethnic minority groups and individuals are able to assert and negotiate their desired ethnic identities. But these assertions and negotiations are also informed and constrained by images, discourses, and practices at the level of society and institutions. Furthermore, it is important to examine individual perceptions and self-understandings. Social processes of identity maintenance and negotiation are related to psychological processes of identity development. Self-understandings can differ from social assignments, a difference which might lead to a sense of ethnic identity that is disrupted, insecure, and negative. Psychologically, one's ethnicity can become a central and distracting issue; socially, one can face the problem of establishing and affirming an acceptable ethnic identity. Ethnic identity is socially defined and negotiated but also provides a horizon for self-understanding, a source for positive and negative self-feelings, and an interior substance with which to engage with the world.

The diversity within social psychology has an additional potential benefit for the study of ethnic identity. The different methodologies favoured by the various approaches allow for a variety of systematic, rigorous empirical research. In the social sciences, much of the contemporary writing on ethnicity is theoretical and ethnographic. The power of ethnographic work is that it gives a rich, in-depth description of people's situated actions and the everyday practices that make up their lives. Such description, however, lacks the generalizability of theory and the specificity of empirical methods. One often has to take on trust the conclusions of ethnographic work because the evidence on which they are based cannot be assessed. Social psychologists have developed theories and more rigorous research methods. Discursive psychologists, for example, have developed fine-grained techniques for detailed studies of social interactions and practices, and situated talk in particular. Others have focused on social representations and the shared, pre-existing, but flexible, interpretative resources with which people build their accounts in order to achieve particular ends. These lines of work have a strong empirical focus in which the critical analytic question, 'How do you know?', is a recurrent one.

In addition, in discourse approaches, the issue of consequences and effects is central. Discursive psychologists examine consequences in terms of the sequential organization of conversations or the visible consequentiality in social interactions, whereas critical studies tend to examine consequences by unmasking discourses or making textual deconstructions. In many of these studies, however, the investigation of the central issue of consequences and effects is not without restrictions. The consequences of particular discourses or interpretations may go beyond the sequential organization of talk in a particular setting, and the extent to which discourses and interpretations actually affect people's understandings and reactions is largely left unexamined in studies of textual deconstructions. Moreover, it is often difficult to determine which particular aspects of interpretations affect people's reactions. The experimental technique is a powerful social psychological device for investigating causal relationships. In Chapter 7, we have seen that it can be used to examine whether ethnic identification is affected by different ideological notions, and whether the group and the cultural context affect self-stereotyping. Obviously, experiments, like all methods, have their limits and restrictions, such as an often questionable ecological validity. However, they do allow for controlled studies that are not necessarily far from social reality. After all, there are often moments in people's lives where a relatively simple response is required to a particular construction of a complex reality, such as for elections, referenda, policy decisions, and practical recommendations. Ethnic and immigration issues, for example, can be framed, by politicians or others, in a variety of ways, and it is possible to examine the effects of this in a controlled way (Augoustinos & Quinn, 2003; Verkuyten, 2005).

Social psychology can improve our understanding of questions and issues surrounding ethnicity. In addition, there are benefits to social psychology in studying these issues. This includes the introduction of relatively new topics such as immigration, hybridity, and diaspora, and the possibility to critically examine implicit assumptions, established theories, and popular concepts. In trying to understand the complexities of real-world ethnic phenomena, one becomes keenly aware of the fact that social psychology has to move forward and open up. Some of the field's key assumptions and models are restrictive and limited. I have given examples of this in the preceding chapters. For example, social psychologists tend to examine ethnicity in terms of general processes and as just another social category. The focus is on the basic cognitive mechanisms and motivations that act upon categories such as ethnicity, or on common discursive devices and strategies of identity management and negotiation. This focus is important and useful, but, as a result, ethnicity as such is not theorized, and the question of what is typical of ethnic identity is not asked.

Other disciplines, particularly anthropology, have a strong interest in ethnicity. Hence, the topic of ethnic identity offers social psychology the opportunity to consider anthropological work in which ethnicity has been a key concept since the late 1960s. I have discussed some of this work in Chapter 3 and elsewhere throughout the book. There is a close relationship between anthropology and social psychology, and the former can make a valuable contribution to social psychological thinking (and vice versa). This is particularly so in view of social psychologists' increased interest in content, culture, interaction, and context. Ethnic studies can give a useful impetus to this development. Anthropologists have shown that historical notions and ideas about common ancestry as well as (assumed) cultural characteristics play a central role in ethnic identity and interethnic relations in particular settings. Hence, social psychology increasingly should find adequate ways to study issues related to history, culture, interactions, and contexts.

Another example of the need for social psychology to broaden its scope is related to the limits of a simple, dualist majority–minority distinction that is central in most social psychological thinking. As we have seen, this is a very useful framework but only for some situations and for some questions. It tends to ignore, for example, the diversity of social comparisons, the flexible definitions of in-groups and out-groups, important within-group differences, and the central role of the members of one's own ethnic group or co-ethnics. Personal agency regarding the assertion of ethnic identity is constrained and influenced not only by majority group stereotyping and discrimination but also by the meanings, politics, and practices of recognition and authenticity within minority groups. People negotiate their ethnic identities in relation to both out-group and in-group members, outsiders and insiders, in a multitude of contexts. A further problem with the dualist model is that the focus is implicitly on the nation state. As a result, there is often no adequate basis for analysing and understanding particular localities and places, such as inner-city areas, but also no room for the transnational spaces in which many immigrant groups operate.

In addition, social psychological theories and approaches are not very adequate for examining the messier categories of social life, in which mixing and blending occur and hybrid identities develop that transgress dualist and binary ways of thinking. Social identities typically tend to be taken as 'pure' categories that make people think and act in homogeneous ways. In contrast, notions of syncretism and hybridity stress the complexities of identities and cultures, and question ideas and approaches that assume or impose clear boundaries. Social psychology must stay in touch with the rapid social changes of our times, in which mixing and transgression are increasingly common phenomena, if it is, as a discipline, to remain able to make sense of people's lives and move the field as a whole forward.

Dualistic thinking

Banks (1996) shows that most theories about ethnic identity are based on an opposition in which one of the two sides is presented as the adequate one. Ethnic identity, for example, is seen as a question of interests or of enduring emotions, of change or continuity, of similarities or differences, of society or the individual. In many approaches, the emphasis is on one of the two aspects, and the other is predominantly used as a negative example. The possibility that each of these positions can offer valuable understandings is ignored. For example, a reference to the emotional and more permanent, habitual aspects of ethnic identity is typically rejected and branded as essentialist and primordialist. The result of this is that it becomes difficult to handle the strong emotions, loyalties, and sentiments that are often associated with ethnicity in everyday life. The dualist thinking of an either/or approach stresses that the one or the other has to be true, thereby ignoring the possibility that both can be true. Ethnic identities are treated as being either by definition variable, multiple, fragmented, and situational, or as being stable, unified, homogeneous, and permanent.

In the social and behavioural sciences, a dualist way of thinking tends to predominate, as in the antitheses between the expressive and pragmatic aspects of language, between perception and action, between process and content, between stability and variability, between structure and agency, and between methods and epistemological positions. I have discussed these forms of dualist thinking throughout the book. Approaches and questions are, typically, conceived in terms of *either* one option *or* another, whereby one of them is defended as the correct one and (implicitly) defined in contrast to the (misguided) other. However, alternatives that are presented as in competition are not necessarily oppositional. The research I have discussed differs in terms of background, theory, design, and methodology. I have tried to show that social psychologists can examine ethnic identity in different ways. Each approach has its own emphasis and makes limiting and fruitful assumptions. Differences in approaches can be seen as alternative perspectives rather than as incommensurable standpoints leading to fierce and unsolvable debates.

In part, these debates are fuelled by conceptual unclearness and conceptual differences, as for example, in relation to terms such as identity, ethnicity, and race. There are many ways in which these concepts are understood and used analytically. Ethnic identity is examined in terms of discourses and identity options that are available in a group or society, or as positions and locations that are taken up and negotiated in actual social interactions, as well as in terms of a sense of ethnic identity and the development of an ethnic self. In addition, terms such as 'identification' and 'self-categorization' are used. These different understandings and terms can lead to misunderstandings and misinterpretations among scholars. By using the same term, different phenomena are examined, and the same phenomena are investigated by the use of different concepts. This situation makes conceptual clarity all the more important. In the wake of postmodernism, there is sometimes some sympathy with definitional looseness and a rejection of prior definitions. Identity phenomena are said to be contradictory and constantly undergoing transformation; therefore, the fixation of meanings in definitions should be avoided. However, for the very same reasons, a clear understanding of specific contents is often imperative. An undefined or inflated concept of identity (or ethnicity or race) stands in the way of insight and invites muddled thinking. It is important and useful to explain how key concepts are used. This makes it clear what the argument is about and offers the opportunity to disagree and criticize. Therefore, in Chapters 2 and 3, I have discussed the key concepts of 'identity' and 'ethnicity'. I also argued that conceptual distinctions, such as those between identity and sense of identity, and identification and orientation, are important for improving our understanding.

When we come to assess the dualisms and debates mentioned, it is also important to keep in mind that the aim of the research and the related research questions can differ. For example, the emphasis can be on normative accounts and what the interactants themselves consider relevant and define as meaningful. In that case, performance or how people do things is examined. The analytic interest is in discursive strategies for managing and negotiating identities. Psychological states and characteristics are not studied as underlying causes of people's behaviour but as topics for analysis in the discourses—how these are implicated and appealed to in the social action performed in talk. In such work, however, the question of why people are saying or doing the things they say and do is de-emphasized. The inner life is downplayed, and, implicitly, an image of an unsocialized actor tends to be used.

The emphasis can also be on trying to understand causalities, motives, feelings, and competences. Describing discursive strategies does not tell us much about why subject positions are taken up or abandoned, why others are ignored or embraced, to what extent a stigmatized position affects people's well-being, and which skills and knowledge are needed to adapt to a new cultural environment. People come to a situation with all kinds of things in mind, such as expectations, feelings, stereotypes, beliefs, and self-understandings. These are important for understanding their inner life, but also for their involvement in practices and actual interactions. Furthermore, beliefs, stereotypes, self-understandings, and so on are invoked selectively, depending on the context and the issue at hand. And their invocation does not ensure acceptance but requires management and negotiation. It is in interactions that understandings of oneself and others are formed, modified, assigned, and asserted. These assignments are influenced by socially shared ideas, images, and beliefs, and asserting and exercising one's sense of identity depend on internalized characteristics and resources.

A focus on action and interaction leads to other questions and emphases than does a focus on dispositions and feelings. The former typically stresses the variable, flexible, and contextual nature of identity constructions, whereas the latter is more concerned with relatively stable self-understandings. A difference in emphasis does not mean, however, a difference in adequacy or accuracy. For example, in examining the role of culture, a distinction can be made between treating culture as a 'text' or a 'conversation' (Fay, 1996). Both approaches offer ways of examining ethnic issues. The first one is more system-oriented in seeing culture as a relatively stable and more or less characteristic system of shared meanings that influence or inform perceptions and behaviour. This approach is typically taken when different ethnic groups are compared, for example, in their endorsement of collectivist, individualist, and family values (e.g. Gaines et al., 1997). Cultural features are identified and used to explain social psychological phenomena among and between ethnic minority groups. Many social psychological studies in cross-cultural psychology take this stance. The culture-as-system approach attempts to describe relatively enduring patterns of meaning. Inconsistencies and changes are not denied or ignored, but a more structural and long-term perspective is taken (Kashima, 2000). In Chapter 6, I indicated that more gradual psychological and behavioural changes as a result of sustained contact with members of other cultural groups are examined in research on acculturation.

The second view on culture is practice-oriented and tends to examine concrete, short-term interactions and context-dependent actions that (re)produce meanings. This view is adopted by those who are concerned with everyday processes in which cultural meanings are defined, challenged, and negotiated. Here, the focus is on the dynamic nature of culture as an ongoing process in which people are not just culture-bearers, but they also appropriate and alter the meanings by which they live. Furthermore, it is also possible to investigate how the notion of 'culture' itself is used when people talk and argue about ethnicity and ethnic relations. Using a discourse-analytic perspective means that it is possible to show how 'culture' is used in defining and explaining interethnic conflicts and the assumed lack of integration and social disadvantage of minority groups (Verkuyten, 1997b; Wetherell & Potter, 1992).

These different understandings of culture have their pros and cons. Treating culture as a 'text' tends to obscure the interactive, changing, and conflicting character of cultures. Cultures are interactive because norms and practices are adjusted and (re)confirmed in everyday interactions. People are not merely passive carriers of culture, but they are also involved in the continuous construction of new meanings. There are ongoing changes in which cultural characteristics are used, mixed, and transformed in relation to the circumstances in which people live. Furthermore, cultures have numerous rules, convictions, and values permitting divergent and conflicting interpretations. Often, cultural meanings are not self-evident, but are objects of debate and negotiation.

In turn, treating culture as a 'conversation' tends to ignore more stable meanings and the habitual horizon of understandings that is learnt and internalized in a process of enculturation. From a cultural point of view, everything is not in motion to the same extent. Cultures have structural and continuous characteristics that are grounded in institutions and practices and expressed in central values, norms, symbols, and language. And the fact that enculturation is not cultural cloning or photocopying does not imply that no unconscious and conscious cultural learning occurs. Culture and ethnicity are things people are socialized in, but that they can, of course, also grow out of.

In relation to ethnicity, Vermeulen (2001) makes a distinction between culture as a way of life and as a lifestyle. The notion of culture as a way of life refers to the body of beliefs, values, and knowledge at the level of the collectivity that is internalized by the individual. In this sense, we are all products of our culture, and we tend to perceive the world from the lens or point of view that this culture offers. 'Culture is what we carry with us, even when we want to get rid of it. And what we lose, even when we want to preserve it' (Vermeulen, 2001, p. 14). In contrast, culture as a lifestyle involves the use or creation of images, symbols, stories, and arterfacts to distinguish ourselves from others. Here, culture is a tool used in interaction for asserting and constructing difference and identity.

Situational and contextual approaches to ethnic identity do not have to replace an interest in more general processes and underlying tendencies. A social psychological understanding of ethnic minority identity can focus on both contextual meanings and experiences of particular groups and on the delineation of underlying processes and structures for different groups. It is obvious that between ethnic identities and situations there are many differences that are significant for understanding. Hence, the focus can be on the unique characteristics of identities and the particular cultural, historical, political, and local circumstances that give rise to them. This strategy adopts a 'birds of a different feather' approach and is predominantly found in anthropological and discourse approaches.

Another strategy is to examine the similarities and general principles underlying the multifaceted nature of ethnic identities. Here, a 'brothers under the skin' approach is adopted, and it implies goals such as testing the generality of existing knowledge and theories, or exploring and explaining variations across situations as to how more general processes are developed and deployed. This strategy is common in mainstream social psychology in which a conceptualization in terms of underlying cognitive and motivational processes is favoured. The specific meanings and differences between social identities are considered less important than their underlying psychological similarities.

Dualisms and differences in approaches are often related to levels of analysis. Critical discourse analysts tend to focus on the level of society in which discursive formations and regimes are analysed in terms of the oppressive and normalizing effects of social assignments. Discursive psychologists are more concerned with the level of situated interactions at which identities are asserted and negotiated, and accountability is produced. And mainstream social psychologists tend to emphasize mental processes and individual differences. The three levels of society, interaction, and subjectivity are interdependent, but also distinct. Sociological social psychologists (e.g. House, 1977, 1981), social psychologists (e.g. Doise, 1986), and sociologists (Berger & Luckmann, 1966) have argued and shown that a distinction between levels of analysis is important. For example, Doise (1997, p. 72) argues that 'Articulating analyses of different levels is an essential aspect of social psychologists' scientific endeavor. Complementing explanations located at one level of analysis by explanations at another level does not only extend the validity of socio-psychological analyses, it also produces a more cumulative science by integrating findings obtained by models at different levels.' The one level cannot be reduced to the other. For example, even though perceptions, thoughts, and feelings are socially shaped, shared, and used, they are also psychological realities that can conflict with social expectations and demands. The relation between individual and collective understandings is never perfect because images, ideas, and discourses are appropriated and internalized in relation to specific circumstances and unique experiences. And the idea of agency implies the capacity to conform to or to oppose and disregard social and cultural definitions and understandings.

Different approaches tend to focus on particular levels of analysis, and there is nothing wrong with that. It is problematic, however, when one level of analysis is used to replace or colonize analyses on other levels. For example, when the complexities and richness of ethnic choices and interactions in everyday life are explained with a few assumptions about cognitive and motivational processes. Or, when the inner life and ethnic self are defined as inaccessible or of little importance in understanding people's social actions because priority is given to the constructed nature of descriptions and expressions rather than to what is being described and expressed. An analysis in terms of internal mechanisms and processes cannot replace an analysis of the regularities at the level of interactions or of society, and a focus on situated interactions does not replace an analysis of mental processes and psychological tendencies.

The debate between discourse-oriented and mainstream social psychologists tends to lead to independent frameworks in which one side's favoured approach is contrasted with that of the other. Mainstream social psychologists emphasize that discursive psychologists ignore important cognitive and affective processes, whereas discursive psychologists argue that mainstream approaches fail to address the practical activities undertaken by people in interactions. A focus on action and interaction, however, does not invalidate approaches that examine cognitive and affective processes and the ethnic self. As I have tried to argue throughout this book, theories that model capacities and mental processes as well as theories that focus on actual interactions and performances are both important for social psychological analyses of ethnicity. A view that focuses exclusively on one sort of theory leaves certain types of questions and therefore certain types of phenomena unaccounted for.

Engagement and reconciliation

By using various empirical examples from our work, I have tried to identify and articulate not only the distinctive features of different approaches, but also their possible commonalities and combinations. To understand questions and issues related to ethnic identity, I have always found it necessary to use more than one perspective and theory, and more than one method. To me, the need for this is clear as soon as one tries to understand and explain the complexities of ethnic identity in the context of the actual lives of people. No one approach, theory, or method provides an image that fully satisfies. By the use of multiple approaches, it should be possible to create fuller and more elaborate images.

However, many of these approaches seem to rest on fundamentally different and frequently irreconcilable premises. This raises the question of the possibility of engagement and reconciliation. In the literature, this question is addressed in different ways, comparable to ideas about the management of ethnic and cultural diversity. Some claim that social psychological approaches are in conflict and that reconciliation or integration is not very easy or helpful (e.g. Stainton Rogers, 2003). Segregation and 'living apart together' seem the preferred strategy here. It is also possible to follow more of an assimilationist approach, for example, by encapsulating discourse-oriented studies into the researcher's own favoured paradigm and treating them as having a secondary, preparatory role for the 'real' work. Furthermore, it is possible to argue for a strategy of integration in which it is considered possible and necessary to combine and synthesize approaches (e.g. Jost & Kruglanski, 2002). In addition, one can argue for 'togetherness in difference' or a kind of 'critical multiculturalism'. Here, differences are considered instructive and useful for a creative rhetorical engagement (Potter, 2002). Instead of dominating or ignoring others, we use diversity as a basis for challenging, revising, and relativizing notions and assumptions.

These different views on engagement and reconciliation are related to differences in epistemological positions and the role of language. I have discussed this in Chapter 1, so I will not repeat it here. However, my use of different perspectives, theories, and methods might raise questions about consistency and coherence. Consistency between epistemological and theoretical assumptions and interpretations is important. In Chapter 1, I have rejected both relativistic and positivistic approaches to knowledge in favour of the dialectical one. This position has a long philosophical tradition (e.g. Fay, 1996; Morris, 1997) and reflects the idea that what we are dealing with is a two-way process: reality constructs the person and the person constructs reality. Knowledge is always a relationship between description and the world, between person and reality, and *neither of the two* should be prioritized or ignored. There is no unmediated access to reality, and many historical, cultural, and political conditions influence research and knowledge. But that does not imply that all knowledge claims are subjective and relative, depending only on these social conditions. These claims are constrained by facts as they can be best ascertained, and some claims are more valid or true than others.

As I have indicated in Chapter 1, doing research from a particular perspective is not the same as being subjective or biased. As the Gulbenkian Commission on the Restructuring of the Social Sciences write in *Open the Social Sciences* (1996, p. 93), 'In short, the fact that knowledge is socially constructed also means that more valid knowledge is socially possible. The recognition of the social bases of knowledge is not at all in contradiction to the concept of objectivity.' This epistemological position makes it possible to include different social psychological approaches as, for example, Campbell and McGuire have demonstrated (see Jost & Kruglanski, 2002). From this position, the differences between the approaches are a matter of perspective and relative emphasis rather than a matter of principle.

But of course, cultural bias and ethnocentrism are never far away, particularly not when addressing questions of ethnicity. For example, studies may implicitly play a role in sustaining ethnic categorizations and understandings by taking ethnic categories for granted. They may render ethnicity natural and suggest that ethnicity inevitably characterizes social formations (Goldberg, 1993; Reicher, 2001). Furthermore, existing theories have arisen in particular circumstances which they reflect (see Duckitt, 1992). The specific social and historical contexts in which theories have been developed leave their traces in the questions asked and explanations given. Throughout this book, I have argued that different theoretical paradigms might represent distinctive contributions to the understanding and explanation of ethnic identity. However, these paradigms do not only offer different analytic tools; they also contain (implicit) moral or political positions. There are practical implications, and research is used to support or question identity politics and other forms of diversity management, such as multiculturalism. For example, a conceptualization of ethnic identity in terms of basic human needs defines the recognition of identity as central to human well-being (Taylor, 1992). However, by using intergroup theories the potential divisive and antagonistic consequences of multiculturalism can also be emphasized. And it has been argued that critical discourse analysis has a one-sided perspective on ethnic relations, because it tends to assume that there is a dominant discourse through which ethnic minority positions are confirmed rather than changed (e.g. Jacobs, 2000). Such a perspective would neglect the political negotiation, positioning, and alliance building that go on in debates about belonging and identity, as well as the existence of majority discourses that aim to improve the position of migrants and minorities.

In addition, there is a potential tension between scholarly and political uses of ethnic identity, essentialism, and social constructions. For quite some time, social scientists have been struggling over whether there is a way to talk about 'making culture' or 'becoming ethnic' without making or becoming enemies of the people studied (e.g. Jackson, 1989). People may think of their attachment to a particular ethnic (minority) identity as pervasive and ineffable, grounded in their 'blood', whereas researchers are bound to think otherwise. They will point out that cultures and ethnic identities change, are never fixed, and can be manipulated by outsiders and ethnic entrepreneurs. What is seen to be natural and essential by actors is understood by scholars as socially constructed. The tension between academic and political commitments and responsibilities is not always easy to resolve.

Future challenges

For social psychologists studying ethnic minority groups, there are several related challenges. I have already mentioned some of these, such as finding alternative and adequate ways to study history, culture, ideology, power, and contexts. These are important issues that increasingly attract social psychologists' attention after being neglected for quite some time. These issues can be studied in a number of ways and at different levels of analysis. Theoretically and empirically, one of the challenges is to include these issues and to develop these levels and their relationships. Work in sociological social psychology, as well as social-representation theory and discourse approaches, is helpful here.

A further challenge is the balance between examining similarities across ethnic groups and considering particular meanings and experiences related to specific groups and situations. A social psychological understanding of ethnic minority identity can focus both on the delineation of underlying processes and structures for different groups and on the examination of contextual meanings and experiences of particular groups. Both approaches are useful, and a combination of the two may raise new theoretical and empirical questions. The work by Sellers and colleagues (1998) on African-American racial identity is a good example. Their multidimensional model of racial identity represents a synthesis of the strengths of approaches that focus on general cognitive and affective processes, and approaches that focus on the unique cultural and historical experiences of African-Americans.

In doing so, it is also important to take into account that not all ethnic minority groups are perceived, positioned, and treated in the same way and that there are important within-group differences. Studies in various countries, including the Netherlands, have found that different minority groups enjoy varying degrees of social acceptability (see Hagendoorn, 1995; Owen et al., 1981). Ethnic hierarchies indicate that groups are located differently within the ethnic landscape and that minority groups are also in the process of distancing themselves from lower-status positions, and this can result in interethnic tensions between these groups. In addition, attention to between-group differences should not lead to overlooking within-group heterogeneity (Celious & Oyserman, 2001). The way minority group members react to and perceive their situation varies. Understanding the implications of ethnicity for the shifting and variable ways in which people live their lives requires that we view it as a heterogeneous category.

Another challenge for social psychology is to examine not only the major and accessible groups but also groups that are more difficult to reach. For example, despite the growing importance of the situation of asylum seekers and refugees, hardly any social psychological research exists on them. There is a dearth of information about their experiences, perceptions, and behaviour. One reason is that it is difficult to establish contact with asylum seekers and political refugees. Generally, they suffer from high levels of uncertainty and fear about their legal status and the risk of being repatriated. In this situation, questions about personal opinions, attitudes, and practices are often met with reluctance and suspicion (Daniel & Knudsen, 1995).

Furthermore, there is the question of to what extent social psychological theories are useful and adequate for understanding situations of fierce and violent ethnic conflicts, including ethnic cleansing and genocide. In the past decades, there have been several of these conflicts, and ethnic violence continues to be a distressing global phenomenon. Interethnic, but also interreligious, violence raises important issues and questions for social psychologists. In social psychological research as well as in this book, the focus is on questions of ethnic identity and interethnic relations in relatively harmonious Western societies. This research is important, but it is unclear to what extent it adds to our understanding of ethnic hatred and violence. For such an understanding, it seems necessary to broaden the scope and study, for example, dangerous ideas (Eidelson & Eidelson, 2003), the roots of evil (Staub, 1989), extreme bigotry (Billig, 2002), and world politics (Tetlock, 1998).

For social psychologists studying ethnicity, there is much to do, but also much to be gained. Arguably, ethnicity is one of the more important and relevant topics of our times. According to Hall (1993, p. 361; his italics), 'The capacity to *live with difference* is . . . the coming question of the twenty-first century.' Social psychologists should try to make a contribution by finding viable and productive ways of living with diversity, by improving interethnic relations, and by bettering the situation of minority groups and immigrants. And the study of ethnicity is not only important for practical reasons but also for the potential benefits to social psychology in its continuous development into a dynamic, open, and challenging science.

Notes

Chapter 2

1　Wentholt has developed his ideas in several unpublished papers. These papers and particularly a paper by Wentholt and Verkuyten (1999) have been used here. The latter paper is available on request.

2　This example is taken from Wentholt and Verkuyten (1999).

3　Note the different meaning again, a third one, employed here. Identity as identicalness, in the sense of 'being identical with', is hardly the same meaning of the word as in 'the essence of who you are'.

4　For this, see, for example, Coté & Levine (2002), Deaux (1996), Gecas & Burke (1995), Jenkins (1996), Simon (2004), and Weigert et al. (1986).

5　Banton's distinction provides a neat picture but is not without problems. Ethnic identity does not have to be 'voluntary' at all, and racial identity is not necessarily the product of oppression. Furthermore, ethnicity and race often overlap, and a group may move from a racial category to an ethnic one over time (see Chapter 6 and Cornell & Hartmann, 1998).

6　A striking example is a deaf lesbian couple that chose to have a deaf baby through artificial insemination with a deaf donor. The baby was born in November 2001 and was indeed deaf. In an interview with *The Lancet* (2002, p. 1315) the couple argued, 'Most of the ethical issues that have been raised in regard to our story centre on the idea that being deaf is a negative thing. From there, people surmise that it is unethical to want to create deaf children, who are, in their view, disabled. Our view, on the other hand, is that being deaf is a positive thing, with many wonderful aspects. We don't view being deaf along the same lines as being blind or mentally retarded; we see it as paralleling being Jewish or black or a member of any minority group. We don't see members of those minority groups wanting to "eliminate" themselves.'

7　In *Vrij Nederland*, 'The History of Norbert Elias', 1984, no. 48.

8　These statements, however, can be interpreted in different ways, and I will discuss this in Chapters 6 and 7.

9　An obvious example is the distinction between collectivism and individualism. This distinction is used in many cross-cultural studies (see Fiske et al., 1998).

10　The literature on the self is extensive. Psychologists, social psychologists, and sociologists, among others, all address a variety of questions and issues related to the self (see Coté & Levine, 2002).

11　There are different theoretical approaches that use the concept of identification, such as the social learning approach, the cognitive development approach, and psychoanalytic thinking (Damon, 1983).

12　Phinney (1990) uses the term 'ethnic self-identification' for this; other terms used are 'ethnic self-description' and 'ethnic self-categorization'.

13 Identity theory focuses on self-definitions that are related to structural role positions. Roles are considered the basis of identity because they carry specific sets of behavioural expectations. This focus on roles has led sociological social psychologists to argue that social categories such as gender and ethnicity are not elements of identity (Hoelter, 1985; Stryker, 1987). Broader social categories are assumed to have consequences for the self and for action only in conjunction with an identity. Identity theorists, however, do not agree about how to treat social categories (see Hogg et al., 1995). For example, White and Burke (1987, p. 327) study ethnic identity and argue that self-identification based on roles does not differ from self-identification based on social categories. They state, 'Identities, whatever their sources, are still the meanings that we have to ourselves as a member of a socially defined category. Roles are only one type of social category on which to base an identity.' For differences and commonalities between identity theory as developed in the USA and social-identity theory as developed in Europe, see Hogg et al. (1995) and Hogg and Ridgeway (2003).

Chapter 3

1 For elaborate and good introductions, see, for example, Banks (1996), Cornell and Hartmann (1998), Eriksen (1993), Fenton (2003), Hutchinson and Smith (1996), and Jenkins (1997).
2 Anderson's notion of 'imagined communities' has similarities with Tajfel's concern for large-scale social categories.
3 See, for example, Cornell (1996), Grosby (1994), Horowitz (2000), Hutnik (1991), Roosens (1994), and Vermeulen and Govers (1997). Anderson points out that nationalism has more in common with religion and kinship than with ideologies such as liberalism and socialism.
4 See Cornell and Hartmann (1998).
5 See different examples in Govers and Vermeulen (1997).
6 See, for example, Peel (1989) and Smith (1986).
7 Barth speaks about ethnicity when people are being categorized in terms of their 'basic, most general identity, presumptively determined by background and origin' (1969, p. 13), and 'the constraints on a person's behaviour which spring from his ethnic identity . . . tend to be absolute' (1969, p. 17). Hence, some scholars accuse Barth of implicitly having a primordial and static idea about ethnicity (e.g. Cohen, 1974).
8 Interestingly, in social psychological research, the family tree is sometimes used to make ethnicity salient. For example, Mullen et al. (2003) instructed their participants to write the name of their ethnic group into three boxes labelled 'father', 'mother', and 'you'.
9 One reason for this is, perhaps, the continued influence of Kurt Lewin's ahistorical approach. Lewin stressed that social psychological explanations should focus on the contemporaneous field of forces acting on the person rather than on 'historical' or 'genetic' factors. Although Lewin referred to the life history of the individual, his proscription taken more generally stresses the role of current social factors. As a consequence, 'not only has the life history of the individual been left to developmental psychologists, but the past of social groups has been left for historians. In contrast, social and cultural anthropologists viewing culture as, in part, something that one generation passes to the next, have been much more inclined to see a group's history as important to understanding its present organization and functioning' (Ashmore et al., 2001, p. 217).
10 See, for example, Eller and Coughlan (1993) and Grosby (1994). Banks (1996), Cornell and Hartmann (1998), and Fenton (2003) discuss the different aspects of this debate and the various interpretations that exist.
11 In the anthropological literature, many terms are used, such as situationalism, instrumentalism, and circumstantialism. These terms are used in various ways but often

are very much related. Circumstantialism and situationalism are concerned with the conditions that determine whether ethnicity matters and what the meaning of ethnicity is. Instrumentalism typically refers to the material and political reasons for the deployment of ethnic identity (see Fenton, 2003).

12 A fourth account is a sociobiological one (e.g. van den Berghe, 1981).

13 An interesting example of the political meaning of kinship occurred when, in 2002, the Japanese emperor, Akihito, argued that he felt a close bond to South Korea because of actual family ties between the Japanese royal family and the royal family of Paekche that used to live in the south-western part of the Korean peninsula. Akihito stated: 'I know that the mother of Emperor Kanmu was a descendant of King Muryong of Paekche and *therefore* I feel a bond with Korea' (my italics).

14 The philosopher Margalit (2002) makes an interesting distinction between 'ethics' and 'morality'. The former would be typical of 'thick' relations that are grounded in attributes such as parent, family, and fellow countryman, and anchored in a shared past or a community of memory. Feelings of loyalty and betrayal are central here. The latter would be typical of 'thin' relations with strangers and the remote. Being human is the key attribute here, and questions of respect and humiliation are central. As he writes, 'Because it encompasses all humanity, morality is long on geography and short on memory. Ethics is typically short on geography and long on memory. Memory is the cement that holds thick relations together, and community of memory is the obvious habitat for thick relations and thus for ethics' (p. 8).

15 Hence, he entitled his book *Two-Dimensional Man*.

Chapter 4

1 Cross-cultural studies tend to emphasize that an in-group focus is more typical of collectivist cultures and migrant or minority groups that have a group-oriented outlook on life (see Yuki, 2003).

2 Oppositional identities are of course closely related to social conditions, such as increased stigmatization and discrimination. On 10 March 2004, the Home Secretary presented a report on 'Jihad recruits' to the Dutch parliament. The report was from the Dutch National Information and Security Council (AIVD: Algemene Inlichtingen-en Veiligheidsdienst), which concluded that an increasing number of Islamic (particularly Moroccan) young people feels rejected and excluded by the growing anti-Islamism in public discourse. As a result, they are inclined to define their identity in oppositional and radical terms.

3 See, for details, Verkuyten, van de Calseijde, and De Leur (1999). Here, it is important to point out that the participants were asked to cooperate in a study on 'Moluccan identity'. The interviews were designed to explore a range of different issues related to this. These issues set the discursive environment and determined the task for the participants. We wanted them to engage in both descriptive and interpretative work, and we were interested in the accounts that were given. The context in which the responses were produced meant that participants' responses were also indicative of their interpretations of what is appropriate language when talking about Moluccan identity with an ethnic Dutch researcher. Here I treat the interviews as conversations or interactions rather than as elicitations; that is, I adopt a more interaction-based, analytic stance towards the interviews, considering both the interviewee(s) and the interviewer to be responsible for any interaction, although from a different position.

4 It is estimated that at present there are about 40,000 people of Moluccan origin living in the Netherlands.

5 The distinction between 'real' and 'less real' Moluccans was not made in political terms. The former were not presented as more committed to the Republic Maluku Selatan than the latter. On the contrary, some participants said that 'half-castes' were sometimes more fanatical than 'real' Moluccans.

6 See Chapter 7 for an analysis of the way that this distinction between 'being' and 'feeling' can function discursively.

7 This is similar to what we have found in studies among Dutch people (Verkuyten, 1997b).

8 See also Verkuyten (2005).

9 For methodological and analytic details as well as the full results, see Verkuyten (1997a).

10 Claims about the existence of discrimination are often problematic and can be challenged by presenting ethnic minority group members as oversensitive and unjustly accusing majority members of racism (Bonilla-Silva & Forman, 2000; Kaiser & Miller, 2001). There is some evidence of Lloyd's orientation towards these possible rhetorical counters. For example, his question for clarification in line 2 suggests that he is not preoccupied with ethnic discrimination; he does not immediately interpret discrimination in ethnic terms. Furthermore, in several places, he refers to the possible unconscious nature of discrimination by the Dutch. Mentioning the nonintentional nature of discrimination might, if read within the context of his being interviewed by an ethnically Dutch person, be understood as a strategy to soften his accusation of the Dutch.

11 See the report by the Sociaal Cultureel Planbureau (2002) entitled 'Trouwen over de grens' ('Marrying Across the Border').

12 These relationships are also supported by governmental policies and agencies in the countries of origin. In Turkey and Morocco, for example, there are Departments of Migration affairs that establish contacts with diaspora communities. These contacts are also supported by embassies, and religious, cultural, and migrant organizations. For economic and political reasons these countries want to have an influence on emigrants. Furthermore, the Moroccan government has always taken the position of 'Once a Moroccan, always a Moroccan' and this is reflected in the impossibility of renouncing Moroccan nationality.

13 The continuing links with the (imaginary) homeland is central in transnationalism and diaspora. These links can be politicized and can have a major influence in international politics. Hence, diaspora communities have been studied as interest groups and people living in diaspora as political actors (Esman, 1994). In his book *The Spectre of Comparison*, Anderson (1998) develops the idea of 'long-distance nationalism'. The term refers to the ideology of a migrant group that politically orientates itself not to the state in which it is located but to the country of origin. This long-distance nationalism can be exploited by homeland politicians. Links are not only political, however. There may be important economic, social, and cultural activities carried out with the homeland and with ethnic group members in other countries (Portes et al., 1999). In addition, there are identifications that locate people in a space that goes beyond the nation state, and there are sentiments that connect people to others in various territorial locations.

14 To capture these transnational and diasporic connections, Clifford (1997) uses the metaphor of 'travel', and in his book *The Black Atlantic*, Gilroy chooses the image of a ship.

15 This study was conducted by Professors Burgers, Engbersen, Entzinger, and Snel at the Erasmus University Rotterdam. I made a small contribution to this study by theorizing and operationalizing the concept of ethnic identification.

16 For each situation of group identification, we used nine questions that were taken from previous studies in the Netherlands (Verkuyten, 1999). The questions formed a homogeneous scale for the different groups of participants, and in the three situations, alpha was >.81.

17 For the three measures, $p < .001$. The post-hoc tests (Scheffé) showed significant differences ($p < .01$) between the Iraqis and the Antilleans and Moroccans.

Chapter 5

1 The study was conducted by Professors Hagendoorn of Utrecht University and Sniderman of Stanford University.

2 These results also imply, of course, that the great majority of the Dutch do not agree with these racist statements.

3 The correlations were approximately .33 ($p < .001$).

4 The equation between ethnicity and culture is not simply stated, however, but is also made acceptable and factual. The speaker does this by introducing his evaluation as very obvious; by giving concrete and detailed examples; by using modalizing terms such as 'anything', 'entirely', and 'never' (Pomerantz, 1986); and by demonstrating his concern with the facts by correcting himself (Edwards & Potter, 1992).

5 I use the term 'essentialism' because it is common in social psychology. However, this term has a complex philosophical history and is used in various ways. For example, it is sometimes used to refer to crucial defining or 'essential' feautures of an object or phenomenon, without any assumption about underlying psychological characteristics. It is also used to refer to overgeneralization about group characteristics and experiences. Hence, I tend to agree with Blum (2002) that the term 'inherentism' is more appropriate.

6 This is also an issue in some of the debates in the USA about multicultural education and the 'cultural war' (see Hochschild, 1999). From an Afro-centric perspective, it is sometimes argued that because of essential racial differences, blacks and whites should be educated separately. Afro-Americans would have distinct psychological and cultural characteristics, including a particular style of learning.

7 There are a number of books on the Amish such as those by Hostetler (1980) and Kraybill (2001).

8 Here, I follow the analysis presented by Galenkamp (1998).

9 Abou Jahjah has argued that the AEL's focus on 'identity' is what makes them different from Marxist-oriented analyses and strategies.

10 There is a similarity here to extreme right-wing groups which also emphasize 'identity'. For example, the official party magazine of the British National Party is entitled *Identity*.

11 For details about the procedure, measures, and full results, see Verkuyten and Brug (2004).

12 Although our focus was on the comparison between the ethnic majority and ethnic minority group participants, we also examined whether there were mean differences between the three ethnic minority groups. There was a significant difference for ethnic identification. Scheffé's test indicated that the Surinamese participants had lower ethnic identification than the Turks and Moroccans. However, no differences were found for the endorsement of multiculturalism, in-group essentialism, and out-group essentialism. This lack of differences may be indicative of a shared low-status position.

13 For both groups of participants, in- and out-group essentialism showed a similar positive correlation (.33, $p < .01$). The association shows that the responses to both measures are not independent. However, the measures are not completely redundant, because around 10% of their variance is shared. Hence, there is some overlap among the measures, but they also elicit somewhat different pieces of information.

14 In the analysis, a measure of the Protestant ethic was also included. See Verkuyten and Brug (2004).

15 See, for example, the debate in *Current Anthropology* (2001, vol. 42, p. 42) in relation to Gil-White's paper, in which he examined why ethnic actors are typically essentialists.

16 Several influential Dutch scholars and commentators argue that it is necessary to go beyond multiculturalism (e.g. Entzinger, 2002) or that assimilation is the only option (e.g. Cliteur, 2002; Schnabel, 2000). Furthermore, in recent years (from 2001 onwards), the idea of multiculturalism has been ridiculed and abandoned by most Dutch political parties and by the right-wing government.

17 According to Blum (2002, p. 212), Herder influenced DuBois' egalitarian, racialist view of the spirit of the white, the black, and other races. DuBois studied Herder's work when he stayed for two years in Berlin in the 1890s.

Chapter 6

1 Nederveen Pieterse (2001) talks about 'the anti-hybridity backlash'.
2 Friesland is a province in the north of the Netherlands with its own flag, language, and traditions.
3 The term 'ethnically mixed marriages' presupposes a categorical distinction. The 'ingredients' that are mixed are socially identifiable and result in a socially defined way of living. However, not every 'mixed' marriage is considered mixed in the same way. A marriage between a white Dutch man and a white British woman will be treated as an ethnically mixed marriage less quickly than a marriage between a black man and a white woman or a Turkish man and a Dutch woman. Furthermore, in the former cases, the emphasis will often be put on the advantages for children of being raised in a bicultural and bilingual environment, whereas in the latter cases disadvantages and problems of uncertainty and confusion are typically envisioned.
4 The material quoted was on the BNP site in April 2003 (www.bnp.org.uk).
5 Acculturation responses have been described by various terms with their own particular connotations. Berry prefers acculturation 'attitudes' and 'strategies'. Others have used the terms 'styles' or 'modes'. Here, I use the term 'positions'.
6 However, Hutnik developed her model independently of Berry's work.
7 With the exception of the Turkish and Kurdish adults, perceived discrimination was not measured among the other groups. For the adult sample, no association between ethnic identification and discrimination was found.
8 For the other samples, no measure of collectivist orientation was used.
9 But see, for example, Bourhis et al. (1997), Piontkowski et al. (2000), van Oudenhoven et al. (1998), Verkuyten and Thijs (2002), Zagefka and Brown (2002), and Zick et al. (2001).
10 Examples are MAVIN and AMEA (Association of MultiEthnic Americans).
11 Quotation from the International Voice website (http://www.webcom.com/~intvoice).
12 In our research, none of the participants took an exclusively white position.
13 This percentage is close to what Rockquemore and Brunsma (2002) found.
14 This is very similar to the 'alternation model' proposed by LaFromboise et al. (1993).
15 But they can of course also be interpreted in psychological terms, such as identity confusion and insecurity. This will be discussed in Chapter 7.
16 Details of this research and the main results can be found in Cieslik and Verkuyten (2004). All credit for collecting the data and analysing the material should go to Anna Cieslik.
17 Most readers will not be familiar with the history of the Polish Tatars, and therefore I give a short description (see Baranowski, 1950; Borawski & Dubinski, 1986, Miskiewicz, 1990, 1993). The Tatars' main presence in Poland dates back to the beginning of the fourteenth century. At that time, the first voluntary settlers arrived with the Golden Horde of Genghis Khan. They were the descendants of Mongolian tribes who adopted Islam from the Turkish peoples who had conquered them. The Tatars had two vital reasons to settle in the territory of the kingdom of Poland and Lithuania. Firstly, they were given land and the right to build mosques in exchange for their military service. Secondly, with the passage of time, the Golden Horde faced internal power struggles, which ended with the disintegration of the empire in the fifteenth century.
  The Tatars fought on the Polish side in many important battles, including the famous struggle with the Teutonic Knights of the Cross in 1410. The Polish kings employed Tatars as translators and diplomats in mediations with the Crimean khans. The golden

age for the Polish Tatars was the sixteenth century. They were allowed to build mosques and religious schools, and they had property rights equal to those of the Polish nobility. These special entitlements were withdrawn in the seventeenth century, bringing about the slow decline of the Tatars in Poland. The reign of Zygmunt III was characterized by religious intolerance and persecution. Problems with payment of the Tatar military units resulted in the Tatar rebellion of 1673. A number of outraged Tatar soldiers joined the Turkish side in the war that was going on at the time. Despite this, incidents of political disagreement between the Polish authorities and the Tatars were rare. During the period of the Polish partitions, between the end of the seventeenth and the beginning of the twentieth century, the Tatars participated in the uprisings resulting in national liberation, and they remained loyal to the Poles, despite the efforts of the Russian authorities. They also served Poland during the two world wars, and in 1935 the Tatar Knight Legion was established as part of the Polish army.

Under communism, the Tatar ethnic group was treated as an exotic 'tourist' attraction. They were protected by the Polish authorities in the hope of enhancing relations with Islamic states, such as Egypt and Saudi Arabia. In the 'new' Poland, they are given all the rights of a minority group, but since the Polish economy is not very stable, they do not receive much financial assistance to protect and promote their culture. For example, the Polish government did not respond favourably to the group's request for funding for the celebrations of the 600th anniversary of the Tatars' settling in Poland (Kosc, 2001).

Over time, the number of Tatars in Poland has decreased considerably, from around 60,000 in the seventeenth century to approximately 30,000 in the nineteenth century, and to from 5000 to 6000 at the time of writing. The Tatars are organized into six religious communities. There are old mosques in small villages in the eastern part of the country, and in 1990 a new mosque was build in Gdańsk. In addition, there are prayer houses in Warsaw and Białystok. Before the collapse of the communist system, the only Tatar organization was the Muslim Religious Association. This association underlines the Tatar cultural features of Polish Islam and distinguishes itself from other more recent Muslim associations in Poland, such as the Association of Muslim Unity. In 1992, and out of a growing concern with the Tatars' distinctive ethnic character, the Association of Polish Tatars was founded. Both the Muslim Religious Association and the Association of Polish Tatars are active in social, religious, and cultural life. They publish magazines, arrange exhibitions, and organize conferences.

18 Both magazines are published by the Tatar community in Poland. First, *The World of Islam* is published by a team of people in the small town of Sokolka (eastern Poland). They cooperate with academic specialists from the field and Muslim students from the Arabic states. Second, *The Tatar Life* is published by a branch of the Association of Polish Tatars in cooperation with Tatar cultural centers in Białystok, Gdańsk, and Warsaw. Both magazines are mostly self-funded, but some issues of *The World of Islam* are sponsored by different institutions, such as local industries, cultural institutions of the Polish government, and Islamic organizations. For further information on the data and analysis, see Cieslik and Verkuyten (2004).

19 In addition, the symbolic character of the story is made obvious in the layout of some of the issues of the magazines. For example, several covers of *The World of Islam* have images of mosques from all over the world. In it, the colourful marble minarets from other countries intermingle with simple wooden Polish and Lithuanian mosques. The palm trees and turquoise skies of the Middle East are complemented by the oak trees and grey horizons of eastern Europe. These images present a clear religious link between the Polish Tatars and the Islamic states. It is the unity in faith that brings together the Polish Tatars and their Muslim brothers abroad. This is the most obvious reading of the images. What also seems to be the case is that the contrasting characteristics between the 'here' and the 'there', the richness versus modesty, the abundance versus simplicity, increase the distance between the reality of Poland and the fairy-tale qualities of the

Orient. Furthermore, in some subtitles and quotations in the articles Arabic script from the Koran is used. The Tatars lost their native language in the seventeench century when they started speaking Polish or Belorussian vernacular. Less than 1% of them can actually understand Arabic. Yet, the connection to the language of the Koran seems to play an important role in representing their community. Because Polish Tatars cannot read the Koran in Arabic, the Polish translation always has to be provided. Thus, there is a contrast between the known and the unknown. Polish is understandable and clear; Arabic is beautifully mysterious. The fairy-tale-like quality of mystery is accorded to the Oriental myth.

20 This is also apparent in the two magazines. For example, one of the readers of *The World of Islam* explains, 'I am Polish, but I try to practise Islam as well as I can, so I wear a headscarf.' The use of the conjunction 'but' indicates that the woman herself perceives a difference between being Polish and being Muslim. Similarly, another person complains that many of the participants of the Tatar annual meeting were not Muslims. She writes, 'Most of the participants were Catholics—which seems to be a paradox!' There is, therefore, a potential tension and conflict between Islamic Tatars and Catholic Poles. The question is how these two identities can be accommodated or reconciled.

21 They acted as translators, guides, negotiators, messengers, and informants in the service of the Polish kings. With the passage of time, the significance of this role dwindled. The Turkish Empire ceased to exist, and the Tatar population in Poland decreased.

Chapter 7

1 In addition, it was found that in-group favouritism was affected by the comparative context. In the intergroup context, participants reported higher in-group favouritism than in the intragroup condition (see Verkuyten & De Wolf, 2002b).

2 This cross-cultural research on the self is rather recent. A relevant older paper is by Nobles (1973) on the 'black self-concept'. He argues that the African world-view suggests that 'I am because *we* are and because *we* are, therefore I am'. . . . Unlike Western conceptions which examine independent and individual selves, research involving the African world-view cannot make a critical distinction between the self (I) and one's people (we)' (p. 24).

3 The assumption of multidimensionality is common, but there is not necessarily consensus as to what the dimensions might be. Various dimensions are distinguished and different labels for the (same) dimensions are used. In addition, terms such as 'components', 'elements', 'facets', 'aspects', and 'dimensions' are used interchangeably to describe social identity's 'multinature'.

4 Brewer's (1991) 'optimal distinction theory' proposes a social psychological model of these processes and the conditions that determine the contrasting tendencies for assimilation and differentiation.

5 Kuhn and MacPartland's (1954) well-known Twenty Statements Test was used.

6 Furthermore, the idea of multiplicity and clusters also suggests the need to think about variations among different types of identity (Brewer & Gardner, 1996; Deaux et al., 1995).

7 But the fact that a distinction is possible does not imply independence. In their meta-analysis of 62 studies from different countries involving more than 15,000 participants, Bat-Chava and Steen (1997) found a moderate overall effect size of .34, which was robust across ethnicities, genders, and age groups. Similar correlations have been reported in research on the relationship between group identity-related self-esteem and global self-esteem (e.g. Crocker & Luhtanen, 1990; Luhtanen & Crocker, 1992; Verkuyten, 1995b). One way of looking at this relationship is to see ethnic identity as part of the self-concept, and thereby as one of the contributing components to or sources of global self-esteem. Multifaceted and hierarchical models of the self-concept have been proposed by different authors and examined in various studies (e.g. Byrne &

Shavelson, 1996; Fleming & Courtney, 1984; Harter, 1999; Marsh & Shavelson, 1976). These structural models portray global self-esteem as the apex and different specific self-evaluations, such as the academic self and the social self, as sources for global self-esteem. In these models and studies, the focus is predominantly on various dispositions and personal attributes, and not on group identity evaluations (but see Hoelter, 1986; Rosenberg, 1979).

8   For further details of the study, see Verkuyten and Thijs (2001).

9   One possible reason for stability in self-esteem is that personality appears to be related to genetically determined stability (McGue et al., 1993; McGuire et al., 1996).

10 In addition, cultural values may also affect self-esteem (Twenge & Crocker, 2002). At the individual level, positive correlations have been found between collectivism and psychological well-being. Triandis et al. (1985) reported that collectivists in the USA know little anomie, alienation, and loneliness. In the Netherlands, Verkuyten and Kwa (1994) found a positive correlation between collectivism and life satisfaction among Chinese adolescents. Hence, high collectivists who value their in-group may experience more social support and a more positive sense of self than low collectivists.

11 Various measures have been developed such as the Implicit Association Test, the 'who-said-what' paradigm, preferences for own-name letters and birthday numbers, and subtle language biases (see Greenwald & Banaji, 1995; Maass et al., 2000).

12 Hetts et al. (1999, p. 528) conclude from their study that 'Easterners emigrating to a Western culture may possess two conflicting sets of beliefs about themselves. At a conscious level, they generally appear to endorse the kind of favourable conceptions of the self that are promoted in individualistic cultures. At an unconscious level, however, their self-evaluations appear to be more consistent with the beliefs and values of collectivist cultures. The reports of immigrants that they feel torn between the values of two different social worlds . . . are consistent with this interpretation. Our findings suggest, however, that the crux of this dilemma may revolve around a conflict between implicit and explicit belief systems.'

13 To attain more implicit and indirect measures of self-esteem, we asked the participants about their feelings towards four words; 'I', 'me', 'we', and 'us' (e.g. Hetts et al., 1999; Perdue et al., 1990). The questions were rated on a 7-point Likert-type scale, ranging from three minus signs ($- - -$) to three plus signs ($+ + +$) and with the number '0' in the middle. For measuring implicit personal self-esteem, participants were also asked to choose and evaluate six letters from a random presentation of the alphabet on a separate page (see Nuttin, 1987). This task was used to assess how well the participants like their initials relative to other letters. To the extent that participants feel favourably toward their initials, they can be thought to possess high implicit personal self-esteem. This measure has been used successfully among children and generalizes over languages, alphabets, and cultures (e.g. Hoorens et al., 1990; Kitayama & Karasawa, 1997; Nuttin, 1987). Furthermore, in investigating the reliability and validity of seven implicit self-esteem measures, Bosson et al. (2000) conclude that the initials-preference task is one of the most stable and predictive ones (see also Koole et al., 2001). In the present study, we focused on the initial of the own first name. Explicit personal self-esteem was measured by the Rosenberg scale (Rosenberg, 1965), and for measuring explicit ethnic self-esteem, the private subscale of Luhtanen and Crocker's (1992) collective self-esteem scale was used. For details of this study, see Verkuyten (2004c).

14 Developmental approaches often use terms such as 'crisis', 'conflict', and '(in)secure' identity. However, some of these terms are also used in social psychology. For example, Jackson and Smith (1999) define a person with a secure sense of social identity as someone who is attracted to the in-group but does not feel a common fate and perceives the intergroup context in a favourable light. In contrast, a person with an insecure sense of identity expresses pride in the in-group but believes that his or her fate is tied to that of the group and perceives the intergroup context in terms of conflict and competition. They found that particularly the insecure type predicted in-group bias.

15 These models are comparable but do not match exactly. They make different assumptions and propose somewhat different paths of development.

16 It is also interesting to note that, as in social-identity theory, Cross argues that personal and group identity comprise functionally distinct domains within the individual.

17 Helms (1995), who has been elaborating on the Cross model, argues that the different statuses of racial identity development are probably similar across racially marginalized groups, such as Native Americans, Asian-Americans, and Hispanic Americans. However, she also acknowledges that the racism experiences of different, visible racial and ethnic groups vary, so that the content of the different statuses may differ across these groups.

18 In addition, it has been argued that 'mixed' or multiracial people go through stages of development. For example, Kich (1992) proposes three stages, including an initial awareness of being different, a wish to be accepted by others, and a gradual acceptance of oneself as a multiracial person. These three stages would describe the transition 'from a questionable, sometimes devalued sense of self to one where an interracial self-conception is highly valued and secure' (p. 305).

19 A similar analysis for personal self-esteem indicated that, in total, 75.5% had secure high self-esteem and 24.5% had defensive high self-esteem. However, there was no significant difference between the three groups of participants.

20 See also McGuire and McGuire (1981), and McGuire et al. (1986).

References

Adam, B. D. (1978). Inferiorization and 'self-esteem'. *Social Psychology, 41*, 47–53.

Ahmad, A. (1995). The politics of literary post coloniality. *Race and Class, 36*, 1–20.

Al-Ali, N., Black, R., & Koser, K. (2001). The limits of 'transnationalism': Bosnian and Eritrean refugees in Europe as emerging transnational communities. *Ethnic and Racial Studies, 24*, 578–600.

Alba, R. D., & Nee, V. (1997). Rethinking assimilation theory for a new era of immigration. *International Migration Review, 31*, 826–874.

Albert, S. (1977). Temporal comparison theory. *Psychological Review, 84*, 485–503.

Allport, G. W. (1954). *The nature of prejudice*. Reading, MA: Addison-Wesley.

Ambady, N., Shih, M., Kim, A., & Pittinsky, T. L. (2001). Stereotype susceptibility in children: Effects of identity activation on quantitative performance. *Psychological Science, 12*, 385–390.

American Psychological Association. (2003). Guidelines on multicultural education, training, research, practice and organizational change for psychologists. *American Psychologist, 58*, 377–402.

Anderson, B. (1983). *Imagined communities*. London: Verso.

Anderson, B. (1998). *The spectre of comparison: Nationalism, South East Asia and the world*. London: Verso.

Ang, I. (2001). *On not speaking Chinese: Living between Asia and the West*. London: Routledge.

Antaki, C., & Widdicombe, S. (Eds.). (1998). *Identities in talk*. London: Sage.

Anthias, F. (1998). Evaluating 'diaspora': Beyond ethnicity? *Sociology, 32*, 557–580.

Anthias, F. (2001). New hybridities, old concepts: The limits of 'culture'. *Ethnic and Racial Studies, 24*, 619–641.

Anzaldua, G. (1987). *Borderlands/La Frontera: The new mestiza*. San Francisco: Aunt Lute Books.

Appiah, K. A. (1997). The multiculturalist misunderstanding. *New York Review of Books, 44*, 30–36.

Arends-Tóth, J., & van de Vijver, F. J. R. (2000). Multiculturalisme: Spanning tussen ideaal en werkelijkheid. *Nederlands Tijdschrift voor de Psychology, 55*, 159–168.

Arends-Tóth, J., & van de Vijver. F. J. R. (2003). Multiculturalism and acculturation: Views of Duth and Turkish-Dutch. *European Journal of Social Psychology, 33*, 249–266.

Armistead, N. (Ed.). (1974). *Reconstructing social psychology*. Harmondsworth, UK: Penguin.

Arroyo, C. G., & Zigler, E. (1995). Racial identity, academic achievement, and the psychological well-being of economically disadvantaged adolescents. *Journal of Personality and Social Psychology, 69*, 903–914.

Asch, S. E. (1952). *Social psychology*. Englewood Cliffs, NJ: Prentice-Hall.

Ashmore, R. D., Deaux, K., & McLaughlin-Volpe, T. (2004). An organizing framework for collective identity: Articulation and significance of multidimensionality. *Psychological Bulletin, 130*, 80–114.

Ashmore, R. D., Jussim, L., Wilder, D., & Heppen, J. (2001). Conclusion: Towards a social identity framework for intergroup conflict. In R. D. Ashmore, L. Jussim, & D. Wilder (Eds.), *Social identity, intergroup conflict and conflict reduction* (pp. 213–249). New York: Oxford University Press.

Atkinson, D., Morten, G., & Sue, D. W. (1990). *Counseling American minorities*. Dubuque, IA: William C. Brown.

Auer, P., & Di Luzio, A. (Eds.). (1992). *The contextualization of language*. Amsterdam: John Benjamins.

Augoustinos, M., & Quinn, C. (2003). Social categorization and attitudinal evaluations: Illegal immigrants, refugees or asylum seekers? *New Review of Social Psychology, 2*, 29–37.

Augoustinos, M., & Walker, I. (1998). The construction of stereotypes within social psychology: From social cognition to ideology. *Theory and Psychology, 8*, 629–652.

Back, L. (1996). *New ethnicities and urban culture: Racisms and multiculture in young lives*. London: UCL Press.

Bagley, C. (1979). Self-esteem as a pivotal concept in race and ethnic relations. In C. Bagley-Marrett & C. Leggon (Eds.), *Research in race and ethnic relations* (Vol. 1, pp. 127–167). Greenwich, CT: Jai Press.

Balibar, E. (1991). Is there a neo-racism? In E. Balibar & I. Wallerstein (Eds.), *Race, nation, class: Ambiguous identities* (pp. 17–28). London: Verso.

Banaji, M. R., & Prentice, D. A. (1994). The self in social contexts. In L. Porter & M. Rosenzweig (Eds.), *Annual review of psychology* (Vol. 45, pp. 297–332). Palo Alto, CA: Annual Reviews, Inc.

Banks, M. (1996). *Ethnicity: Anthropological constructions*. London: Routledge.

Banton, M. (1988). *Racial consciousness*. London: Longman.

Banton, M. (1998). *Racial theories* (2nd ed.). Cambridge: Cambridge University Press.

Baranowski, B. (1950). *Znajomosc Wchodu w Dwanej Polsce do XVII wieku*. Łódź.

Barker, M. (1981). *The new racism*. London: Junction Books.

Barker, M. (1989). *Comics: Ideology, power and the critics*. Manchester: Manchester University Press.

Barnes, E. J. (1980). The Black community as a source of positive self-concept for Black children: A theoretical perspective. In R. Jones (Ed.), *Black psychology* (pp. 123–147). New York: Harper & Row.

Barreto, M., Spears, R., Ellemers, N., & Shahinper, K. (2003). Who wants to know? The effect of audience on identity expression among minority group members. *British Journal of Social Psychology, 42*, 299–318.

Barry, B. (2001). *Culture and equality*. Cambridge: Polity Press.

Barth, F. (1969). Introduction. In F. Barth (Ed.), *Ethnic groups and boundaries: The social organization of cultural difference*. London: Allen & Unwin.

Barth, F. (1994). Enduring and emerging issues in the analysis of ethnicity. In H. Vermeulen & C. Govers (Eds.), *The anthropology of ethnicity: Beyond 'ethnic groups and boundaries'* (pp. 11–32). Amsterdam: Spinhuis.

Basch, L., Glick Schiller, N., & Szanton Blanc, C. (1994). *Nations unbound: Transnational projects, postcolonial predicaments, and deterritorialized nation-states*. Basel, Switzerland: Gordon and Breach.

Bat-Chava, Y., & Steen, E. M. (1997). *Ethnic identity and self-esteem: A meta-analytic review*. Unpublished manuscript, New York State University.

Bauböck, R. (1998). The crossing and blurring of boundaries in international migration: Challenges for social and political theory. In R. Bauböck & J. Rundell (Eds.), *Blurred boundaries: Migration, ethnicity, citizenship* (pp. 17–52). Aldershot, UK: Ashgate.

Baumann, G. (1996). *Contesting culture: Discourses of identity in multi-ethnic London*. Cambridge: Cambridge University Press.

Baumeister, R. F., & Leary, M. R. (1995). The need to belong: Desire for interpersonal attachments as a fundamental human motivation. *Psychological Bulletin, 117*, 497–529.

Becker, E. (1974). *The birth and death of meaning: An interdisciplinary perspective on the problem of man* (2nd ed.). London: Penguin.

Bekerman, Z. (2002). The discourse of nation and culture: Its impact on Palestinian-Jewish encounters in Israel. *International Journal of Intercultural Relations, 26*, 409–427.

Bell, V. (Ed.). (1999). *Performativity and belonging*. London: Sage.

Bendle, M. F. (2002). The crisis of 'identity' in high modernity. *British Journal of Sociology, 53*, 1–18.

Benet-Martínez, V., Leu, J., Lee, F., & Morris, M. W. (2002). Negotiating biculturalism: Cultural frame switching in biculturals with oppositional versus compatible cultural identities. *Journal of Cross-Cultural Psychology, 33*, 492–516.

Bentley, C. G. (1987). Ethnicity and practice. *Comparative Studies in Society and History, 29*, 24–55.

Berger, P., & Luckmann, T. (1966). *The social construction of reality*. Harmondsworth, UK: Penguin.

Berry, J. W. (1984). Cultural relations in plural societies: Alternatives to segregation and their sociopsychological implications. In N. Miller & M. B. Brewer (Eds.), *Groups in contact* (pp. 11–27). San Diego, CA: Academic Press.

Berry, J. W. (1990). Psychology of acculturation. In J. J. Berman (Ed.), *Nebraska Symposium on Motivation, 1989. Vol. 37. Cross-cultural perspectives* (pp. 201–234). Lincoln: University of Nebraska Press.

Berry, J. W. (1997). Immigration, acculturation, and adaptation. *Applied Psychology: An International Review, 46*, 5–34.

Berry, J., & Kalin, R. (1995). Multicultural and ethnic attitudes in Canada: An overview of the 1991 national survey. *Canadian Journal of Behavioural Science, 27*, 301–320.

Berry, J. W., & Sam, D. L. (1996). Acculturation and adaptation. In J. W. Berry, M. H. Segall & C. Kagitcibasi (Eds.), *Handbook of cross-cultural psychology, Vol. 3, Social behavior and applications* (2nd ed.). Boston: Allyn & Bacon.

Bettencourt, B. A., Dorr, N., Charlton, K., & Hume, D. L. (2001). Status differences in in-group bias: A meta-analytical examination of the effects of status stability, status legitimacy, and group permeability. *Psychological Bulletin, 127*, 520–542.

Bhaba, H. (1990). The third space. In J. Rutherford (Ed.), *Identity* (pp. 207–221). London: Lawrence & Wishart.

Bhatia, S. (2002). Acculturation, dialogical voices and the construction of the diasporic self. *Theory and Psychology, 12*, 55–77.

Bhatia, S., & Ram, A. (2001). Rethinking 'acculturation' in relation to diasporic cultures and postcolonial identities. *Human Development, 44*, 1–18.

Biernat, M., & Thompson, E. R. (2002). Shifting standards and contextual variation in stereotyping. In W. Stroebe & M. Hewstone (Eds.), *European review of social psychology* (pp. 103–137). London: Wiley.

Biernat, M., Vescio, T. K., Theno, S. A., & Crandall, C. S. (1996). Values and prejudice: Toward understanding the impact of American values on outgroup attitudes. In C. Seligman, J. M. Olson, & M. P. Zanna (Eds.), *The psychology of values: The Ontario Symposium, Vol. 8* (pp. 153–189). Mahwah: NJ: Lawrence Erlbaum Associates, Inc.

Billig, M. (1987). *Arguing and thinking: A rhetorical approach to social psychology.* Cambridge: Cambridge University Press.

Billig, M. (1988). The notion of 'prejudice': Some rhetorical and ideological aspects. *Text, 8,* 91–110.

Billig, M. (1995). *Banal nationalism.* London: Sage.

Billig, M. (1997a). Discursive, rhetorical, and ideological messages. In C. McGarty & S. A. Haslam (Eds.), *The message of social psychology* (pp. 36–53). Oxford: Blackwell.

Billig, M. (1997b). The dialogical unconscious: Psychoanalysis, discursive psychology and the nature of repression. *British Journal of Social Psychology, 36,* 139–160.

Billig, M. (2002). Henri Tajfel's 'cognitive aspects of prejudice' and the psychology of bigotry. *British Journal of Social Psychology, 41,* 171–188.

Billig, M., Condor, S., Edwards, D., Gane, M., Middleton, D., & Radley, A. (1988). *Ideological dilemmas: A social psychology of everyday thinking.* London: Sage.

Billig, M., & Sabucedo, J. (1994). Rhetorical and ideological dimensions of common sense. In J. Siegfried (Ed.), *The status of common sense in psychology* (pp. 121–145). Norwood, NJ: Ablex.

Birnbaum, P. (1996). From multiculturalism to nationalism. *Political Theory, 24,* 33–45.

Blokland, T. (2003). Ethnic complexity: routes to discriminatory repertoires in an inner-city neighbourhood. *Ethnic and Racial Studies, 26,* 1–24.

Blu, K. L. (1980). *The Lumbee problem: The making of an American Indian people.* Cambridge: Cambridge University Press.

Blum, L. (2002). *"I'm not a racist but . . . ": The moral quandary of race.* Ithaca, NY: Cornell University Press.

Bochner, S. (1982). The social psychology of cross-cultural relations. In S. Bocher (Ed.), *Cultures in contact: Studies in cross-cultural interaction* (pp. 5–44). Oxford: Pergamon.

Bond, M. H., & Hwang, K.-K. (1986). The social psychology of Chinese people. In M. H. Bond (Ed.), *The psychology of Chinese people* (pp. 213–266). New York: Oxford University Press.

Bonilla-Silva, E., & Forman, T. A. (2000). "I am not a racist but . . . ": Mapping White college students' racial ideology in the USA. *Discourse and Society, 11,* 50–85.

Bonnett, A. (1993). Forever white? Challenges and alternatives to a 'racial' monolith. *New Community, 20,* 173–180.

Bonnett, A. (2000). *Anti-racism.* London: Routledge.

Borawski, P., & Dubinski, A. (1986). *Tatarzy Polscy: Dzieje, Obrzedy, Legendy, Tradycje.* Warsaw: Iskry.

Bosma, H. A., & Graafsma, T. L. G. (1982). *De ontwikkeling van identiteit in de adolescentie.* Nijmegen, the Netherlands: Dekker & van de Vegt.

Bosson, J. K., Swann, W. B., & Pennebaker, J. W. (2000). Stalking the perfect measure of implicit self-esteem: The blind men and the elephant revisited? *Journal of Personality and Social Psychology, 79,* 631–643.

Bourdieu, P. (1987). What makes a social class? On the theoretical and practical existence of groups. *Berkeley Journal of Sociology, 23,* 1–17.

Bourhis, R. Y., Moïse, L. C., Perreault, S., & Senécal, S. (1997). Towards an interactive acculturation model: A social psychological approach. *International Journal of Psychology, 32,* 369–386.

Brah, A. (1992). Difference, diversity and differentiation. In J. Donald & A. Rattansi (Eds.), *'Race', culture and difference* (pp. 126–144). London: Sage.

Brah, A. (1996). *Cartographies of diaspora*. London: Routledge.

Branch, C. W., Tayal, P., & Triplett, C. (2000). The relationship of ethnic identity and ego identity status among adolescents and young adults. *International Journal of Intercultural Relations, 24*, 777–790.

Branscombe, N. R., Schmitt, M. T., & Harvey, R. D. (1999). Perceiving pervasive discrimination among African-Americans: Implications for group identification and well-being. *Journal of Personality and Social Psychology, 77*, 135–149.

Brewer, M. B. (1991). The social self: On being the same and different at the same time. *Personality and Social Psychology Bulletin, 17*, 475–482.

Brewer, M. B. (1997). The social psychology of intergroup relations: Can research inform practice? *Journal of Social Issues, 53*, 197–211.

Brewer, M. B. (2001). Ingroup identification and intergroup conflict: When does ingroup love becomes outgroup hate? In R. D. Ashmore, L. Jussim, & D. Wilder (Eds.), *Social identity, intergroup conflict and conflict reduction* (pp. 17–41). New York: Oxford University Press.

Brewer, M. B., & Gardner, W. (1996). Who is this 'we'? Levels of collective identity and self representations. *Journal of Personality and Social Psychology, 71*, 83–93.

Brewer, M. B., Ho, H.-K., Lee, J.-Y., & Miller, N. (1987). Social identity and social distance among Hong Kong schoolchildren. *Personality and Social Psychology Bulletin, 13*, 156–165.

Bromley, R. (2000). *Narratives of a new belonging*. Edinburgh: Edinburgh University Press.

Brown, A. R. (1999). *Political languages of race and the politics of exclusion*. Aldershot, UK: Ashgate.

Brown, L. M. (1998). Ethnic stigma as a contextual experience: A possible selves perspective. *Personality and Social Psychology Bulletin, 24*, 163–172.

Brown, R. (1995). *Prejudice: Its social psychology*. Oxford: Blackwell.

Brown, R. (2000). Social identity theory: Past achievements, current problems and future challenges. *European Journal of Social Psychology, 30*, 745–778.

Brown, R., & Haeger, G. (1999). 'Compared to what?': Comparison choice in an international context. *European Journal of Social Psychology, 29*, 31–42.

Brown, R., Hinkle, S., Ely, P. G., Fox-Cardamone, L., Maras, P., & Taylor, L. A. (1992). Recognizing group diversity: Individualist-collectivist and autonomous-relational social orientations and their implications for intergroup processes. *British Journal of Social Psychology, 31*, 327–342.

Brown, R. H. (1987). *Society as text: Essays on rhetoric, reason and reality*. Chicago: University of Chicago Press.

Brubaker, R., & Cooper, F. (2000). Beyond "identity". *Theory and Society, 29*, 1–47.

Bryman, A. (1992). The debate about quantitative and qualitative research: A question of method or epistemology? *British Journal of Sociology, 35*, 75–92.

Buriel, R. (1987). Ethnic labeling and identity among Mexican Americans. In J. S. Phinney & M. J. Rotheram (Eds.), *Children's ethnic socialization: Pluralism and development* (pp. 134–152). Newbury Park, CA: Sage.

Burman, E., & Parker, I. (1993). Introduction—discourse analysis: The turn to the text. In E. Burman & I. Parker (Eds.), *Discourse analytic research: Repertoires and readings of texts in action* (pp. 1–13). London: Routledge.

Burr, V. (1995). *An introduction to social constructionism*. London: Routledge.

Burr, V. (2002). *The person in social psychology*. London: Psychology Press.

Buss, A. R. (1975). The emerging field of the sociology of psychological knowledge. *American Psychologist, 30*, 988–1002.

Buss, A. R. (1978). The structure of psychological revolutions. *Journal of the History of the Behavioral Sciences, 14*, 57–64.

Byrne, B. M., & Shavelson, R. J. (1996). On the structure of social self-concept for pre-, early, and late adolescents: A test of the Shavelson, Hubner, and Stanton (1976) model. *Journal of Personality and Social Psychology, 70*, 599–613.

Cameron, D. (1998). Gender, language and discourse: A review essay. *Signs, 23*, 945–973.

Cameron, J. E., & Lalonde, R. N. (1994). Self, ethnicity, and social group memberships in two generations of Italian Canadians. *Personality and Social Psychology Bulletin, 20*, 514–520.

Campbell, D. T. (1958). Common fate, similarity, and other indices of the status of aggregates of persons as social entities. *Behavioural Science, 3*, 14–25.

Celious, A., & Oyserman, D. (2001). Race from the inside: An emerging heterogeneous race model. *Journal of Social Issues, 57*, 149–165.

Chapman, M. (1993). Social and biological aspects of ethnicity. In M. Chapman (Ed.), *Social and biological aspects of ethnicity* (pp. 18–32). Oxford: Oxford University Press.

Chazbijewicz, S. (1989). Muzulmanie, Polscy Taterzy: Skad przyszlismy, kim jestesmy, dkad idziemy. *Zycie Muzulmanskie, 3*, 14–23.

Christian, J., Gadfield, N. J., Giles, H., & Taylor, D. M. (1976). The multidimensional and dynamic nature of ethnic identity. *International Journal of Psychology, 11*, 281–291.

Christiansen, F., & Hedetoft, U. (2004). *The politics of multiple belonging: Ethnicity and nationalism in Europe and East Asia*. Aldershot, UK: Ashgate.

Chryssochoou, X. (2000). Multicultural societies: Making sense of new environments and identities. *Journal of Community and Applied Social Psychology, 10*, 343–354.

Chryssochoou, X. (2003). *Cultural diversity: Its social psychology*. Oxford: Blackwell.

Cieslik, A., & Verkuyten, M. (2004). National, ethnic and religious identities: Hybridity and the case of the Polish Tatars. *National Identities* (in press).

Clark, K. B., & Clark, M. P. (1947). Racial identification and preference in Negro children. In T. M. Newcombe & E. L. Hartley (Eds.), *Readings in social psychology* (pp. 169–178). New York: Holt, Rinehart & Winston.

Clay, A. (2003). Keepin' it real: Black youth, hip hop culture, and Black identity. *American Behavioral Scientist, 46*, 1346–1358.

Clifford, J. (1997). *Routes: Travel and translation in the late twentieth century*. Cambridge, MA: Harvard University Press.

Cliteur, P. (2002). *Moderne Papoea's: Dilemma's van een muliculturele samenleving*. Amsterdam: De Uitgeverspers.

Coan, R. W. (1979). *Psychologists: Personal and theoretical pathways*. New York: Irvington.

Cohen, A. (1969). *Custom and politics in urban Africa*. London: Routledge.

Cohen, A. (1974). *Two-dimensional man*. London: Tavistock.

Cohen, A. P. (1994). *Self consciousness: An alternative anthropology of identity*. London: Routledge.

Cohen, R. (1978). Ethnicity: Problem and focus in anthropology. *Annual Review of Anthropology, 7*, 379–404.

Cohen, R. (1997). *Global diasporas: An introduction*. London: UCL Press.

Condor, S. (1996). Social identity and time. In W. P. Robinson (Ed.), *Social groups and identities: Developing the legacy of Henri Tajfel* (pp. 285–316). Oxford: Butterworth-Heinemann.

Condor, S. (2000). 'Pride and prejudice': Management in English people's talk about 'this country'. *Discourse and Society, 11*, 175–205.

Connor, W. (1993). Beyond reason: The nature of the ethnonational bond. *Ethnic and Racial Studies, 16*, 373–398.

Connor, W. (1994). *Ethnonationalism: The quest for understanding.* Princeton, NJ: Princeton University Press.

Conquergood, D. (1994). For the nation! How street gangs problematize patriotism. In H. W. Simons & M. Billig (Eds.), *After postmodernism: Reconstructing ideology critique* (pp. 200–221). London: Sage.

Cornell, S. (1996). The variable ties that bind: Content and circumstance in ethnic processes. *Ethnic and Racial Studies, 19*, 265–289.

Cornell, S., & Hartmann, D. (1998). *Ethnicity and race: Making identities in a changing world.* London: Pine Forge.

Coté, J. E., & Levine, C. G. (2002). *Identity formation, agency, and culture: A social psychological synthesis.* Hillsdale, NJ: Lawrence Erlbaum Associates, Inc.

Craig, A. P. (1997). Postmodern pluralism and our selves. *Theory and Psychology, 7*, 505–527.

Crisp, R. J., & Hewstone, M. (2000). Multiple categorization and social identity. In D. Capozza & R. Brown (Eds.), *Social identity processes: Trends in theory and research* (pp. 149–166). London: Sage.

Cristiane, S. (1998). 'Biological' Christianity and ethnicity: Spain's construct from past centuries. In J. Leman (Ed.), *The dynamics of emerging ethnicities: Immigrant and indigenous ethnogenesis in confrontation* (pp. 115–147). Frankfurt am Main, Germany: Peter Lang.

Crocker, J. (1999). Social stigma and self-esteem: Situational construction of self-worth. *Journal of Experimental Social Psychology, 35*, 89–107.

Crocker, J., & Luhtanen, R. (1990). Collective self-esteem and ingroup bias. *Journal of Personality and Social Psychology, 58*, 60–67.

Crocker, J., & Major, B. (1989). Social stigma and self-esteem: The self-protective properties of stigma. *Psychological Review, 96*, 608–630.

Cross, W. E. (1991). *Shades of black: Diversity in African-American identity.* Philadelphia: Temple University Press.

Cross, W. E., & Strauss, L. (1998). The everyday functions of African American identity. In J. K. Swim & C. Stangor (Eds.), *Prejudice: The target's perspective* (pp. 267–279). San Diego, CA: Academic Press.

Damon, W. (1983). *Social and personality development.* New York: Norton.

Daniel, E. V., & Knudsen, J. (Eds.). (1995). *Mistrusting refugees.* Berkeley: University of California Press.

Daniel, G. R. (1996). Black and white identity in the new millennium: Unsevering the ties that bind. In M. Root (Ed.), *The multiracial experience* (pp. 121–139). Thousand Oaks, CA: Sage.

Davies, B., & Harré, R. (1990). Positioning: The discursive production of selves. *Journal for the Theory of Social Behaviour, 20*, 43–63.

Deaux, K. (1993). Reconstructing social identity. *Personality and Social Psychology Bulletin, 19*, 4–12.

Deaux, K. (1996). Social identification. In E. T. Higgins & A. W. Kruglanski (Eds.), *Social psychology: Handbook of basic principles* (pp. 777–798). New York: Guilford.

Deaux, K., & Martin, D. (2003). Interpersonal networks and social categories: Specifying levels of context in identity processes. *Social Psychology Quarterly, 66*, 101–117.

Deaux, K., & Philogene, G. (Eds.). (2001). *Representations of the social: Bridging theoretical traditions.* Oxford: Blackwell.

Deaux, K., Reid, A., Mizrahi, K., & Ethier, K. A. (1995). Parameters of social identity. *Journal of Personality and Social Psychology, 68,* 280–291.

De Jong, W., & Verkuyten, M. (1996). Urban renewal, housing policy, and ethnic relations in Rotterdam. *New Community, 22,* 689–705.

De la Garza, M. F., Newcomb, M. D., & Myers, H. F. (1995). A multidimensional measure for cultural identity for Latino and Latina adolescents. In A. M. Padilla (Eds.), *Hispanic psychology: Critical issues in theory and research* (pp. 26–42). London: Sage.

De Vos, G. A. (1995). Ethnic pluralism: Conflict and accommodation. In L. Romanucci-Ross & G. De Vos (Eds.), *Ethnic identity: Creation, conflict, and accommodation* (pp. 15–47). Walnut Creek, CA: Alta Mira.

Dickerson, P. (2000). 'But I'm different to them': Constructing contrasts between self and others in talk-in-interaction. *British Journal of Social Psychology, 39,* 381–398.

Dixon, J. A., & Reicher, S. (1997). Intergroup contact and desegregation in the new South Africa. *British Journal of Social Psychology, 36,* 361–381.

Doise, W. (1986). *Levels of explanation in social psychology.* Cambridge: Cambridge University Press.

Doise, W. (1997). Organizing social-psychological explanations. In C. McGarty & S. A. Haslam (Eds.), *The message of social psychology* (pp. 63–76). Oxford: Blackwell.

Dominguez, V. (1994). A taste for 'the other': Intellectual complicity in racializing practices. *Current Anthropology, 35,* 333–338.

Doosje, B., Branscombe, N. R., Spears, R., & Manstead, A. S. R. (1998). Guilt by association: When one's group has a negative history. *Journal of Personality and Social Psychology, 75,* 872–886.

Dovidio, J. F., & Esses, V. M. (2001). Immigrants and immigration: Advancing the psychological perspective. *Journal of Social Issues, 57,* 375–387.

Duckitt, J. (1992). *The social psychology of prejudice.* Westport, CT: Praeger.

Duijzing, G. (1997). The making of Egyptians in Kosovo and Macedonia. In C. Govers & H. Vermeulen (Eds.), *The politics of ethnic consciousness* (pp. 194–222). London: Macmillan.

Ebaugh, H. R. F. (1988). *Becoming an ex: The process of role exit.* Chicago: University of Chicago Press.

Edley, N. (2001a). Analysing masculinity: Interpretative repertoires, ideological dilemmas and subject positions. In M. Wetherell, S. Taylor, & S. J. Yates (Eds), *Discourse as data: A guide for analysis* (pp. 189–228). London: Sage.

Edley, N. (2001b). Unravelling social constructionism. *Theory and Psychology, 11,* 433–441.

Edwards, D. (1991). Categories are for talking: On the cognitive and discursive bases of categorization. *Theory and Psychology, 1,* 515–542.

Edwards, D. (1997). *Discourse and cognition.* London: Sage.

Edwards, D., & Potter, J. (1992). *Discursive psychology.* London: Sage.

Eidelson, R. J., & Eidelson, J. I. (2003). Dangerous ideas: Five beliefs that propel groups toward conflict. *American Psychologist, 58,* 182–192.

Eiser, J. R. (1990). *Social judgement.* Buckingham: Open University Press.

Ellemers, N. (1993). The influence of socio-structural variables on identity enhancement strategies. In W. Stroebe, & M. Hewstone (Eds.), *European Review of Social Psychology,* (Vol. 4, pp. 27–57). Chichester, UK: Wiley.

Ellemers, N., Kortekaas, P., & Ouwerkerk, J. W. (1999). Self-categorisation, commitment to the group and group self-esteem as related but distinct aspects of social identity. *European Journal of Social Psychology, 29*, 371–389.

Ellemers, N., Spears, R., & Doosje, B. (Eds.). (1999). *Social identity: Context, commitment, content*. Oxford: Blackwell.

Eller, J., & Coughlan, R. (1993). The poverty of primordialism: The demystification of ethnic attachments. *Ethnic and Racial Studies, 16*, 183–202.

Entzinger, H. (2002). *Voorbij de multiculturele samenleving*. Assen, the Netherlands: van Gorcum.

Epstein, A. L. (1978). *Ethos and identity: Three studies in ethnicity*. London: Tavistock.

Eriksen, T. H. (1993). *Ethnicity and nationalism: Anthropological perspectives*. London: Pluto.

Eriksen, T. H. (2001). Ethnic identity, national identity and intergroup conflict: The significance of personal experiences. In R. D. Ashmore, L. Jussim, & D. Wilder (Eds.), *Social identity, intergroup conflict and conflict reduction* (pp. 42–68). New York: Oxford University Press.

Erikson, E. H. (1966). The concept of identity in race relations: Notes and queries. *Daedalus, 95*, 145–177.

Erikson, E. H. (1968). *Identity: Youth and crisis*. New York: Norton.

Esman, M. J. (1994). *Ethnic politics*. Ithaca, NY: Cornell University Press.

Essed, P. (1991). *Understanding everyday racism*. Newbury Park, CA: Sage.

Ethier, K. A., & Deaux, K. (1994). Negotiating social identity when contexts change: Maintaining identification and responding to threat. *Journal of Personality and Social Psychology, 67*, 243–251.

Faist, T. (2000). *The volume and dynamics of international migration and transnational social spaces*. Oxford: Oxford University Press.

Favell, A. (1998). *Philosophies of integration: Immigration and the idea of citizenship in France and Britain*. London: Macmillan.

Fay, B. (1996). *Contemporary philosophy of social science*. Oxford: Blackwell.

Fazio, R. H., & Olson, M. A. (2003). Implicit measures in social cognition research: Their meaning and use. *Annual Review of Psychology, 54*, 297–327.

Fearon, J. D., & Laitin, D. D. (2000). Violence and social construction of ethnic identities. *International Organization, 54*, 845–877.

Fenton, S. (2003). *Ethnicity*. Cambridge: Polity.

Fischer, E. F. (1999). Cultural logic and Maya identity. *Current Anthropology, 40*, 473–488.

Fishman, J. (1980). Social theory and ethnography. In P. Sugar (Ed.), *Ethnic diversity and conflict in Eastern Europe* (pp. 84–97). Santa Barbara, CA: ABC-Clio.

Fiske, A. P. (1992). The four elementary forms of sociality: Framework for a unified theory of social relations. *Psychological Review, 99*, 689–723.

Fiske, A. P., Kitayama, S., Markus, H. R., & Nisbett, R. E. (1998). The cultural matrix of social psychology. In D. T. Gilbert, S. T. Fiske, & G. Lindzey (Eds.), *The handbook of social psychology*, 4th ed., Vol. 2, pp. 915–981). Boston: McGraw-Hill.

Fleming, J. S., & Courtney, B. E. (1984). The dimensionality of self-esteem: Hierarchical facet model for revised measurement scale. *Journal of Personality and Social Psychology, 46*, 404–421.

Flick, U. (1998). *The psychology of the social*. Cambridge: Cambridge University Press.

Flowers, B. J., & Richardson, F. C. (1996). Why is multiculturalism good? *American Psychologist, 51*, 609–621.

Foote, N. N. (1951). Identification as a basis for a theory of motivation. *American Sociological Review, 26*, 14–21.

Fordham, S. (1988). Racelessness as a factor in Black students' school success: Pragmatic strategy or pyrrhic victory? *Harvard Educational Review, 58*, 54–84.

Fordham, S., & Ogbu, J. U. (1986). Black students' school success: "Coping with the burden of 'acting white'". *Urban Review, 18*, 176–206.

Forsythe, D. (1989). German identity and the problem of history. In E. Tonkin, M. McDonald, & M. Chapman (Eds.), *History and ethnicity* (pp. 137–156). London: Routledge.

Foucault, M. (1977). *Discipline and punish*. London: Allen Lane.

Frankenberg, R. (1993). *The social construction of whiteness: White women, race matters*. Minneapolis, MN: University of Minnesota Press.

Frankl, V. E. (1962). *Man's search for meaning*. Boston: Beacon Press.

Fredrickson, G. M. (1999). Models of American ethnic relations: A historical perspective. In D. A. Prentice & D. T. Miller (Eds.), *Cultural divides: Understanding and overcoming group conflict* (pp. 23–34). New York: Russell Sage Foundation.

Freeman, M. A. (2003). Mapping multiple identities within the self-concept: Psychological constructions of Sri Lanka's ethnic conflict. *Self and Identity, 2*, 61–83.

Freud, S. (1955). *Civilization, society and religion: 'Group psychology', 'Civilization and its discontents', and other works*. Middlesex, UK: Penguin.

Friedman, J. (1997). Global crises, the struggle for cultural identity and intellectual porkbarreling: Cosmopolitans versus locals, ethnics and nationals in an era of de-hegemonisation. In P. Werbner & T. Modood (Eds.), *Debating cultural hybridity* (pp. 70–89). London: Zed Books.

Friedman, J. (1999). The hybridization of roots and the abhorrence of the bush. In M. Featherstone & S. Lash (Eds.), *Spaces of culture: City–nation–world* (pp. 230–255). London: Sage.

Frosh, S., Phoenix, A., & Pattman, R. (2003). Taking a stand: Using psychoanalysis to explore the positioning of subjects in discourse. *British Journal of Social Psychology, 42*, 39–53.

Gaines, S. O., Marelich, W. D., Bledsoe, K. L., Steers, W. N., Henderson, M. C., Granrose, C. S., et al. (1997). Links between race/ethnicity and cultural values as mediated by racial/ethnic identity and moderated by gender. *Journal of Personality and Social Psychology, 72*, 1460–1476.

Galenkamp, M. (1998). Collectieve rechten in de praktijk: De Amish als paradigma? *Recht der Werkelijkheid, 19*, 37–54.

Gans, H. J. (1979). Symbolic ethnicity: The future of ethnic groups and cultures in America. *Ethnic and Racial Studies, 2*, 9–17.

Gans, H. J. (1999). Toward a reconciliation of 'assimilation' and 'pluralism': The interplay of acculturation and ethnic retention. In C. Hirschman, P. Kasinitz, & J. DeWind (Eds.), *The handbook of international migration: The American experience* (pp. 161–171). New York: Russell Sage Foundation.

Garcia Coll, G., Lamberty, G., Jenkins, R., McAdoo, H. P., Crnic, K., Wasik, B. H., et al. (1996). An integrative model for the study of developmental competencies in minority children. *Child Development, 67*, 1891–1914.

Gecas, V., & Burke, P. J. (1995). Self and identity. In K. S. Cook, G. A. Fine & J. S. House (Eds.), *Sociological perspectives on social psychology* (pp. 41–67). Boston: Allyn and Bacon.

Geense, P., & Pels, T. (1998). *Opvoeding in Chinese gezinnen in Nederland*. Assen, the Netherlands: van Gorcum.

Geertz, C. (1973). *The interpretation of cultures*. New York: Basic Books.

Georgas, J. (1989). Changing family values in Greece: From collectivist to individualist. *Journal of Cross-Cultural Psychology, 20*, 80–91.

Georgas, J., Berry, J. W., Shaw, A., Christakopoulou, S., & Mylonas, K. (1996). Acculturation of Greek family values. *Journal of Cross-Cultural Psychology, 27*, 329–338.

Georgas, J., Christakopoulou, S., Poortinga, Y. H., Angleitner, A., Goodwin, R., & Charalambous, N. (1997). The relationship of family bonds to family structure and function across cultures. *Journal of Cross-Cultural Psychology, 28*, 302–320.

Gergen, K. J. (1991). *The saturated self: Dilemmas of identity in contemporary life*. New York: Basic Books.

Giles, H., Taylor, D. M., Lambert, W. E., & Albert, G. (1976). Dimensions of ethnic identity: An example from northern Maine. *Journal of Social Psychology, 100*, 11–19.

Gilroy, P. (1993). *The Black Atlantic: Modernity and double consciousness*. London: Verso.

Gil-White, F. (1999). How thick is blood? The plot thickens . . . : If ethnic actors are primordialist, what remains of the circumstatialist/primordialist controversy? *Ethnic and Racial Studies, 22*, 789–820.

Gil-White, F. (2001). Are ethnic groups biological "species" to the human brain? Essentialism in our cognition of some social categories. *Current Anthropology, 42*, 515–554.

Gitlin, T. (1995). *The twilight of common dreams: Why America is wracked by cultural wars*. New York: Henry Holt.

Glazer, N., & Moynihan, D. A. (1963). *Beyond the melting pot*. Cambridge, MA: Harvard University Press.

Glazer, N., & Moynihan, D. P. (1975). Introduction. In N. Glazer & D. P. Moynihan (Eds.), *Ethnicity: Theory and experience* (pp. 1–26). Cambridge, MA: Harvard University Press.

Gleason, P. (1983). Identifying identity: A semantic history. *Journal of American History, 69*, 910–931.

Goffman, E. (1959). *The presentation of self in everyday life*. New York: Doubleday.

Goldberg, D. T. (1993). *Racist culture: Philosophy and the politics of meaning*. Oxford: Blackwell.

Goldberg, D. T. (Ed.). (1994). *Multiculturalism: A critical reader*. Oxford: Blackwell.

Goodman, M. E. (1952). *Race awareness in young children*. New York: Macmillan.

Goodstein, R., & Ponterotto, J. G. (1997). Racial and ethnic identity: Their relationship and their contribution to self-esteem. *Journal of Black Psychology, 23*, 275–292.

Goodwin, C., & Duranti, A. (1992). Rethinking context: An introduction. In A. Duranti & C. Goodwin (Eds.), *Rethinking context: Language as an interactive phenomenon* (pp. 1–42). Cambridge: Cambridge University Press.

Gordon, L. R. (1995). Critical 'mixed race'? *Social Identities, 1*, 381–395.

Govers, C., & Vermeulen, H. (1997). *The politics of ethnic consciousness*. London: Macmillan.

Graham, D. (1972). *Moral learning and development*. London: Batsford.

Gramsci, A. (1973). *Selections from prison notebooks*. London: Lawrence and Wishart.

Grasmuck, S., & Grosfoguel, F. (1998). 'Coloniality of power' and racial dynamics: Caribbean diasporas in New York City. *Identities, 5*, 78–92.

Gray-Little, B., & Hafdahl, A. R. (2000). Factors influencing racial comparisons of self-esteem: A quantitative review. *Psychological Bulletin, 126*, 26–54.

Greenberger, E., & Chen, C. (1996). Perceived family relationships and depressed mood in early and late adolescence: A comparison of European and Asian Americans. *Developmental Psychology, 32*, 707–716.

Greenwald, A. G., & Banaji, M. R. (1995). Implicit social cognition: Attitudes, self-esteem, and stereotypes. *Psychological Review, 102*, 4–27.

Greenwald, A. G., Banaji, M. R., Rudman, L. A., Farnham, S. D., Nosek, B. A., & Mellott,

D. S. (2002). A unified theory of implicit attitudes, stereotypes, self-esteem, and self-concept. *Psychological Review, 109*, 3–25.

Greenwald, A. G., Bellezza, F. S., & Banaji, M. R. (1988). Is self-esteem a central ingredient of the self-concept? *Personality and Social Psychology Bulletin, 14*, 34–45.

Greenwald, A. G., & Pratkanis, A. R. (1984). The self. In R. S. Wyer & T. K. Srull (Eds.), *Handbook of social cognition* (Vol. 3, pp. 129–178). Hillsdale, NJ: Lawrence Erlbaum Associates, Inc..

Griffiths, D. J. (2002). *Somali and Kurdish refugees in London*. Aldershot, UK: Ashgate.

Grosby, S. (1994). The verdict of history: The inexpungeable tie of primordiality—a response to Eller and Coughlan. *Ethnic and Racial Studies, 17*, 164–171.

Grossberg, L. (1996). Identity and cultural studies: Is that there all there is? In S. Hall & P. du Gay (Eds.), *Questions of cultural identity* (pp. 143–172). London: Sage.

Guimond, S., & Dambrun, M. (2002). When prosperity breeds intergroup hostility: The effects of relative deprivation and relative gratification on prejudice. *Personality and Social Psychology Bulletin, 28*, 900–912.

Gulbenkian Commission on the Restructuring of the Social Sciences (1996). *Open the social sciences*. Stanford, CA: Stanford University Press.

Gurin, P., Hurtado, A., & Peng, T. (1994). Group contacts and ethnicity in the social identities of Mexicanos and Chicanos. *Personality and Social Psychology Bulletin, 20*, 521–532.

Hacking, I. (1999). *The social construction of what?* Cambridge, MA: Harvard University Press.

Hagendoorn, L. (1995). Intergroup bias in multiple group systems: The perception of ethnic hierarchies. In W. Stroebe & M. Hewstone (Eds.), *European Review of Social Psychology* (Vol. 6, pp. 199–228). London: Wiley.

Hall, S. (1988). New ethnicities. In K. Mercer (Ed.), *Black film, British cinema* (pp. 27–31). London: ICA.

Hall, S. (1993). Culture, community, nation. *Cultural Studies, 7*, 349–363.

Hall, S. (1996). Introduction: Who needs 'identity'? In S. Hall & P. du Gay (Eds.), *Questions of cultural identity* (pp. 1–17). London: Sage.

Halualani, R. T. (2000). Rethinking "ethnicity" as structural-cultural project(s): Notes on the interface between cultural studies and intercultural communication. *International Journal of Intercultural Relations, 24*, 579–602.

Hammersley, M. (2003). Conversation analysis and discourse analysis: Methods or paradigms? *Discourse and Society, 14*, 751–781.

Hannerz, U. (1992). *Cultural complexity: Studies in the social organization of meaning*. New York: Columbia University Press.

Harré, R., & Gillett, G. (1994). *The discursive mind*. London: Sage.

Harter, S. (1999). *The construction of the self: A developmental perspective*. New York: Guilford Press.

Hartstone, M., & Augoustinos, M. (1995). The minimal group paradigm: Categorization into two versus three groups. *European Journal of Social Psychology, 25*, 179–194.

Haslam, N., Rothschild, L., & Ernst, D. (2000). Essentialist beliefs about social categories. *British Journal of Social Psychology, 39*, 113–127.

Haslam, N., Rothschild, L., & Ernst, D. (2002). Are essentialist beliefs associated with prejudice? *British Journal of Social Psychology, 41*, 87–100.

Haslam, S. A., Turner, J. C., Oakes, P. J., McGarty, C., & Hayes, B. K. (1992). Context-dependent variation in social stereotyping. I. The effects of intergroup relations as mediated by social change and frame of reference. *European Journal of Social Psychology, 22*, 3–20.

Heatherton, T. F., & Polivy, J. (1991). Development and validation of a scale for measuring state self-esteem. *Journal of Personality and Social Psychology, 60*, 895–910.

Heine, S. J., Kitayama, S., & Lehman, D. R. (1999). Cultural differences in self-evaluation: Japanese readily accept negative self-relevant information. *Journal of Cross-Cultural Psychology, 32*, 434–443.

Helms, J. E. (Ed.). (1990). *Black and white racial identity: Theory, research and practice.* Westport, CT: Greenwood Press.

Helms, J. E. (1995). An update of Helm's White and People of Color racial identity models. In J. Ponterotto, J. M. Casas, L. A. Suzuki, & C. M. Alexander (Eds.), *Handbook of multicultural counseling* (pp. 181–198). Thousand Oaks, CA: Sage.

Henry, J. M., & Bankston, C. L., III (1998). Propositions for a structuralist analysis of creolism. *Current Anthropology, 39*, 558–566.

Henry, J. M., & Bankston, C. L., III (2001). Ethnic self-identification and symbolic stereotyping: The portrayal of Louisiana Cajuns. *Ethnic and Racial Studies, 24*, 1020–1045.

Hermans, H., & Kempen, H. (1993). *The dialogical self: Meaning as movement.* San Diego, CA: Academic Press.

Herz, L., & Gullone, E. (1999). The relationship between self-esteem and parenting style: A cross-cultural comparison of Australian and Vietnamese Australian adolescents. *Journal of Cross-Cultural Psychology, 30*, 742–761.

Hetts, J. J., Sakuma, M., & Pelham, B. W. (1999). Two roads to positive regard: Implicit and explicit self-evaluation and culture. *Journal of Experimental Social Psychology, 35*, 512–559.

Hewitt, J. P. (2003). *Self and society: A symbolic interactionist social psychology* (9th ed.). Boston: Allyn and Bacon.

Hewitt, R. (1986). *White talk, black talk.* Cambridge: Cambridge University Press.

Hewstone, M., Islam, M. R., & Judd, C. M. (1993). Models of crossed categorization and intergroup relations. *Journal of Personality and Social Psychology, 64*, 779–793.

Higgins, E. T. (1996). The 'self-digest': Self-knowledge serving self-regulatory functions. *Journal of Personality and Social Psychology, 71*, 1062–1083.

Hirschfeld, L. (1996). *Race in the making: Cognition, culture and the child's construction of human kinds.* Cambridge, MA: Bradford.

Hochschild, J. I. (1999). Affirmative action as cultural war. In M. Lamont (Ed.), *The cultural territories of race: Black and white boundaries* (pp. 342–368). Chicago: University of Chicago Press.

Hodgson, D. (2002). Introduction: Comparative perspectives on the indigenous rights movement in Africa and the Americas. *American Anthropologist, 104*, 1037–1049.

Hoelter, J. W. (1985). The structure of self-conception: Conceptualization and measurement. *Journal of Personality and Social Psychology, 49*, 1392–1407.

Hoelter, J. W. (1986). The relationship between specific and global evaluations of self: A comparison of several models. *Social Psychology Quarterly, 49*, 129–141.

Hofstede, G. (1980). *Culture's consequences: International differences in work-related values.* London: Sage.

Hofstede, G. (1991). *Cultures and organizations: Software of the mind.* New York: McGraw-Hill.

Hogg, M. A., & Abrams, D. (1988). *Social identifications.* London: Routledge.

Hogg, M. A., & Ridgeway, C. L. (2003). Social identity: Sociological and social psychological perspectives. *Social Psychology Quarterly, 66*, 97–100.

Hogg, M. A., Terry, D. J., & White, K. M. (1995). A tale of two theories: A critical comparison of identity theory and social identity theory. *Social Psychology Quarterly,* *58,* 255–269.

Hogg, M. A., & Turner, J. C. (1987). Intergroup behaviour, self-stereotyping and the salience of social categories. *British Journal of Social Psychology, 26,* 325–340.

Hollan, D. (1992). Cross-cultural differences in the self. *Journal of Anthropological Research, 48,* 283–300.

Holland, D., Lachicotte, W., Skinner, D., & Cain, C. (2001). *Identity and agency in cultural worlds.* Cambridge, MA: Harvard University Press.

Hollinger, D. (1995). *Postethnic America.* New York: Basic Books.

Hollinger, D. (2000). *Postethnic America: Beyond multiculturalism* (2nd ed.). New York: HarperCollins.

Hollis, M. (1977). *Models of man: Philosophical thoughts on social action.* Cambridge: Cambridge University Press.

Hollway, W. (1989). *Subjectivity and method in psychology: Gender, meaning and science.* London: Sage.

Hong, Y.-Y., Chan, G., Chiu, C.-Y., Wong, R. Y. M., Hansen, I. G., Lee, S.-L. et al. (2003). How are social identities linked to self-conception and intergroup orientation? The moderating effect of implicit theories. *Journal of Personality and Social Psychology, 85,* 1147–1160.

Hong, Y.-Y., Morris, M. W., Chiu, C.-Y., & Benet-Martínez, V. (2000). Multicultural minds: A dynamic constructivist approach to culture and cognition. *American Psychologist, 55,* 709–720.

Hoorens, V., Nuttin, J. M., Herman, I. E., Pavakanun, U. (1990). Mastery pleasure versus mere ownership: A quasi-experimental cross-cultural and cross-alphabetical test of the name letter effect. *European Journal of Social Psychology, 20,* 181–205.

Hopkins, N., & Murdoch, N. (1999). The role of the 'other' in national identity: Exploring the context-dependence of the national ingroup stereotype. *British Journal of Social Psychology, 9,* 321–338.

Hopkins, N., Regan, M., & Abell, J. (1997). On the context dependence of national stereotypes: Some Scottish data. *British Journal of Social Psychology, 36,* 553–563.

Hopkins, N., Reicher, S., & Kahani-Hopkins, V. (2003). Citizenship, participation and identity construction: Political mobilization amongst British Muslims. *Psychologica Belgica, 43,* 33–54.

Hopkins, N., Reicher, S., & Levine, M. (1997). On the parallels between social cognition and 'new racism'. *British Journal of Social Psychology, 36,* 305–329.

Horenczyk, G. (1996). Migrant identities in conflict: Acculturation attitudes and perceived acculturation ideologies. In G. M. Breakwell & E. Lyons (Eds.), *Changing European identities: Social psychological analyses of social change* (pp. 241–250). Oxford: Butterworth-Heinemann.

Horenczyk, G., & Munayer, S. (2003). Complex patterns of cultural allegiances: The ethnic identity of Palestinian Christian Arab adolescents in Israel. In P. Weinreich & W. Saunderson (Eds.), *Analysing identity: Cross-cultural, societal and clinical contexts* (pp. 171–189). London: Routledge.

Horowitz, D. L. (2000). *Ethnic groups in conflict* (2nd ed.). Berkeley: University of California Press.

Horowitz, E. L. (1939). Racial aspects of self-identification in nursery school children. *Journal of Psychology, 7,* 91–99.

Hostetler, J. A. (1980). *Amish society* (3rd ed.). Baltimore: Johns Hopkins University Press.

House, J. S. (1977). The three facets of social psychology. *Sociometry, 40*, 161–177.

House, J. S. (1981). Social structure and personality. In M. Rosenberg & R. H. Turner (Eds.), *Social psychology: Sociological perspectives* (pp. 525–561). New York: Basic Books.

Huddy, L. (2001). From social to political identity: A critical examination of social identity theory. *Political Psychology, 22*, 127–156.

Hughes, M., & Demo, D. H. (1989). Self-perceptions of Black Americans: Self-esteem and personal efficacy. *American Journal of Sociology, 95*, 132–159.

Huiberts, A. M., Vollebergh, W. A. M., & Meeus, W. (1999). Individualisme en collectivisme bij Nederlandse, Turkse en Marokkaanse jongeren. *Tijdschrift voor Orthopedagogiek, 38*, 342–356.

Huntington, S. P. (1993). The clash of civilizations? *Foreign Affairs, 72*, 22–49.

Hurtado, A., Gurin, P., & Peng, T. (1994). Social identities, a framework for studying the adaptations of immigrants and ethnics: The adaptations of Mexicans in the United States. *Social Problems, 41*, 129–151.

Hutchinson, J., & Smith, A. D. (Eds.). (1996). *Ethnicity.* Oxford: Oxford University Press.

Hutnik, N. (1991). *Ethnic minority identity: A social psychological perspective.* Oxford: Clarendon.

Hutnyk, J. (1997). Adorno and Womad: South Asian crossovers and the limits of hybridity talk. In P. Werbner & T. Modood (Eds.), *Debating cultural hybridity* (pp. 106–136). London: Zed Books.

Ibanez, T., & Iniguez, L. (1997). *Critical social psychology.* London: Sage.

Isaacs, H. R. (1975). Basic group identity: The idols of the tribe. In N. Glazer & D. P. Moynihan (Eds.), *Ethnicity: Theory and experience* (pp. 29–52). Cambridge, MA: Harvard University Press.

Iyer, A., Leach, C. W., & Crosby, F. J. (2003). White guilt and racial compensation: The benefits and limits of self-focus. *Personality and Social Psychology Bulletin, 29*, 117–129.

Jackson, J. E. (1989). Is there a way to talk about making culture without making enemies? *Dialectical Anthropology, 14*, 127–144.

Jackson, J. S., Brown, K. T., & Kirby, D. C. (1998). International perspectives on prejudice and racism. In J. L. Eberhardt & S. T. Fiske (Eds.), *Confronting racism: The problem and the responses* (pp. 101–135). Thousand Oaks: Sage.

Jackson, J. W. (2002). Intergroup attitudes as a function of different dimensions of group identification and perceived intergroup conflict. *Self and Identity, 1*, 11–33.

Jackson, J. W., & Smith, E. R. (1999). Conceptualising social identity: A new framework and evidence for the impact of different dimensions. *Personality and Social Psychology Bulletin, 25*, 120–135.

Jacobs, D. (2000). Giving foreigners the vote: Ethnocentrism in Dutch and Belgian political debates. In J. Ter Wal & M. Verkuyten (Eds.), *Comparative perspectives on racism* (pp. 117–138). Aldershot, UK: Ashgate.

Jahoda, G. (1982). *Psychology and anthropology: A psychological perspective.* London: Academic Press.

James, W. (1890). *The principles of psychology* (Vol. 1). London: Macmillan.

Jasinskaja-Lahti, I., & Liebkind, K. (1999). Exploration of the ethnic identity among Russian-speaking immigrant adolescents in Finland. *Journal of Cross-Cultural Psychology, 30*, 527–539.

Jenkins, A. H. (2001). Individuality in cultural context: The case for psychological agency. *Theory and Psychology, 11*, 347–362.

Jenkins, R. (1996). *Social identity.* London: Routledge.

Jenkins, R. (1997). *Rethinking ethnicity: Arguments and explorations.* London: Sage.

Jetten, J., Postmes, T., & Mcauliffe, B. J. (2002). 'We're *all* individuals': Group norms of individualism and collectivism, levels of identification and identity threat. *European Journal of Social Psychology, 32*, 189–207.

Jones, J. M. (1997). *Prejudice and racism* (2nd ed.). New York: McGraw-Hill.

Jordan, C. H., Spencer, S. J., Zanna, M. P., Hoshino-Browne, E., & Correll, J. (2003). Secure and defensive high self-esteem. *Journal of Personality and Social Psychology, 85*, 969–978.

Jost, J. T., & Banaji, M. R. (1994). The role of stereotyping in system-justification and the production of false consciousness. *British Journal of Social Psychology, 33*, 1–27.

Jost, J. T., & Kruglanski, A. W. (2002). Estrangement of social constructionism and experimental social psychology: history of the rift and prospects for reconciliation. *Personality and Social Psychology Review, 6*, 168–187.

Jost, J. T., & Major, B. (Eds.). (2001). *The psychology of legitimacy: Emerging perspectives on ideology, justice, and intergroup relations.* Cambridge: Cambridge University Press.

Judd, C. M., Park, B., Ryan, C. S., Brauer, M., & Kraus, S. (1995). Stereotypes and ethnocentrism: Diverging interethnic perceptions of African American and White American youth. *Journal of Personality and Social Psychology, 69*, 460–481.

Kaiser, C. R., & Miller, C. T. (2001). Stop complaining! The social costs of making attributions to discrimination. *Personality and Social Psychology Bulletin, 27*, 254–263.

Karlsson, B. G. (2003). Anthropology and the 'indigenous slot': Claims to and debates about indigenous peoples' status in India. *Critique of Anthropology, 23*, 403–423.

Kaplan, H. B. (1982). Prevalence of the self-esteem motive. In M. Rosenberg & H. B. Kaplan (Eds.), *Social psychology of the self-concept* (pp. 139–151). Arlington Heights, IL: Harlon Davidson.

Kappus, E.-N. (1997). Changing history: Ethnic identity management in Trieste. In C. Govers & H. Vermeulen (Eds.), *The politics of ethnic consciousness* (pp. 90–120). London: Macmillan.

Kardiner, A., & Ovesey, L. (1951). *The mark of oppression.* New York: Norton.

Kashima, Y. (2000). Conceptions of culture and person for psychology. *Journal of Cross-Cultural Psychology, 31*, 14–32.

Katz, I., & Hass, R. G. (1988). Racial ambivalence and American value conflict: Correlational and priming studies of dual cognitive structures. *Journal of Personality and Social Psychology, 55*, 893–905.

Keesing, R. (1982). Prologue: Toward a multidimensional understanding of male initiation. In G. H. Herdt (Ed.), *Rituals of manhood* (pp. 2–43). Berkeley: University of California Press.

Kelman, H. C. (1958). Compliance, identification and internalization: Three processes of attitude change. *Journal of Conflict Resolution, 2*, 51–60.

Kelman, H. C. (2001). The role of national identity in conflict reduction: Experiences from Israeli-Palestinian problem-solving workshops. In R. D. Ashmore, L. Jussim, & D. Wilder (Eds.), *Social identity, intergroup conflict, and conflict reduction* (pp. 187–213). New York: Oxford University Press.

Kemper, F. (1996). *Religiositeit, etniciteit en welbevinden bij mannen van de eerste generatie Marokkaanse moslimmigranten.* Nijmegen, the Netherlands: KU Nijmegen.

Kernis, M. H., & Paradise, A. W. (2002). Distinguishing between secure and fragile forms of high self-esteem. In E. L. Deci & R. M. Ryan (Eds.), *Handbook of self-determination research* (pp. 339–360). Rochester, NY: University of Rochester Press.

Kich, G. K. (1992). The developmental process of asserting a biracial, bicultural identity. In M. Root (Ed.), *Racially mixed people in America* (pp. 304–317). Newbury Park, CA: Sage.

Kinket, B., & Verkuyten, M. (1997). Levels of ethnic self-identification and social context. *Social Psychology Quarterly, 60*, 338–354.

Kitayama, S., & Karasawa, M. (1997). Implicit self-esteem in Japan: Name letters and birthday numbers. *Personality and Social Psychology Bulletin, 23*, 736–742.

Kitwood, T. (1983). Self-conception among young British-Asian Muslims: Confutation of a stereotype. In G. Breakwell (Ed.), *Threatened identities* (pp. 129–149). London: Wiley.

Kivisto, P. (2001). Theorizing transnational immigration: A critical review of current efforts. *Ethnic and Racial Studies, 24*, 549–577.

Koole, S. L., Dijksterhuis, A., & van Knippenberg, A. (2001). What's in a name: Implicit self-esteem and the automatic self. *Journal of Personality and Social Psychology, 80*, 669–685.

Kosc, W. (2001). Tartar source: After six centuries, Poland's Muslims are still misunderstood. *Central Europe Review, 3*, 1–4.

Kosmitzki, C. (1996). The reaffirmation of cultural identity in cross-cultural encounters. *Personality and Social Psychology Bulletin, 22*, 238–248.

Krauss, R. M., & Chiu, C. Y. (1998). Language and social behaviour. In D. T. Gilbert, S. T. Fiske, & G. Lindzey (Eds.), *The handbook of social psychology* (4th edn, Vol. 2, pp. 41–88). Boston: McGraw-Hill.

Kraybill, D. B. (2001). *The riddle of Amish culture*. Baltimore: Johns Hopkins University Press.

Kraybill, D. B., & Nolt, S. M. (1995). *Amish enterprise: From plows to profits*. Baltimore: Johns Hopkins University Press.

Kryczynski, O. (1932). Ruch nacjonalistyczny a Tatarzy litewscy. *Rocznik Tatarski, 1*, 5–21.

Kuhn, M. H., & McPartland, T. S. (1954). An empirical investigation of self-attitudes. *American Sociological Review, 19*, 68–76.

Kunneman, H. (1996). *Van theemutscultuur naar walkman-ego: Contouren van postmoderne individualiteit*. Meppel, the Netherlands: Boom.

Kymlicka, W. (1995). *Multicultural citizenship*. Oxford: Clarendon.

Laclau, E., & Mouffe, C. (1985). *Hegemony and socialist strategies*. London: Verso.

LaFromboise, T., Coleman, H., & Gerton, J. (1993). Psychological impact of biculturalism: Evidence and theory. *Psychological Bulletin, 114*, 395–412.

Lange, A. (1989). Identifications, perceived cultural distance and stereotypes in Yugoslav and Turkish youth in Stockholm. In K. Liebkind (Ed.), *New identities in Europe: Immigrant ancestry and the ethnic identity of youth* (pp. 169–218). Aldershot, UK: Gower.

Lange, A., & Westin, C. (1985). *The generative mode of explanation in social psychological theories of race and ethnic relations*. Stockholm: Centre for Research in International Migration and Ethnicity, University of Stockholm.

Laroche, M., Kim, C., Hui, M., & Joy, A. (1996). An empirical study of multidimensional ethnic change: The case of French Canadians in Quebec. *Journal of Cross-Cultural Psychology, 27*, 114–131.

Lee, D. (1987). The semantics of 'just'. *Journal of Pragmatics, 11*, 377–398.

Leeman, Y. (1994). *Samen jong: Nederlandse jongeren en lessen over inter-etnisch samenleven en discriminatie*. Utrecht, the Netherlands: Jan van Arkel.

Lentz, C. (1997). Creating ethnic identities in north-western Ghana. In C. Govers & H. Vermeulen (Eds.), *The politics of ethnic consciousness* (pp. 31–89). London: Macmillan.

Levin, S., Sidanius, J., Rabinowitz, J. L., & Federico, C. (1998). Ethnic identity, legitimizing ideologies, and social status: A matter of ideological asymmetry. *Political Psychology, 19*, 373–404.

Liang, X. (2004). Intermarriage and the construction of ethnic identity: European overseas Chinese community leaders' marriage ideals. In F. Christiansen & U. Hedetoft (Eds.), *The politics of multiple belonging: Ethnicity and nationalism in Europe and East Asia* (pp. 109–124). Aldershot, UK: Ashgate.

Lickel, B., Hamilton, D. L., & Sherman, S. J. (2001). Elements of a lay theory of groups: Types of groups, relational styles, and the perception of group entativity. *Personality and Social Psychology Review, 5*, 129–140.

Lickel, B., Hamilton, D., Wieczorkowska, G., Lewis, A. C., Sherman, S. J., & Uhles, A. N. (2000). Varieties of groups and the perception of group entativity. *Journal of Personality and Social Psychology, 78*, 223–246.

Liebkind, K. (1992). Ethnic identity: Challenging the boundaries of social psychology. In G. M. Breakwell (Ed.), *Social psychology of identity and the self-concept* (pp. 147–185). London: Surrey University Press.

Liebkind, K. (2001). Acculturation. In R. Brown & S. L. Gaertner (Eds.), *Blackwell handbook of social psychology: Intergroup processes* (pp. 386–407). Oxford: Blackwell.

Linville, P. W. (1985). Self-complexity and affective extremity: Don't put all your eggs in one cognitive basket. *Social Cognition, 3*, 94–120.

Linville, P. W. (1987). Self-complexity as a cognitive buffer against stress-related depression and illness. *Journal of Personality and Social Psychology, 52*, 663–676.

Lorenzo-Hernández, J., & Ouellette, S. C. (1998). Ethnic identity, self-esteem, and values in Dominicans, Puerto Ricans, and African Americans. *Journal of Applied Social Psychology, 28*, 2007–2024.

Luhtanen, R., & Crocker, J. (1992). A collective self-esteem scale: Self-evaluation of one's social identity. *Personality and Social Psychology Bulletin, 18*, 302–318.

Lui, J. H., Wilson, M. S., McClure, J., & Higgins, T. R. (1999). Social identity and the perception of history: Cultural reprsentations of Aotearoa/New Zealand. *European Journal of Social Psychology, 29*, 1021–1047.

Maass, A., Catelli, L., & Arcuri, L. (2000). Measuring prejudice: Implicit versus explicit techniques. In D. Capozza & R. Brown (Eds.), *Social identity processes* (pp. 96–116). London: Sage.

Mac an Ghaill, M. (1999). *Contemporary racisms and ethnicities: Social and cultural transformations.* Buckingham: Open University Press.

Mackie, D. M. & Smith, E. R. (1998). Intergroup relations: Insights from a theoretically integrative approach. *Psychological Review, 105*, 499–529.

Major, B., Quinton, W. J., & McCoy, S. K. (2002). Antecedents and consequences of attributions to discrimination: Theoretical and empirical advances. In M. P. Zanna (Ed.), *Advances in experimental social psychology* (Vol. 34, pp. 251–330). New York: Academic Press.

Marcia, J. E. (1966). Development and validation of ego identity status. *Journal of Personality and Social Psychology, 3*, 551–558.

Margalit, A. (2002). *The ethics of memory.* Cambridge, MA: Harvard University Press.

Mark, C. (2001). *Multiracial identity: An international perspective.* New York: St Martin's Press.

Markus, H. R. (1977). Self-schemata and processing information about the self. *Journal of Personality and Social Psychology, 35,* 63–78.

Markus, H. R., & Kitayama, S. (1991). Culture and self: Implications for cognition, emotion, and motivation. *Psychological Review, 98,* 224–253.

Markus, H. R., Kitayama, S., & Heiman, R. J. (1996). Culture and 'basic' psychological principles. In E. T. Higgins & A. W. Kruglanski (Eds.), *Social psychology: Handbook of basic principles* (pp. 915–981). New York: Guilford.

Marsh, H. W., & Shavelson, R. (1976). Self-concept: Its multifaceted, hierarchical structure. *Educational Psychologist, 20,* 107–123.

Marshall, H., Stenner, P., & Lee, H. (1999). Young people's accounts of personal relationships in a multi-cultural East London environment: Questions of community, diversity and inequality. *Journal of Community and Applied Social Psychology, 9,* 155–171.

Martens, E. P., & Verweij, A. O. (1997). *Turken in Nederland: Kerncijfers 1996.* Rotterdam: ISEO.

Mason, D. (1994). On the dangers of disconnecting race and racism. *Sociology, 28,* 845–858.

McCall, G. J., & Simmons, J. L. (1978). *Identities and interactions: An examination of human associations in everyday life.* New York: Free Press.

McCarthy, J., & Yancey, W. C. (1971). Uncle Tom and Mr Charlie: Metaphysical pathos in the study of racism and personal disorganization. *American Journal of Sociology, 76,* 648–672.

McConahay, J. B. (1986). Modern racism, ambivalence, and the modern racism scale. In F. J. Dovidio & S. L. Gaertner (Eds.), *Prejudice, discrimination and racism* (pp. 91–126). Orlando, FL: Academic Press.

McDonald, M. (1989). *'We are not French': Language, culture and identity in Brittany.* London: Routledge.

McGarty, C., Haslam, S. A., Hutchinson, K. J., & Grace, D. M. (1995). Determinants of perceived consistency: The relationship between group entativity and the meaningfulness of categories. *British Journal of Social Psychology, 34,* 237–256.

McGue, M., Bacon, S., & Lykken, D. T. (1993). Personality stability and change in early adulthood: A behavioral genetic analysis. *Developmental Psychology, 29,* 96–109.

McGuire, S., Neiderhiser, J. M., Reiss, D., Hetherington, E. M., & Plomin, R. (1996). Genetic and environmental influences on perceptions of self-worth and competence in adolescence: A study of twins, full siblings and step-siblings: Erratum. *Child Development, 67,* 3417.

McGuire, W. J., & McGuire, C. V. (1981). The spontaneous self-concept as affected by personal distinctiveness. In M. D. Lynch, A. A. Norem-Hebeisen & K. J. Gergen (Eds.), *Self-concept: Advances in theory and research.* Cambridge, MA: Ballinger.

McGuire, W. J., McGuire, C. V., & Cheever, J. (1986). The self in society: Effects of social contexts on the sense of self. *British Journal of Social Psychology, 25,* 259–270.

McGuire, W. J., McGuire, C. V., Child, P., & Fujioka, T. (1978). Salience of ethnicity in the spontaneous self-concept as a function of one's ethnic distinctiveness in the social environment. *Journal of Personality and Social Psychology, 36,* 511–520.

McKay, J. (1982). An exploratory synthesis of primordial and mobilizationist approaches to ethnic phenomena. *Ethnic and Racial Studies, 5,* 395–420.

Medin, D. L. (1989). Concepts and conceptual structure. *American Psychologist, 44,* 1469–1481.

Michael, M. (1996). *Constructing identities.* London: Sage.

Migdal, M. J., Hewstone, M., & Mullen, B. (1998). The effects of cross-categorization on intergroup evaluations: A meta-analysis. *British Journal of Social Psychology, 37*, 303–324.

Miles, R. (1989). *Racism*. London: Routledge.

Miller, D. (1994). *Modernity: An ethnographic approach: Dualism and mass consumption in Trinidad*. Providence, RI: Berg.

Milner, D. (1983). *Children and race: Ten years on*. London: Ward Lock Educational.

Mills, C. (1997). *The racial contract*. Ithaca, NY: Cornell University Press.

Miskiewicz, A. (1990). *Tartarzy Polscy 1918–1939*. Warsaw: PWN.

Miskiewicz, A. (1993). *Tatarska Legenda: Tartarzy Polscy 1945–1990*. Białystok: KAW.

Modood, T. (1998). Anti-essentialism, multiculturalism, and the 'recognition' of religious groups. *Journal of Political Philosophy, 6*, 378–399.

Modood, T., Beishon, S., & Virdee, S. (1994). *Changing ethnic identities*. London: Policy Studies Institute.

Moghaddam, F. M., & Taylor, D. (1987). The meaning of multiculturalism for visible minority immigrant women. *Canadian Journal of Behavioural Science, 19*, 121–136.

Montreuil, A., & Bourhis, R. Y. (2001). Majority acculturation orientations toward "valued" and "devalued" immigrants. *Journal of Cross-Cultural Psychology, 32*, 698–719.

Morawska, E. (1994). In defense of the assimilation model. *Journal of American Ethnic History, 13*, 76–87.

Morin, F., & Saladin d'Anglure, B. (1997). Ethnicity as a political tool for indigenous peoples. In C. Govers & H. Vermeulen (Eds.), *The politics of ethnic consciousness* (pp. 157–193). London: Macmillan.

Morris, B. (1997). In defence of realism and truth: Critical reflections on the anthropological followers of Heidegger. *Critique of Anthropology, 17*, 313–340.

Moscovici, S. (1984). The phenomenon of social representations. In R. M. Farr & S. Moscovici (Eds.), *Social representations* (pp. 3–69). Cambridge: Cambridge University Press.

Moscovici, S., & Paicheler, G. (1978). Social comparison and social recognition: Two complementary processes of identification. In H. Tajfel (Ed.), *Differentiation between social groups* (pp. 251–266). London: Academic Press.

Mullen, B., Migdal, M. J., & Rozell, D. (2003). Self-awareness, deindividuation, and social identity: Unraveling theoretical paradoxes by filling empirical lacunae. *Personality and Social Psychology Bulletin, 29*, 1071–1081.

Mummendey, A., Klink, A., Mielke, R., Wenzel, M., & Blanz, M. (1999). Socio-structural characteristics of intergroup relations and identity management strategies: Results from a field study in East Germany. *European Journal of Social Psychology, 29*, 259–285.

Mummendey, A., & Wenzel, M. (1999). Social discrimination and tolerance in intergroup relations: Reactions to intergroup differences. *Personality and Social Psychology Review, 3*, 158–174.

Mussweiler, T., Gabriel, S., & Bodenhausen, G. V. (2000). Shifting social identities as a strategy for deflecting threatening social comparisons. *Journal of Personality and Social Psychology, 79*, 398–409.

Nagel, J. (1994). Constructing ethnicity: creating and recreating ethnic identity and culture. *Social Problems, 41*, 152–176.

Nakashima, C. (1996). Voices from the movement: Approaches to multiraciality. In M. Root (Ed.), *The multiracial experience* (pp. 79–100). London: Sage.

Nederveen Pieterse, J. (1995). Globalization as hybridization. In M. Featherstone, S. Lash, & R. Robertson (Eds.), *Global modernities* (pp. 45–68). London: Sage.

Nederveen Pieterse, J. (2001). Hybridity, so what? The anti-hybridity backlash and the riddles of recognition. *Theory, Culture and Society, 18*, 219–245.

Nesdale, D., & Mak, A. S. (2000). Immigrant acculturation attitudes and host country identification. *Journal of Community and Applied Social Psychology, 10*, 483–495.

Niranjana, T. (1992). *Siting translation: History, post-structuralism and the colonial context.* Berkeley, CA: University of California Press.

Nobles, W. W. (1973). Psychological research and the Black self-concept: A critical review. *Journal of Social Issues, 29*, 11–31.

Nuttin, J. M. (1987). Affective consequences of mere ownership: The name letter effect in twelve European languages. *European Journal of Social Psychology, 17*, 381–402.

Oakes, P. J., Haslam, S. A., & Turner, J. C. (1994). *Stereotyping and social reality.* Oxford: Blackwell.

Ogbu, J. (1990). Minority status and literacy in comparative perspective. *Daedalus, 119*, 141–168.

Ogbu, J. U. (1993). Differences in cultural frame of reference. *International Journal of Behavioral Development, 16*, 483–506.

Okamura, J. Y. (1981). Situational ethnicity. *Ethnic and Racial Studies, 4*, 452–465.

Owen, C., Eisner, H., & McFaul, T. (1981). A half-century of social distance research: National replication of the Bogardus studies. *Sociology and Social Research, 66*, 80–98.

Oyserman, D., & Swim, J. K. (2001). Stigma: An insider's view. *Journal of Social Issues, 57*, 1–14.

Parekh, B. (2000). *Rethinking multiculturalism: Cultural diversity and political theory.* London: Macmillan.

Parham, T. A. (1989). Cycles of psychological nigrescence. *The Counseling Psychologist, 17*, 187–226.

Park, R. E. (1928). Human migration and the marginal man. *American Journal of Sociology, 5*, 881–893.

Parker, D., & Song, M. (Eds.). (2001). *Rethinking "mixed race".* London: Pluto Press.

Parker, I. (1992). *Discourse dynamics: Critical analysis for social and individual psychology.* London: Routledge.

Parker, I. (1997). Discourse analysis and psychoanalysis. *British Journal of Social Psychology, 36*, 479–495.

Peel, J. D. Y. (1989). The cultural work of Yoruba ethnogenesis. In E. Tonkin, M. McDonald, & M. Chapman (Eds.), *History and ethnicity* (pp. 198–215). London: Routledge.

Pelham, B. W., & Hetts, J. J. (1999). Implicit and explicit personal and social identity: toward a more complete understanding of the social self. In T. R. Tyler, R. M. Kramer & O. P. John (Eds.), *The psychology of the social self* (pp. 115–143). Mahwah, NJ: Lawrence Erlbaum Associates, Inc.

Perdue, C., Dovidio, J., Gurtman, M., & Tyler, R. (1990). Us and them: Social categorization and the process of intergroup bias. *Journal of Personality and Social Psychology, 59*, 475–486.

Pettigrew, T. F. (1978a). Placing Adam's argument in a broader perspective: Comment on Adam paper. *Social Psychology, 41*, 58–61.

Pettigrew, T. F. (1978b). Three issues in ethnicity: Boundaries, deprivations and perceptions. In J. M. Yinger & S. J. Cutler (Eds.), *Major social issues: Multidisciplinary views* (pp. 25–49). New York: Free Press.

Pettigrew, T. F., & Meertens, R. (1995). Subtle and blatant prejudice in Western Europe. *European Journal of Social Psychology, 25*, 57–75.

Phalet, K., van Lotringen, C., & Entzinger, H. (2000). *Islam in de multiculturele samenleving: Opvattingen van jongeren in Rotterdam (Islam in the multicultural society: Attitudes of young people in Rotterdam)*. Utrecht, the Netherlands: Ercomer.

Philogene, G. (1994). 'African American' as a new social representation. *Journal for the Theory of Social Behaviour*, *24*, 89–109.

Phinney, J. (1989). Stages of ethnic identity development in minority group adolescents. *Journal of Early Adolescence*, *9*, 34–49.

Phinney, J. (1990). Ethnic identity in adolescents and adults: A review of research. *Psychological Bulletin*, *108*, 499–514.

Phinney, J. S. (1991). Ethnic identity and self-esteem: A review and integration. *Hispanic Journal of Behavioral Sciences*, *13*, 193–208.

Phinney, J. S. (1992). The multigroup ethnic identity measure: A new scale for use with adolescents and young adults from diverse groups. *Journal of Adolescent Research*, *7*, 156–176.

Phinney, J. S. (1996). When we talk about American ethnic groups, what do we mean? *American Psychologist*, *51*, 918–927.

Phinney, J. S., & Alipuria, L. (1990). Ethnic identity in college students from four ethnic groups. *Journal of Adolescence*, *13*, 171–183.

Phinney, J. S., Madden, T., & Santos, L. J. (1998). Psychological variables as predictors of perceived ethnic discrimination among minority and immigrant adolescents. *Journal of Applied Social Psychology*, *28*, 937–953.

Phinney, J. S., & Tarver, S. (1988). Ethnic identity search and commitment in Black and White eighth graders. *Journal of Early Adolescence*, *8*, 265–277.

Pinderhughes, E. (1995). Biracial identity: Asset or handicap? In H. W. Harris, H. C. Blue, & E. E. H. Griffith (Eds.), *Racial and ethnic identity: Psychological development and creative expression* (pp. 73–93). New York: Routledge.

Pinel, E. C. (1999). Stigma consciousness: The psychological legacy of social stereotypes. *Journal of Personality and Social Psychology*, *76*, 114–128.

Piontkowski, U., Florack, A., Hoelker, P., & Obdrzálek, P. (2000). Predicting acculturation attitudes of dominant and non-dominant groups. *International Journal of Intercultural Relations*, *24*, 1–26.

Pomerantz, A. (1986). Extreme case formulations: A new way of legitimating claims. *Human Studies*, *9*, 219–230.

Portes, A., Guarnizo, L. E., & Landolt, P. (1999). The study of transnationalism: Pitfalls and promise of an emergent research field. *Ethnic and Racial Studies*, *22*, 217–237.

Portes, A., & MacLeod, D. (1996). What shall I call myself? Hispanic identity formation in the second generation. *Ethnic and Racial Studies*, *19*, 523–547.

Postmes, T., & Branscombe, N. R. (2002). Influence of long-term racial environment composition on subjective well-being in African Americans. *Journal of Personality and Social Psychology*, *83*, 735–751.

Potter, J. (1996). *Representing reality: Discourse, rhetoric and social construction*. London: Sage.

Potter, J. (2002). Experimenting with reconciliation: A comment on Jost and Kruglanski. *Personality and Social Psychology Review*, *6*, 192–193.

Potter, J., & Wetherell, M. (1987). *Discourse and social psychology*. London: Sage.

Prentice, D. A., & Miller, D. T. (Eds.). (1999). *Cultural divides: Understanding and overcoming group conflict*. New York: Russell Sage Foundation.

Procter, N. G. (2000). *Serbian Australians in the shadow of the Balkan war*. Aldershot, UK: Ashgate.

Pryke, S. (2003). British Serbs and long distance nationalism. *Ethnic and Racial Studies, 26*, 152–171.

Rapley, M. (1998). 'Just an ordinary Australian': Self-categorisation and the discursive construction of facticity in 'new racist' political rhetoric. *British Journal of Social Psychology, 37*, 325–344.

Rapley, M. (2001). 'How to do X without doing Y': Accomplishing discrimination without 'being racist'—'doing equity'. In M. Augoustinos & K. J. Reynolds (Eds.), *Understanding prejudice, racism and social conflict* (pp. 231–251). London: Sage.

Reicher, S. (2001). Studying psychology studying racism. In M. Augoustinos & K. J. Reynolds (Eds.), *Understanding prejudice, racism and social conflict* (pp. 273–298). London: Sage.

Reicher, S., & Hopkins, N. (2001). *Self and nation: Categorization, contestation and mobilization*. London: Sage.

Reicher, S., Spears, R., & Postmes, T. (1995). A social identity model of deindividuation phenomena. *European Review of Social Psychology, 6*, 161–198.

Roccas, S. (2003). The effects of status on identification with multiple groups. *European Journal of Social Psychology, 33*, 351–366.

Roccas, S., & Brewer, M. B. (2002). Social identity complexity. *Personality and Social Psychology Review, 6*, 88–106.

Rockquemore, K. A. (1999). Between black and white: Exploring the biracial experience. *Race and Society, 1*, 197–212.

Rockquemore, K. A., & Brunsma, D. L. (2002). Socially embedded identities: Theories, typologies, and processes of racial identity among black/white biracials. *Sociological Quarterly, 43*, 335–356.

Roosens, E. (1989). *Creating ethnicity: The process of ethnogenesis*. Newbury Park, CA: Sage.

Roosens, E. (1994). The primordial nature of origins in migrant ethnicity. In H. Vermeulen & C. Govers (Eds.), *The anthropology of ethnicity: Beyond 'ethnic groups and boundaries'* (pp. 81–104). Amsterdam: Spinhuis.

Roosens, E. (1998). *Eigen grond eerst? Primordiale autochtonie: Dilemma van de multiculturele samenleving*. Leuven, Belgium: Acco.

Rosenberg, M. (1965). *Society and the adolescent self-image*. Princeton, NJ: Princeton University Press.

Rosenberg, M. (1979). *Conceiving the self*. New York: Basic Books.

Rosenberg, M. (1985). Self-concept and psychological well-being in adolescence. In R. L. Leaky (Ed.), *The development of the self* (pp. 205–246). New York: Academic Press.

Rosenberg, M. (1986). Self-concept from middle childhood through adolescence. In J. Suls & A. G. Greenwood (Eds.), *Psychological perspectives on the self* (pp. 107–136). Hillsdale, NJ: Greenwald Lawrence Erlbaum.

Rosenthal, D. A., & Hrynevich, C. (1985). Ethnicity and ethnic identity: A comparative study of Greek-, Italian- and Anglo-Australian adolescents. *International Journal of Psychology, 20*, 723–742.

Rothbart, M., & Taylor, M. (1992). Category labels and social reality: Do we view social categories as natural kinds? In G. R. Semin & K. Fiedler (Eds.), *Language, interaction and social cognition* (pp. 11–36). London: Sage.

Rothberger, H., & Worchel, S. (1997). The view from below: Intergroup relations from the perspective of the disadvantaged group. *Journal of Personality and Social Psychology, 73*, 1191–1205.

Rubin, M., & Hewstone, M. (1998). Social identity theory's self-esteem hypothesis: A review and some suggestions for clarification. *Personality and Social Psychology Review, 2,* 40–62.

Rudmin, F. W. (2003). Critical history of the acculturation psychology of assimilation, separation, integration, and marginalization. *Review of General Psychology, 7,* 3–37.

Rumbaut, R. G. (1994). The crucible within: Ethnic identity, self-esteem, and segmented assimilation among children of immigrants. *International Migration Review, 28,* 795–820.

Ryder, A. G., Alden, L. E., & Paulhus, D. L. (2000). Is acculturation unidimensional or bidimensional? A head-to-head comparison in the prediction of personality, self-identity, and adjustment. *Journal of Personality and Social Psychology, 79,* 49–65.

Saharso, S. (1992). *Jan en alleman: Etnische jeugd over etnische identiteit, discriminatie en vriendschap.* Utrecht, the Netherlands: Jan van Arkel.

Sampson, E. E. (1993). Identity politics: Challenges to psychology's understanding. *American Psychologist, 48,* 1219–1230.

Sánchez, J. I., & Fernández, D. M. (1993). Acculturative stress among Hispanics: A bidimensional model of ethnic identification. *Journal of Applied Social Psychology, 23,* 654–668.

Sani, F., & Reicher, S. (1998). When consensus fails: An analysis of the schism within the Italian Communist Party (1991). *British Journal of Social Psychology, 28,* 623–645.

Sansone, L. (1992). *Schitteren in de schaduw: Overlevingsstrategieën, subcultuur en etniciteit van Creoolse jongeren uit de lagere klasse in Amsterdam 1981–1990.* Amsterdam: Spinhuis.

Savin-Williams, R. C., & Demo, D. H. (1983). Conceiving and misconceiving the self: Issues in adolescent self-esteem. *Journal of Early Adolescence, 3,* 121–140.

Schegloff, E. A. (1997). Whose text? Whose context? *Discourse and Society, 8,* 165–187.

Schlesinger, A. M. Jr. (1992). *The disuniting of America.* New York: Norton.

Schmitt, M. T., & Branscombe, N. R. (2002). Meaning and consequences of perceived discrimination in advantaged and privileged social groups. In W. Stroebe & M. Hewstone (Eds.), *European Review of Social Psychology* (Vol. 12, pp. 167–199). London: Wiley.

Schnabel, P. (2000). *De multiculturele illusie: Een pleidooi voor aanpassing en assimilatie.* Utrecht, the Netherlands: Forum.

Schuyt, C. J. M. (1986). *Filosofie van de sociale wetenschappen.* Leiden, the Netherlands: Martinus Nijhoff.

Schuyt, C. J. M. (1995). *Kwetsbare jongeren en hun toekomst: Beleidsadvies gebaseerd op literatuurverkenning.* Rijswijk, the Netherlands: Ministerie van VWS.

Scott, G. (1990). A resynthesis of the primordial and circumstancialist approaches to ethnic group solidarity: Towards an explanatory model. *Ethnic and Racial Studies, 13,* 147–171.

Scott, W. A., Scott, R., & McCabe, M. (1991). Family relationships and children's personality: A cross-cultural, cross-source comparison. *British Journal of Social Psychology, 30,* 1–20.

Sears, D. (1988). Symbolic racism. In P. A. Katz & D. A. Taylor (Eds.), *Eliminating racism: Profiles in controversy* (pp. 53–84). New York: Plenum.

Sellers, R. M., Smith, M. A., Shelton, J. N., Rowley, S. A. J., & Chavous, T. M. (1998). Multidimensional model of racial identity: A reconceptualization of African American racial identity. *Personality and Social Psychology Review, 2,* 18–39.

Shek, D. T. L. (1999). Parenting characteristics and adolescent psychological well-being:

A longitudinal study in a Chinese context. *Genetic, Social, and General Psychology Monographs, 125,* 27–44.

Shelton, J. N. (2000). A reconceptualization of how we study issues of racial prejudice. *Personality and Social Psychology Review, 4,* 374–390.

Sherif, M. (1936). *The psychology of social norms.* New York: Harper.

Sherif, M. (1948). *An outline of social psychology.* New York: Harper and Row.

Sherif, M., & Sherif, C. (1969). *Social psychology.* New York: Harper and Row.

Sherman, S. J., Hamilton, D. L., & Lewis, A. C. (1999). Perceived entativity and the social identity value of group memberships. In D. Abrams & M. Hogg (Eds.), *Social identity and social cognition* (pp. 80–110). Oxford: Blackwell.

Shore, C. (1993). Inventing the 'people's Europe': Critical approaches to European community 'cultural policy'. *Man, 28,* 779–800.

Shotter, J., & Gergen, K. J. (Eds.). (1989). *Texts of identity.* London: Sage.

Sidanius, J., & Pratto, F. (1999). *Social dominance: An intergroup theory of social hierarchy and oppression.* Cambridge: Cambridge University Press.

Simmons, R. G. (1978). Blacks and high self-esteem: A puzzle. *Social Psychology, 41,* 54–57.

Simon, B. (1997). Self and group in modern society: Ten theses on the individual self and the collective self. In R. Spears, P. J. Oakes, N. Ellemers, & S. A. Haslam (Eds.), *The social psychology of stereotyping and group life* (pp. 318–335). Oxford: Blackwell.

Simon, B. (2004). *Identity in modern society: A social psychological perspective.* Oxford: Blackwell.

Sinclair, S., Sidanius, J., & Levin, S. (1998). The interface between ethnic and social system attachment: The differential effects of hierarchy-enhancing and hierarchy-attenuating environments. *Journal of Social Issues, 54,* 741–757.

Sinnerbrink, I., Silvone, D., Field, A., Steel, Z., & Manicavasagar, V. (1997). Compounding of premigration trauma and postmigration stress in asylum seekers. *Journal of Psychology, 131,* 463–470.

Smaje, C. (1997). Not just a social construction: Theorising race and ethnicity. *Sociology, 31,* 307–327.

Smith, A. (1986). *The ethnic origins of nations.* Oxford: Blackwell.

Smith, A. (1992). Chosen peoples: Why ethnic groups survive. *Ethnic and Racial Studies, 15,* 440–449.

Smith, D. E. (1978). 'K is mentally ill': The anatomy of a factual account. *Sociology, 12,* 23–53.

Smith, E. R., Murphy, J., & Coats, S. (1999). Attachment to groups: Theory and measurement. *Journal of Personality and Social Psychology, 77,* 94–110.

Smith, M. B. (1994). Selfhood at risk: Postmodern perils and the perils of postmodernism. *American Psychologist, 49,* 405–411.

Snauwaert, B., Soenens, B., Vanbeselaere, N., & Boen, F. (2003). When integration does not necessarily imply integration: Different conceptualizations of acculturation orientations lead to different classifications. *Journal of Cross-Cultural Psychology, 34,* 231–239.

Sniderman, P. M., & Tetlock, P. E. (1986). Symbolic racism: Problems of motive attribution in political analysis. *Journal of Social Issues, 42,* 129–150.

Solomon, S. Greenberg, J., & Pyszczynski, T. (1991). A terror management theory of social behavior: The psychological functions of self-esteem and cultural worldviews. In M. P. Zanna (Ed.), *Advances in experimental social psychology* (Vol. 24, pp. 93–159). San Diego, CA: Academic Press.

Solomos, J., & Back, L. (1994). Conceptualising racisms: Social theory, politics and research. *Sociology, 28*, 143–161.

Song, M. (2003). *Choosing ethnic identity*. Cambridge: Polity.

Spencer, J. M. (1997). *The new colored people*. New York: New York University Press.

Stainton Rogers, W. (2003). *Social psychology: Experimental and critical approaches*. Buckingham: Open University Press.

Stallaert, C. (1998). 'Biological' Christianity and ethnicity: Spain's construct from past centuries. In J. Leman (Ed.), *The dynamics of emerging ethnicities: Immigrant and indigenous ethnogenesis in confrontation* (pp. 115–148). Frankfurt am Main, Germany: Peter Lang.

Stapleton, K., & Wilson, J. (2003). Grounding the discursive self: A case study in ISA and discursive psychology. In P. Weinreich & W. Saunderson (Eds.), *Analysing identity: Cross-cultural, societal and clinical contexts* (pp. 195–212). London: Routledge.

Staring, R. (2001). *Reizen onder regie: Het migratieproces van illegale Turken (Planned travel: Migration of illegal Turks)*. Amsterdam: Spinhuis.

Staub, E. (1989). *The roots of evil: The origins of genocide and other group violence*. Cambridge: Cambridge University Press.

Steijlen, F. (1996). *RMS: Van ideaal tot symbool. Moluks nationalisme in Nederland 1951–1994*. Amsterdam: Spinhuis.

Stoler, A. (1995). 'Mixed bloods' and the cultural politics of European identity in colonial Southeast Asia. In J. Nederveen Pieterse & B. Parekh (Eds.), *The decolonization of imagination: Culture, knowledge and power* (pp. 128–148). London: Zed Books.

Stone, G. P. (1962). Appearance and the self. In A. M. Rose (Ed.), *Human behavior and social processes*. Boston: Houghton Mifflin.

Stonequist, E. V. (1935). The problem of marginal man. *American Journal of Sociology, 7*, 1–12.

Stryker, S. (1980). *Symbolic interactionism: A social structural version*. Palo Alto: Benjamin/Cummings.

Stryker, S. (1987). Identity theory: Development and extensions. In K. Yardley & T. Honess (Eds.), *Self and identity* (pp. 89–104). New York: Wiley.

Sue, D. W., Bingham, R. P., Porché-Burke, L., & Vasquez, M. (1999). The diversification of psychology: A multicultural revolution. *American Psychologist, 54*, 1061–1069.

Sue, S. (1999). Science, ethnicity, and bias: Where have we gone wrong? *American Psychologist, 54*, 1070–1077.

Sussman, N. M. (2000). The dynamic nature of cultural identity throughout cultural transition: Why home is so sweet. *Personality and Social Psychology Review, 4*, 355–373.

Taguieff, P. A. (1988). *La Force du préjugé: Essai sur le racisme et ses doubles*. Paris: La Decouverte.

Tajfel, H. (1978). *The social psychology of minorities*. London: Minority Rights Group.

Tajfel, H. (1981). *Human groups and social categories*. Cambridge: Cambridge University Press.

Tajfel, H. & Turner, J. C. (1986). The social identity theory of intergroup behavior. In S. Worchel & W. Austin (Eds.), *Psychology of intergroup relations* (pp. 7–24). Chicago: Nelson-Hall.

Taylor, C. (1992). *Multiculturalism and the politics of recognition*. Princeton, NJ: University of Princeton Press.

Taylor, D. M., & Lambert, W. E. (1996). The meaning of multiculturalism in a culturally diverse urban American area. *Journal of Social Psychology, 136*, 727–740.

Taylor, D. M., Moghaddam, F. M., & Bellerose, J. (1989). Social comparison in an intergroup context. *Journal of Social Psychology*, *129*, 499–515.

Taylor, D. M., Wright, S. C., Moghaddam, F. M., & Lalonde, R. N. (1990). The personal/group discrimination discrepancy: Perceiving my group, but not myself, to be a target of discrimination. *Personality and Social Psychology Bulletin*, *16*, 254–262.

Taylor, D. M., Wright, S. C., & Porter, L. E. (1994). Dimensions of perceived discrimination: The personal/group discrimination discrepancy. In M. P. Zanna & J. M. Olson (Eds.), *The psychology of prejudice: The Ontario Symposium*, (Vol. 7, pp. 233–255). Hillsdale, NJ: Lawrence Erlbaum Associates, Inc.

Taylor, S. E., & Brown, J. (1988). Illusion and well-being: Some social psychological contributions to a theory of mental health. *Psychological Bulletin*, *103*, 193–210.

Tesser, P. T. M., van Dugteren, F. A., & Merens, A. (1996). *Rapportage Minderheden 1996: Bevolking, arbeid, onderwijs en huisvesting*. Rijswijk, the Netherlands: Sociaal Cultureel Planbureau.

Tetlock, P. (1998). Social psychology and world politics. In D. T. Gilbert, S. T. Fiske & G. Lindzey (Eds.), *The handbook of social psychology* (4th ed., Vol. 2, pp. 868–912). Boston: McGraw-Hill.

Tizard, B., & Phoenix, A. (1993). *Black, white or mixed race: Race and racism in the lives of young people of mixed parentage*. London: Routledge.

Tololyan, K. (1986). Narrative culture and the motivation of the terrorist. In J. Shotter & K. J. Gergen (Eds.), *Texts of identity* (pp. 99–118). London: Sage.

Törrönen, J. (2001). The concept of subject position in empirical social research. *Journal for the Theory of Social Behaviour*, *31*, 313–329.

Triandis, H. C. (1989). The self and social behavior in different cultural contexts. *Psychological Review*, *93*, 506–520.

Triandis, H. C., Bontempo, R., Betancourt, H., Bond, M., Leung, K., Brenes, A., et al. (1986). The measurement of the etic aspects of individualism and collectivism across cultures. *Australian Journal of Psychology*, *38*, 257–267.

Triandis, H. C., Leung, K., Villareal, M., & Clack, F. (1985). Allocentric vs. idiocentric tendencies: Concergent and discriminant validation. *Journal of Research in Personality*, *19*, 395–415.

Tropp, L. R., & Wright, S. C. (2001). Ingroup identification as the inclusion of ingroup in the self. *Personality and Social Psychology Bulletin*, *27*, 585–600.

Trzesniewski, K. H., Donnellan, M. B., & Robins, R. W. (2003). Stability of self-esteem across the life span. *Journal of Personality and Social Psychology*, *84*, 205–220.

Tully, J. (1995). *Strange multiplicity: Constitutionalism in an age of diversity*. Cambridge: Cambridge University Press.

Turner, J. C. (1982). Towards a cognitive redefinition of the social group. In H. Tajfel (Ed.), *Social identity and intergroup relations* (pp. 15–40). Cambridge: Cambridge University Press.

Turner, J. C. (1991). *Social influence*. Milton Keynes, UK: Open University Press.

Turner, J. C. (1999). Some current issues in research on social identity and self-categorization theories. In N. Ellemers, R. Spears, & B. Doosje (Eds.), *Social identity: Context, commitment, content* (pp. 6–34). Oxford: Blackwell.

Turner, J. C., Hogg, M. A., Oakes, P. J., Reicher, S. D., & Wetherell, M. (1987). *Rediscovering the social group: A self-categorization theory*. Oxford: Blackwell.

Turner, J. C., Oakes, P. J., Haslam, S. A., & McGarty, C. (1994). Self and collective: Cognition and social context. *Personality and Social Psychology Bulletin*, *20*, 454–463.

Turner, J. C., & Onorato, R. S. (1999). Social identity, personality, and the self-concept: A self-categorization perspective. In T. R. Tyler, R. M. Kramer, & O. P. John (Eds.), *The psychology of the social self* (pp. 11–46). Hove, UK: Lawrence Erlbaum Associates Ltd.

Turner, T. (1993). Anthropology and multiculturalism: What is anthropology that multiculturalists should be mindful of it? *Cultural Anthropology, 8*, 411–429.

Twenge, J. M., & Crocker, J. (2002). Race and self-esteem: meta-analyses comparing Whites, Blacks, Hispanics, Asians and American Indians and comment on Gray-Little and Hafdahl (2000). *Psychological Bulletin, 128*, 371–408.

Ullah, P. (1987). Self-definition and psychological group formation in an ethnic minority. *British Journal of Social Psychology, 26*, 17–23.

Ullah, P. (1990). Rhetoric and ideology in social identification: The case of second generation Irish youth. *Discourse and Society, 1*, 167–188.

Unger, R. K., Draper, R. D., & Pendergrass, M. L. (1986). Personal epistemology and personal experience. *Journal of Social Issues, 42*, 67–79.

Urban, L. M., & Miller, N. M. (1998). A theoretical analysis of cross-categorization effects: A meta-analysis. *Journal of Personality and Social Psychology, 74*, 894–908.

van de Vyver, G. (1998). Ethnicity and historicity in Transylvania. In J. Leman (Ed.), *The dynamics of emerging ethnicities: Immigrant and indigenous ethnogenesis in confrontation* (pp. 87–114). Frankfurt am Main, Germany: Peter Lang.

van den Berg, H. (2003). Contradictions in interview discourse. In H. van den Berg, M. Wetherell, & H. Houtkoop-Steenstra (Eds.), *Analyzing race talk: Multidisciplinary approaches to the interview* (pp. 119–137). Cambridge: Cambridge University Press.

van den Berghe, P. (1978). Race and ethnicity: A sociobiological perspective. *Ethnic and Racial Studies, 1*, 401–411.

van den Berghe, P. (1981). *The ethnic phenomenon*. New York: Elsevier Press.

van Dijk, T. (1984). *Prejudice in discourse*. Amsterdam: John Benjamins.

van Dijk, T. (1987). *Communicating racism: Ethnic prejudice in thought and talk*. Newbury Park, CA: Sage.

van Dijk, T. (1992). Discourse and the denial of racism. *Discourse and Society, 3*, 87–118.

van Heelsum, A. (1997). *De etnische-culturele positie van de tweede generatie Surinamers*. Amsterdam: Spinhuis.

van Knippenberg, A. (1989). Strategies of identity management. In J. P. van Oudenhoven & T. Willemsen (Eds.), *Ethnic minorities: Social psychological perspectives* (pp. 59–76). Amsterdam: Swets & Zeitlinger.

van Langenhove, L., & Harré, R. (1994). Cultural stereotypes and positioning theory. *Journal for the Theory of Social Behaviour, 24*, 359–372.

van Niekerk, M. (2001). Becoming Dutch and staying Surinamese: Culture as a way of life and as a lifestyle. In F. Lindo & M. van Niekerk (Eds.), *Dedication and detachment: Essays in honour of Hans Vermeulen* (pp. 179–192). Amsterdam: Spinhuis.

van Oudenhoven, J. P., Prins, K. S., & Buunk, B. P. (1998). Attitudes of minority and majority members towards adaptation of immigrants. *European Journal of Social Psychology, 28*, 995–1013.

Veenhoven, R. (1984). *Conditions of happiness*. Dordrecht, the Netherlands: Reidel.

Verdery, K. (1994). Ethnicity, nationalism, and state-making. In H. Vermeulen & C. Govers (Eds.), *The anthropology of ethnicity: Beyond 'Ethnic groups and boundaries'* (pp. 33–58). Amsterdam: Spinhuis.

Verkuyten, M. (1988). *Zelfbeleving en identiteit van jongeren uit etnische minderheden*. Arnhem, the Netherlands: Gouda Quint.

Verkuyten, M. (1990). Self-concept in cross-cultural perspective: Turkish and Dutch adolescents in the Netherlands. In N. Bleichrodt & P. J. D. Drenth (Eds.), *Contemporary issues in cross-cultural psychology* (pp. 185–195). Amsterdam: Swets & Zeitlinger.

Verkuyten, M. (1992). *Zelfbeleving van Jeugdige Allochtonen: Een Socio-Psychologische Benadering*. Lisse, the Netherlands: Swets & Zeitlinger.

Verkuyten, M. (1994). Self-esteem among ethnic minority youth in Western countries. *Social Indicators Research, 32,* 21–47.

Verkuyten, M. (1995a). Self-esteem, self-concept stability, and aspects of ethnic identity among minority and majority youth in the Netherlands. *Journal of Youth and Adolescence, 24,* 155–175.

Verkuyten, M. (1995b). Symbols and social representations. *Journal for the Theory of Social Behaviour, 25,* 263–284.

Verkuyten, M. (1997a). Discourses of ethnic minority identity. *British Journal of Social Psychology, 36,* 565–586.

Verkuyten, M. (1997b). *'Redelijk racism': Gesprekken over allochtonen in oude stadswijken*. Amsterdam: Amsterdam University Press.

Verkuyten, M. (1998). Personhood and accounting for racism in conversation. *Journal for the Theory of Social Behaviour, 28,* 147–167.

Verkuyten, M. (1999). *Etnische identiteit: Theoretische en empirische benaderingen*. Amsterdam: Spinhuis.

Verkuyten, M. (2001a). 'Abnormalization' of ethnic minorities in conversation. *British Journal of Social Psychology, 40,* 257–278.

Verkuyten, M. (2001b). Global self-esteem, ethnic self-esteem, and family integrity: Turkish and Dutch early adolescents in the Netherlands. *International Journal of Behavioral Development, 25,* 357–366.

Verkuyten, M. (2002). Perceptions of ethnic discrimination by minority and majority early adolescents in the Netherlands. *International Journal of Psychology, 37,* 321–332.

Verkuyten, M. (2003). Discourses about ethnic group (de-)essentialism: Oppressive and progressive aspects. *British Journal of Social Psychology, 42,* 371–391.

Verkuyten, M. (2004a). Accounting for ethnic discrimination: A discursive study among minority and majority group members. *Journal of Language and Social Psychology* (in press)

Verkuyten, M. (2004b). Ethnic group identification and group evaluations among minority and majority groups: Testing the multiculturalism hypothesis. *Journal of Personality and Social Psychology* (in press).

Verkuyten, M. (2004c). *Explicit and implicit self-esteem among ethnic minority and majority early adolescents*. Utrecht, the Netherlands: Ercomer.

Verkuyten, M. (in press). Immigration discourses and their impact on multiculturalism: a discursive and experimental study. *British Journal of Social Psychology*.

Verkuyten, M., & Brug, P. (2002). Ethnic identity achievement, self-esteem, and discrimination among Surinamese adolescents in the Netherlands. *Journal of Black Psychology, 28,* 122–141.

Verkuyten, M., & Brug, P. (2004). Multiculturalism and group status: The role of ethnic identification, group essentialism and Protestant ethic. *European Journal of Social Psychology* (in press).

Verkuyten, M., De Jong, W., & Masson, C. N. (1994). Racial discourse, attitude, and rhetorical manoeuvres: race talk in the Netherlands. *Journal of Language and Social Psychology, 13,* 278–298.

Verkuyten, M., & De Wolf, A. (2002a). 'Being, feeling and doing': Discourses and ethnic self-definitions among minority group members. *Culture and Psychology, 8,* 371–399.

Verkuyten, M., & De Wolf, A. (2002b). Ethnic minority identity and group context: Self-descriptions, acculturation attitudes and group evaluations in an intra- and intergroup situation. *European Journal of Social Psychology, 32,* 781–800.

Verkuyten, M., Hagendoorn, L., & Masson, K. (1996). The ethnic hierarchy among minority and majority youth in the Netherlands. *Journal of Applied Social Psychology, 26,* 1104–1118.

Verkuyten, M., & Kwa, G. K. (1994). Ethnic self-identification and psychological well-being among ethnic minority youth in the Netherlands. *International Journal of Adolescence and Youth, 5,* 19–34.

Verkuyten, M., & Kwa, G. A. (1996). Ethnic self-identification, ethnic involvement, and group differentiation among Chinese youth in the Netherlands. *Journal of Social Psychology, 136,* 35–48.

Verkuyten, M., & Masson, K. (1996). Culture and gender differences in the perception of friendship by adolescents. *International Journal of Psychology, 31,* 207–217.

Verkuyten, M., & Nekuee, S. (1999a). Ingroup bias: The effect of self-stereotyping, identification and group threat. *European Journal of Social Psychology, 29,* 411–418.

Verkuyten, M. & Nekuee, S. (1999b). Subjective well-being, discrimination and cultural conflict: Iranians living in the Netherlands. *Social Indicators Research, 47,* 281–306.

Verkuyten, M., & Pouliasi, K. (2002). Biculturalism among older children: Cultural frame switching, attributions, self-identification and attitudes. *Journal of Cross-Cultural Psychology, 33,* 596–608.

Verkuyten, M., & Thijs, J. (1999). Multiculturalism among minority and majority adolescents in the Netherlands. *International Journal of Intercultural Relations, 26,* 91–108.

Verkuyten, M., & Thijs, J. (2001). Peer victimization and self-esteem of ethnic minority group children. *Journal of Community and Applied Social Psychology, 11,* 227–234.

Verkuyten, M., & Thijs, J. (2002). Multiculturalism among minority and majority adolescents in the Netherlands. *International Journal of Intercultural Relations, 26,* 91–108.

Verkuyten, M., & Thijs, J. (in press). Global and ethnic self-esteem in school context: Minority and majority groups in the Netherlands. *Social Indicators Research, 67,* 253–281.

Verkuyten, M., van de Calseijde, S., & De Leur, W. (1999). Third generation South Moluccans in the Netherlands: The nature of ethnic identity. *Journal of Ethnic and Migration Studies, 25,* 63–79.

Vermeulen, H. (2001). *Etnisch-culturele diversiteit als 'feit' en norm.* Amsterdam: Vossius.

Vermeulen, H., & Govers, C. (1994). *The anthropology of ethnicity: Beyond 'ethnic groups and boundaries'.* Amsterdam: Spinhuis.

Vermeulen, H., & Govers, C. (1997). From political mobilization to the politics of consciousness. In C. Govers & H. Vermeulen (Eds.), *The politics of ethnic consciousness* (pp. 1–30). London: Macmillan.

Vertovec, S. (1999). Conceiving and researching transnationalism. *Ethnic and Racial Studies, 22,* 447–462.

Vollebergh, W. A. M., & Huiberts, A. (1996). Welbevinden en etnische identiteit bij allochtone jongeren. *Pedagogisch Tijdschrift, 21,* 357–372.

Ward, C., & Rana-Deuba, A. (1999). Acculturation and adaptation revisited. *Journal of Cross-Cultural Psychology, 30,* 422–442.

Warminska, K. (1997). Polish Tartars: Ethnic ideology and state policy. In C. Govers & H. Vermeulen (Eds.), *The politics of ethnic consciousness* (pp. 343–366). London: Macmillan.

Waters, M. (1990). *Ethnic options: Choosing identities in America*. Berkeley: University of California Press.

Waters, M. C. (1994). Ethnic and racial identities of second-generation Black immigrants in New York City. *International Migration Review, 28*, 795–820.

Watson, D. R., & Weinberg, T. S. (1982). Interviews and the interactional construction of accounts of homosexual identity. *Social Analysis, 11*, 56–78.

Weber, M. (1968). *Economy and society: An outline of interpretive sociology*. New York: Bedmeister (original 1922).

Weigert, A. J., Smith-Teitge, J., & Teitge, D. W. (1986). *Society and identity: Towards a sociological psychology*. Cambridge: Cambridge University Press.

Weinreich, P. (1986). The operationalisation of identity theory in racial and ethnic relations. In J. Rex & D. Mason (Eds.), *Theories of race and ethnic relations* (pp. 299–344). Cambridge: Cambridge University Press.

Weinreich, P., Bacova, V., & Rougier, N. (2003). Basic primordialism in ethnic and national identity. In P. Weinreich & W. Saunderson (Eds.), *Analysing identity: Cross-cultural, societal and clinical contexts* (pp. 115–169). London: Routledge.

Wells, L. E., & Marwell, G. (1976). *Self-esteem: Its conceptualization and measurement*. London: Sage.

Wentholt, R. (1991). *Membership identity: Structure and dynamics*. Rotterdam: Erasmus University.

Wentholt, R., & Verkuyten, M. (1999). *Meanings of the term identity: That, who, what and how you are*. Utrecht, the Netherlands: Ercomer.

Werbner, P. (1997). Introduction: The dialectics of cultural hybridity. In P. Werbner & T. Modood (Eds.), *Debating cultural hybridity: Multi-cultural identities and the politics of anti-racism* (pp. 1–26). London: Zed Books.

Werbner, P., & Modood, T. (Eds.). (1997). *Debating cultural hybridity: Multi-cultural identities and the politics of anti-racism*. London: Zed Books.

Wetherell, M. (1998). Positioning and interpretative repertoires: conversation analysis and post-structuralism in dialogue. *Discourse and Society, 9*, 387–412.

Wetherell, M., & Potter, J. (1992). *Mapping the language of racism*. London: Harvester-Wheatsheaf.

Wetherell, M., Stiven, H., & Potter, J. (1987). Unequal egalitarianism: A preliminary study of discourses concerning gender and employment opportunities. *British Journal of Social Psychology, 26*, 59–71.

White, C. L., & Burke, P. J. (1987). Ethnic role identity among black and white college students: An interactionist perspective. *Sociological Perspectives, 30*, 310–331.

Widdicombe, S., & Wooffitt, R. (1990). 'Being' versus 'doing' punk: On achieving authenticity as a member. *Journal of Language and Social Psychology, 9*, 257–277.

Widdicombe, S., & Wooffitt, R. (1995). *The language of youth subcultures: Social identity in action*. London: Harvester Wheatsheaf.

Wieviorka, M. (1995). *The arena of racism*. London: Sage.

Willig, C. (2001). *Introducing qualitative research in psychology: Adventures in theory and mind*. Buckingham: Open University Press.

Wilson, A. (1987). *Mixed race children: A study of identity*. London: Allen and Unwin.

Wilson, T. D., Lindsey, S., & Schooler, T. Y. (2000). A model of dual attitudes. *Psychological Review, 107*, 101–126.

Wolsko, C., Park, B., Judd, C. M., & Wittenbrink, B. (2000). Framing interethnic ideology: Effects of multicultural and color-blind perspectives on judgments of groups and individuals. *Journal of Personality and Social Psychology, 78*, 635–654.

Wrong, D. (1961). The oversocialized conception of men in modern sociology. *American Sociological Review, 26*, 183–193.

Wrong, D. H. (1997). Cultural relativism as ideology. *Critical Review, 11*, 291–300.

Yabiku, S. T., Axinn, W. G., & Thornton, A. (1999). Family integration and children's self-esteem. *American Journal of Sociology, 104*, 1494–1524.

Yancey, W., Ericksen, E., & Juliani, R. (1976). Emergent ethnicity: A review and reformulation. *American Sociological Review, 41*, 391–403.

Young, R. J. C. (1995). *Colonial desire: Hybridity in theory, culture and race*. London: Routledge.

Yuki, M. (2003). Intergroup comparison versus intragroup relations: A cross-cultural examination of social identity theory in North American and East Asian cultural contexts. *Social Psychology Quarterly, 66*, 166–183.

Yuval-Davis, N. (1997). *Gender and nation*. London: Sage.

Yzerbyt, V., Castano, E., Leyens, J.-P., & Paladino, M.-P. (2000). The primacy of the ingroup: The interplay of entativity and identification. In W. Stroebe & M. Hewstone (Eds.), *European review of social psychology* (Vol. 11, pp. 257–295). London: Wiley.

Yzerbyt, V., Corneille, O., & Estrada, C. (2001). The interplay of subjective essentialism and entativity in the formation of stereotypes. *Personality and Social Psychology Review, 5*, 141–155.

Yzerbyt, V., Rocher, S., & Schadron, G. (1997). Stereotypes as explanations: A subjective essentialistic view of group perception. In R. Spears, P. J. Oakes, N. Ellemers & S. A. Haslam (Eds.), *The social psychology of stereotyping and group life* (pp. 20–50). Oxford: Blackwell.

Zack, N. (1996). On being and not-being Black and Jewish. In M. Root (Ed.), *The multiracial experience* (pp. 140–151). London: Sage.

Zagefka, H., & Brown, R. (2002). The relationship between acculturation strategies and relative fit and intergroup relations: Immigrant-majority relations in Germany. *European Journal of Social Psychology, 32*, 171–188.

Zick, A., Wagner, U., van Dick, R., & Petzel, T. (2001). Acculturation and prejudices in Germany: Majority and minority perspectives. *Journal of Social Issues, 57*, 541–557.

Author Index

Subject Index